Year of the Heroic Guerrilla

YEAR OF THE HEROIC GUERRILLA

World Revolution and Counterrevolution in 1968

ROBERT V. DANIELS

Harvard University Press
Cambridge, Massachusetts
London, England

First Harvard University Press paperback edition, 1996

Library of Congress Cataloging-in-Publication Data

Daniels, Robert Vincent.
    Year of the heroic guerrilla: world revolution and
counterrevolution in 1968/Robert V. Daniels.
    p. cm.
    Bibliography: p. 263
    Includes index.
    ISBN 0-674-96451-9 (pbk.)
    1. United States—Politics and government—1963–1969.
2. Violence—United States—History—20th century. 3. World
politics—1965–1975. 4. Revolutions—History—20th century.
5. Counterrevolutions—History—20th century.   I. Title.
E846.D36   1989
973.923—dc20   89–42521

CONTENTS

PREFACE   *vii*

1. The Spirit of '68   3

2. Saigon   17

3. Haight-Ashbury   43

4. New Hampshire   67

5. Memphis and Washington   95

6. Morningside Heights   127

7. Paris   149

8. Peking   167

9. Prague   187

10. Chicago   213

11. The World Social Revolution   235

NOTES   249

BIBLIOGRAPHY   263

INDEX   273

PREFACE

YEAR OF THE HEROIC GUERRILLA looks back at the events of the late 1960s from a perspective of two decades that highlights the extraordinary social upheaval experienced by the United States and many other countries during those times. In just one year, 1968, there was an amazing confluence of revolutionary currents and crises all around the globe. It was a time that truly must be understood in terms of revolution, if we are to sort out the issues that we have inherited from it. Out of this retrospective awareness I was led to write this book, narrating in close-up detail the critical national and world events of 1968 and putting them in their historical context to explain the nature, successes, and failures of those incredible days.

I came to the subject of 1968 and its revolutions in a roundabout way. My actual specialty—the subject that I have studied, taught, and written about for the last forty years—is the history of the Russian Revolution and the Soviet Union, that is, the revolution of the Old Left. From this base, I have broadened my work in recent years to include the comparative history of revolution in modern times and the role of successive revolutionary movements and ideas in shaping the world we live in today. (Future works on these themes are already in progress.) In this book, I apply my approach to describe and interpret the events of 1968 as the climax of a new kind of revolutionary process. Although this "Sixties Revolution" was not the kind that succeeds in overthrowing governments, it had as much impact around the world on prevailing values and modes of thinking—and as much disappointment in its ultimate aspirations—as did any of the classic revolutions of history.

In executing this project, I have had the benefit of a host of valuable works of reportage and interpretation, the most pertinent of which are listed in the bibliography. (Endnotes are used only to document quotations or other specific data whose sources are not clear from the text.) In addition, many friends, relatives, and colleagues have contributed valuable comments on particular portions of the manuscript. I would like especially to acknowledge the help of my sons, Robert H. Daniels and

Thomas L. Daniels, and my daughter, Helen L. Turcotte—all children of the 1960s—who gave me the benefit of their generational perspective. I am also indebted to Carolyn Elliott, Jean Hennessey, Philip Hoff, John Otto Johansen, Michal and Tamara Reiman, and Peter Seybolt for their comments on various parts of the book. Above all, I wish to thank my wife, Alice M. Daniels, who read the entire manuscript critically and contributed immeasurably to its readability. I am further indebted both to her and to Diann Varricchione for accomplishing the difficult task of rendering my handwritten yellow pads into a workable typescript, especially in the light of countless revisions. Finally, I want to express my appreciation for the help and encouragement of my editor at Basic Books, Steven Fraser, in bringing this project to fruition.

R. V. D.
Burlington, Vermont
February 1989

Year of the Heroic Guerrilla

1

The Spirit of '68

WHEN Fidel Castro proclaimed in his New Year's speech that 1968 would be "the year of the heroic guerrilla," he probably had no inkling of how accurate his histrionic forecast would prove to be in the short term. 1968 was the year of defiant heroics by youthful rebels all over the world, the year when the gathering forces of antiestablishment, anti-imperialist, and antielitist protest peaked from the campuses of Peking to the streets of Paris and to the hippie pads of San Francisco. As students were seizing buildings at Columbia University and preparing to derail the Democratic "Convention of Death" in Chicago, building barricades in the streets of the Latin Quarter, interrogating and humiliating the family of the president of the People's Republic of China, and fighting Russian tanks in Prague with gasoline and graffiti, many people could well believe that the worldwide structure of power, within and among nations, was at the point of collapse.

It was not to be. Within months, it was the Sixties Revolution that failed instead—splintered, discredited, or rudely snuffed out in one country after another. 1968 turned out to be not the year of the revolution's victory but the beginning of the end, ushering in a long era of counterrevolutionary doldrums. In the United States, public opinion recoiled from all the excesses of 1960s radicalism that television made so visible—black nationalism, countercultural nose-thumbing, rioting students, Vietcong flags. In staggering contrast to the landslide presidential

3

election of Lyndon Johnson over Barry Goldwater in 1964, Democratic rule and the Great Society came to grief at the hands of Richard Nixon, while ten million voters, Northern as well as Southern, endorsed the racist, ultranationalist, anti-intellectual appeal of George Wallace. Student uprisings in Europe, Japan, and Latin America flamed out, leaving only small groups of terrorists to go on discrediting the Left. Student power in China yielded to army power and eventually to Peking's sweeping compromise with the capitalist world. Soviet force in Eastern Europe dashed hopes for a "socialism with a human face." Yet for all this, the worldwide surge in the 1960s for a new kind of revolutionary change in the social order bequeathed a compelling legacy, not of power but of principle. It was heroic to some, sinister to others, but to all it made the years since then different from what went before.

Twenty years or so has become a common time frame for nostalgia and living anniversaries. The late 1980s thus began a time for recollections and retrospectives about the era of the 1960s. Yet it is not enough to recount and recall these years from a personal or journalistic standpoint. True understanding of the era demands a more comprehensive attempt at explaining it in the broad perspectives of modern history—revolution and counterrevolution, national and racial struggles for freedom and equality, modern social transformations, humanity's long struggle to realize its emergent ideals. Such an attempt at historical interpretation of the Sixties Revolution is the aim of this book.

Oddly enough, the focal point of this global upheaval was the country that had long been regarded as the most stable and the most powerful on earth, the United States of America. Values and traditions that stood beyond questioning in America for generations suddenly came under direct and often violent attack. Obviously, there was no new American Revolution in the sense of a forcible attempt to overthrow the government, but the attitude toward established norms and institutions in many sectors of society and especially among youth clearly became revolutionary. The consequences of this disaffection and the issues and aspirations it injected into American public life are still with us, partially offsetting the quest for personal security and the retreat into tradition that have marked the national scene in more recent years.

Nothing in the Sixties Revolution was a sudden development or the implementation of some nefarious plot, tempting as such an explanation might be to anxious partisans of the old order. The black civil rights movement and the counterculture had their roots in the 1950s, and radical student agitation commenced in the early 1960s. John Kennedy's "New Frontier" of 1961 presaged Lyndon Johnson's Great Society and

War on Poverty. What focused and radicalized all these movements in the later 1960s, more than anything else, was the war in Vietnam.

If any one event signaled the end of America's post–World War II mood of complacent conservatism and patriotic solidarity, it was the election of John F. Kennedy to the presidency in 1960. But public expectations changed even more than governmental leadership. Quite abruptly, the times began to be perceived as an opportunity to press for radical alternatives in the social order and even in the conventions of personal life.

For those who lived through it, it is easy enough to recall the intensity and the breadth of defiance that welled up in American society during those years. Central to it all was the Vietnam War and the escalating waves of protests—above all by the young and draftable—against United States involvement in what was perceived as a fruitless and even immoral conflict. Intertwined with the antiwar movement was the broader spirit of alienation from the whole contemporary way of life, manifested most visibly first by the counterculture and its expression in mind-altering drugs and rock music, and then by the unprecedented series of violent student uprisings on the most famous American university campuses. Partly antedating these modes of protest and then running as a constant counterpoint to them was the uniquely American struggle over equal rights for the black minority, producing what virtually became a revolution in microcosm.

There was a striking common denominator to the upheavals of 1968, wherever they erupted. Unlike the revolutionary movements of the nineteenth century and the early decades of the twentieth, the movements of 1968 were not directed primarily against absolute monarchies or unfettered capitalists. Rather, the target of rebellion was power—power over people and power over nations, power exercised on the international plane by great imperial states, by governments within nations, or by people in positions of dominance over the powerless under them, from the industrial bureaucracy to the university classroom. The primary aim of the era was equality, but a form of equality that no revolution of the past had achieved. It was a drive for equality in direct social relationships, which meant racial equality in America, national equality in Eastern Europe, equality of administrators and administered in Western Europe and China, and everywhere the equality of male and female, the old and the young, the teacher and the learner, the expert and the zealot. In many places the revolution had an antitechnology, almost Luddite, character.

Although the New American Revolution stands out in our consciousness, it was only one component of an extraordinary international surge of radical emotion. Like the amazing year 1848 in Europe, with its rash of democratic uprisings from the Channel to the Russian border, or the upheaval of 1917–1919 spearheaded by the Russian Revolution in the wake of World War I, 1968 was one of those rare moments in history when revolutionary lightning flashes nearly everywhere on the international landscape. There is no obvious explanation, certainly no world-wide plot, to account for the confluence of all the diverse movements of the year or to show why it happened at this particular time. Says Tom Hayden in his memoir, "I know of no historian who has adequately explained the simultaneous nature of these intercontinental developments."[1]

One explanation credits the modern news media, which telegraphed each episode of defiance around the world and disseminated revolutionary example and inspiration. But these upheavals were long in preparation, not spur-of-the-moment affairs. The war in Vietnam gave extra intensity to the issues of social protest in Western Europe and America, but anti-imperialism had been a growing sentiment everywhere, in the East as well as the West. Some writers see a common revolutionary element in the demographic surge of the post–World War II generation and the bulge in the numbers of postadolescent youth, which, indeed, is a unique circumstance of the 1960s. But a deeper underlay of the trouble was a growing unrest over the hierarchical conservatism in the societies of the major world powers, afflicting both the East and the West in their distinctive ways.

All of the movements of protest in the 1960s, within the United States and around the world, were interrelated. Common circumstances—the widening urbanization, education, and technological impersonality of modern society; rising expectations for economic progress and personal freedom; and the perception of oppressive authority in school, street, and workplace, whether in the hands of one's own rulers or of alien races and governments—readied potential rebels for action. Mutual encouragement of rebellion flowed back and forth among countries as well as among constituencies. The same principles of personal liberation and equality found revolutionary expression in diverse places and in a variety of issues, all coming together in an extraordinary sequence of rebellions in the year 1968.

When the New Year dawned in January of 1968, the United States was already experiencing an escalating sense of crisis. President Lyndon Johnson declared in his State of the Union speech, "Our country is being challenged at home and abroad," and he took note of "a certain restlessness, a questioning." Two circumstances in particular were driving the nation to a confrontation with itself—the civil rights movement and the war in Vietnam. President Kennedy's traumatic assassination in November 1963 had already attuned the nation to violence as a threat to the social order. By 1967, violence in the black ghettos, following in the wake of the extraordinary nonviolent civil rights movement of the early 1960s, had aroused acute concern, reflected in President Johnson's creation of the National Advisory Commission on Civil Disorders, chaired by Governor Otto Kerner of Illinois. Antiwar protests verged on the illegal and sometimes went beyond to incur prosecution. More peacefully, the counterculture of the hippies was attracting youthful adherents and shocking their elders with the unconventional life-style it exhibited in many urban bohemias, universities, and rural communes. At the same time, President Johnson and his administration were still engaged in a massive effort to fulfill the unachieved promise of Franklin Roosevelt's New Deal. Caught in the typical quandary of reformers in a time of revolution, they were being overtaken (and, in the minds of many, discredited) by the direct action that the new agendas of social change and antiauthority defiance inspired.

It was events in Vietnam that turned this time of tension into a time of crisis and ran like a thundering accompaniment to all the shocking episodes punctuating the year 1968. Violence in Vietnam set the tone for violence and defiance on the American home front. The Tet Offensive launched by the North Vietnamese and the Vietcong at the end of January on the day of the Vietnamese New Year, although militarily more embarrassing than decisive, compelled Americans to rethink the cost and purposes of their Indo-Chinese adventure. The immediate result was to upset the political future of President Johnson, when he suffered an unacceptably close call in the New Hampshire presidential primary and decided to remove himself from the race for reelection. The next victim was the Democratic party, as it wallowed through the spectacle of the Chicago nominating convention and on to defeat at the hands of Richard Nixon.

The intensity of feeling that Vietnam aroused, pro and con, reflected the tendency in America since World War II for both the Left and the Right to use issues of foreign policy to express basic sentiments about the country's institutions and power structure. Debates about foreign policy provide an outlet for both Left and Right political extremes that is more acceptable to Americans than European-style ideologies. The Left believes that the existing power structure can do no right and uses

7

international embarrassment as a point of attack. The Right believes that anyone who questions the economic and social status quo is a subversive or a traitor, and it makes the most dubious foreign policy adventures and allies a litmus test of loyalty. We have seen the same attitudes projected on Central America today.

Along with the violent, political side of the Sixties Revolution, American society was deeply unsettled by an undertow of changing social mores that called into question the old patriarchal and puritanical verities. The trend was sharpened and magnified in the 1960s by the emergence of the counterculture and its expression of the profound alienation felt by many youth from the mainstream of American society, in such centers of hippie life as the Haight-Ashbury district of San Francisco.

More physically threatening to the fabric of American life were the eruptions of mass violence in the spring of 1968 among blacks and among university students. Neither development was new. Both represented the culmination of angry defiance that had been taking shape since the middle of the decade, but in both cases the troubles of 1968 registered the most severe, most nearly revolutionary points reached by these movements. The new surge of direct action among blacks was triggered by the tragic and mysterious assassination of the charismatic civil rights leader Martin Luther King, Jr. Reaction to this atrocity expressed itself in a frightening series of urban riots, worst of all in the nation's capital, followed by anticlimactic and self-destructive efforts to advance the black cause by demonstrations and encampments. For the students, the spring (the natural season for campus unrest) saw an unprecedented revolutionary event at Columbia University, as young radicals endeavored to turn the antiwar movement into a physical seizure and transformation of the institution. For manifold reasons, an entire youthful generation, or certainly its best educated and most politically conscious segment, appeared to be defecting massively from what mainstream America had thought to be the basic norms of patriotism, duty, and self-discipline.

The most intense role in the Sixties Revolution was shared by two countries at opposite ends of the earth and in totally different circumstances, which nevertheless faced radical challenges of a remarkably similar character. One of these was France, chafing under General de Gaulle's semiauthoritarian government, a social system of hierarchical privilege, and an ossified and bureaucratic educational structure. In May 1968, Paris was the scene of a student uprising with working-class support that seemed so severe for a time as to have the makings of a real revolution. The other center of radicalism was Communist China, where for two years past an analogous youth rebellion against the bureaucratic power structure of society, sponsored by none other than the country's leader Mao Tse-tung, had been gathering steam under the rather inappropriate banner of a "cultural revolution." Now, at its high point, the rebellion was turned back, despite the efforts of university students to sustain the revolutionary momentum. Elsewhere in the Western world, particularly in Germany, in Italy, and even in Latin America, the chorus of youthful radicalism was echoed, if not quite paralleled, and the themes of anti-imperialism and revulsion against the American war in Vietnam resounded everywhere. In Communist Eastern Europe, the spirit of protest targeted the heavy hand of Soviet domination and Communist puppet governments of twenty years standing. In this case, however, the aims of the reformers—above all as articulated in the Prague Spring in Czechoslovakia before it was nipped in August by the early frost of the Soviet occupation—had more in common with the values of democracy and national independence that the West took for granted than with the often exotic ideology of Western protest movements.

Can we still speak of revolution in 1968 when in no major instance was a government toppled by force? The nearest case was China, where revolutionaries seized power locally and briefly, but the initiative for their actions came from above. Czechoslovakia, perhaps, went the farthest in changing the character of its regime, but it did so without resort to force. In France, the revolutionaries came near to forcing a political crisis and the formation of a cabinet by the parliamentary opposition, but this was still within constitutional procedures. No one in America came close to changing the governmental leadership, and even a McCarthy victory, like any likely outcome in France, would have remained within constitutional channels.

But this is not the point. Revolution is more than the violent seizure of power; indeed, the mere transfer of power without fundamental changes in society and its values is no revolution at all but only a pointless coup. Revolution's essence is a turnabout, whether temporary or permanent, in the basic values that hold a society or a significant segment of society together and legitimize its character. To what end should power be exercised? How should rewards be distributed in society? What kinds of relations should prevail among individuals and groups? Struggles over such bedrock questions are not resolved overnight, but involve long and often intricate processes of political conflict

9

and transformation. Here the systems of both the West and the East were vulnerable, as the modern bureacratic evolution of both kinds of societies veered away from the original legitimizing principles of democratic individualism in the West and collectivist equalitarianism in the East and national self-determination for both. These inconsistencies prompted the revolutionaries in America, France, China, and Czechoslovakia to try to hold the powers that be to their professed principles, and then to reject those powers as hypocrites when they were proved unwilling to uphold those principles. Most striking in many cases was the revolutionaries' perception that technology, extolled by the dominant ideologies as the salvation of humanity, could be the accomplice of bureaucracy and the bane of a free and equal society. The technocrats, for their part, from French cabinet ministers and American generals to Soviet and Chinese party bosses, proved themselves consistently unable to understand what their adversaries were agitated about.

Throughout the world, the revolutionary upheaval of the late 1960s replicated the classic model of revolution as a step-by-step development, growing in intensity over a period of time. The process was most clearly etched in the United States, where, as in the literal revolutions of the classic series—seventeenth-century England, eighteenth-century France, twentieth-century Russia—there was a distinct sequence of phases and styles of political action succeeding one another. It began with liberal reform, stimulated initially by President Kennedy's nebulous but high-sounding New Frontier. As resistance was met and deeper animosities were activated, particularly in the civil rights movement, radicals demanded total and sometimes forcible reconstruction of the social order in the form of "black power," "student power," or, more vaguely, the New Left slogan of "power to the people." In 1968, the growth of defiance reached its climax as a result of the Vietnam War and the focusing effect of the presidential election campaign. Then, radical protest rapidly provoked its own undoing, as it splintered the various movements for social change, on the one hand, and on the other galvanized the "silent majority" of more tradition-bound Americans into often not-so-silent resistance to these disturbing challenges. Thus did the revolutionary forces of the 1960s rise, peak, divide, and fall before their own counterrevolutionary antithesis in the manner of the classic revolutionary cycle.

The revolutions of 1968, if they were in fact true revolutions, were unlike any of the great revolutions of the past in the social forces that supported them. They were, more than ever before in history, generational revolutions of youth, of those in their late teens and early twenties.

They were not by and large movements of the most oppressed and downtrodden—the American black movement came closest to this description—and they were not primarily movements based on the working class like the whole revolutionary tradition of the previous century and a quarter. This is a paradox that many writers have tried to address in terms of the alienation of the sons and daughters of the privileged—not unlike the Russian revolutionary movement of the nineteenth century. In both cases, rebellion was an act, above all, of the recently educated and those still being educated—in other words, students. In the 1960s, students all over the world were in the vanguard, often so little supported by traditional revolutionary elements that the New Left tried to devise theories of the students as the true revolutionary class, morally and psychologically oppressed by the academic discipline that they had to endure. In fact, workers (if they weren't too young) often proved to be the most available force at the service of the authorities or the counterrevolutionaries to fight against student radicals. So it was with the Wallace movement in America, Mao's 1968 reaction in China, and even to a limited extent in Czechoslovakia. France was a notable exception.

The revolutionary acts of 1968 were not the outcome of economic crisis or impoverishment. Quite the contrary—1968 was the culmination of an unprecedented era of economic expansion and of affluence that was growing and spreading throughout the industrialized world. The progress of the American economy during the 1960s brought living standards to an all-time high. Between 1960 and 1968, incomes rose 51 percent, while the big price inflation due to the Vietnam War was yet to come. Real per capita income in 1958 dollars reached $2,473, compared with $1,883 in 1960 and only $2,557 in 1980.[2] The stock market also reflected national progress: on 2 January 1968, the Dow-Jones Industrial Average stood at 906.84, compared with 679.06 in January 1960; it peaked at 985.21 before the year ended, demonstrating that revolution is not necessarily bad for the economy. The market was more sensitive to the prospects for peace in Vietnam.

All of this economic success fits the classic story: revolution is most likely to occur not when a society is in a state of hopelessness but when it is developing dynamically and enjoying rising expectations. It then experiences frustration and outrage as social and economic advance encounters the obstinacy of entrenched government or custom. Too many determined and articulate people refuse to accept these limits. Just those elements of American society—youth, women, and minorities—who felt most keenly the promise and the obstacles of the new era of prosperity were the most likely to turn to radical forms of protest.

11

Economic gains did not necessarily mean social progress or ease. Crime rates in America were climbing precipitously, proving to some that the Great Society or the new life-styles were undermining the social order, but in fact simply reflecting a surge in the numbers of the youth generation born in the baby boom of the 1940s and 1950s. Other social indicators gave reason for concern as well—the divorce rate in 1968 was 2.9 per 1,000 as compared to 2.3 in 1960, and the rate of illegitimate births rose from 5.3 percent in 1960 to 9 percent in 1968. (These figures are modest compared to those for 1980—divorces at 5.2 per 1,000 and illegitimacies at 18.4 percent.) Clearly, neither revolution nor counter-revolution had the cure for the processes of decay that were at work in the foundations of modern society.

Why did the issues and animosities of the 1960s not lead to a total revolution of the classic type in the United States? There were, in fact, local outbreaks of a vividly revolutionary character among blacks and students—microrevolutions, so to speak. David Burner and Thomas West attribute to the 1960s "the sense that private lives were partaking of something of the energy and direction of public events"[3]—which is typical of a society undergoing revolution. Overall, however, this was a revolution in values rather than a revolution in institutions. Revolutionary overthrow of the national government was not in prospect because constitutional systems, themselves the product of revolutions in the past, are normally flexible and responsive enough to yield to public pressures and ease the head of revolutionary steam. As for the general direction of national policies, revolutionary crises in advanced countries tend to generate more popular support for counterrevolution than for a consummation of revolutionary radicalism: witness Central Europe and the rise of Fascism and Nazism between the two world wars. In the end, a majority of the American public turned against the radicals and against further social change, laying the basis for the long conservative era in American political life in the 1970s and 1980s.

The diverse movements of protest that climaxed in 1968 did share certain common principles. These new social values give the Sixties Revolution a distinctive place in the sequence of revolutionary up-heavals that have shaped modern civilization during the last several hundred years. The revolutions of the seventeenth and eighteenth centuries in England, France, and America centered on values of religious liberty and political equality that became deeply woven into the fabric of the American Republic. The Russian Revolution and the socialist movement from which it emerged had a very different value focus: the economic liberation of the ordinary individual from domination by private wealth, that is, capitalism, whatever the de facto political tyranny that might supplant it. The same urge underlay movements of less radical reform—democratic socialism and the American New Deal—even though they had nothing in common politically with Soviet-style dictatorship. One recalls Franklin Roosevelt's declaration of war on "economic royalists." A cycle of semirevolutionary upheaval, described by the surge and ebb of New Deal liberalism, could easily be seen in America during the 1930s and 1940s.

How did the revolutionary wave of the 1960s differ from all these antecedents? Most contemporaries, both proponents and enemies of the revolution, were really not sure. The terms *liberal* and *Left* seemed to cover the aspirations of the new protest movements as well as the unfinished business of economic reform bequeathed by the first half of the century. Even today's political alignments and analyses are confused because they do not make proper distinctions between the value issues of the 1960s and those of an earlier generation—the agenda of the New Left as opposed to the Old Left in its various manifestations. Actually, the Old Left of the Marxist persuasion knew well enough that the young radicals represented something fundamentally different. "Werewolves" were what an official Soviet commentator called the fanatics of the New Left.[4]

In distinction to the Old Left, the New Left, liberal or radical, represented a different form of the old urge for liberation and equalization, this time not so much in the economic respect as in the realm of face-to-face personal relationships. The revolutionary movement of the 1960s attacked relationships of hierarchy and dominance-submission wherever they appeared. Here was the common denominator of the civil rights movement for black-white equality, the rising feminist movement for female-male equality, the student movement for liberation of the ignorant from the authority of the learned, the youthful rejection of the authority of their elders ("Don't trust anyone over 30"). In Europe, the New Left centered on a rejection of meritocracy and the managerial authority of the experts and bureaucrats, and the same targets—"expertise in command"—were assailed by the Cultural Revolution in China. In the Third World, the implied superiority of the West over native cultures came widely under attack by radical nationalists, though they were not averse to their own forms of authoritarianism in the name of national self-assertion. Western radical sympathy for the Third World had a hard time dealing with this contradiction.

It is paradoxical in timing that anti-imperialist sentiment peaked all over the world in the 1960s, for imperialism, in the strict sense of colonial rule, had been in full retreat ever since World War II. It is equally paradoxical that anti-imperialism should be a rallying cry within the formerly imperialist countries as much as in their former colonies. The target broadened from specifically colonial overlordship to the exercise of power—economic and cultural as well as military—by large nations over small ones. Thus, imperialism became the common enemy of Third World nationalists and of dissidents within the major states of the West who could identify domestic power structures—or the power structure of the most powerful Western state—with the role of international bully. Here the war in Vietnam was decisive. Imperialism, even the memory of imperialism, served to "de-authoritize" the ruling generation in the minds of youth, as Lewis Feuer expresses it in *The Conflict of Generations*.[5] Similar attitudes even cropped up in the Communist bloc: East Europeans rebelled at every opportunity against the local representatives of Soviet power, while Communist China denounced the "social imperialism" of the Russians and experimented with an alternative to the "capitalist road" of bureaucratic authoritarianism that it perceived in the Soviet Union.

Anti-imperialist nationalism was central to the unification struggle of the Vietnamese that stimulated social protest in the United States during the second half of the 1960s. In a symbolic way, the Vietnam War was a catalyst to the worldwide revolutionary mood of the era. By discrediting and destabilizing previously accepted authority and values in the United States, Vietnam bore out the adage that war—especially unsuccessful war—is the mother of revolution. For the first time in the history of the American Republic, apart from the crisis of the Civil War, widespread doubts emerged about the virtue of the American record and the legitimacy of the American enterprise. The emotional lodestone of nationalism had failed, at last, to pull the nation together as it had in all previous wars of the twentieth century. Vietnam became a cause that many if not most Americans found unworthy of sacrifice on either political or strategic grounds, and the veterans who fought there found themselves more often shunned than lionized. Americans' confidence, not only in the policies of their leadership but in the very institutions of government as well, began a slide from which it has not even now fully recovered.

This was the atmosphere of 1968. Every element of American society that felt itself deprived or abused began to assert its claims for a new form of social justice. The most impatient in each group began to assert those claims by confrontation and violence. At the same time, the Vietnam War and the political polarization it provoked spelled failure for a great attempt to achieve that social justice through the constituted governmental process. Just as Lyndon Johnson had feared, the war cut progress toward his dream of the Great Society to a slow crawl. It also put an end to his own career as a national leader.

American society survived the challenge of 1968 as well as the aftershocks of protest and controversy that continued for the next few years. The rest of the world—Western Europe, China, the Soviet bloc—also stood off their respective challengers who attempted to defy the authority of the prevailing order. In short, the international revolutionary drive of the 1960s was a failure.

Yet the post-1960s world would never be the same. This was especially true for the United States. Even though the protest movements of the era fell short of their most radical goals, they succeeded in irreversibly changing national thinking and expectations. Neither the Vietnam War nor any other exercise in the exertion of national power could again command the automatic solidarity of the American people. Racial equality became a principle that could not be publicly challenged, and programs were pushed to make amends for past discrimination. Feminism and the sexual revolution moved to the center of the political agenda for the decade that followed. The youth revolution and student radicalism ran their course, as a politicized generation moved on into middle age and economic affluence, but the values of the counterculture in personal self-expression and disdain for old mores continued to percolate through society as a whole. None of these effects were altered by the popular majority at the polls that swung behind the rejection of social experiment and the endorsement of a long counterrevolutionary phase in the American political cycle.

Abroad, 1968 left the world recovering from a state of shock. Western Europe continues to look back on that year as a watershed between the old political struggles and the new crisis of disbelief. For Eastern Europe it remains a symbol of hope and despair. For China it was the beginning of a long transition from revolutionary fever to cooler pragmatism. For all, perhaps, 1968 stands for the futility of untempered idealism.

The revolution that peaked so widely and dramatically in 1968 was a failure and it was not a failure. This is the contradictory destiny of revolutions. The revolutionary approach to change, however understandable in terms of the frustrations that fuel it, is inherently self-defeating. At the same time, the momentary shock it gives the social order cannot easily be forgotten. Unfinished revolutions can keynote the agenda for a nation or even for the international community for many decades to come. The last echoes of 1968 are still to be heard.

2

Saigon

2:45 A.M., WEDNESDAY, JANUARY 31. It is the day after Tet, the Vietnamese New Year's Day, ushering in the Year of the Monkey. Saigon is resting after a noisy celebration. Fireworks have been going off all evening. Although Vietcong trouble is expected and even reported up north in I Corps Area, security is routine.

In the moonless dark, a taxi and a truck crammed with men of the C–10 Vietcong City Sapper Battalion—the Saigon Underground—approach the walled compound of the American Embassy on tree-lined Thong Nhut ("Reunification") Boulevard. Without warning, shots burst from the taxi toward two American MPs guarding the embassy gate— S–4 Charles Daniel of Durham, N.C., and Pfc William Sebast of Albany, N.Y. The MPs bolt the gate closed and radio for help, while the sleepy Vietnamese police sentries outside the embassy flee for their lives. The vehicles come to a stop and discharge their passengers, who move quickly to the wall, plant a bomb, and blast their way through onto the embassy grounds. In an exchange of automatic rifle fire, their two lead men and the two MPs are killed. Two more MPs, responding in a jeep to the radio call for help, are shot dead as they approach the gate. The VC assailants lay siege to the brand new embassy chancery building with their hand-held rocket launchers.

The commando unit is woefully inadequate for its presumed task of seizing this symbol of the American presence, but it has no idea that the embassy is virtually undefended except for three marines and some communications personnel. Ambassador Ellsworth Bunker and most embassy officials are asleep at their respective residences several blocks away. (Bunker, who has not been privy to the intelligence about a possible attack, is spirited out of his house at 3 A.M. by marines in an armored personnel carrier and taken to a more secure location.) The attackers fail to storm the solidly built chancery, as early news reports assumed they did, though the firing goes on incessantly. Marine Sergeant Ronald Harper of Cambridge, Minnesota, alone at the guard desk awaiting the VC assault, receives a telephone call from the headquarters of General William Westmoreland, commander of all United States forces in Vietnam.

"You're not scared or anything, are you, Sergeant?"

"You bet your ass I am."[1] (Sergeant Harper wins the Bronze Star for remaining at his post throughout the attack.)

The first American relief unit to arrive at the scene, off-duty marine guards, find themselves locked out of the Embassy grounds. In the dark, they do not notice the hole in the wall. Some of the marines rush into buildings opposite the embassy and exchange fire with the VC on the grounds. The marines have no grenades. One of them is killed—the fifth and last American fatality in the embassy action. The nearest Vietnamese police station refuses to help.

Because the defense of Saigon has been officially turned over to the ARVN (Army of the Republic of Vietnam), the only serious American military unit inside the city is the 716th MP Battalion. Although the battalion lacks heavy equipment, commander Lt. Col. Gordon Rowe endeavors to implement his "disaster plan" in response to the torrent of calls for help. He receives orders from General Westmoreland to make the situation at the embassy his first priority, but when his MPs reach the embassy compound, they, like the marines, cannot get inside.

At 5 A.M. helicopters finally arrive from Bien-hoa air base with a company of airborne infantry, intending to land on the chancery roof (made famous for this purpose by the final American evacuation in 1975). Fire from the VC within the embassy compound drives the helicopters off, and Lt. Gen. Frederick Weyand, commanding United States ground forces around Saigon, orders them to wait until daybreak. At dawn, the MPs finally break through the compound gate and a helicopter full of paratroopers at last lands on the embassy roof, but they find that most of the VC squad are dead or dying, picked off one by one by the marines and MPs. Two VC are taken alive, while four Vietnamese employees of the embassy (one apparently turned traitor) are killed in the crossfire. The last of the attackers charges into an old house on the Embassy grounds occupied by retired colonel George Jacobson, special assistant to the ambassador. Pfc Paul Healy pitches a .45 through a window to Jacobson, and the colonel gets his man before the VC can turn his AK–47 on him.

Despite a multitude of news reports to the contrary, the VC have not penetrated the chancery building. The embassy is declared secure in time for breakfast, and General Westmoreland arrives to inspect the scene of battle. One reporter likens the locale, with the dead still strewn about the gardens, to "a butcher shop in Eden."[2] Westmoreland tells the press that despite the "deceitful" attack, "the enemy's well-laid plans went afoul," and that "the enemy, by coming into the open . . . was inviting defeat."[3]

The VC assault on the American Embassy in Saigon, carried off under the noses of a huge American news-gathering establishment, became a headline newspaper and television sensation back home. In perspective, however, it was only a minor action among the coordinated nationwide series of attacks by which the North Vietnamese and the Vietcong hoped to seize the psychological initiative and open the way to victory in their war of national unification. Their strategy was not a frontal assault, which would have been suicidal on any large scale against the fire power and air supremacy of the American and South Vietnamese forces. Instead, the Communists relied on the guerrilla warfare methods they had practiced so successfully for years, carrying their attack out of the jungles and into the cities. Part of their offensive force was already in place as a clandestine urban underground. Reinforcements from the rural areas filtered into the cities by disguising themselves as civilians returning from holiday visits to the villages of their ancestors. They brought in weapons hidden in vegetable carts.

Units of the Vietcong opened the attack on January 30 in the northern sector of South Vietnam. Infiltrating the city of Da Nang and other points, they attempted to seize government buildings and command posts. However, the VC in this area had jumped the gun, due to confusion over their orders. Their actions prompted the joint command in Saigon to cancel observance of the Tet cease-fire and to alert their forces. But the warning, like many previous ones, was not taken seriously.

To American intelligence, a general Communist offensive occurring around the time of Tet was a likely prospect. The National Security Agency revealed during the *Westmoreland* v. *CBS* libel trial in 1984 that its new means of electronic surveillance had detected substantial movements of North Vietnamese troops down the Ho Chi Minh trail through the jungles of Laos and into South Vietnam beginning in November

1967.[4] In a 1981 interview with CBS, President Johnson's national security advisor Walt Rostow confirmed that the White House had been fully briefed:

> I sent out early in December of '67 a cable saying evidently we're going to see a maximum effort. . . . Saigon sent back a cable saying this is a maximum effort. We will never have seen anything like it before. The CIA said no, it's more—rather more the same.[5]

Where intelligence failed was not in anticipating the offensive but in predicting its direction. The American command was sure that the main effort would come on the battlefield farther north. Saigon itself had never before been the object of a serious Communist attack. "We did not surmise the true nature or the scope of the countrywide attack . . . ," admitted General Westmoreland. "It did not occur to us that the enemy would undertake suicidal attacks in the face of our power."[6] General Weyand had fortunately persuaded General Westmoreland to delay his plan to commit their main force out in the jungles. According to Neil Sheehan, "Weyand was convinced afterwards as was [John Paul] Vann, that . . . Saigon would have fallen had he not objected to sending his troops up to the Cambodian frontier. 'It would have been an absolute disaster. . . .' "[7]

The main wave of the Tet attacks came, as planned, in the early hours of January 31, as infiltrators from the countryside joined the underground Vietcong forces in cities all over South Vietnam. The plan was to seize key government buildings and public facilities, isolate the military bases, and incite a general popular uprising against the South Vietnamese regime. Highways were blocked to obstruct the movement of American and ARVN forces. Every significant South Vietnamese city, including thirty-six of the forty-four provincial capitals, was hit on January 30 or 31.

In Saigon, nearly every major public building and military installation was an objective of the Vietcong commando squads, about four thousand men in all. At most key points, including the heavily guarded presidential palace, they were driven off, only to assume sniper positions in nearby buildings until they were blasted out or hunted down, sometimes days later. Cho-lon, the Chinese quarter of Saigon, was densely infiltrated by VC and half destroyed in the counterattacks to root them out.

One temporary success for the attackers was the seizure of the Saigon radio station by a VC unit, which intended to broadcast tapes announcing the general insurrection. A new "Alliance of National and Peace

Forces" was supposed to supplant the American-backed government and form a coalition with the National Liberation Front, the Communist-run political arm of the Vietcong. Fortunately for the government, however, the link to the transmitter outside of town was cut, leaving the VC voiceless except for their clandestine transmitter (called "Liberation Radio") in the jungle. Meanwhile, some of the most serious Communist blows were aimed at the nearby American air bases of Tan Son Nhut and Bien-hoa, where the VC rocketed planes on the ground, and at the ground forces base at Long Binh, where they blew up an ammunition dump.

Along with their assault on the cities, the Vietcong stepped up their pressure on American and ARVN outposts in the countryside. What it was like for the grunts in their bunkers only 20 kilometers north of Saigon is vividly described by a 20-year-old First Division rifleman who later went on to become an accomplished writer:

> At midnight our perimeter came under small arms and automatic weapons fire. The green tracers came flying in at us and bullets began popping, thudding, and ricocheting into and around the bunker. Next came some *whoosh-crack-booms* of RPGs [rifle-propelled grenades] or rockets and the flashes lit up the area around us. Whoever I was with was saying, "Hey man, something big's comin' down!" I fired a few bursts from my rifle into the enemy tracers. Firing felt good, the empty shells spewing out, the rifle warm. . . .
>
> In our bunker we kept taking incoming rounds, and several times I spotted movement out in front.
>
> "My God! Those are Viet Cong out there!"
>
> I opened fire in the weird, surreal light of flares. Because of clumps of bushes and uneven ground, it was hard to tell whether I was hitting them. At 2:05 A.M. a helicopter overhead spotted seventy-five more heavily-armed enemy lying face down to avoid being seen, and called in artillery and airstrikes on them. All around us, the night was erupting with the artillery's high explosive shells, the firing machine-guns and rockets of the gunships, and the enemy tracers flying every which way.[8]

In the initial shock of the surprise Tet attacks, South Vietnamese authority, both civil and military, was badly shaken. Even before, the Saigon government was a fragile entity, theoretically a parliamentary democracy but actually a personal dictatorship under Ngo Dinh Diem from independence in 1954 to his assassination in 1963. Advised by his wily brother Ngo Din Nhu and the so-called "Dragon Lady," Madame Nhu, Diem depended heavily on the Catholic minority, primarily refugees from the North, and was repeatedly embroiled with the national Buddhist leadership centered at the ancient capital city of Hué. After Diem was eliminated in an American-approved military coup, politics in

South Vietnam remained fluid and personalized, without any clear system of parties. The leadership in Saigon passed rapidly from one egocentric military figure to another—the lackadaisical General Duong Van Minh ("Big Minh") to 1964, the unstable General Nguyen Khanh to 1965, and the flamboyant Air Marshal Nguyen Cao Ky to 1967. These men were typically upper-class Vietnamese, more often natives of the North or the central provinces than of the South, who had risen through the ranks of the French puppet army fighting against Ho Chi Minh.

In 1967, a new American-style constitution was put into effect, and the Americans pressured the two leading presidential rivals onto a single ticket—the devious former chief of staff General Nguyen Van Thieu for president, and Air Marshal Ky for vice president. (These were not enthusiastic choices; Assistant Secretary of State William Bundy later called the Thieu–Ky team "absolutely the bottom of the barrel."[9]) Even with military manipulation of the rural vote in the September 1967 election, the official ticket won by a plurality of only 35 percent against a splintered field of oppositionists (which moreover excluded anyone accused of being a Communist or a "neutralist"). Thieu's first act in office was to jail the leading opposition candidate.

In mid-1967, in the face of American claims of steady progress in the campaign to pacify South Vietnam, the North Vietnamese leadership decided on a spectacular and heroic campaign to destroy the political base of the Saigon government and demonstrate the futility of American intervention. For the next six months Hanoi and COSVN (the Communist Central Office for South Vietnam that ran the war for Hanoi) secretly pursued detailed military preparations, while the National Liberation Front dusted off its democratic-sounding program and tried to line up supporters for a prospective coalition government. There was no doubt about North Vietnamese control over all aspects of the operation, political as well as military; the First Secretary of COSVN, Pham Hung, was a member of the ruling Politboro of the Vietnam Workers party (that is, the Communists) in Hanoi. The aging Ho Chi Minh made a·rare public appearance in December 1967 to recharge enthusiasm for the war, appealing to all Vietnamese as "thirty-one million resistance fighters, fearing neither hardships nor sacrifice, going forward in the wake of their victories to accomplish even greater feats of battle."[10] The upshot was Tet, launched after this order was read to the waiting units:

> All cadres and combatants of all South Vietnam Liberation Armed Forces should move forward to carry out direct attacks on all the headquarters of the enemy, to disrupt the United States imperialists' will for aggression and to smash the Puppet Government and Puppet Army, the lackeys of the United States, restore power to the people, completely liberate the fourteen million

people of South Vietnam, fulfill our revolutionary task of establishing democracy throughout the country. It will be the greatest battle ever fought throughout the history of our country. . . . It will decide the fate and survival of our Fatherland and will shake the world and cause the most bitter failure to the imperialist ringleaders.[11]

When the shooting started at Tet, President Thieu was on vacation and had to be flown into Saigon in an American helicopter to join Vice President Ky and the Joint General Staff. Some South Vietnamese generals in the Delta towns panicked and went into hiding, including the regional commander. Other South Vietnamese officials lashed out in rage, such as National Police Chief Nguyen Ngoc Loan, the man caught in a memorable photograph by AP's Eddie Adams the day after the offensive began, in the act of shooting a captive VC suspect at point-blank range. The ARVN experienced its worst wave of desertions of the entire war prior to the final collapse in 1975, and there were outbreaks of looting as well. In most situations, what saved the day was a vigorous reponse by American forces on the ground and in the air, pounding the Vietcong penetrators into oblivion. Unfortunately, victory was gained at the cost of vast civilian damage and the generation of hundreds of thousands of new refugees.

In the meantime, taking advantage of President Thieu's absence at the start of the Tet offensive, Vice President Ky attempted a personal coup by forming a "National Reconstruction Committee" to take over the government. Thieu quickly elbowed Ky aside, and announced a purge of selected military and provincial chiefs on ostensible grounds of corruption, but actually for their links with the vice president. He followed this with further arrests of political oppositionists and suspected neutralists, including the head of the South Vietnamese Confederation of Labor. But in the crazy quilt of South Vietnamese politics—half authoritarian and half stubbornly individualistic—the National Assembly in late February denied Thieu's request for the declaration of a national emergency. A CIA report warned, "Further military defeats could cause a sudden swing away from the government. . . . Its ability to provide energetic leadership throughout the country and at all levels is in serious doubt."[12]

While Saigon tried to go on with politics as usual, the rural pacification program, supposed to implant government authority in the countryside, was left in a shambles after South Vietnamese troops pulled back from the hamlets to secure the urban centers. The Joint Chiefs of Staff chairman, General Earle Wheeler, acknowledged in his report a month later, "The enemy is operating with relative freedom in the countryside, probably recruiting heavily and no doubt infiltrating NVA

[North Vietnamese Army] units and personnel. . . . There is no doubt that the RD [Revolutionary Development] Program has suffered a severe setback."[13] This was a major blow to American hopes for a self-reliant South Vietnam, already called into question just a few days before Tet when Saigon's head of pacification resigned to protest corruption and nepotism in the program. The chief American advisor to the program, Robert Komer, still defended the effort ten years later and blamed its troubles on the politicians: "What failed was the Vietnam government and its armed forces. It turned out that all the investment we made in them could not compensate for a single fact, which was that they simply lacked effective leadership from the top to the bottom."[14] Not long after Tet, an Agency for International Development study of corruption in South Vietnam was disclosed by Senator Ernest Gruening:

> Corruption in Vietnam is an ever-present fact of life, permeating all echelons of government and society, corroding the vitality of this nation, eroding the framework of government, and unnecessarily prolonging the war. Unless it is substantially reduced on a broad scale, and very soon at that, there are serious doubts that this war can ever be really "won."[15]

The Tet offensive was particularly savage in the Mekong Delta region southwest of Saigon, the densely populated rice bowl of the country where the South Vietnamese authorities had insisted on fighting their own war without the aid of American combat forces. In city after city, the ARVN command was paralyzed by fear, and American advisors had to take charge. Only by massive artillery fire and air bombardment were the VC attackers ultimately subdued. The press was taken to view the results at the provincial center of Ben Tre, where over a thousand civilians had been killed by these tactics. An American officer offered the unforgettable explanation, "It became necessary to destroy the town to save it."[16] In his history of the Tet offensive, Don Oberdorfer of the *Washington Post* comments:

> The United States claimed to be fighting to build a nation and protect the freedom of a people, but the immense weight of its modern weaponry was destroying Vietnam in the process. The Viet Cong, whose military means were more closely tailored to political ends, placed strict limitations on the use of their firepower. They killed for a purpose, and put a high value on the good will of the people. . . . The United States and South Vietnamese government forces, on the other hand, were indiscriminate in their use of firepower, and seemed to value their own safety far beyond the political purpose (if any) for which they fought.[17]

24

In most locations, the Tet attacks turned out to be militarily futile suicide missions. Surprisingly enough, too few Communist troops were committed to the daring task set for them, and success—as is so familiar in modern military actions—hinged too much on elaborate plans working out without such mishaps as units getting lost and leaders getting killed. Typically, the attackers were isolated and confined to sniping activity wherever they were holed up, until American firepower could be brought in to dispose of them. Most estimates claim that about half of the 80,000 or so Vietcong troops committed to the Tet offensive were killed in action, as compared to roughly 1,000 Americans and 5,000 South Vietnamese (excluding civilians). The day after the attack was launched, an assessment by COSVN conceded, "We failed to seize a number of primary objectives. . . . We also failed to hold the occupied areas. In the political field we failed to motivate the people to stage uprisings and break the enemy's oppressive control."[18]

Between February 18 and 20, the Communists launched a second wave of attacks, but this effort, mostly shelling and mortaring, was less daring and less effective. On February 21, COSVN ordered suspension of offensive action against South Vietnamese cities in order to concentrate their efforts again in the rural areas. North Vietnamese sources admitted after the war that they had lost their best Southern cadres in the Tet offensive and that the core of the subsequent war effort had to be North Vietnamese regulars. As described by Communist General Tran Van Tra, the objectives of the offensive were "beyond our actual strength" and stemmed from

> an illusion based on our subjective desires. . . . We suffered large losses in materiel and manpower. . . . We were not only unable to retain the gains we had made but had to overcome a myriad of difficulties in 1969 and 1970 so that the revolution could stand firm in the storm.[19]

Despite North Vietnamese admissions of failure, the psychological shock of Tet was devastating both to the South Vietnamese and to the Americans. The contrasting reactions of confidence within the military hierarchy, and of futility among the journalists and ordinary GI's, underscore how far the military technocrats were out of touch with the powerful though subtle realities of the human realm. Robert Shaplen of the *New Yorker* reported (March 23) "a continuing erosion of morale and a growing sense of foreboding." Wrote Michael Herr of *Esquire* magazine, "We took a huge collective nervous breakdown."[20]

One major target of the Tet offensive was an exception to the pattern of failure—the ancient capital city of Hué, just south of the Demilitarized Zone and the North Vietnamese boundary. With a heavy commitment of forces and successful planning, as well as the background of Buddhist disaffection, the Vietcong and North Vietnamese attackers took the entire city and held all or part of it for three weeks. Their regime was one of unabashed terror; some three thousand civilians connected with the Saigon government were executed and buried in mass graves. American marines and ARVN troops fought their way back through Hué in a bloody spectacle that became nightly fare on American television. Finally, on February 24, the last Communist resistance in Hué was overcome, suspect VC collaborators were liquidated by the Saigon forces, and the Tet offensive was brought to an end.

At the time the Tet offensive was launched, U.S. combat forces had been in action in South Vietnam for more than two and a half years, helping the Saigon government resist what was variously described as a war of aggression or a nationalist revolutionary movement waged by the Vietcong. It had been nearly three and a half years since Congress passed the "Gulf of Tonkin Resolution," which authorized the president to use American armed force in "retaliation" against the North Vietnamese for an alleged torpedo boat attack on two American destroyers. (The ships were, in fact, supporting South Vietnamese raids on the North Vietnamese coast.) It was a full three years since President Johnson had ordered American air forces to begin bombing North Vietnam on the pretext of a Communist attack on American advisors at the South Vietnamese mountain base of Pleiku.

Even now we cannot define with certainty the American motive for engagement in Vietnam—so entangled are the strategic reasons and the political myths. The strategic concern had its roots in the victory of the Communists in China in 1949, putting them in a position to aid Ho Chi Minh's Communist-led Viet Minh independence movement that had been fighting the French colonial rulers since the end of World War II. To contain Communism in Asia and to encourage France's cooperation in Europe, the Truman administration began to provide logistical aid to the French in Indo-China. The outbreak of the Korean War, in June 1950, multiplied American worries about the Pacific region, but the experience of Chinese intervention in Korea in November of that year lent a dimension of caution lest Peking be provoked into a similar action in Vietnam. By 1954, when a whole division was trapped and besieged by Ho's troops at the northern mountain town of Dien Bien Phu, the French faced defeat. Paris appealed for direct American air strikes. The

Eisenhower administration even debated the use of nuclear weapons against the Viet Minh, but was dissuaded from this extreme by congressional leaders (including Senator Lyndon Johnson) and the British.

At the Geneva Conference of 1954, the war-weary French, stunned by the surrender of their garrison at Dien Bien Phu, accepted de facto partition of Vietnam between Ho Chi Minh's Communist government in Hanoi and the former French puppet regime under Emperor Bao Dai in Saigon. Ostensibly, this was only a temporary military disengagement pending elections in two years of a government for all of Vietnam. The Eisenhower administration denounced the agreement and instead recognized the Saigon authorities as the sole Vietnamese government, guaranteeing their security as the French pulled out and eventually encouraging them to repudiate the proposed elections. In line with President Eisenhower's "Domino Theory"—that the first country in Southeast Asia to fall to Communism would cause all the others to topple—Washington dispatched American military advisors and economic aid to Saigon. The United States remained undeterred when Bao Dai's prime minister Ngo Din Diem overthrew the playboy emperor and proclaimed a republic under his own authoritarian rule.

To justify its involvement with Saigon, the United States government shifted its political rationale. Instead of rolling back Communism and overthrowing the Hanoi regime, Washington now sought to defend an allegedly separate and independent nation, South Vietnam, against Communist bloc "aggression." In 1955, Secretary of State John Foster Dulles set up the Southeast Asia Treaty Organization (SEATO), a paper entity modeled on NATO, to legitimate the American commitment to Saigon. Ten years later the argument had not changed. Speaking to an audience at Johns Hopkins University in April 1965, President Johnson declared, "We fight because we must fight if we are to live in a world where every country can shape its own destiny. . . . North Vietnam has attacked the independent nation of South Vietnam. Its object is total conquest." General Westmoreland went so far as to liken the Tet offensive to North Korea's surprise attack on South Korea in 1950. President Reagan epitomized the lingering popular confusion over this mission when he tried in 1982 to justify his policy of defending El Salvador against Nicaragua by comparing it to American intervention to help Saigon: "North and South Vietnam had been, previous to colonization, two separate countries."[21] Reagan thought the election called for by the Geneva Agreement was to decide whether the two supposed nations would unite, and claimed that Ho Chi Minh was the one who rejected it. Arguments like these left no room for comprehending the common

Vietnamese nationalism that linked the southern Vietcong, a residue of the anti-French war, with the Hanoi government in a civil struggle against the Saigon clients, first of the French and later of the Americans.

The revolutionary war in Indo-China was not a unique or isolated phenomenon. Rather, it was part of a vast anticolonial and anti-imperialist movement that had been sweeping the Third World since the end of World War II. Castro's revolution in Cuba in 1959 opened a new phase in this upheaval, including sweeping decolonization in Africa, new radical movements in the Middle East inspired by "Arab Socialism," and the extraordinary period of revolutionary extremism in Communist China during the Cultural Revolution when Peking denounced the Soviets for taking the "capitalist road." Coincidentally, guerrilla warfare was resumed by the Communists in South Vietnam, ending the half-dozen years of truce after Geneva. Chinese encouragement may have played a part in starting the war up again, but the driving force for the Vietnamese Communists was always their own revolutionary nationalist urge to expel the foreigners and reunite the country under the government in Hanoi. Between 1960 and the onset of massive American intervention in 1965, the Vietcong guerrillas, under the political umbrella of the National Liberation Front, made steady progress toward this end, while the South Vietnamese regime backed by the United States tottered from one coup to another.

These historical subtleties were not foremost in President Johnson's mind when he decided to escalate in Vietnam. He had a more pragmatic concern for his political flanks at home. After he retired he told his biographer Doris Kearns:

> I knew from the start that I was bound to be crucified either way I moved. If I left the woman I really loved—the Great Society—in order to get involved with that bitch of a war on the other side of the world, then I would lose everything at home. All my programs. All my hopes to feed the hungry and shelter the homeless. All my dreams to provide education and medical care to the browns and the blacks and the lame and the poor. But if I left that war and let the Communists take over South Vietnam, then I would be seen as a coward and my nation would be seen as an appeaser and we would both find it impossible to accomplish anything for anybody anywhere on the entire globe. . . . I knew that if we let Communist aggression succeed in taking over South Vietnam, there would follow in this country an endless national debate—a mean and destructive debate—that would shatter my Presidency, kill my administration, and damage our democracy. I knew that Harry Truman and Dean Acheson had lost their effectiveness from the day that the Communists took over in China. I believed that the loss of China had played a large role in the rise of Joe McCarthy. And I knew that all of these problems, taken together, were chickenshit compared with what might happen if we lost Vietnam . . . [including the awful specter of] Robert Kennedy out in front

leading the fight against me, telling everyone that I had betrayed John Kennedy's commitment to South Vietnam.[22]

Following the initial landing of the First Marine Division at Da Nang in June 1965, the American government poured combat troops into South Vietnam in a two-year buildup to save the Saigon government from the Communist insurgency, while United States Air Force and Navy planes continued their punitive bombardment of North Vietnam. The man in charge since 1964 was General Westmoreland, a proud and stubborn South Carolinian, at one time the youngest major general in the army and, just prior to his assignment to Saigon, the superintendent of the Military Academy at West Point. With half a million Americans at his disposal and a South Vietnamese army of nearly a million (some good, some not so good), Westmoreland claimed steady progress over the enemy through his search-and-destroy operations and the rural pacification program. (Operation Phoenix, designed to target suspected Communist leaders and agents for assassination, came later, a response to the Tet crisis.) Meanwhile, the Johnson administration, committed not to lose the war and hoping not to have to widen it, put out off-again, on-again peace feelers to Hanoi, culminating in the president's "San Antonio Formula" of September 1967: "The United States is willing to stop all aerial and naval bombardment of North Vietnam when this will lead promptly to productive discussions," with the undefinable proviso that "North Vietnam would not take advantage of this bombing cessation or limitation."

About the same time, advised of growing misgivings about the war on the home front and in Congress, General Westmoreland put the best possible face on his intelligence estimates to minimize the presumed enemy capacity to continue the war.* "The people we work for are in

---

* Westmoreland's approach to the intelligence estimates in 1967–1968 became the main issue in one of the more controversial reverberations of the Vietnam War. The media, blamed by prowar apologists for America's withdrawal of support for South Vietnam, were returning to the war theme to feed the public's appetite for an explanation of what went wrong. On 23 January 1982, CBS aired a documentary on General Westmoreland's intelligence estimates called "The Uncounted Enemy: A Vietnam Deception."

The trouble with the estimates of Vietcong strength went back to 1966, when CIA intelligence analyst Sam Adams (a descendant of the presidential family), using captured VC documents, worked out projections of guerrilla strength far in excess of the official estimates in Saigon. Rebuffed by the intelligence bureaucracy but vindicated in his own mind by the Tet surprise, Adams eventually published his story in *Harper's* magazine ("Vietnam Cover-up," May 1975), from which CBS developed the idea of the documentary. Through interviews conducted with former intelligence officers by Mike Wallace and George Crile, the program argued that Westmoreland's headquarters had systematically held back information on growing North Vietnamese and Vietcong troop strength in 1967, so as not to upset the optimism of official Washington. To this end, CBS claimed, there was "a conscious effort—indeed a conspiracy at the highest levels of American military intelligence—to suppress and alter critical intelligence on the enemy in the year

the business of reelecting President Johnson in November," explained an unnamed American official in Saigon to the *New York Times*.[23] Westmoreland prevailed on the CIA not to count local VC supporters in the official "Order of Battle" assessment of enemy strength, after he and Ambassador Bunker had cabled the White House, "We have been projecting an image of success over the recent months. The self-defense militia must be removed [from the OB], or the newsmen will immediately seize on the point that the enemy force has increased."[24] "During 1967," Westmoreland stated in his year-end assessment to the Pentagon, "the enemy lost control of large sectors of the population. . . . The year ended with the enemy increasingly resorting to desperation tactics in attempting to achieve military/psychological victory; and he has experienced only failure in these attempts. . . ." He expressed "optimism for increased successes in 1968," thanks in part to "a greatly improved intelligence system."[25] Returning to Washington to report personally in November 1967, Westmoreland gave assurance—in those never-to-be-forgotten words—that he saw "light at the end of the tunnel."[26] Journalist Michael Herr quotes the response of one battle-hardened grunt who had made a specialty of ferreting VC out of their tunnel hideouts: "What does that asshole know about tunnels?"[27]

Whatever the arguments for assessing victory or defeat, Tet clearly heightened the anxiety level of American forces searching out the Vietcong in the jungles. This was the immediate background of the My Lai

---

leading up to the Tet offensive." Westmoreland had allegedly imposed a "ceiling" of 300,000 on estimates of Vietcong guerrilla strength, although testimony on this point was never definitive.

The now-retired Westmoreland, attributing the dispute over the figures to technicalities of intelligence evaluation, held a press conference in Washington on 26 January 1982, to denounce the CBS program as a "vicious, scurrilous and premeditated attack on my character and personal integrity," and filed a libel suit against CBS for $120 million. He claimed that all he did was exclude VC village auxiliaries from the enemy troop total on the ground that they had no offensive value. After its own internal investigation of the program, CBS offered to retract the "conspiracy" charge and give Westmoreland a chance for rebuttal, but he chose to press on with the libel suit. Finally coming to trial late in 1984, the case was abruptly settled out of court with a pro-forma apology to the general. An account of the trial by Renata Adler, published first in a *New Yorker* magazine series and then in her book *Reckless Disregard* (New York: Knopf, 1986), denounced CBS for riding roughshod over the truth in the interest of theatrical sensationalism. As it did in response to the earlier study of the broadcast in *A Matter of Honor* by Don Kowet (New York: Macmillan, 1984), CBS protested to the *New Yorker* and tried to get Knopf to make prepublication changes in the book, only to incur further charges of bias and intimidation. In the face of all this, an in-house reexamination by CBS producer Burton Benjamin, later expanded into a book, found the broadcast "seriously flawed" and "out of balance" (Burton Benjamin, *Fair Play: CBS, General Westmoreland, and How a Television Documentary Went Wrong*, New York: Burlingame/Harper & Row, 1988, p. 160, 163). In this, as in so many other facets, the Vietnam War is far from over in America.

massacre of 16 March 1968. Due to a cover-up by the United States Army, My Lai did not enter into history and become a political issue for an entire year after it occurred. Ultimately, Seymour Hersh of the *New York Times* recounted it in two books: *My Lai 4* (New York: Random House, 1970) and *Cover-Up: The Army's Secret Investigation of the Massacre at My Lai 4* (New York: Random House, 1972). The basic story is now well known. Dropped by helicopter early in the morning on a typical search-and-destroy mission, C Company of the 20th Infantry, Americal Division, entered the My Lai cluster of hamlets in VC-infested Quang Ngai Province south of Da Nang. One American soldier shot a suspect and then, as if on signal, the unit went berserk and annihilated every villager in sight—old men, women, and children, 347 in all according to the official Army investigation that finally took place. The victims were meanwhile chalked up as VC combatants in the body count of enemy dead.

My Lai was not altogether exceptional as a consequence of the American attempt to impose a military solution on Vietnam. When it finally came to light, it laid bare the moral crisis that afflicted the United States war effort. The issue was not merely whether a worthy end can justify the means, but whether this particular end was compelling enough to justify the means that American forces were driven to use in a struggle where anyone could be the enemy. For the Pentagon, the end was ultimately self-justification; although charges of responsibility for My Lai were brought against the entire chain of command up to the division commander, most were eventually dropped. Five members of the offending company were tried by court-martial; one, platoon leader Lt. William Calley, was found guilty and sentenced to twenty years' imprisonment. Nobody was convicted for the nearly identical massacre, perpetrated simultaneously at the adjacent village of My Khe by B Company of the same regiment, which came to light during the My Lai investigation.

The contention that Tet was a Communist defeat, however cruelly inflicted, is the major premise in the argument that the United States could have gone on to win the war had it not been for the alleged media myth of a Communist triumph. President Johnson recalled the episode in his memoirs:

> The media seemed to be in competition as to who could provide the most lurid and depressing accounts. Columnists unsympathetic to American involvement in Southeast Asia jumped on the bandwagon. Some senatorial critics and numerous opponents of America's war effort added their voices to the chorus of defeatism. The American people and even a number of officials

in government, subjected to this daily barrage of bleakness and near panic, began to think that we must have suffered a defeat.[28]

But Johnson, then as later, failed to grasp the reason why Tet had such a decisive political effect. Tet came at a time of rising doubts about the prosecution of the war, both in the government and among the American public. It shook the theory of outside aggression and underscored the element of civil war within South Vietnam. North Vietnam's legendary commander Vo Nguyen Giap told the renowned interviewer Oriana Fallaci shortly after Tet, "The Liberation Front shows that it is able to attack them whenever it wants, wherever it wants. . . . The Americans finally admit that this war is a strategic error. Johnson admits it, McNamara admits it."[29] As Stanley Karnow observes in his history of the war, "Public 'support' for the war had been slipping steadily for two years prior to Tet—a trend influenced by the mounting casualties, rising taxes, and, especially, the feeling that there was no end in view."[30]

The initial, media-fed impact of Tet was actually to revive patriotic support of the war, but with time for reflection, doubt set in again. Tet did not create these doubts, it only confirmed them: that Communist persistence would not easily be ground down; that the South Vietnamese regime, on its own, was too ineffective and corrupt to be worth supporting; and that the war represented no critical strategic purpose for the United States. Senator George Aiken declared on the floor of the Senate on January 19, eleven days before the Tet offensive, "We are fighting nationalists first in Vietnam. . . . To make out that the North Vietnamese and the Viet Cong even today are integral parts of a unified and monolithic world communism is simply self-destructive fantasy." He described the lack of any believable policy rationale: "By clinging to its inventions, the Administration is simply duping Americans at home and undermining credibility abroad in the sincerity of our purposes and the efficiency of our diplomacy." Henry Brandon of *The Times* of London commented, "Politically, the U.S. failed because President Johnson and his military leaders thought they could ignore public opinion."[31]

Opposition to the war in Vietnam had been growing in direct proportion to the extent of American involvement. In 1964, when only two senators—Wayne Morse of Oregon and Ernest Gruening of Alaska—voted against the Tonkin Gulf Resolution, its implications were not yet widely apparent. Lyndon Johnson overwhelmingly won election to his first full term on a platform of peace and prosperity against the perceived right-wing extremist Barry Goldwater. After Johnson began the bombing of North Vietnam in February 1965 and committed American combat troops, disillusionment quickly set in, most visibly on college campuses. Students for a Democratic Society organized the first big antiwar demonstration in Washington in April 1965. In preparation for this event, University of Michigan protestors started the "teach-in" movement of marathon lectures and discussions about the war (so named by their mentor, philosophy professor Arnold Kaufman). In October of that year, David John Miller, a member of the pacifist Catholic Worker Group, set a new trend of protest by publicly burning his draft card and defiantly going to jail for his transgression.

Even within the government there were a few early voices of dissent. Undersecretary of State George Ball had opposed committing an American land army since the Kennedy years. Retired Lt. Gen. James Gavin, the former U.S. Army planning chief who had directed a study of the French phase of the war, spoke as early as 1966 of his policy of "enclaves," key areas to which the American forces would fall back while the South Vietnamese government sought a negotiated settlement with the guerrillas. Senator Aiken used this same theme in a memorable speech of October 1966, but added the notion that the United States could consider this a victory, giving rise to the exaggerated recollection that he had urged the country to "declare victory and go home."[32]

As American ground involvement escalated during 1966 and 1967, so did the extent and magnitude of antiwar protests. By the spring of 1967, Martin Luther King was brought by events to denounce "the madness of Vietnam." Speaking at the Riverside Church in New York on April 4, he called for "a revolution of values" in America, "to get on the right side of the world revolution." Sparked by black civil rights groups, the Spring Mobilization to End the War (the "Mobe") organized marches in New York and San Francisco, enlisting hundreds of thousands of protesters in both cities. The draft personalized the war for millions of young men and became a prime focus of opposition, more so, ironically, among college students who enjoyed deferments than among working-class youth (disproportionately black) who were called on to fight. In New York's Central Park, a group of Cornell University students assembled to burn their draft cards. Selective Service Director General Lewis Hershey only poured oil on the fire by ordering that protesting students and ministers lose their deferments.

Throughout the United States the more volatile elements of the student movement and the black civil rights movement were deeply radicalized by the war. The National Secretary of Students for a Democratic Society, Greg Calvert, citing Cuba's ideologist Che Guevara, declared, "We are working to build a guerrilla force. . . . We are actively organizing sedition."[33] In September 1967, a delegation of thirty antiwar activists organized by SDS past president Tom Hayden and pacifist leader David Dellinger went to Bratislava, Czechoslovakia, to meet a North Vietnamese and Vietcong delegation and promote solidarity between the American peace movement and Hanoi. While there, Hayden reportedly declaimed, "We are all Viet Cong" (a statement he later disavowed).[34] Afterward, he flew on to Hanoi with SDS organizer Rennie Davis and several others to negotiate the release of American prisoners held by the Vietcong, and actually returned with three men—an apparent gesture of the Communists' willingness to negotiate. The group came back from North Vietnam believing that they had seen a New Jerusalem of mass revolutionary devotion. Rennie Davis reported, "North Vietnam had an impact on me. . . . In Hanoi we saw things that *no one* in the country was aware of . . . , incredible human struggle. . . . The Vietnamese really did identify with and believe in the American Revolution."[35] Alarmed by such sentiments, C. L. Sulzberger of the *New York Times* warned in the wake of the Tet crisis (1 March 1968), "Our enemies call for two, three, many Vietnams inside the United States itself. . . . The distorted 'Revolutionary Warfare' virus might well spread in the racially bewildered USA. . . ."

Meanwhile, the "Mobe"—now the National Mobilization Committee to End the War in Vietnam—together with the San Francisco–based "Resistance" proclaimed "Stop the Draft Week" for October and scheduled a protest march in Washington. Fifty to a hundred thousand people at the Lincoln Memorial heard David Dellinger call for civil disobedience and confrontation, while hot-headed elements in the crowd crossed the Potomac and tried physically to storm the Pentagon. Norman Mailer, chronicling the encounter in *The Armies of the Night*, described it as "a rite of passage" for "unnamed saints"; America was exposed as "a beauty with a leprous skin."[36]

Actions to resist the draft went on almost continuously until the end of 1967, prompting the authorities to fight back with stiff legal measures. The Black Muslim boxing champion Muhammad Ali was denied conscientious objector status, tried and convicted for refusing induction, and officially stripped of his heavyweight title by the Boxing Association. On 5 January 1968, a federal grand jury indicted the noted baby-book author Dr. Benjamin Spock and Yale chaplain William Sloan Coffin, along with several others, for conspiring to promote draft evasion.

Until Tet, all these cries of protest found the government deaf and the public resentful. After Tet, the depth of youthful and radical disaffection brought on by the war would become astonishingly clear and undeniable.

At the time of the Tet offensive, President Johnson was already on edge because of the *Pueblo* affair of barely a week before, when the North Koreans' seizure of the American electronic intelligence ship by that name met with a chorus of national outrage. His immediate response to the new crisis in Vietnam was to order a public relations blitz in Washington and Saigon in order to restore public confidence. At his press conference on February 2, the President asserted, "The stated purposes of the general uprising have failed." Privately, as Joint Chiefs of Staff chairman General Wheeler acknowledged, the reaction in Washington was more like the mood after the Battle of Bull Run.[37] Johnson railed against the media for making Tet look like a Communist triumph. Yet to a reporter who saw him up close, "It was a heartbreaking period for the President. Victory suddenly looked remoter than ever. There was a mood of desperation between the lines of what he said to me that day [February 4], but it only seemed to reinforce his determination to win that coonskin."[38]

The president and the Joint Chiefs of Staff feared further embarrassing setbacks after the shock of Tet. They were particularly worried about the exposed American base of Khe Sanh just south of the DMZ near the Laotian border. Khe Sanh was where Westmoreland had expected the main Communist attack, rather than the cities. "I don't want any damn Dinbinphoo," Johnson warned the Joint Chiefs.[39] Although North Vietnamese pressure on Khe Sanh proved to be only a diversionary action, it looked serious to the command in Saigon and Washington when on February 7 the North Vietnamese, using tanks for the first time in the war, overwhelmed a Special Forces camp of American Montagnard allies at Lang Vei just outside Khe Sanh. The U.S. Marines and South Vietnamese at Khe Sanh itself held on through a gruelling seige, supplied only by air. Ironically, four months later, after enemy pressure had eased, they were ordered to abandon the post as a strategic liability.

American military leaders viewed the Tet offensive, whether setback or victory, as an opportunity to adopt a new and more aggressive strategy. JCS chairman Wheeler cabled Westmoreland, "The United States is not prepared to accept a defeat in South Vietnam. In summary, if you need more troops, ask for them."[40] Westmoreland had felt confident that he could make do with the troops he had, but in response to Wheeler's broad suggestion, he told the Army historian Herbert Schandler, "It seemed to me that for political reasons or otherwise, the president and the Joint Chiefs of Staff were anxious to send me reinforcements. . . . My first thought was not to ask for any, but the signals from Washington got stronger."[41] Westmoreland therefore formulated a request for reinforcements possibly in excess of the 525,000-man ceiling currently limiting American forces in Vietnam—"not because I fear defeat if I am not reinforced but because I do not feel·I can fully grasp the initiative from the recently reinforced enemy without them. On the other hand, a setback is fully possible if I am not reinforced. . . ."[42]

Backed up by the president's authority, Wheeler responded immediately and ordered new units, still within the 525,000 limit, to enplane for the war zone. Johnson flew to Fort Bragg, North Carolina, to exhort the departing troops of the 82nd Airborne Division, and then on to California to see off a marine unit, pray with the sailors of the aircraft carrier *Constellation*, and confer with ex-president Eisenhower. He reiterated a now familiar theme: "In Vietnam today, the foes of freedom are making ready to test America's will."[43] For their part, the Joint Chiefs evidently hoped to use the Tet crisis to justify a real national mobilization, and they revised their estimates of continued Communist fighting capabilities upward. According to Herbert Schandler:

> The chairman of the Joint Chiefs of Staff, in stressing the negative aspects of the situation in Vietnam, again saw Tet and the reaction to it as an opportunity, perhaps the last opportunity, to convince the Administration to call up the reserve forces to reconstitute a military capability within the United States that would allow some military flexibility to meet other contingencies.[44]

Westmoreland later confirmed this motive in an interview with BBC reporter Michael Charlton: "When the enemy's hurting you increase the pressure, don't decrease it. . . . The 200,000 troop plan was not a request for deployment but an input to a contingency plan associated with a more aggressive strategy under consideration in Washington."[45] As it turned out, this was a misbegotten maneuver. Lawrence Korb, the historian of the JCS, observes, "Their attempt to expand the American commitment would not only fail but also would galvanize those forces within the administration who were opposed to the war."[46]

On February 23, General Wheeler flew to Saigon to work out the actual escalation plan—a request to expand total military personnel by 206,000, with half of them slated immediately to expand the forces in Vietnam. Upon his return on February 28, he went directly to the White House to submit his report to the president. He had drafted it on the plane, in terms even more pessimistic for the United States than the Communists' own claims:

> There is no question in the mind of MACV [Military Assistance Command, Vietnam; that is, Westmoreland] that the enemy went all out for a general offensive and general uprising and apparently believed that he would succeed in bringing the war to an early successful conclusion.

The enemy failed to achieve his initial objective but is continuing his effort. Although many of his units were badly hurt, the judgment is that he has the will and the capability to continue. . . . His determination appears to be unshaken. . . .

The initial attack nearly succeeded in a dozen places, and defeat in those places was only averted by the timely reaction of U.S. forces. In short, it was a very near thing.

On the basis of his analysis, Wheeler concluded:

Forces currently assigned to MACV, plus the residual Program Five forces yet to be delivered [that is, within the administration's set limit] are inadequate in numbers. . . . To contend with, and defeat, the new enemy threat, MACV has stated requirements for forces over the 525,000 ceiling imposed by Program Five. The add-on requested totals 206,756 spaces. . . .[47]

While the plan for a major increase in United States force in Vietnam was still under wraps, a barrage of I-told-you-so criticism burst out from members of Congress who already had misgivings about the war. Senator Robert Kennedy, chagrined that just one day before Tet he had abjured running against President Johnson "in any foreseeable circumstances," spoke in Chicago on February 8 to denounce the entire war policy as a "lengthy and consistent chronicle of error." The war was unwinnable. To claim Tet as an American victory was "as if James Madison were able to claim a great victory in 1812 [*sic*—it was in 1814] because the British only burned Washington instead of annexing it to the British Empire."

In the next two weeks, Kennedy was echoed by a distinguished chorus on the floor of the Senate. Albert Gore, Mike Mansfield, John Sherman Cooper, and J. William Fulbright all called for a new approach in Vietnam. Fulbright, chairman of the Foreign Relations Committee, initiated a retrospective staff study of the Gulf of Tonkin Resolution, concluding that the resolution was based on "misrepresentation" by the Johnson administration and therefore "null and void." Mansfield, Johnson's successor as Senate majority leader, noting the dependence of the Saigon regime on the United States as revealed by Tet, challenged the administration's key political assumption: "From the outset, it was not an American responsibility, and it is not now an American responsibility, to win a victory for any particular Vietnamese group, or to defeat any particular Vietnamese group." There could be no success in negotiations "if the conflict is defined as a simple case of aggression on the part of the North against the South." Cooper, the ranking Republican on the Foreign Relations Committee, backed Mansfield on negotiations and warned that further escalation would only provoke intervention by the

Chinese and the Soviets. Senator Gore of Tennessee called for a negotiated withdrawal from "the morass in Vietnam," disputed the rationale
of "containing Chinese expansion," and warned, "We are destroying
the country we profess to be saving. . . . We are also seriously damaging,
if we are not in danger of destroying, ourselves." The hawks suddenly
found themselves outtalked; protested Russell Long of Louisiana, "The
American people are getting disgusted of this talk of a pause, or pulling
your punches when the enemy is slugging you. I for one hope General
Westmoreland will be provided with all the troops he requests." George
Murphy of California, the former actor, added, "The military decisions
should be left to the military," while Senator James Eastland of Mississippi proposed to extend the law on treason to anyone offering "aid and
comfort" to North Vietnam.

The media took their cue from the predominant new mood in Congress. The *Wall Street Journal*, for example, surprised its readers on
February 23 with the warning, "Be prepared for the bitter taste of a
defeat beyond America's power to prevent." One of the biggest blows
to Johnson's self-assurance was dealt by Walter Cronkite, arguably the
second most influential man in America, who made his own fact-
finding trip to Vietnam and reported on CBS television on February 27:

> To say that we are mired in stalemate seems the only realistic, yet unsatisfac-
> tory conclusion. On the off chance that military and political analysts are
> right, in the next few months we must test the enemy's intentions, in case this
> is indeed his last gasp before negotiations. But it is increasingly clear to this
> reporter that the only rational way out then will be to negotiate, not as victors,
> but as an honorable people who lived up to their pledge to defend democ-
> racy, and did the best they could.

The Johnson administration itself was not immune to misgivings
about the war, even prior to Tet. Defense Secretary Robert McNamara,
the paragon of the technocrats, was the first highly placed member of
the team to grasp the futility of the Vietnam effort, particularly the air
war against North Vietnam. Documents declassified in the course of
General Westmoreland's 1982 libel suit against CBS News underscored
the depth of McNamara's doubts by 1967 and the support he drew for
his views from impartial CIA analyses of the situation. In his growing
skepticism, McNamara set in motion the secret in-house study of the
war that four years later was leaked to the press by Defense Department
consultant Daniel Ellsberg and became publicly known as *The Pentagon
Papers*. He advised the president to curb the bombing and to negotiate.
The suggestion infuriated the Joint Chiefs of Staff, who called his suggestion an "aerial Dienbienphu" and threatened to resign en masse.[48]

Under pressure from congressional hawks and increasingly impatient with what he regarded as McNamara's defeatism, Johnson called in his own team of "Wise Men"—former officials whose advice he trusted—to discuss ways of stiffening public support for the war. Meeting on 2 November 1967, the group (including, among others, former secretary of state Dean Acheson, former national security advisor McGeorge Bundy, the perennial Clark Clifford, and former Saigon ambassadors Henry Cabot Lodge and Maxwell Taylor) gave the war policy a vote of confidence. So did General Westmoreland and Ambassador Bunker when summoned home for the same purpose later in the month. Prodded by this hostile consensus, McNamara had to walk the plank, though only to fall into the open presidency of the World Bank.[49] On 29 November 1967, the day before Senator Eugene McCarthy announced his presidential candidacy, the secretary of defense made known his intent to resign effective 1 March 1968. His designated successor was Clifford, one-time chief of staff to Harry Truman, well-known Washington attorney and Cold Warrior, and frequent advisor to Johnson. Clifford was confirmed by the Senate for his prospective job one day before Tet erupted.

A month later, shocked now by the Pentagon's troop requests and unnerved by the brouhaha in the Senate and in the media, the president turned to the new defense secretary–designate (just two days before he was officially to take office) to set up another high-level study group for an "A to Z" reassessment of Vietnam. Clifford immediately brought together a policy team including, among others, Secretary of State Dean Rusk, National Security Advisor Walt Rostow, General Wheeler, and former Ambassador Taylor, as well as the retiring McNamara and his undersecretary Paul Nitze (once a noted Cold Warrior in Truman's State Department, and more recently President Reagan's chief arms negotiator).

The crash efforts of Clifford's panel and the new secretary's own turnaround on the war are recounted in detail by Herbert Schandler, himself a staff participant in this work and the principle author of the 1968 portion of *The Pentagon Papers*.[50] Clifford convened the group on February 28 in the secretary's private dining room at the Pentagon. Rostow urged immediate reinforcements for Westmoreland. Treasury Secretary Henry Fowler supported Rostow's suggestion, but also warned of the heavy economic price the Great Society would have to pay for further national mobilization. Clifford assigned policy papers to each of the agencies represented, though the bulk of the work went to the deputies whom he had inherited from McNamara.

Critical memos were drawn up overnight. On Leap Day the 29th, Assistant Secretaries Paul Warnke (International Security Affairs), Alain Enthoven (Systems Analysis), and Phil Goulding (Public Affairs) presented their misgivings about American strategy and the viability of the Saigon government. The discussion conjured up a ghostly recall of an old proposal and an almost psychic anticipation of a new policy—General Gavin's "enclaves" and Richard Nixon's "Vietnamization"—though skeptical estimates of Saigon's ability to shoulder the main burden foreshadowed South Vietnam's ultimate collapse. "The Tet offensive demonstrated," said Enthoven in his paper, "not only that the U.S. had not provided an effective shield, it also demonstrated that the GVN [Government of Vietnam] and RVNAF [Republic of Vietnam Armed Forces] had not made real progress in pacification."[51] Goulding reviewed the divisive effects on American public opinion of all options except a change of strategy to concentrate on the defense of populated areas. Warnke, who had Clifford's ear more than anyone else in the Pentagon, presented the secretary and the JCS on March 1 with an even more pessimistic assessment from his own team of experts (drawing in part from a memo by Daniel Ellsberg). The GVN, this document maintained,

> will not move toward a Government of National Union. Current arrests of oppositionists further isolate and discredit it. . . . The Saigon leadership shows no signs of a willingness—let alone an ability—to attract the necessary loyalty or support of the people. . . . Even if the political makeup of the GVN should change for the better, it may well be that VC penetration in the cities has now gone or will soon go too far for real non-Communist political mobilization to develop.[52]

Any troop increase, Warnke's advisors concluded, would only prompt a corresponding build-up by the North Vietnamese and result in "the total Americanization of the war." Therefore, the group endorsed the "demographic strategy," a modified enclave approach to defend the thickly populated areas of the Delta and the coast, while giving up the search-and-destroy operations of which Westmoreland was so enamored. They would "buy the time during which ARVN and the GVN can develop effective capability."[53]

General Wheeler, armed with optimistic cables from General Westmoreland, continued to urge the build-up for offensive operations. But what Clifford heard confirmed his own growing doubts about the war. "I couldn't get hold of a plan to win the war, there was no plan for winning the war," he recalled. "It was a dead end."[54] According to the then Undersecretary of the Air Force Townsend Hoopes:

> In the Pentagon, the Tet offensive performed the curious service of fully revealing the doubters and dissenters to each other, as in a lightning flash.

Nitze suddenly spoke out on "the unsoundness of continuing to reinforce weakness. . . ." Warnke thought Tet showed that our military strategy was "foolish to the point of insanity."[55]

Faced with a widening chasm between the military and the Pentagon civilians, Clifford's panel told Warnke and Goulding to work out a compromise position, which they submitted on March 3. In it they recommended an emergency troop increase of 20,000, a call-up of the Reserves, and an in-depth study of long-range strategy, subject to signs of improvement among the South Vietnamese. On the basis of this proposal, Warnke and Assistant Secretary of State William Bundy drafted the final report for the president, which was submitted to him on Monday, March 4. Although much detail was appended on the use of United States forces, the need to galvanize the South Vietnamese, and various negotiating options, the hastily prepared document still put off to the future the real review of strategy that Johnson had wanted. As Schandler expressed it in *The Pentagon Papers*, the assumption was to "furnish what we can presently furnish without disrupting the normal political and economic life of the nation, while we study the situation as it develops."[56]

The Clifford group met at the White House on the evening of March 4 to discuss its report with the president. Rostow panned the document for its pessimism and Johnson himself was "troubled" by "its totally negative approach to any possible negotiations."[57] At this juncture, Dean Rusk, up to then an outspoken hawk, stepped in decisively to sway the president against escalation by suggesting an unconditional halt in the bombing of most of North Vietnam and the tactic of "fighting and negotiating." His hope, as Schandler summarized it, was "to restore the Administration's credibility and thereby make it domestically tolerable to continue the war until the enemy realized that he could not prevail militarily."[58]

In the face of this advice, Johnson made his decision about the troop request. He said to General Wheeler, "Tell him [Westmoreland] to forget the 100,000. . . . Tell him 22,000 is all we can give at the moment." He observed to his assembled advisors that they were making "a rather basic change in strategy," putting the onus finally on the South Vietnamese themselves.[59] Meanwhile, rumors of the now passé proposal for a massive troop increase spread on Capitol Hill. On Sunday, March 10, the *New York Times* had the story, uncovered by Hedrick Smith and Neil Sheehan: "Westmoreland Requests 206,000 More Men, Stirring Debate in Administration." And the New Hampshire primary was just two days away.

3

Haight-Ashbury

SUNDAY, FEBRUARY 18, a balmy 60-degree day in San Francisco's famous counterculture district in the center of the city. Haight Street, the east-west commercial axis of Haight-Ashbury, is described by observers Martin Lee and Bruce Shlain as "center stage," where the spectator-participant is "bombarded by a perpetual parade of stimuli—wild costumes, spontaneous theater, assorted antics, wandering minstrels."[1] "The Haight" has become a tourist attraction, a "swinging, psychedelic sector," according to Frommer's *West Coast* guidebook. As depicted by the hippie organ, *The Haight-Ashbury Oracle*, "Walking barefooted with hair askew, hand-made robes over torn blue jeans, the young people wander from noon until early two [A.M.]. . . . The street can be a classroom, a zoo, a stage, an asphalt padded cell, a whorehouse, a folksong, or the traverse of Scorpio."[2]

What makes the hippies of Haight-Ashbury so intriguing is the lure of the forbidden. The counterculture rejects almost every rule of polite society in industry, sobriety, monogamy, cleanliness, and decorum of dress and language, in favor of self-indulgence in leisure, drugs, promiscuity, slovenliness, and spontaneity. The *Haight-Ashbury Maverick*, an underground monthly, writes:

> The tourist from Corn Pone, Iowa, or Possum Trot, Alabama, approaches Haight Street with many misgivings, but they are drawn there by an irresistable magnet. . . . They want to see the sin that their Man of God told them

43

about. . . . They see young people of all ages doing exactly what they wish they had the courage to do—to drop out of the rat race that keeps them on the treadmill day after day.[3]

Good weather on this particular winter afternoon has brought an unusually large number of the young and curious to Haight-Ashbury. Although days like this have usually passed without serious disorder among the hippies, crime is on the upswing in the area and the city fathers have become increasingly unhappy with the district's defiance of customary social norms, particularly illegal drug use.

Suddenly, a dog darts out of the crowd and into the traffic on Haight Street. One of the voyeurs driving by has to slam on his brakes and screech to a halt. Although the dog is unhurt, its young owner, perhaps in a drug-induced state of excitement, rushes out angrily to berate the driver and then sits down on the pavement in the path of the car. Friends and bystanders promptly join the aggrieved youth, blocking traffic as a crowd of several hundred denizens of the district gathers. Guitars are produced, and some of the multitude take advantage of the occasion to launch an impromptu street dance.

This sort of behavior is not unusual in the district. In the words of its historian Charles Perry, Haight-Ashbury is "participatory theater," where everyone is set on "making the scene" and eagerly awaiting the next "happening."[4] But also part of the routine is the arrival of the neighborhood police from the Park Station on Stanyan Street. These local officers are accustomed to the hippies. As the Park Station sergeant tells an inquiring journalist, L. H. Whittemore, "We just don't want to rock the boat. I think you'll agree that cops don't like work any more than the next guy. We don't go out there and advertise for business. We just want to keep the trouble low, not let things get out of hand."[5] Nevertheless, since the previous summer, the Park Station force has conducted periodic sweeps of Haight Street, checking ID and, according to a report by *Rolling Stone* magazine (February 24), arresting people who "cannot satisfactorily answer a policeman's questions." On this particular occasion the police again manage to disperse the crowd quietly for the time being.

Meanwhile, word of the uproar on Haight Street has reached Mayor Joseph Alioto, recently elected under the banner of "an all-out war on crime." Although Alioto has professed to listen to all sides, he has been increasingly pressured about the crime wave and drug use in Haight-Ashbury. Nerves are already taut in City Hall because of an ongoing newspaper strike and an impending teachers' strike, and the mayor has

44

just launched a police campaign against marijuana sales in the city's high schools. In an apparently unnecessary but politically nervous response to the Haight Street commotion, Alioto orders in the San Francisco Tactical Squad.

The Tactical Squad is San Francisco's answer to the prevailing anxiety of urban America about riot control, sharpened everywhere by the black riots during the long, hot summer of 1967. The squad is described by Dr. David Smith, a founder of the Haight-Ashbury Free Clinic, and his collaborator John Luce as "an allegedly elite corps of two-hundred-pound-plus bruisers trained in hand-to-hand combat and riot control."[6] "Compared to the members of the tactical patrol force," says Whittemore, the regular patrolmen whom he interviewed "felt like ultrasensitive social workers in police uniforms." Members of the Tactical Squad "wear black leather jackets, white crash helmets, and big gun belts with equipment that jangles as they stride in and out of the station house. Though their physiques are huge, their faces seemed to me clean and blank, as if they were in some kind of occupational limbo, waiting for something to happen so that their big, restless bodies could go into motion again."[7] Like most police officers, the members of the Tactical Squad are nonplussed by the hippies' tactics of defiance and ridicule, and dislike them even more than they do common criminals: "You feel like vomiting."[8] According to Smith and Luce, some of the riot police "seemed to be as sadistic and impulsive as the people they were paid to help control."[9]

The intervention of the Tactical Squad on February 18 is the first of many violent mass confrontations between the hippies and the authorities in Haight-Ashbury. Upon arriving at Haight Street, the Tactical Squad forms its customary wedge to sweep the area. Smith and Luce describe the scene:

> Some members of the thirty-eight-man special unit marched down the street with their faces concealed under Plexiglas helmets, spraying tear gas and Mace before them. Others mounted motorcycles and roared down the sidewalk, scattering street people like bowling pins and clubbing them with riot sticks, cowboy style.[10]

Some of the hippies fight back by throwing bricks and bottles. Patrolman James Christman is taken to a hospital with glass fragments in both eyes from a shattered bottle. The Free Clinic provides first aid for over a hundred individuals, mostly for scalp wounds or for Mace and tear gas in their eyes.

By 6 P.M., after night has fallen and the usual Pacific fog has rolled in, the Tactical Squad has cleared the street and imposed a curfew. But the youthful rebels again flock back into Haight Street, this time holding handkerchiefs drawn over their noses because of the lingering tear gas. One long-haired hippie even has his own gas mask. Some of them scatter tacks on the pavement, let the air out of the tires of cars, stop moving vehicles and rock them back and forth. The police reappear, bark through their bullhorns for the crowd to disperse, and then attack again with tear gas and night sticks. They hurl gas grenades randomly into shops along the street, even into the Straight Theater (an abandoned movie house converted into a communal theater and dance hall). One police officer tries to throw a grenade through a window of the Free Clinic but it bounces off the windowsill. "Too bad we missed," he shouts, "but we'll get you assholes next time."[11] According to varying accounts, between sixty-five and ninety persons (including a number of unhip and startled sightseers) are arrested and booked for inciting a riot or failing to disperse. When interviewed by the press, the police can only explain the disturbance as "just spontaneous." A writer who happened to be in the crowd tells a reporter, "They were just dancing in the street and everything was cool until a riot squad came and started tossing tear gas bombs."[12]

The next day, Mayor Alioto says that the police "acted correctly" and accuses the hippies (not the police, as the *Maverick* notes sarcastically) of "storm-trooper tactics."[13] He warns, "When love and peace turn to hatred and violence, then police have no recourse but to restore peace."[14] However, a few days later the *San Francisco Chronicle* (March 3 and 4), reports, "The mayor's office reached the conclusion that giving the hippies their day on the street would relieve the tensions developing in the Haight area." The following Sunday Alioto begins the weekly practice of closing Haight Street to traffic so that "hippies and hippie-watchers," as the *Chronicle* (March 3) styles them, can congregate freely to pursue their diversions. It is well that he takes this step, for some of the Haight-Ashbury crowd are reportedly getting hold of firearms to prepare for their next confrontation with the law. For a time Haight Street becomes, in the *Chronicle*'s words, an "arcade of pleasure" occupied by "a singing, strolling, dancing crowd" smoking pot and listening to rock groups.

All this notwithstanding, the hippies, ordinarily unaggressive people even when they are not sedated by drugs, are shocked and frightened by their experience with the organized force of mainstream America. February 18 proves to be the beginning of the end of the Haight-Ashbury love-in, though not of the counterculture and its manifold impact on American civilization.

46

Haight-Ashbury

Haight-Ashbury is a distinctly self-contained neighborhood of roughly five by five city blocks, near the exact geographical center of the city, framed between Golden Gate Park and its "Panhandle" extension on the west and north, and steep hills on the south and east. During the 1960s, the area succumbed to urban blight but was temporarily revived by a mass influx of youthful refugees from civilization. The district's counterculture colony had its origins in the early 1960s, when some of San Francisco's literary and artistic bohemia—the so-called "Beat Generation"—moved there from the North Beach area around Fisherman's Wharf to escape rising rents and crime. In the mid-1960s, hippies settled in communal droves in the three-story wooden Victorian houses that are typical of the older residential parts of San Francisco. In the words of Lee and Shlain, the hippies made Haight-Ashbury "a small psychedelic city-state,"[15] a concentrated drug-driven enclave of the counterculture, asserting an alternative life-style that rejected every conceivable value of traditional American society.

Social movements like that of the hippies almost defy explanation. Without organization or leadership except for the most informal local type, ties of common emotional involvement may take hold among thousands of people with amazing swiftness, like the crystallization of a lake's surface that is ready to freeze. What this phenomenon reveals is that the society of the status quo is under great though unrecognized tension, and that its prevailing values are vulnerable to a strong challenge. The effect on public life can be revolutionary in the sense of basic changes in society and its values, even without the actual seizure of political power. This distinction is essential to understanding the impact of the youth rebellion all over the world in the 1960s.

Apart from a few superannuated gurus, the counterculture revolt was distinctly a youth movement, accentuated by the sheer number of late adolescents and young adults born in the post-World War II baby boom. Their repudiation of their elders was prefigured by Henry David Thoreau: "I have lived some thirty years on this planet, and I have yet to hear the first syllable of valuable or even earnest advice from my seniors."[16] Lewis Feuer recounts the long series of youth rebellions in modern history, and attributes them to circumstances, often governmental failures, that de-authoritize the status quo and the older generation that presides over it. In the words of Thoreau, "One generation abandons the enterprises of another like stranded vessels."[17] For many young Americans the Vietnam War was the delegitimizing event, although the beginnings of the counterculture antedate the escalation of the war into an object of mass disaffection. The two circumstances reinforced each other: the counterculture challenged the traditional values to which President Johnson's war policy consciously appealed, while the war gave added weight to this challenge and generated new recruits for the counterculture.

As in all the classic revolutions of history, the ground of opinion for the Counterculture Revolution was prepared beforehand by a small number of bold intellectual critics of the old order. Like the French *philosophes* of the eighteenth century who paved the way intellectually for the French Revolution and its democratic offshoots all over Europe, the writers and artists of the Beat Generation of the late 1950s and early 1960s set the ideological stage for the hippie movement and all its defiant challenges to the existing moral order. In line with these critiques, the counterculture expressed a highly self-conscious alienation from the form of society that had evolved in America. Charles Reich observed "a universal sense of powerlessness. We seem to be living in a society that no one created and that no one wants."[18] According to J. M. Yinger, the counterculture was "both behavioral and symbolic . . . , a combination of deviance and criticism of the social order. . . . It is when the two merge, as in the United States and Western Europe during the 1960s, in England in the 1640s and 1650s [during the Puritan Revolution], or in the Roman Empire in the second century A.D., that major countercultural movements occur."[19]

Poets and novelists (such as Allen Ginsberg, Lawrence Ferlinghetti, Jack Kerouac), philosophers (such as Herbert Marcuse, Paul Goodman, Norman O. Brown), and psychologists (such as Fritz Perls and William Schutz of the Esalen Institute, and Abraham Maslow of peak-experience and self-actualization fame) all set out to repudiate the forms and constraints that in the minds of the rebels hopelessly crippled the traditional life-style. As Theodore Roszak pointed out, psychological questing replaced class conflict as the basis for protest: "Sociology has been forced to yield progressively to psychology as the generative principle of revolution."[20]

Other circumstances contributing to the youth revolution had a more physical basis, namely psychoactive drugs and the rock music craze. Timothy Leary had popularized LSD by the time of his ouster from the Harvard faculty in 1963, and the Beatles began a revolution in American popular entertainment when they arrived in the United States in 1964. Imitators of both found a congenial base in Haight-Ashbury as well as in New York City's East Village, from which the new fashions spread all over the country.

Haight-Ashbury's years of creative joy coincided with the escalation of the Vietnam War in 1966 and 1967. Beginning with the opening of the world's first psychedelic shop on Haight Street on New Year's Day in 1966, the district became a beacon to the disaffected and the disaffiliated, the drop-outs and the plain psychotic. LSD, vigorously promoted by the writer Ken Kesey and his entourage of "Merry Pranksters," had been tried by an estimated 10,000 individuals by the time the State of California ruled it illegal in the fall of 1966.[21] Some 10,000 hippies gathered at Golden Gate Park on 14 January 1967, at the instigation of John Starr Cooke and his followers—the Psychedelic Rangers—for a "Human Be-in," a sort of mass LSD picnic embellished with incessant rock music. One historian of the movement called it "a love riot in fancy dress."[22] The 1967 "Summer of Love," so proclaimed by its promoters, attracted many more thousands of restless and curious youth, along with a growing criminal element that inevitably followed the drug trade.

Numerically, the hard-core counterculture was a modest phenomenon even at its peak. In 1968, sociologist-participant Lewis Yablonsky estimated, there were "about 200,000 core visible and identifiable total hippie drop-outs in the United States," along with "at least another 200,000 visible teeny-boppers, part-time, summer and weekend hippies." He also noted "several hundred thousand invisible 'Clark Kent' hippies . . . , students, young executives, and professional people who use psychedelic drugs, interact, and closely associate with totally dropped-out hippies, yet maintain nine-to-five jobs or student status." Beyond all these, Yablonsky asserted, "There are millions of hippie 'fellow-travelers' in the United States," mainly university types and the hapless but supportive parents of hippies.[23] By 1968, approximately 75,000 hippies had lived in Haight-Ashbury at one time or another (although the district could only have accomodated about 10,000 people at any one time).[24] As for the sex ratio among Haight-Ashbury hippies, the figure was somewhere between 3–5 males to every female, which inevitably limited sexual opportunity despite the free-love ethic of the movement. According to a study by Ross Speck and his colleagues, the average participant spent only a year or so in the hippie environment.[25] This phenomenon of transient protest had its counterpart in the easily exhausted radicalism of many people in the contemporaneous student movement.

In terms of social background, the hippie movement in Haight-Ashbury and elsewhere drew almost exclusively from the WASP and Jewish middle class, the rebellious children of an uptight affluent society. The hippies idealized the blacks and the American Indians, at least in theory; they self-consciously drew much of their musical inspiration from the former group, and ideas about drugs (notably the peyote cult) from the latter. In actuality there were few residents of Haight-Ashbury representing racial minorities, and relations between the hippie district and the ghetto area adjoining it to the east were strained at best. In New Mexico and Manhattan, hippie communities were sometimes the object of physical attack by their Hispanic or European-immigrant neighbors. Those who hoped to rise in American society were not excited by movements that repudiated its fundamentals.

Within the more or less spontaneous mass of the counterculture in Haight-Ashbury there were a few small but singular groups who stood out because of their antics or ideas. Ken Kesey's Merry Pranksters were a peripatetic commune (made famous by the novelist Tom Wolfe in *The Electric Kool-Aid Acid Test*) who distinguished themselves by traveling around the country in a psychedelic bus spray-painted in Day-Glo hues, and injecting farce into political protest demonstrations. Another far-out group was the Psychedelic Rangers, devoted like Kesey's followers to the promotion of LSD as society's panacea. The Hell's Angels motorcycle clan found a home from time to time in the Haight, where their own violent proclivities were endured by the ever-tolerant hippies. Considerably more sinister was the figure of Charles Manson, an ex-con (forgery) who assembled a personal harem in the Haight by means of drugs and his evident powers of fascination. Manson moved on to Los Angeles in 1968 and then to the heinous mass murder of actress Sharon Tate and her entourage of guests the following year.

One submovement in Haight-Ashbury stood out as the bearer of a consistent, if unworldly, utopian vision—the Diggers, an offshoot of the San Francisco Mime Troupe, themselves artists of theatrical protest. Formed in 1966 by Emmett Grogan, a self-styled filmmaker from Brooklyn, the Diggers assumed the name and philosophy of that radical communitarian sect in the English Revolution of the seventeenth century, but with an added meaning—those who "dug" (that is, truly appreciated) the values of the counterculture. Charles Perry calls them "the only psychedelic political movement."[26] Rejecting all claims of the achievement-oriented society around them, the Diggers carried the antimaterialist attitude of the hippies one step further, calling for the free distribution of all goods. In the seriously absurd way that could only happen in the world of the counterculture, the Diggers practiced what they preached, opening a free store and serving free meals in the Panhandle Park. (Stocks for this largess seem to have come mainly from the generosity of the more conventional local merchants—that is, shakedowns—or by theft.) "A group of Diggers on the move give off an electric energy that is shocking to middle-class liberals," wrote Leonard

Wolf, a hippie sympathizer from the English Department at San Francisco State University. "Their program is to live *now* as if the revolution were already won."[27] In April 1967, with the slogan "The streets belong to the people," the Diggers led thousands of enthusiasts to demonstrate for LSD. Disillusioned by the crime, hard drugs, gawkers, and runaways that the Summer of Love drew to Haight-Ashbury, they joined other organizations in the district to proclaim "the death of the hippie" and held an elaborate mock funeral in the fall of 1967. By 1968, the Diggers had changed their name to the "Free City Collective" and were struggling to keep the old Haight-Ashbury spirit alive, allying themselves with minority gangs in the adjacent neighborhoods and conducting demonstrations and poetry readings at San Francisco City Hall. Their last act before giving up in the summer of 1968 was to hold a "Free City Convention" to parody the national parties, after which they could only escape to the commune movement in the wilds of northern California and New Mexico.

One of the more positive activities in the Haight was Happening House, a sort of educational outreach center set up by Leonard Wolf. At the time of the February riot, the center had just been disrupted by its founder's arrest and abortive trial for "contributing to the delinquency of minors" when some hippies broke into a meeting he was conducting and staged a nude dance. The authorities seemed to target the private social agencies that attempted to minister to the hippie population.

Without any formal organization or leadership, the countersociety of Haight-Ashbury rapidly spawned a series of entities that attempted to address the physical and psychological needs of the hippies. Wolf saw the basis of the community in four institutions—the Psychedelic Shop of the Thelin brothers, the I and Thou Coffee Shop of David Rothkop, the *Haight-Ashbury Oracle*, and the Avalon and Fillmore dance halls. Happening House, Huckleberry's (for runaway kids), the Switchboard (for emergency referrals), the Free Clinic, and the Hip Job Co-op (for those who cared to seek employment) were among the positive efforts giving some social coherence to the Haight up to 1968. All Saints Episcopal Church, under the ministry of Father Leon Harris, provided encouragement and operating premises for some of these efforts.

Father Harris called the hippies "a manifestation of a major social revolution that may be the most significant development of the twentieth century.[28] According to Wolf:

Haight Street became the Main Street of a village of children. It was a village made paranoid by the constant threat of arrest. It was a village where feeling necessarily fluctuated wildly because the central community experience was drugs. On the one hand, there was the acid experience that helped to produce an ethic of affection and help, and on the other there was the reality that you could not trust anyone. The "nark" was everywhere. . . .[29]

As a modern social movement, the youth culture symbolized by Haight-Ashbury was unique in drawing its energy and vision from a chemical source. The counterculture was inseparable from the drug culture. Not only did the hippies manifest their enthusiasms and achieve their joy under the mass influence of marijuana and LSD; the most ardent of them became messianically convinced that the straight society around them needed to be—and could only be—subverted and reconstructed by the general dissemination of mind-altering drugs.

There is a certain irony in the confluence of hallucinogenic drugs and the Cultural Revolution of the 1960s. Marijuana had long been available, though illegal, but LSD (first discovered in Switzerland in 1943) became widely known only through experimental work done under the aegis of the United States government. According to Lee and Shlain:

> Nearly every drug that appeared on the black market during the 1960s—marijuana, cocaine, heroin, PCP, amyl nitrate, mushrooms, DMT, barbiturates, laughing gas, speed, and many others—had previously been scrutinized, tested, and in some cases refined by CIA and army scientists. But of all the techniques explored by the Agency in its multimillion-dollar twenty-five-year quest to conquer the human mind, none received as much attention or was embraced with such enthusiasm as LSD-25.[30]

In pharmacology, as in the prosecution of the Vietnam War, government agencies were zealously pursuing what they conceived to be in the national interest. The result in both respects was profound disaffection from the very idea of national interest among a vocal segment of the nation's youth that would be expected to carry that interest forward.

LSD failed to prove itself a reliable agent for purposes of intelligence or psychological warfare, or a safe tool of psychotherapy as was briefly hoped. Nevertheless, psychologists Timothy Leary and Richard Alpert at Harvard saw in it a path to new levels of experience and perception. Leary claimed that LSD could produce "the most intense religious experience." Given the right setting, an "intense mystical or revelatory experience can be expected in from 40 to 90 percent of subjects ingesting psychedelic drugs."[31] By the time their experiments and proselytizing precipitated the Harvard purge of 1963, both the preparation and the effect of LSD were becoming widely known among the bohemians of the east and west coasts. Users claimed that the "acid trip" gave them an experience that was difficult to verbalize because it was so intensely personal and overwhelming. One veteran LSD user told an interviewer:

> The first time I took a mind-expanding drug, it became very clear to me why it was called mind-expanding. I was no longer limited to my old perceptions. I could see I was connected in essence to all around me, not separate. With that realization I felt a flood of love, as if I were in a sea of love, and there were no boundaries.[32]

To the nonparticipant the effects of LSD looked more like a temporary psychosis.

Widespread LSD use within the hippie community began when Ken Kesey and his confreres began to promote the drug through "acid tests" demonstrated at public gatherings in Haight-Ashbury in 1965. At about the same time, Berkeley chemist Augustus Owsley Stanley, IV, set up its mass production; "Owsley" is said to have produced four million hits over a two-year period, most of which were sold in Haight-Ashbury at $2 apiece. Ten thousand hippies "tripping" once a week would account for a quarter of his output, but this was only part of his market. Lee and Shlain estimated that four million people in the United States and Canada sampled LSD before the decade was out.[33]

Until the State of California moved against LSD use in October 1966 (just prior to the election of Ronald Reagan as governor), no law curbed the production or consumption of the drug, even though it was far more potent and hazardous than the long-banned marijuana. Early in 1966, the Thelin brothers of the Psychedelic Shop and their co-worker Allen Cohen started a weekly paper, the *Oracle*, with the avowed aim of promoting Timothy Leary and LSD. In October of the same year, despite growing public alarm over the behavioral and genetic consequences of LSD use (including birth defects), the *Oracle* successfully organized a so-called "Love Pageant Rally" in the Panhandle, at which thousands of participants tripped on LSD. The Psychedelic Rangers entered the Haight-Ashbury picture to announce their aim "to psychedelicize the radical left."[34]

Ultimately, drugs proved the greatest single factor in the undoing of the counterculture as a self-contained community. Their use put the counterculture legally at odds with the authorities and invited attacks by the forces of law and order, who were only too happy to make drugs the excuse for physical assaults on those elements who challenged public codes of decency and propriety. Drug busts became everyday occurrences in 1967 and 1968. "These days," commented the radical journal

Ramparts in November 1967, "California's marijuana laws are sometimes used like its vagrancy laws, to put socially undesirable people out of sight." "Spanish lady, come to me," sang the Grateful Dead,

> I was like to blown away.
> But the Heat came round and busted me
> For smiling on a cloudy day.[35]

More serious were the inherently debilitating effects of drug use that were undermining Haight-Ashbury society. This was particularly evident after the summer of 1967, when the new generation of residents turned to intravenous use of amphetamines as well as adulterated or ersatz forms of LSD that cropped up after the drug was made illegal. New and even more powerful drugs became available—methedrine, manufactured by the Love Conspiracy Commune; STP (Serenity, Tranquility, Peace), a form of amphetamine; and PCP (Phencyclidine); the last two being escaped products of U.S. Army experimentation. In the face of this deluge, the movement suffered a symbolic shock when the Psychedelic Shop closed its doors in October 1967 out of frustration and disillusionment over the disintegration of the hippie ideal.

Research on the impact of hallucinogenic drug use shows no consensus about the positive contribution it might have made to the Counterculture Revolution. Ross Speck and his associates, who studied communes in Philadelphia contemporary with those in Haight-Ashbury, arrived at the "central discovery . . . that the use of so-called psychedelic drugs, currently so disapproved of by the larger society, represents a sort of training process for a new society."[36] Lee and Shlain, however, were more skeptical about drug users: "There was a sense that LSD had changed all the rules, that the scales had been lifted from their eyes and they'd never be the same. The drug was thought to provide a short cut to a higher reality."[37] If Communism can be viewed as the excess that tarnished American radicalism in the 1930s, then drugs were the corresponding excess that corroded the new radicalism of the 1960s.

Closely linked with the drug culture, though more nearly universal in its appeal, was the rock music movement. Like the use of psychedelic drugs, the new music was incubated in a few counterculture centers, above all in Haight-Ashbury. From these cells of innovation it erupted to change the sounds that the whole world listened to.

The origins of the San Francisco Sound, the acid rock distinguished by its sensuous 4/4 time with a heavy backbeat and pounding decibels

of electric guitars, go back as far as the philosophy of the Beat Generation. However, a great leap occurred in the ideas associated with the
music, leaving behind the old rock-and-roll style and essentially no-
message entertainment offered by such popular idols as Elvis Presley
and the early Beatles (when they first arrived in the United States in
1964 and immortalized themselves on the Ed Sullivan Show with "I
Wanna Hold Your Hand."). As far as national awareness was concerned, the Beatles were the bridge from the old rock-and-roll style to
the new rock being generated by the counterculture. Robert Pielke, a
chronicler of rock music, sees the advent of the Beatles so soon after the
assassination of President Kennedy as a trigger of cultural revolution in
America. Their words and music, he suggests, entered into a void of
unfulfilled values and precipitated "a change of consciousness."
"Beatlemania" had the impact of a new religion; it was a "phenomenon
of mass conversion."[38]

The groups that sprang up in California in the mid-1960s in imitation
of these models—whether acid rock, folk rock, country rock, or hard
rock—were committed to the new message of social and political protest: "Turn on, tune in, drop out," was Timothy Leary's slogan, picked
up by the Beatles. The Monterey Pop Festival of June 1967 was the great
breakthrough of the new genre to national fame. "Suddenly," notes the
historian Robert Rosenstone, "popular music began to deal with civil
rights demonstrations and drug experiences, with interracial dating and
war and explicit sexual encounters, with, in short, the real world in
which people live."[39] For millions of foot-soldiers of the social revolution in America, rock concerts took the place of political demonstrations; the stage replaced the barricades. Rock music became the gospel
chorus of the antiwar movement and the new generational
millenium.

The link of the new-wave music with the drug culture in Haight-
Ashbury applied to performers as well as to audiences. Among the
former—the Family Dog, the Jefferson Airplane, the Grateful Dead,
Janis Joplin with Big Brother and the Holding Company, the most
famous of the groups to emerge in the Haight in 1965 and 1966, as well
as the Beatles by 1967—psychedelic drugs became a source both of
inspiration in their compositions and of energy in their executions. The
Grateful Dead, originally called the Warlocks, first came to fame by
providing the music for Ken Kesey's "acid tests." The Beatle's 1967 hit
album, *Sergeant Pepper's Lonely Hearts Club Band*, was "the counterculture's first publicly certified work of art," according to Richard Har-
rington of the *Washington Post* (31 May 1987). It was "the album that

made rock respectable," commented Jon Pareles of the *New York Times* (also 31 May 1987). "Sergeant Pepper" was immediately recognized as a thinly disguised endorsement of LSD, with song titles like "Lucy in the Sky with Diamonds" and lyrics like "I get high with a little help from my friends" and "I'd love to turn you on."[40] Even more explicitly drug-oriented was the Jefferson Airplane's "White Rabbit" on the album *Surrealistic Pillow*, also of 1967: "One pill makes you larger, one pill makes you small. . . ."[41]

For the audiences at Avalon Hall or Fillmore Auditorium near Haight-Ashbury, or for those in the district's parks, the music plus the drugs plus the innovative use of psychedelic lighting produced an overwhelming sensory experience, rivaling the most ecstatic religious frenzy. As participant-observer Helen Perry described it:

> After my first visit to the Fillmore Auditorium, I had a strange physical reaction unrelated to any intake of drugs. The light show at the Fillmore and the beat of the music, the young lovely bodies dancing in fluid hope and caught in quick flashes of light as in the jerk of an old movie produced something in me akin to a conversion experience. . . . It invaded all the senses. . . . I had been turned on to the hope still left in me for a better world than any I had ever known.[42]

"If rock-dope had become a new American religion," suggest Lee and Shlain, "then the musicians were akin to prophets."[43] *Head* magazine (April 1978) retrospectively compared the Beatles of *Sergeant Pepper* with the early Christians and the medieval Troubadours.

Most radical about the rock movement of the 1960s was not the quality of its sound but its incorporation of political and cultural protest into a medium of mass entertainment. Critic Jonathan Eisen attributed to rock

> a kind of visceral anarchism, an anti-authoritanianism. . . . The rock movement is most involved with the idea that freedom is *not* that which lies in such codes as equal protection of the laws, but in liberating that which has been repressed, even if it means the disruption of the on-going processes of our social institutions. . . . Rock music was profoundly subversive.[44]

"We are all outlaws in the eyes of America," sang the Jefferson Airplane.[45] Another freedom of the movement was the freedom from logic, as any glance at the drug-fed, free-associational lyrics of a contemporary rock album attests. In its more coherent forms, especially in the folk vein, popular music had become by 1967 a powerful vehicle of antiwar protest at the hands of such performers as the Kingston Trio ("Where

Have All the Flowers Gone?''), Donovan (''The Universal Soldier''), and Bob Dylan (''Blowin' in the Wind''), as it was already a source of inspiration for the civil rights movement.

Rock music, even more than indulgence in drugs, was the most widely disseminated feature of the counterculture among the public at large. In 1967, the first hip radio station—KMPX in San Francisco—began broadcasting freshly recorded rock, and the first rock magazine —*Rolling Stone*—began publication. But the old familiar phonograph record was the decisive technology of transmission, establishing the musical recording as one of the major forms of mass media along with print and the airwaves. By 1968, record manufacturers and concert tour promoters had awakened to the nationwide appeal of rock, and began signing lucrative contracts with Haight-Ashbury performing groups. These new opportunities came none too soon for the musicians, for their original San Francisco nest was by then disintegrating from the corrosive effects of drugs and crime. In sum, the most vigorous element of the counterculture revolution was being coopted by the System, in return for the permanent implantation of the counterculture's more nonpolitical values of self-expression and self-fulfillment in the center of American life.

Ralph Gleason, cofounder of *Rolling Stone*, wrote in its tenth anniversary issue in 1977 that rock had an impact ''unlike anything in history, yes, even including religion. . . . Music is now in the process of changing the way in which things are seen. In the process it is changing ways in which this generation will relate to everything and, in the ultimate, it will change the nature of our society.'' By the 1970s, it was difficult to turn on the radio any time of day, anywhere in North America, without being assaulted by the sounds of rock. Allan Bloom, the philosopher of educational decadence, sees terrible effects:

> Rock music . . . is *the* youth culture . . . , there is now no other countervailing nourishment for the spirit. . . . I believe it ruins the imagination of young people and makes it very difficult for them to have a passionate relationship to the art and thought that are the substance of liberal education. . . . Rock music provides premature ecstasy and, in this respect, is like the drugs with which it is allied. . . . As long as they have the Walkman on, they cannot hear what the great tradition has to say.[46]

The changes in other cultural media around 1968 were equally striking even if less pervasive. The first rock-musical theater production, *Hair*, with its then shocking glimpses of nudity and its proclamation of love and peace in ''the Age of Aquarius,'' opened on Broadway in June

1968 after a six-months' start in Greenwich Village. About the same time, the first rock mass was recorded by a group called the Electric Prunes, and films began quite suddenly to reflect and project the new life-style. Releases of 1968 included *The Graduate*, satirizing the get-ahead values of the Establishment; Andy Warhol's first widely recognized underground film, *Beyond the Law;* the Beatles' escapist cartoon, *Yellow Submarine;* and the ultimate film of the absurd, Bob Rafelson's *Head*, featuring a pop group, The Monkees. *Bonnie and Clyde*, which made criminal violence seem like a high-spirited romp, won ten 1968 Oscar nominations and two awards. It prompted Pauline Kael to write, "In the spoofs of the last few years, everything is gross, ridiculous, insane."[47]

The ultimate triumph of the counterculture in the arts came in the summer of 1969 with the memorable "Woodstock" rock festival in Upstate New York. Half a million young people—hippies, straights, and in between—congregated in a hay field to listen to a galaxy of by then famous rock groups in the greatest public entertainment spectacle ever staged. Through a three-day weekend of heat, rain, and mud, lightened by drugs, nudity, and public copulating, the mood of participatory ecstasy was sustained. The unexpected numbers swamped all the arrangements for supplying food and handling traffic, but medical services sufficed to handle drug casualties, and no mass violence marred this great generational be-in. The miraculous avoidance of disaster lent support to the utopian hope for a "Woodstock Nation" (the title of Abbie Hoffman's book on the theme). "It was less a festival than a religious convocation," wrote Myra Friedman, the biographer of Janis Joplin. "Its ceremonies were the assertion of lifestyle, and the lifestyle included a celebration of the mystical relationship between drugs and rock."[48]

Four months later came the ultimate countercultural horror at the Altamont race track in Livermore, California, where another promotional rock festival was held. In their haste, the organizers made the fatal mistake of taking on the Hell's Angels as their security force in return for free beer. Drug crises were legion among the crowd, while the Angels freely made mayhem with their clubs and ended by stabbing a young black to death. Three other spectators were killed in drug-related accidents. Thus did the counterculture reach its limits in commercialism and violence.

Beneath all the spectacular forms of political protest and dissent that erupted in the 1960s, America was undergoing a sea change in personal values and behavior. Old assumptions about the most basic kinds of human relationships and the most revered rules of conduct were challenged by the burgeoning movement of the counterculture. With an "angry no" and a "transcendent yes,"[49] the counterculture was the life-style component of the many-sided revolutionary experience sweeping the country. The hippies were waging a cultural guerrilla war against the mainstream, using ridicule and farce and visible nonconformity as their sharpest weapons. The mainstream felt the challenge acutely and fought back by every means of coercion available within the law.

Sex, dirt, and long hair were the distinguishing marks of the counterculture in the minds of the majority left behind by the revolution. As Herbert Robb of Queens College described it:

> Hippiedom in the spirit of "love" and "nature" supported free sexuality, ragged or unkempt clothing, beards and long hair, body painting and tattooing, beads, bells, earrings and flowers even for males; scorned money (except for survival needs) and jobs; often welcomed drugs (though most cannot be considered addicts); sought refuge in Eastern philosophy and esoteric Asian music. Hippies rejected military power, offering "flower power" instead.[50]

As a gesture of cultural defiance, long hair on males generated more popular disgust than even drug use, especially among school authorities who were still trying to impose dress and appearance codes on teenagers. Norwalk, Connecticut, found itself in the first mass court case over hairstyles, after fifty-three high school students were suspended in January 1968 for violating a ban on this particular form of deviance. The courts upheld the school. A Concord, New Hampshire, parochial school went so far as to hire a barber to cut students' hair forcibly. A hair case from Dallas was taken all the way to the Supreme Court, until the Court, over Justice Douglas' dissent, declined to hear the students' appeal.

Issues of appearance symbolized a challenge that the counterculture posed to the values of bourgeois America. San Francisco State sociologist Fred Davis summarized the "core values" of the hippies—freedom, expressiveness, immediacy, naturalness and spontaneity, the primitive and the mystical, the egalitarian and the communal—as a "peculiarly reactive quality." The hippies rejected not only the most fundamental American premises of consumerism and the work ethic, but also patriotic solidarity around the supposed national interest. "Practically all that the dominant middle class culture openly admires is scorned or ridiculed in the hippie ideology."[51]

The counterculture found its most advanced form in the creation of communes, which sprouted like mushrooms on the West Coast and in the Northeastern states in the hospitable climate of generational protest. Estimates of the total number of communes in the United States in the late 1960s run as high as two to three thousand. In the words of one participant-surveyor of the movement, the communes were "an intense reaction against a fragmented, commercialized society whose institutions—from the family on up to the community—had, they were convinced, lost vital, unifying vision. . . . The contemporary commune was the outward form of a movement in consciousness."[52] Observes another student of the movement, "For them, the lesson of the sixties is the futility of political reform, and the only viable radical alternative is to begin to create a new society in microcosm."[53] A woman who participated in the commune set up by the Diggers in 1968 explained, "It was one of the experiments in life style. The idea was sharing space, time, property, feelings, lovers, relationships—just about anything that you could share."[54]

Typically, the initial core of a commune came out of a countercultural center such as Haight-Ashbury, when groups of hippies transplanted themselves into a rural locale where their antimaterialist and back-to-nature values could be more realistically practiced. These circumstances, as a practical matter, often shifted the communal life-style toward more conventional forms. "The entire counterculture began as an exercise in protest and symbolic rage," notes an observer team, "but the rural commune people had left that thinking behind." At "The Ranch," a Northern California commune spawned in 1968 from Haight-Ashbury, "people were simply not involved in the world of image-making, hyperbole, mental gymnastics, and self-consciousness."[55]

As a system of values repudiating the fundamental axioms of the old order, the counterculture became the equivalent of a new religion. As such, it put belief, feeling, and commitment ahead of rational argument and scientific demonstration. For its adherents, it filled the void in faith created by the materialistic, technocratic, competitive, and egoistic civilization of the twentieth century. Charles Reich hailed what he called "Consciousness III," based on "liberation," "self," "the absolute worth of every human being," and "genuine relationships with others," as contrasted with the nineteenth-century individualism of "Consciousness I" and the "corporate state" of "Consciousness II."[56] To the philosopher Nathan Adler, the counterculture was an "antinomian" movement (that is, above the rules of the old system), similar to the early Christians in Rome. The hippies were "pilgrims between the dying world and the world not yet born."[57] Robert McAfee Brown of the

Stanford University Religion Department opined in 1967 that the hippies were "a good deal closer to the early Christian movement than the churches."[58] Another minister sermonized, "Philosophically, Jesus Christ was a hippie. . . . These young people are in revolution against society, they are saying pretty successfully that they are only trying to relate what Christians teach, but are unwilling to practice."[59]

Facilitated as it was by music and drugs and the group solidarity of the faithful, the counterculture vision was the next thing to a religious conversion experience, complete with a "new consciousness," "ritual communication" among the faithful, and an urge to proselytize.[60] For some, the attachment to the new faith was a consequence of the ossification of traditional religion. A May 1968 Gallup poll found that the proportion of Americans who believed that religion was losing ground in the United States had risen from 14 percent in 1958 to an astonishing 67 percent.[61] This trend was furthered by the "God is dead" controversy going on among theologians in the mid-1960s. Meanwhile, among young people there was a growing void of emotional commitment waiting to be filled. "In the late sixties," observed William O'Neill, "faith was expressed by not going to church."[62]

Often the religious bent in the counterculture took the form of a conscious seeking for a new theology, usually found in Oriental religion—Zen Buddhism or the Hare Krishna cult, among others. Transcendental Meditation became all the fashion with the visit of the Maharishi Maheesh Yogi to the United States in March 1968. (The Beatles had already tried his method in India during their "Magical Mystery Tour" the year before.) The Princeton University Press was overwhelmed by orders (some 50,000 in 1968 alone) for the ancient Chinese collection of philosophical sayings, the *I Ching*.[63] Various bizarre forms of occultism, including witches and warlocks and Satanism, took hold among the hippies, and astrology enjoyed a new surge of interest among youth at large.

The Eastern outlook of mystical transcendence over reality fit nicely with the counterculture's rejection of the rationalist and technological tradition of the West and the alleged reduction of the human individual to a mere instrument, a cog in the system. Theodore Roszak signaled this radical change of worldview in *The Making of a Counter-Culture* with his attack on the "myth of objective consciousness." "The joyous and voluntary poverty of Buddhism becomes a positive force," wrote one convert, to whom the cultures both of capitalism and of Communism were "contradictory, repressive, and productive of violent and frustrated personalities." He went on to find justification for the hippies' sexual ethics: "The belief in a serene and generous fulfillment of natural loving desires destroys ideologies which blind, maim, and repress, and points the way to a kind of community which would amaze 'moralists' and eliminate armies of men who are fighters because they cannot be lovers."[64]

So vigorous was the counterculture in the religious context that it even percolated into the traditional churches, through such practices as rock masses and Oriental readings. Haight-Ashbury offered ample illustration of the readiness of the mainline churches to engage the counterculture and provide any service that society's drop-outs would accept. The most zealous forms of traditional religion—"Jesus freaks" and religious communes—were readily absorbed into the countercultural communities. More broadly, the fashionable search for personal peace and fulfillment through psychology acquired a religious character with its distinctive cults (notably the Encounter Movement at Esalen). In turn, the psychological quest was absorbed by the mainline churches as a major part of their offering.

One of the most serious limitations of the counterculture, paralleling the Oriental outlook so popular among the hippies, was its lack of a sense of the future. Neither in the personal nor in the public realm were the hippies working toward any definable future goal. As the Jefferson Airplane's lyrics in "The Other Side of This Life" put it,

> I don't know where I'm going next,
> I don't know why I'm going to be.[65]

The hippie values of escapist individualism were to be expressed and enjoyed in the here and now. The revolution was in your head. Once you turned on with acid, tuned in to rock, and dropped out of the rat race, there was nothing more to aspire to. This blind alley helps account for the rapid turnover of participation in the hippie life and the self-destructive pursuit of kicks among those who stayed in it too long. It also helps explain the absolute disgust for the counterculture felt by those in the achievement-oriented world outside.

By the end of 1968, the early centers of the counterculture had gone into terminal decline. Haight-Ashbury was never the same after the violence of February 18. The original, philosophically committed hippies moved out, leaving the district to addicts, psychotics, teenage runaways, and criminals. More dangerous types of drugs and more of them, particularly amphetamines, became the rule. The police grew harsher during and after the resurgence of rioting on July 16 and 17, remembered as the "siege of Haight-Ashbury." L. H. Whittemore describes the changing scene:

> A nightmare of frustration, anger, disillusionment, despair, racial conflict, and disease swirled about Haight Street, turning it into a tension-filled area, simmering with hostility. Fights, holdups, muggings, and rapes were common. Clamorous, raunchy mobs milled about on the sidewalks. Youngsters, many barely out of their teens, emaciated and wild-eyed, stood or sat in doorways alongside sleeping derelicts. Without enthusiasm they whispered their offers of sale to passers-by: "Acid" (LSD) . . . "Speed" (methamphetamine) . . . "Smack" (heroin) . . . "Pot" (marijuana). Violence-prone white hoodlums on motorcycles declared they would beat up any black men they saw with white women. Meanwhile, young Negroes stood on the sidewalk and taunted passing white girls. A scarcity of marijuana had led to an increased use of hard drugs. The "home of the flower children and refuge of youth" had become a magnet for hate.[66]

The final blow, four days before year's end, was the vicious murder of a hippie girl by the motorcyclists.

Apologists for the counterculture often blamed the media for the corruption and destruction of the hippie life. Haight-Ashbury began to decline soon after the press zeroed in on it in the summer of 1967 and stimulated an influx of thrill-seekers. Ironically, in causing the breakup of the hippie communities the media also multiplied the impact of their example. Not long after the Haight Street riot, the *San Francisco Chronicle* published a random sidewalk poll on the future of the hippies (February 29). Some of the answers were highly perceptive: "The real hippies have already left," but "it will become some other ism"; "I'll always be a hippie but I'll stop roaming around"; "There will always be free thinkers. . . . They won't be centered in San Francisco but they'll still be all over"; "Hippies were a product of the news media"; "Hippies will be everywhere in five years but they'll be disguised." Lee and Shlain comment, "Like a cueball scattering the opening shot, the media laserbeam broke open the energy cluster that had coalesced in these hip enclaves and spread the psychedelic seed throughout the country. Soon there were love-ins and be-ins in nearly every major city in the U.S. as hippie colonies sprang up across the land."[67]

It is not unusual in the history of revolutions for the initial centers of a movement to lose their idealistic vitality even while the influence of the movement is still spreading. People in any number can sustain the spirit of revolution for only a limited period of time, after which they become divided or corrupted or just plain tired out. In this respect, Haight-

Ashbury was the microcosmic paradigm for society at large, which went through a longer revolutionary experience but eventually came to the point where radical exhortation roused more antagonism than enthusiasm.

The Counterculture Revolution dovetailed with all the other movements of protest and social change that were coming to a head in the United States in this era. At the same time, challenging all conventional values, the counterculture remained distinct from radicalism of a more political sort. It was sympathetic to blacks but did not on any large scale draw their sympathy. It attracted rebellious young women without truly coming to terms with the sexual revolution (often stopping at the phase that merely liberated men to use women). It fed the antiwar movement but often embarrassed political protest by its social nonconformity, and it blended with the student protest movement in its preference for drugs and music over ideology. Still, to the outside observer, the American rebel movements of the 1960s were all part of one remarkable tide. "Today in America," wrote the French journalist Jean-François Revel, "a new revolution is rising. It is *the* revolution of our time. It is . . . a total affirmation of liberty for all in place of archaic prohibitions."[68]

The counterculture and the New Left have often been confused in conservative minds because of their overlap in attitudes, styles, and even individuals. Actually, those young people who took their politics most seriously eschewed the more extreme forms of life-style deviance, particularly hard drugs. Conversely, those most dedicated to repudiation of the cultural status quo included politics—radical as well as mainstream—in their rejection.

Where the counterculture and the New Left did coincide, they produced an extreme that was as embarrassing as it was entertaining. This was embodied in the Youth International Party—the "Yippees"— launched by Jerry Rubin and Abbie Hoffman in January 1968, after their encounters with the Haight-Ashbury people. As Richard Neville described them:

> The Yippees are politicized acid freaks. . . . Instead of painstakingly acquiring a textbook ideology and seeking to feed society into its vision machinery, the Yippees found their politics and their freedom through a life style. They extracted their world view from an intense, electrifying generational communion, which taunted authority, and like a poultice, brought out the worst in it.[69]

They were "a parody of left-wing politics," in the view of Lee and Shlain, "the first group on the Left to define themselves solely through the media projections of their flamboyant leaders."[70] The Yippees continued to capture headlines throughout 1968, culminating in the Chicago demonstrations and the trial of the Chicago Seven.

It says something about American society, that the element of the New Revolution enjoying the most widespread and lasting influence was not its political side in the New Left but the side of the counterculture. The New Left, embodied largely in the radical student movement, was in a state of disintegration and collapse as early as 1969. "The older militant youth who believed in the principle of 'sacrifice now for the new society which is coming' have almost disappeared," wrote the sociologist James Drane in 1973. "Much more enduring are the nonpolitical hippies of the sixties who believe that the only way to bring in the new society is to start enjoying it right now."[71]

With the triumphant spread of the musical component of the counterculture came the divorce of entertainment and political protest, so ostentatiously combined in the rock movement up to 1968. Such stars of the revolution as Bob Dylan and the Beatles signaled this shift by abandoning political lyrics and repudiating extremist views. The Beatles turned conservative (on the advice of their business manager, according to *Ramparts*) in their *White Album* of late 1968:

> You say you want a revolution
> . . . But when you talk about destruction
> Don't you know that you can count me out. . . .[72]

According to the radical sociologist Jerold Starr, Woodstock was a victory for the "romantic conservatism" that substituted drugs and music for revolution.[73] The most symbolic moment at Woodstock came when Abbie Hoffman, by now of Chicago Seven fame, attempted to climb up onto the stage to make a political statement while The Who were performing. The group's leader, Pete Townshend, bashed Hoffman with his guitar and drove him off.

For the purest devotee of the counterculture, the mentality of self-realization induced by drugs, sex, and sound dissolved any serious political commitment. "If the 'real war' is strictly an internal affair," question Lee and Shlain, "does it not follow that the desire to redress social ills is yet another delusion? In this 'ultimate' scheme of things all sense of moral and political commitment is rendered absurd by definition."[74] The Counterculture Revolution had little or nothing to do with the old struggles of classes and economic interests. Rather, as in the most conservative religious denominations, the state of the individual soul became its primary concern.

4

New Hampshire

TUESDAY, MARCH 12, 8 P.M., a snowy late winter evening in northern New England. The polls are closing in New Hampshire's traditionally first-in-the-nation presidential preference primary. President Johnson, running as a write-in candidate because he has not yet officially entered the lists, is facing the first electoral challenge to his administration and his war policy, mounted by the senior senator from Minnesota, Eugene McCarthy.

The pundits have not expected serious trouble for Johnson here, well off the beaten track of antiwar protest and countercultural defiance. His reelection is firmly backed by the New Hampshire Democratic Establishment, including Governor John King and Senator Thomas McIntyre. But the opinion polls have shown McCarthy coming up rapidly since he filed in the New Hampshire primary on January 3, thanks to the Tet crisis and the debate it triggered around the country, and to the crew of enthusiastic college students who have flocked into the state to work on his campaign (2,000 of them full time and as many as 5,000 more on weekends,[1] plus movie stars Paul Newman and Dustin Hoffman and the poet Robert Lowell). The Johnson people have conceded 35 to 40 percent of the Democratic vote to McCarthy, hoping to hold him below that level. In their anxiety, King and McIntyre have called McCarthy an "appeaser" because of his opposition to the Vietnam War, and have asserted that a McCarthy victory would be "greeted with cheers in

Hanoi." McCarthy has denounced the charges as "a cruel and false attack," and they appear to have backfired, as have the Johnson people's effort to get their supporters to sign loyalty pledges.

Johnson's fortunes are not helped by the press. Late Saturday evening, March 9, the Smith–Sheehan story on the proposed increase in troops for Vietnam appears in the Sunday *Times,* just when the Gridiron Club in Washington is enjoying its annual roast of the nation's leaders. Smith is there: "At about 10 P.M. the news of the story hit the room. It moved like wind through a field of wheat. . . . I could physically see the impact of this story. It was one of the greatest journalistic thrills I've ever had."[2] Commenting on the story, Walter Lippmann returns to his old critique of national overextension:

> Lyndon Johnson thinks he is fighting a limited war because he does not escalate as fast as some of the generals would like him to. The fact is that his war aims are unlimited: he promises the pacification of all of Asia. For such unlimited ends it is not possible to win a war with limited means. Because our aims are limitless, we are sure to be "defeated."[3]

In New Hampshire, McCarthy's antiwar challenge becomes all the more cutting.

As the polls close on the 12th, hundreds of McCarthy supporters gather at their state headquarters, the Sheraton-Wayfarer Motel in Manchester, an old mill town that is New Hampshire's largest city. There is not a bearded or long-haired male among them—they are all "clean for Gene." Voters' responses on the campaign trail have filled them with enthusiasm, and the mood escalates as the returns come in. At Johnson headquarters, set up by the official New Hampshire Democrats at the Sheraton-Carpenter Motel, a total of twenty-six people are counted, and one of the two cash bars has to close. The earliest returns, though scarcely decisive, are exciting for the McCarthyites: Waterville Valley, one of those small communities where everybody votes immediately after midnight on election day, has reported eight votes for McCarthy, two write-ins for Robert Kennedy, zero for Johnson. (On the Republican side, it is Nixon, eight votes; Rockefeller, four write-ins; and one write-in for McCarthy.)

At 11:40 P.M., figures posted at the McCarthy party show the definitive trend: he is drawing 41 percent of the vote, more than anyone's prediction. The youthful crowd shouts "victory" and starts singing "On, Wisconsin" (referring to the next primary). Minutes later McCarthy appears in the room to address his supporters in his uniquely bloodless style: "I'm feeling somewhat better." However, his aide Richard Goodwin (the former Kennedy speechwriter, shortly to return to that camp) observes in McCarthy as he stands before the cheering crowd "an almost physical change, you could see the color come into his face."[4] Meanwhile, Johnson's New Hampshire chairman, former Laconia mayor and small business administrator Bernard Boutin, agonizes over calling Washington with the bad news.

McCarthy beams his message to the youth: "People have remarked that this campaign has brought young people back into the system. But it's the other way around: the young people have brought the country back into the system." He goes on, "I said earlier that I thought I could bridge the generation gap. Your turn will come." McCarthy's essential conservatism shows in the belief that his movement is the antidote to the youthful radicalism that has so distressed the older generation: "If we come to Chicago with this strength, then there will be no riots but a great victory celebration." The vote he has amassed, he says, is "not only encouraging but what we deserve because of the kind of campaign we put on." The final tally gives him 42.4 percent to Johnson's 49.5, but with his Republican write-ins counted in, his total is only 230 votes short of the president's. Thanks to the error of the Johnson people in allowing too many people to file for convention delegate, the McCarthy forces sweep twenty of New Hampshire's twenty-four slots.

Ironically, as exit polls and subsequent analysis show, a substantial portion of McCarthy voters are not even aware of his stand on the Vietnam War, think Johnson is too weak on it, or confuse Eugene with the late Senator Joseph McCarthy; many of the same people will vote for George Wallace in November. On the Republican side, in the meantime, it is a walk-away for Richard Nixon, scoring 80 percent against Michigan governor George Romney, who is still on the ballot even though he has dropped out of the race, and Governor Nelson Rockefeller of New York, who is only an unofficial, write-in candidate. With a sidelong glance at the Haight-Ashburies of the nation, the *New York Times* editorializes on the 14th, "Eugene McCarthy . . . has rekindled the faith of thousands of intelligent young Americans in democratic machinery and the efficacy of the ballot." Yet some of McCarthy's supporters remain frustrated by his stand-offish manner. One recalls, "He spoke quietly. I wanted him to yell and laugh with us, but he only thanked us for our work and in quiet tones said something about the people who had called us a kiddie corps. I had the impression that he did not realize what he had just done."[5]

McCarthy's New Hampshire showing temporarily stuns the nation, but his thunder is quickly stolen. In Washington, as the primary returns manifest President Johnson's discomfiture, all eyes turn to Senator Robert Kennedy. Bobby's dislike of Johnson and his war policy is well established, and many in Democratic circles think he is really the man to knock the president out of the running and go on to win the election. Kennedy thinks so too, though he tells the press, "At the moment my plans haven't changed," and congratulates McCarthy for "bringing out the issues in the campaign clearly and courageously." At 12:30 A.M., he phones McCarthy in Manchester. Although the substance of the conversation is not reported, they agree to get in touch again when McCarthy returns to Washington the following day.

When the press reaches Kennedy the next morning, he announces, "I am reassessing the possibility of whether I will run against President Johnson." He explains that he has held back up to this point for fear of being accused of provoking a split in the Democratic Party, but now the McCarthy vote in New Hampshire has shown that the split is already a fact. Actually, Kennedy has already warned McCarthy the week before, via Richard Goodwin, that he might become a candidate; McCarthy's reply to Goodwin is, "Why don't you tell him that I only want one term, and he can have it next time."[6] Before leaving Manchester for Washington, McCarthy asserts, "I think I can get the nomination," and affirms that he will not drop out of the race in favor of Kennedy.

The two contenders meet in Senator Ted Kennedy's office on the afternoon of March 13. To say the least, the encounter is a cool one. McCarthy repeats his one-term suggestion, "consistent with my effort to depersonalize the presidency. However, I did not ask Senator Kennedy for his support in return for my stepping aside in 1972, . . . I got the definite impression that he was going to run."[7]

In fact Kennedy really has not yet made up his mind. For months he has wrestled with the idea of opposing Johnson, yet to try and fail would destroy his future chances for the presidency. In the wake of the polarization of Democratic factions revealed by the New Hampshire vote, Kennedy attempts one more gambit, first suggested by Chicago's mayor Richard Daley: to urge President Johnson to appoint a special commission to review the entire policy of the Vietnam War. This would give Kennedy credit for turning the country toward peace, and thereby set him up for 1972 without exposing him to the risks of an uphill insurgency in 1968. Late at night on the day after the primary, Kennedy receives word via Daley that Johnson will consider the idea. On the 14th, Kennedy and former JFK assistant Ted Sorensen meet with Clark Clifford at the Pentagon; the dovish direction of the new defense secretary's thinking makes the deal appealing to him. But later the same day, Johnson surprises everyone; he considers the proposal an ultimatum for his own surrender and vetoes the commission idea as a "stacked deck." Kennedy has no choice but to make good on his threat: he decides to run.

The next step for Kennedy is to try to box in the McCarthy campaign. His aides talk with pro-Kennedy people in the McCarthy organization about dividing the primary states between them so as not to split the anti-Johnson vote. Ted Kennedy is deputized to fly to Wisconsin to break the news to McCarthy and to attempt an accommodation, but it is already hours after Walter Cronkite has broadcast the report of Bobby's decision on national television. Teddy gets to Green Bay by chartered plane at 1 A.M. on March 15, and McCarthy is waked up to receive him. Their meeting, recounted in detail in Abigail McCarthy's memoir, is totally inconclusive: Senator Ted broaches the idea of dividing up the primaries, helping McCarthy in some of them in return for his bowing out of others, but McCarthy refuses to deal. Ted flies back to Virginia to report to Bobby early in the morning and blames Abigail for McCarthy's intransigence. The Kennedy advisors make one last effort to dissuade Bobby from announcing at this early date. They want him to wait, if not until 1972 then at least until a date nearer the convention. To no avail. Bobby sees no alternative; as *Time* magazine comments on March 22, "Events were passing him by. Kennedys are supposed to stand for courage; the antiwar parade marshaled by a lonely Gene McCarthy was trampling that profile."

Robert Kennedy meets the press at 9 A.M. on Saturday, March 16—in the same Senate Caucus room where his brother had declared his candidacy eight years before—to read his formal announcement. "I do not run for the presidency merely to oppose any man but to propose new policies," he maintains. "Now that the fight is one over policies which I have long been challenging, I must enter that race." There is still the token nod to McCarthy: "My candidacy would not be in opposition to his but in harmony"—whatever that meant.

Not surprisingly, the response in the McCarthy camp is bitterness and outrage. One distressed McCarthy worker charges, "It is something like trying to steal another dog's bone."[8] Another laments, "We woke up after the New Hampshire primary like it was Christmas Day. And when we went down to the tree, we found Bobby Kennedy had stolen our Christmas presents."[9] McCarthy himself comments, with the caustic wit he sometimes shows, "Other politicians were afraid to come down to the playing field. . . . They were content to stand on the hill and light bonfires and dance by the light of the moon."[10] Observes the columnist

Mary McGrory, "Kennedy thinks that American youth belongs to him as the bequest of his brother. . . . Seeing the romance flower between them and McCarthy, he moved with the ruthlessness of a Victorian father whose daughter has fallen in love with a dustman."[11] In the White House, Johnson is sardonic about the whole business: "Bobby Kennedy has been a candidate since the first day I sat here."[12]

The "Dump Johnson" movement was a direct outgrowth of opposition to the Vietnam War, escalating as the war escalated. But it needed a candidate and a catalyst.

The catalyst appeared first, in the person of Allard Lowenstein, a New York lawyer and indefatigable liberal activist, then in his late 30s. A veteran of the civil rights movement and a former president of the National Student Association, Lowenstein plunged into the antiwar movement. By the spring of 1967, he came to the conclusion that Johnson should and could be denied the Democratic nomination for reelection in 1968, if the right candidate could be found to oppose him.

Lowenstein's personal favorite was Robert Kennedy. Chance put him on a plane with Kennedy in August 1967, and he seized the opportunity to press the idea with the senator. Kennedy demurred: "I've tried to stop the war in every way I can, but Johnson can't be stopped."[13] With the financial backing of the California-based Conference of Concerned Democrats, Lowenstein furiously buttonholed every available liberal in the Senate, including George McGovern, and others outside it, including General Gavin of enclave fame—all without success. Eugene McCarthy responded at first that Kennedy was the only one who could lead the charge. Then he began to nibble at the idea on his own behalf.

McCarthy was a congressional veteran—ten years in the House of Representatives, service in the Senate since 1958. He was, however, hardly the typical politician: a very private and reflective person, with intense inner feelings, not a flaming liberal leader. According to Theodore White, "He bore quiet and long-lasting rancor for Hubert Humphrey, a rancor somehow connected with the feeling that Humphrey had tried to use him as the house Catholic in Minnesota politics." McCarthy's feelings toward both Humphrey and Johnson were evidently exacerbated when the president dangled the vice-presidency before him at the Atlantic City convention in 1964, only to give it to Humphrey. White adds, "He came later to enmity of Bobby Kennedy with an ultimate bitterness that not even Kennedy's death could erase."[14] McCarthy had developed strong feelings against the Vietnam War, partly under the influence of his college-age children.

72

"The moral issue as I saw it," he told British interviewer Michael Charlton, "finally got down to the question of whether there was any proportion between the destruction and what possible good would come out of it."[15] In public, McCarthy has been described as "a man who seemed to find it difficult to be animated, let alone passionate,"[16] though his student audiences in the early part of the campaign were carried away by the fervor his words aroused in them. In any case, he was not the customary presidential candidate, as became painfully clear during his campaign.

In October 1967, McCarthy made up his mind to run. On or about the 17th, he told McGovern, "I think I may do it,"[17] and on October 21, in a meeting in Los Angeles, he told Lowenstein he was ready. As McCarthy self-consciously explained in his low-keyed immodesty, "I didn't think there was anyone who had better knowledge of the issues than I did. . . . I looked around at the other prospects and felt that I was really not—if I became the candidate—I really wasn't offering a bad candidate."[18]

Lowenstein scheduled McCarthy to make his announcement at the national convention of the Conference of Concerned Democrats, opening in Chicago on December 2. McCarthy was leery of the group, which he judged a bit radical, and distanced himself from it by announcing beforehand at a press conference in Washington on November 30. Foremost in his reasons were the administration's plans "for continued escalation and intensification of the war in Vietnam" and its failure to seek any "compromise or negotiated settlement."[19] In his formal speech at the Chicago meeting McCarthy called Vietnam "a war which cannot be defended in the context of the judgment of history . . . , a war which is morally wrong." Invoking the names of Adlai Stevenson and John Kennedy, he bemoaned "the spirit of 1967 . . . , a joyless spirit, a mood of frustration, of anxiety, of uncertainty," and called for trust, dedication, and hope. "Let us sort out the music from the sounds and again respond to the trumpet and the steady drum."

Collaboration between the new candidate and his earliest enthusiastic supporter did not survive this occasion. Angered after Lowenstein stole his thunder in his long introductory speech to the Concerned Democrats, McCarthy turned him down as his campaign manager in favor of the well-connected media executive Blair Clark. It was just as well; Lowenstein was a political free-lance, not an organization man. Caught in the crossfire between McCarthy and Kennedy, he plunged into his own campaign for Congress on Long Island, where he was successful to the extent of one term. Clark, for his part, at first saw the McCarthy effort as a holding action for Kennedy. "All we want to do is get Kennedy in," he told the journalist Seymour Hersh when he hired him to handle press relations for McCarthy.[20]

Shortly before his announcement, McCarthy confided his plans to his former Senate colleague from Minnesota, the vice president. Recalled Humphrey:

> He spoke so casually, as he usually does, that I felt it was just sort of a lark on his part. I asked whether he had thought it through carefully, including the difficulties of unseating an incumbent President. He said, in essence, "Well, I don't have any feeling that I can win, but I don't like the Senate. I've lost interest in it, and I feel very strongly about the war. I guess the best way to show my feelings about it is to go on out and enter the primaries.[21]

According to Kennedy loyalist William Vanden Heuvel, "Eugene McCarthy said when he announced his candidacy that he expected Robert Kennedy to carry the flag to Chicago. Along the way, he decided to try it himself."[22] McCarthy has denied this report.

Initially, McCarthy did not want to run in New Hampshire, preferring to concentrate on larger primary states such as Wisconsin and California where he knew he had strength. His New Hampshire supporters, led by Dartmouth professor David Hoeh and prep-school teacher Gerry Studds (now a congressman from Massachusetts), were convinced of their grass-roots potential and importuned him to enter the primary. "A victory here," they wrote him, "which seems to us far more within the realm of possibility than it did a month ago—would have major national repercussions."[23] With the added urging of Blair Clark and his national staff, McCarthy finally agreed, and his supporters filed his candidacy on January 3. This was the signal for a gathering whirlwind of spontaneous electioneering, done mainly by the locals and the college students who swarmed in from all over the Northeast, under the direction of Curtis Gans, a Lowenstein associate and former Americans for Democratic Action staffer. Richard Goodwin, a White House assistant under Kennedy and Johnson, signed on as chief speechwriter (though he still kept his channels to the Kennedy camp open). A few wealthy sympathizers took care of the budget for a last-minute television blitz. Yet all this effort was scarcely abetted by the candidate—he did not even make a campaign appearance in New Hampshire until January 25. Only after Tet was McCarthy galvanized into making a real effort.

While McCarthy was taking the plunge, Robert Kennedy was agonizing over what course of action would be best for the party, for the country, and for his own career. The antiwar movement was growing stronger and more radical, as evidenced by the October march on the

Pentagon. This gave antiwar liberals reason to fear that protesting youth would be lost to the system, without a strong alternative candidate to win them back. Lowenstein made bold to threaten Kennedy: "We're going to do it without you." To which Kennedy replied, "I just can't do it."[24] Around November 1, Bobby told John Kenneth Galbraith that he thought he could win but couldn't live with the rancor he would arouse; therefore, McCarthy was the only possibility.[25] He continued ever more emotionally to speak out against the war, in a style the antithesis of McCarthy's; he was, in the words of one chronicler of the Kennedys, "a passionate man in an impassioned time."[26] He asserted in a television interview on November 26 that Johnson had turned away from John Kennedy's policy of helping the South Vietnamese defend themselves, and had Americanized the war at great moral cost to ourselves. Yet as late as 30 January 1968, he made that awkward remark at the National Press Club, "I can't conceive of any circumstances in which I would run." He told McCarthy privately that he would not run because he "had to think about his future," which McCarthy took as a firm commitment to stay out of the race.[27]

No more than twenty-four hours after Kennedy's January 30 statement, the circumstances of which he could not conceive came to pass. Under the impact of the Tet crisis and the resulting furor, the pressure upon him and within him to run became altogether irresistible. His impassioned Chicago speech against the war came on February 8: "The first and necessary step is to face the facts . . . , the grim anguish, the reality of that battlefield which was once a nation called South Vietnam, stripped of deceptive illusions. . . . We must actively seek a peaceful settlement." By the end of the month he was seriously reconsidering the presidential race. McCarthy sensed this in an interview he gave the Miami Herald: "He's like Enoch Arden [Alfred Tennyson's character—a measure of McCarthy's poetic erudition]. He won't go away from the window. He just comes back and scratches on the window or scratches on the door. . . . With Bobby, I think there is the sense that he's got, somehow, to do this thing."[28] At lunch with reporters Hugh Sidey and Peter Lisagor, Kennedy was asked about the "no circumstances" statement, and responded, "Did I make a mistake?"[29]

After intense discussions with his friends and aides, and further antagonized by Johnson's disdain for the Kerner Commission report on black-white relations, Kennedy reached a decision in the first week of March: "The question was no longer *whether*, but *how*."[30] He probably would have decided sooner, had it not been for his January 30 statement. George McGovern implored him not to commit the gaffe of announcing on the eve of the New Hampshire primary,[31] and he held back for fear of being thought "ruthless" on the eve of McCarthy's challenge to Johnson. Nevertheless, Kennedy's California supporters filed the necessary statement of intent to get him on the primary ballot there by the March 5 deadline. None of his advisors wanted Kennedy to announce immediately after the New Hampshire primary. But even though he knew how bad it would look, by that time he apparently felt that circumstances left him no other choice if he was to begin a credible campaign.

On the Republican side, it looked at first as though the party might be polarized by the war issue just like the Democrats. The standard-bearer for the liberal, dovish wing was Michigan governor and former auto executive George Romney, backed this time by New York's governor Nelson Rockefeller, who had vainly fought Barry Goldwater for the nomination in 1964. Romney had switched to oppose the war in the summer of 1967, following a trip to Vietnam during which he was effusive in support of the American effort. His excuse for the reversal —that he had been "brainwashed" by the military—was to haunt him for the remainder of his political career.

Romney stood little chance nationwide against the man who was the choice of the Republican Establishment, Richard Nixon. Determined to make up for his cliff-hanger loss to John Kennedy in 1960 and his humiliating failure to win the governorship in California in 1962, Nixon had been campaigning again for the presidency ever since the Republican Right had their day in the Goldwater debacle of 1964. He picked up IOUs by speaking and raising money for Republican candidates everywhere in 1964 and 1966. By 1968, Nixon was again clearly the favorite of organizational Republicans, as the centrist, consensus candidate representing, in this year of crisis and chaos, "dynamic stability"—a neat trick.[32] In other words, Nixon enjoyed much the same position vis-à-vis his own party that Humphrey did—the strategic center—but in a party less divided on the issues of the New Revolution and hence suffering less tension between its wings. The Republicans faced no such danger of a split as Wallace perpetrated and McCarthy threatened among the Democrats. Nixon had only to firm up his support by showing that he could be a winner with the voters for a change. He prepared to run in every state primary.

On February 1, Nixon formally launched his 1968 campaign, and filed in the New Hampshire primary on the Republican side with every prospect of a sweeping victory. Despite Tet, he made his support of the Vietnam War crystal clear, telling his New Hampshire supporters on

February 12, "Our commitment in Vietnam [is] the cork in the bottle of Communist expansion in Asia." The polls left no doubt about the Republican choice—Nixon would trounce Romney ten to one. Romney held out almost to the end, announcing his withdrawal from the presidential contest on February 28. (Long afterwards, he blamed Rockefeller for undercutting him by hinting at his own availability for a convention draft.) Evidently, it was former Romney supporters who gave McCarthy his 5,000 write-ins on the Republican ballot. In the meantime, Romney's place on the Republican Left was taken by an impromptu write-in campaign for Rockefeller, to little avail. The New Hampshire returns on the Republican side gave Rockefeller 11 percent against a crushing 79 percent (and all the convention delegates) for Nixon, the remainder of the popular vote going to Romney (who was still on the ballot) or to McCarthy as a write-in. Rockefeller got the message and announced on March 21 that he would not oppose Nixon for the nomination. For the time being, this left all the excitement on the Democratic side.

President Johnson tried at first to downplay his dismay over New Hampshire. In his memoirs, he blamed his poor showing on his decision to delay announcing that he would not be a candidate, because of the uncertain situation in Vietnam and the fate of his legislative program. "Still," he conceded, "I think most people were surprised that Senator McCarthy rolled up the vote he did. I was much less surprised when Bobby Kennedy announced his candidacy four days later. I had been expecting it."[33]

Meanwhile, the administration's attention was riveted on Vietnam and the issue, raised by Secretary Clifford's reassessment, of whether to escalate or de-escalate. Dean Rusk, testifying to a tense session of the Senate Foreign Relations Committee on March 11 and 12, still represented the war as a commitment to defend the freedom of a small ally against outside invasion. Rusk's rigidity further propelled Robert Kennedy into his decision to oppose Johnson. But the president had finally come so far as to reject the military's request to send 200,000 more troops to Vietnam, settling instead for a mere 30,000.

Johnson was then hit by a series of negative reports from his most trusted advisors, simultaneously with Kennedy's commission ultimatum and announcement. Former Secretary of State Dean Acheson reported the results of the inquiry that the president had permitted him to make: the military plan to win in Vietnam was totally unrealistic, except with an unlimited commitment of resources, and ebbing popular support for the war made this a political impossibility. Chief speechwriter

Harry McPherson and the old Democratic political counselor James Rowe confirmed the growing popular and congressional rejection of the war. "Everyone wants to get out," Rowe told Johnson. "The only question is how."[34] This judgment, or at least the trend, was confirmed by the polls: according to Lou Harris, support for the war was up from 61 to 74 percent immediately after Tet but dropped by late March to only 54 percent.[35] This was the ultimate irony for the president, for he had by his own account escalated the war in order to protect the political flanks of the Great Society. Still, when UN Ambassador Arthur Goldberg sent a memo urging Johnson to halt the bombing to encourage Hanoi to negotiate, he said to his advisors, "Let's get one thing clear. I am not going to stop the bombing. I have heard every argument on the subject, and I am not interested in further discussion. I have made up my mind."[36] The reaction typified Johnson's rejection of dissent and his denial of unpleasant facts. He "bellowed" even at an elder statesman like Acheson when the advice given him was not what he wanted to hear.[37] As Johnson's former press secretary Bill Moyers later told Arthur Schlesinger, "Johnson was by now well sealed off from reality," and indeed "paranoid."[38]

Johnson's belligerent sensitivity can in part be explained by his preoccupation at this point with the U.S. Marines at Khe Sanh, still under siege just south of the DMZ by North Vietnamese regulars. He had become more at home in military command than in politics, and even had a model of the Khe Sanh battlefield set up in the Situation Room in the White House basement, where he personally picked bombing targets. By the end of March the siege was effectively broken by American airpower through the most intense application of explosive force in history, the total exceeding even Hiroshima—only to be followed by the abandonment of the post.

In Congress, Johnson's position deteriorated further after Kennedy's announcement. One hundred thirty-nine representatives signed a resolution on March 18 against continuing the course in Vietnam. Others wanted officially to repeal the Tonkin Gulf Resolution of 1964 that legalized American intervention. (It actually was repealed after Nixon ordered the invasion of Cambodia in 1970.) Clifford thought the president was becoming even more hawkish despite the pressure, and contemplated resigning along with all his civilian assistants, but then persuaded Johnson to reconvene the "Wise Men" who had endorsed his stand in November. The new defense secretary had good reason to believe that the answer would be different now.

On Friday, March 22, Johnson held a press conference, his first since mid-February. Along with extending the term of General Wheeler as JCS chairman, he announced that he was going to bring General Westmoreland back from Vietnam to become chief of staff of the army. The press sniffed the implication of a change of strategy in Vietnam, but the president side-stepped questions in this vein and refused to give any figures on troop increases. He was curt about the political campaign: "I would have no comment on Senator Kennedy's entrance other than to say I was not surprised. And I could have made this statement to you this time last year." About his own candidacy, "When I get to that bridge, I will cross it." General Wheeler was sent off to tell Westmoreland there would be no more troops. Westmoreland professed to see a silver lining: "In effect, it forced the Vietnamization strategy that I had proposed earlier as the only tactical option."[39]

Later that day, Johnson gathered his inner circle to discuss a speech on Vietnam that he would give at the end of March. For the first time in his presence, they debated the idea of a bombing halt. Out of this discussion came a compromise proposal by Harry McPherson, similar to that suggested by Rusk, to announce a bombing halt north of the 20th parallel only (that is, excluding the southern panhandle of North Vietnam through which supplies were funneled to the besiegers of Khe Sanh and the Vietcong).[40] Before Johnson could reject the idea, he received the report of the Wise Men, who had met on March 25 and 26. The nearly unanimous change in their assessments was startling, even to the participants. Acheson reported for the group: "We can no longer do the job we set out to do in the time we have left, and we must take steps to disengage."[41] Walt Rostow was outraged: "I smelled a rat . . . , it was a put-up job," he recalled in an interview. "The American Establishment is dead."[42] "Somebody poisoned the well," Johnson fumed, and tried to blame the briefings that had been given to the group.[43] To Clifford, in contrast, "The meeting with the Wise Men served the purpose that I hoped it would. It really shook the President."[44] Another blow to the status quo came from Postmaster General Larry O'Brien (John Kennedy's campaign manager and the future Democratic chairman at the time of the Watergate break-in in 1972), who advised Johnson of "an ever deepening disenchantment among many segments of the population which have heretofore supported our actions in Vietnam." A desperate president called O'Brien about the trip he had just made to Wisconsin to campaign for the slate of Johnson delegates. O'Brien was brutally candid: "I think you are going to be badly defeated."[45]

By now the dramatic announcements that finally figured in the March

31 speech were taking shape in the president's mind. The hero of the 1964 campaign and the Great Society felt beset from all directions: "The whole situation was unbearable for me," he told Doris Kearns. "After thirty-seven years of public service, I deserved something more than being left alone in the middle of the plain, chased by stampedes on every side."[46] In a series of intense staff meetings on March 28, Johnson at last accepted the idea of a partial bombing halt, and sent word of this intent to Ambassador Bunker and the leaders of Congress. General Wheeler cabled Westmoreland to console him: "It is hoped that this unilateral initiative to seek peace will reverse the growing dissent and opposition within our society to the war."[47]

Although Johnson had been hinting to his intimates for many months that he might not run again for president in 1968, none took him seriously. The truth is that at this particular time no one wanted the job very badly, other than Richard Nixon, of course. Hubert Humphrey has related how the Johnsons appeared at his home that Sunday morning the 31st on their way home from church, just as the Humphreys were getting ready to depart for Mexico City for the signing of the Western Hemisphere Nuclear Non-Proliferation Treaty. Johnson wanted to alert the vice president about his planned speech.

> He showed me two endings drafted for it, saying he had not yet decided which one to use. I could barely believe what I was reading. . . . I urged him not to do it. . . . The President had told me that unless he removed himself from the politics of 1968, his efforts to achieve peace, to enter into negotiations with the North Vietnamese and the Viet Cong, would be attacked as being no more than election politics. Furthermore, he needed to ask Congress for an increase in taxes. He insisted that these two objectives could not be pursued if he was a candidate.[48]

Humphrey's biographer Carl Solberg has reconstructed the conversation:

> HUMPHREY: You're kidding, Mr. President. You can't do this, you can't just resign from office. You're going to be reelected.
> JOHNSON: Hubert, nobody will believe that I'm trying to end this war unless I do just that. . . . If you're going to run, you'd better get ready damn quick.
> HUMPHREY: There's no way I can beat the Kennedy machine.
> JOHNSON: You've got to get moving.[49]

Johnson then remarked poignantly of the record of early death in his family: " 'Even if I should run and be re-elected, I most likely would not live out my term.' "[50] (He lived, in fact, three days past the end of the next presidential term—Nixon's first.) Muriel Humphrey was understandably angered: "There had been no warning for us that permitted rational planning."[51]

The president went on national television at 9 P.M. that Sunday evening. His worries were not only public but personal: his daughter Lynda Byrd had just seen her husband Charles Robb (the future governor of Virginia and U.S. Senator) off for Vietnam, and Luci Baines was about to say good-bye to her husband Patrick Nugent. Until the last minute, no one knew for sure what Johnson was going to say, and the press had mostly scoffed at rumors that he might retire. The text prepared for the newspapers omitted the ending that he would actually use.

"Good evening, my fellow Americans," he began with the usual greeting. "Tonight I want to speak to you of peace in Vietnam and Southeast Asia." He then reviewed the history of his fruitless San Antonio Formula and the Tet offensive. "I renew the offer I made last August—to stop the bombardment of North Vietnam"—excluding "the area north of the demilitarized zone where the continuing enemy build-up directly threatens Allied forward positions." In return, "We ask that talks begin promptly, and that they be serious talks on the substance of peace." Johnson said he would meet in "any forum, at any time," and designated the veteran diplomat and past governor of New York, Averill Harriman, actually the most dovish of the Wise Men, for this responsibility.

But LBJ still meant business about continuing the war effort unless or until Hanoi came to terms: "The United States will not accept a fake solution to this long and arduous struggle and call it peace." He reiterated the official rationale for the American presence to help the South Vietnamese defend their "freedom," claimed that Saigon was accepting responsibility for this goal, and promised increased American contributions of war material. He announced also the decision to send an additional 13,000 "support troops" (artillery, tanks, and airmen) to complement the infantry reinforcements rushed to Vietnam at the time of Tet. To back up the effort, he called on Congress to pass an income tax surcharge to meet the anticipated federal budget deficit and to avert an international collapse of the U.S. dollar.

In his peroration Johnson rehashed his hopes for peace in Southeast Asia and for a response from the North Vietnamese. Then the surprise, the second ending:

> For 32 years in the service of our Nation . . . , I have put the unity of the people first. I have put it ahead of any divisive partisanship. . . . There is divisiveness among us all tonight. And holding the trust that is mine, as

President of all the people, I cannot disregard the peril to the progress of the American people and the hope and the prospect of peace for all peoples. . . . Believing this as I do, I have concluded that I should not permit the Presidency to become involved in the partisan divisions that are developing in this political year. With America's sons in the fields far away, with America's future under challenge right here at home, with our hopes and the world's hopes for peace in the balance every day, I do not believe that I should devote an hour or a day of my time to any personal partisan causes or to any duties other than the awesome duties of this office—the Presidency of your country.

Accordingly, I shall not seek, and I will not accept, the nomination of my party for another term as your President.

Reactions to Johnson's announcement varied all over the map. "There was a mood of euphoria in the capital, the next day," Doris Kearns recalls.[52] Robert Kennedy—"that grandstanding little runt" in Johnson's words[53]—called the withdrawal "truly magnanimous," and flew from New York to pay his respects.[54] "It was all over and I felt better," Johnson later recorded in his memoirs. "The weight of the day and the weeks and the months had been lifted."[55] Eugene McCarthy, though he had now achieved the central purpose of his crusade, declined to be interviewed—"Just tell the TV stations to . . . read a little poetry," he said to the reporter. "This is a night for reading poetry."[56] He let Abigail make the call to the White House. Hubert Humphrey, in Mexico City, knew immediately that he would have to be a candidate himself. "Left-wing opinion," according to the radical *Guardian* of New York (6 April), was "skeptical of Johnson's motives." What was least expected was the word three days later from Hanoi: they would at last meet to discuss the initiation of peace talks.

President Johnson's sensational March 31 announcement did not end the struggle among his advisors to set the shape of Vietnam policy. As Secretary of State George Shultz later observed during the Iran-Contra hearings in July 1987, nothing is ever settled in Washington—the bureaucratic infighting goes on forever. The Vietnam hawks—Rusk, Rostow, and the military—were still wedded to the goal of military victory. Surprised by Hanoi's agreement to talk, they used every opportunity to raise difficulties about the negotiations, starting with the question of a site and later the issue of NLF participation and even the shape of the bargaining table.

Westmoreland, not due to leave his command until June, continued to talk the offensive. He resumed his search-and-destroy operations even though the Pentagon had frozen his strength at 549,500, the maximum of the entire war. Together, the Americans and South Vietnamese launched the much-decried "Phoenix" program to identify and assassinate suspected members of the secret Communist network in the South. Bombing by B-52s from Guam and Thailand went on in the tail of North Vietnam below the 19th parallel more intensively than ever, and to the surprise of the generals (but not Clifford) worked better to slow down infiltration into the South than the previous pattern of raids spread all over the country.

Despite this backdrop, the administration doves—Clifford, Harriman, and most of the Wise Men—thought they had the opening they had sought for a negotiated end to the war. They soon realized that the contest for the president's will was still going on. Acheson wrote to Harriman, "I thought for a while that you had him on course, but I gather Bunker and Westy have fed him some raw meat."[57] The Clifford-Harriman group, aghast at the prospect of a Nixon presidency, considered peace a must for the presidential hopes of Hubert Humphrey. But the president bristled at the "conspiracy" implied by this reasoning; wrote Harriman aide Chester Cooper, "Any implication that Humphrey needed a major switch in Vietnam policy if he were going to win the Democratic nomination and the presidency directly touched exposed nerves at the White House."[58] Privately, Humphrey made it clear that he wanted to speak out for the doves' position—including a total bombing halt over North Vietnam to encourage the start of negotiations—but he allowed himself to remain caught in the middle between his recognition of this necessity and his loyalty to Johnson.

For a month, United States and North Vietnamese representatives, meeting usually in Vientiane, Laos, danced around the question of a site for the formal talks. In his withdrawal speech, Johnson had suggested Geneva "or any other suitable place." Hanoi countered with the capital of Cambodia, Phnom Penh, where the United States had no embassy. It soon became clear that the United States would not meet "anywhere," as the president had earlier proclaimed. Maneuvering continued until the North Vietnamese proposed Paris, a locale that the United States could hardly quarrel with. It was agreed on May 3 to begin the talks in Paris one week later, on May 10. The Vietcong marked the occasion with a new round of mortar and rocket attacks all over South Vietnam, supported by a sortie of North Vietnamese regulars in division strength across the DMZ. Saigon and its environs were besieged almost as they had been during Tet. The May fighting accounted for the highest number of American casualties—2,000 killed—of any month of the war.

On May 13, Ambassador Harriman, backed up by former Deputy

Defense Secretary Cyrus Vance (the future secretary of state under Jimmy Carter) and State Department professional Philip Habib, opened discussions with the North Vietnamese at the Hotel Majestic just off the Champs Elysées in Paris. What had seemed like an ideal location for the talks became somewhat awkward as the May rebellion of French students welled up. Nevertheless, Harriman's instructions from Johnson, as he understood them, were "basically, 'You stay there until they surrender on our terms' "[59]—in other words, the same "fight-talk" strategy attributed to North Vietnam. Hanoi's position was that formal negotiations could not begin until all bombing was unconditionally halted. President Thieu, for his part, refused to participate in the talks if the NLF were represented.

Despite all these difficulties, by July Harriman thought he had the solution—a halt to the bombing and an announcement that the United States was assuming from the current lull in the fighting that Hanoi was showing restraint. He dispatched an assistant to Washington with this suggestion. Unfortunately, Harriman's plan reached the president just as he was returning from a July 19 meeting with President Thieu in Honolulu, at which Saigon was assured of United States backing. Their communique affirmed that the GVN would be a "full participant" in the negotiations and promised that the United States "will not support the imposition of a 'coalition government,' or any other form of government, on the people of South Vietnam." At his next press conference, Johnson pointedly rejected Harriman's proposal and in effect gave Saigon veto power over peace, a concession that would haunt Washington at election time in 1968 as well as four years later. As Clifford observed after it was all over:

> The goal of the Saigon government had become utterly antithetical to the goal of the United States. One, the Saigon government did not want the war to end. Number two, they did not want the Americans to pull out. Number three, they did not want to make any settlement of any kind with Hanoi or with the Viet Cong or the NLF. They preferred it the way they were.[60]

One member of the U.S. delegation in Paris recalled, "It turned out that our most difficult negotiations were with Washington and not Hanoi. . . . We just couldn't convince the President that summer."[61]

Lyndon Johnson's pullout was the third great shock during one of the most turbulent campaign years in American political history, following the two sensations of McCarthy's near-victory in New Hampshire and Kennedy's announcement. His decision immediately threw open the gates of the political field. New candidacies emerged, inside and outside the major parties, and existing ones drew new enthusiasm from the event. The political spectrum was splintered as never before in the experience of the American party system.

On April 1, the day after Johnson's speech, former Alabama Governor George Wallace announced his candidacy for president on the ticket of the American Independent party. Wallace had won national notoriety in 1963 by attempting to "stand in the schoolhouse door" at the University of Alabama to defy a federal desegregation order. He ran in the 1964 Democratic primaries and made a remarkably good showing before he stepped back to give Barry Goldwater the votes of Southern conservatives. Wallace now sought to revive Strom Thurmond's Dixiecrat splinter movement of 1948 but with an added dimension—by appealing to the anti-Communist, antiblack, antihippie, and above all anti-Establishment sentiment of Northern blue-collar workers. He made much of all the "pointy-headed bureaucrats" whom he would throw into the Potomac with their briefcases. He called his party "a movement of the people, and it doesn't make any difference whether top leading politicians endorse this movement or not. I think that if the politicians get in the way in 1968, a lot of them are going to get run over by this average man in the street. . . ."[62] Wallace's law-and-order line of legalized violence against all forms of dissent came at just the right time to be justified in the minds of his listeners by the Martin Luther King riots and the student disorders. At the outset, the polls put him at 10 to 15 percent nationwide, a not insignificant showing that rose to 20 percent after the Chicago convention. Wallace's strength in the South was conceivably sufficient to deny victory to a Democrat and to prevent anyone from getting a majority of the electoral vote, which would throw the election into the House of Representatives. In the actual event, he carried five states in the Deep South, came in second to Nixon in three more, and accounted for the Republican margin in fourteen others.

Vice President Humphrey, of course, was running from the moment Johnson announced his withdrawal. Uncharacteristically, the Happy Warrior began his campaign in a depressed mood, even refusing in Mexico City most of the phone calls from people who wanted him to announce. Johnson, no doubt out of rancor after he was forced to abdicate, failed to offer Humphrey his active support. Even before he left Mexico City to fly back to Washington, Humphrey called Larry O'Brien to ask him to head his campaign. Although O'Brien was torn, his old loyalties to the Kennedys prevailed and he resigned as postmaster general to serve in Bobby's campaign. Humphrey desisted from announcing immediately for fear of seeming too eager to profit from Johnson's withdrawal. Then came the murder of Martin Luther King on April 4, which caused Humphrey to delay his formal declaration and active campaigning even longer in deference to King's memory. In the interim, Kennedy had the gall to send his aide Kenny O'Donnell to offer Humphrey a top post in the next administration if he stayed out of the race; Humphrey quipped that he would only consider heading the Small Business Administration.[63]

A campaign headquarters was opened in Washington by Humphrey supporters on April 11. The vice president chose Senators Walter Mondale of Minnesota and Fred Harris of Oklahoma to co-chair his prospective effort, and Harry Truman, still combative at age 83, became honorary chairman. For the time being, money and organizational support were no problem, given the dislike of Kennedy among major New York business figures. Humphrey's main trouble was disunity and disorganization in the campaign staff. "It was a mess," Harris complained in his memoirs. But Mondale had warned him that all Humphrey campaigns had been like that.[64]

Humphrey finally announced on April 27 at a big bash for the fat cats at Washington's Shoreham Hotel. Finishing his prepared speech, he was carried away by the excitement of the moment and ad-libbed about "the politics of joy"—a phrase, he later claimed, "I did not invent but that was to haunt me."[65] Robert Kennedy quickly threw it back at him: "If you see a small black child starving to death in the Mississippi Delta, as I have, you know this is not the politics of joy. . . . I'm going to tell it like it is."[66] CBS News supported Kennedy's point in the documentary "Hunger in America," which estimated that ten million people were suffering from hunger or malnutrition. Ever the optimist about justice and equality in American society, Humphrey failed to understand fully the reasons for all the national discord at the time: "I did not realize," he later confessed, "how deep the hatred and anger of the young had become, what little effective appeal I could have as a part of the Johnson–Humphrey administration."[67]

Humphrey started too late for most of the primaries except those in which Johnson slates or stand-ins were already filed. In 1968, before the great reform upheaval in the Democratic party's rules, it was still possible to gather a majority of delegates from convention and caucus states, where organizational loyalty counted more than public opinion. These were the locations where Humphrey chose to concentrate, particularly in the South and wherever the old machines still called the tune. He won four-fifths of the delegates chosen by the Pennsylvania state convention, for example, despite McCarthy's run-away victory in the non-binding preferential primary in April against Kennedy and Humphrey–Johnson write-ins. Thus, it was in the organization states that Humphrey racked up his convention majority.

On the Republican side, Johnson's withdrawal encouraged Nelson Rockefeller to get back into the race and make it official. Like Humphrey, Rockefeller would not take a chance in the primaries except where he was unable to control the automatic listing of his name or write-in campaigns organized on his behalf. On April 30, the same day that he formally announced his candidacy, a Rockefeller write-in campaign won in the Massachusetts Republican primary and gave him all of the state's thirty-four delegates, against favorite son Governor John Volpe and a Nixon write-in effort. (In the same primary, on the Democratic side, McCarthy won the entire delegation by default because the Johnson people had failed to file their slate by the March 5 deadline.)

Rockefeller's strategy was to hope for a divided convention and wait to accept a draft. This proved to be unrealistic. Rockefeller was not in the swing position within the party (where a draft might have been conceivable) but on its left wing; he was anathema to the South. He was counterbalanced on the Republican Right by Ronald Reagan, whose presidential aspirations (and those of his ultraconservative entourage) were coming back to life. Nixon held the comfortable middle position, and he was gobbling up delegates much too fast for either candidate of the ideological wings to have any serious hopes. He had his work cut out for him, however: an early April Harris poll showed him behind all three Democratic contenders.[68]

Reagan held back for the time being from an announced candidacy, but allowed himself to be placed on the California primary ballot as a favorite son. His friends worked the non-primary states of the South for delegates and prepared a write-in campaign for him in Oregon. Nixon was sufficiently alarmed by Reagan's Southern foray that he visited Southern Republican leaders himself to assure them that he would slow down the pace of racial integration. In the end, with the instrumental help of Senator Strom Thurmond of South Carolina, Nixon got the lion's share of Southern delegates in the split with Reagan.[69]

Meanwhile, the Wisconsin primary on April 2 pitted McCarthy against the loyalist ticket, with Johnson's name still on the ballot. It was New Hampshire all over again, only more so, with the student volunteers swarming everywhere in the state and party loyalty giving way to disgust with the war. There were wild celebrations among the McCarthy workers at the news of Johnson's withdrawal. Just as Larry

O'Brien had predicted, the Johnson slate lost badly—36 to 58 percent, with the remainder going to Kennedy as write-ins. Alone on the Republican ballot, Nixon ran away with 79 percent of the vote and all of the delegates.

The Kennedy campaign organization was not yet geared up at this point. By the time of the next major primary, in Indiana on May 7, it proved formidable. Indiana was the first head-to-head contest between Kennedy and McCarthy; counting Governor Roger Branigin, who had filed as the stand-in for Johnson before the president withdrew, it was the first with all three factions represented on the ballot. McCarthy thought Johnson's withdrawal deprived Kennedy of his main target: "Up to now, Bobby was Jack running against Lyndon. Now Bobby has to run against Jack" (that is, against the original policy of intervention in Vietnam).[70] Kennedy did not seem bothered by this; drawing on lavish family funds, he reverted to the old technique of the whistle-stop campaign. His train, naturally, was the "Wabash Cannonball." When the Indiana returns came in, Kennedy had garnered 42 percent of the vote against 31 percent for Johnson-Branigin and only 27 percent for McCarthy, reflecting the latter's minimal effort and poor organization in that conservative state. On the same day in the District of Columbia, Kennedy handily beat the administration ticket 62.5 percent to 37.5 percent.

Bobby Kennedy proved to be an extraordinary campaigner, though his approach was as conventional as McCarthy's was eccentric. Making up for lost time, he dashed around the country as frenetic as the audiences he aroused. He actually started his campaign in McCarthy's college territory, at Kansas State University, where he was given a tumultuous reception on March 18, two days after he announced. The Kennedy name gave him only a slight lead among Catholics, but he developed an amazingly charismatic appeal for the poor, blacks, Chicanos, big-city slum dwellers, migrant farm workers—in short, for all the downtrodden and disinherited. Kennedy captured the heritage of the Great Society.

Although Humphrey had devoted himself to that mission far longer and more deeply than Kennedy, the shape of his campaign made him look like the stereotypical candidate of the political hacks, the labor bosses, and the Southern Bourbons. But Kennedy failed to sustain the allure of his name for the intellectuals. These "spiritual heirs of Adlai Stevenson," to quote one observer, thought him ruthless and opportunistic, recalled his service with Joseph McCarthy's investigating committee, and manifested a "lemming-like rush" to Eugene McCarthy.[71]

Americans for Democratic Action endorsed McCarthy as early as February, even though the decision drove some old-time liberals to quit the group. McCarthy ran well ahead with Democratic voters in the middle-class suburbs and among the college-educated.

If McCarthy represented the new politics and Humphrey, perforce, the old, then Kennedy bridged the two. Although both he and McCarthy were lifted by the revolutionary tide of the 1960s, Kennedy understood it better and chose to put himself at the head of it, whereas McCarthy was carried along by his own following toward a radical realm in which he was obviously uncomfortable. By all accounts, Kennedy went through a sort of conversion experience to become the believing liberal that his brother John was not (but as the younger Teddy would also become in his own time). Bobby himself pointed to the shock of the ghetto conditions that he confronted for the first time during his New York senatorial campaign in 1964. In the Senate, his ADA voting score was almost impeccable, distinctly better than McCarthy's. For example, McCarthy had gone along with the Subversive Activities Control Board whereas Kennedy voted for its abolition, and Kennedy, reflecting the tragedy of 1963, supported federal gun control whereas McCarthy opposed it. On the other hand, as the campaign experience and his supporters' pressure radicalized him, McCarthy promised to fire Dean Rusk and J. Edgar Hoover, propositions that the brother of John Kennedy found a bit shocking. McCarthy was enraged by what he regarded as distortions of his record by Kennedy. The bitterness between the two men reached the point where, as Arthur Schlesinger concludes, "Despite Vietnam and the politics of joy, each, I would guess, preferred Hubert Humphrey to the other."[72] In May, McCarthy said as much. The currents of the times were driving the Democrats into a position where anyone who could be nominated for president could not be elected, and anyone who could be elected could not be nominated.

After Wisconsin and Indiana, the primary campaign rolled westward. In Nebraska on May 14, Kennedy beat McCarthy 51.5 percent to 31 percent, with a mere 14 percent for the Johnson ballot and Humphrey write-ins combined. Next was Oregon, on May 28, where McCarthy finally put some steam in his campaigning and traced responsibility for the Vietnam mess back to John Kennedy. McCarthy turned the tables here and bested Robert Kennedy by 45 to 39 percent. It was the first election that a Kennedy had ever lost. Nixon won the Republican ballot in Oregon with a hefty 73 percent but a sign of things to come was the

23-percent write-in vote for Reagan (leaving Rockefeller a mere 4 percent of write-ins).

All eyes then turned to California, the last major primary, where the winner-take-all contest on June 4 pitted Kennedy against McCarthy and another administration stand-in candidate. Nixon chose not to take any chances in the state where he had lost in his bid for the governorship, and Reagan remained the unopposed favorite son for the Republicans. The McCarthy people had a head start in California in organization and fund raising, thanks to the California Democratic Council headed by Gerald Hill (a McCarthy backer from the start) and to the vigorous student movement. Kennedy had the ardent support of the powerful assembly speaker Jesse Unruh, one of the few Democratic bosses anywhere who backed his candidacy. The Kennedy–McCarthy contest grew increasingly bitter, particularly when McCarthy tried to invade what Kennedy regarded as his private following among the poor and the minorities, but the only televised debate between them (June 1) proved to be anticlimactic. Kennedy pulled his punches to avoid looking ruthless. McCarthy was characteristically above it all; the last person he talked with before the debate was Robert Lowell, with whom he reportedly spent the time composing a new "Ode to St. Cecilia's Day."[73] Whatever the day of the patron saint of music had to do with the occasion, it is by eerie coincidence the same day as the assassination of John Kennedy—November 22. In any case, with an edge in money, the regular organization, and labor support, Kennedy gradually pulled ahead. The actual vote was Kennedy, 46 percent, to McCarthy's 42 percent, with the administration ticket a humiliating 12 percent.

Even before the results became firm, that election night saw the fourth and most traumatic shock of the campaign. Robert Kennedy had just finished thanking his celebrating supporters at the Ambassador Hotel in Los Angeles, and was making his way out of the ballroom through a kitchen, when a young Jordanian immigrant by the curious name of Sirhan Sirhan squeezed through the crowd and fired a .22 pistol point-blank at the candidate's head. He went on shooting randomly as kitchen workers tried to restrain him, wounding several more people. No coherent motive was ever established, other than a vague association of Kennedy with Israel. Emergency surgery failed to save the victim, as it had failed in Dallas four and a half years before. A little more than twenty-four hours after the shooting, in the early hours of Thursday, June 6, the doctors pronounced Kennedy dead. Not only the presidential campaign but the whole course of the New American Revolution being carried out by a generation of protesters was suddenly recast.

The wild presidential politics of 1968 were the product of something much deeper than proliferating ambitions and competing parties, much deeper even than the issue of the Vietnam War that generated so much heat. The war had ripped open a wide variety of latent social-cultural-generational fissures in American society. It was these antagonistic cleavages, above all the revolt of the blacks and the revolt of the young against the white adult majority, that made the presidential campaign of 1968 probably the most divisive in American history since the 1860 contest that set off the Civil War.

Under these conditions, the candidates were all forced to become something more than they intended to be. McCarthy was manifestly uneasy from the start with the enthusiasms he had evoked. Swept along by the force of the campaign, he found himself taking more and more controversial positions on issues beyond the war, such as helping blacks move out of the ghettos. David Riesman wrote of McCarthy, "There is a tendency . . . to read ourselves into a condition we 'need' and hence on the part of some of his following to see him as more radical than he is."[74] William O'Neill observed in his history of the time, "McCarthy . . . proved . . . that plain speaking, nerve, and a low profile appealed to a constituency that no one believed existed,"[75] though in many respects it was the Adlai Stevenson constituency of the 1950s. Abigail McCarthy called it "the constituency of thoughtful America and troubled America."[76]

Humphrey, for his part, was trapped as the candidate of the mainstreamers loyal to the Democratic label. Their conservative following among Southerners and Catholics, repelled by protests and disorders, was more and more prone to fall away from the party altogether. It was not entirely accidental that a number of future New Conservatives had been Humphrey staffers at one time or another. All this was quite ironic because Humphrey's instincts, going back to the famous 1948 civil rights plank, had always been more liberal and more activist than McCarthy's. Even on the night of Johnson's withdrawal, Humphrey had lamented to his personal physician, Dr. Edgar Berman, "As much as I've tried to do for the Negro and the poor, even they're against me," adding that only the mayors and governors and labor leaders appreciated his efforts.[77]

Wallace, whose vengeful populism defied traditional classification as Left or Right, triggered a broader response than he probably expected or understood. He was the Man on Horseback without the horse, representing a sort of Perónism, if one may cite the late Argentine dictator's peculiar combination of left-wing economic radicalism and right-wing ideological nostalgia. His support came above all from those social groups—poor farmers and the white ethnic working class—who had benefited most from the New Deal and who were threatened most by the Sixties Revolution. On the other hand, Texas oil money was prominent in his campaign.

Kennedy alone, whether or not for opportunistic reasons, seemed to have grasped the full range of the social unrest of the epoch and to be willing to put himself firmly at the head of it. Only this can explain the meteoric success of his brief presidential campaign with a minimum of support among the regular party organizations and Democratic office-holders. Kennedy's assassination removed the personal force that brought all the currents of protest together and held them within the system, and it exposed the Democratic party to an even more severe, clearly two-way polarization. Radicalism among blacks and the young was already spilling over the banks of peaceful politics. With Kennedy gone and Humphrey on the road to the nomination, there was little to contain revolutionary extremism until it had run its course and splintered the forces of protest that had given it birth.

What happened to the American political process in 1968 underscores the impact of the Sixties Revolution. The antiwar movement would not tolerate Johnson-Humphrey leadership, which, in turn, was the only force that could keep the Democrats' old ethnic working-class base solid. But the clamor on the party's Left only drove the traditionals to seek some other alternative. Meanwhile, impatient youth abandoned the Democrats for the New Left, becoming more and more overtly revolutionary and eschewing all the major party candidates. If any of them had the potential of attracting some of these people back, it was Robert Kennedy, but his assassination eliminated that possibility. Far more serious, numerically, was the counterrevolutionary reaction in Middle America against the excesses of the black movement, the student movement, the antiwar movement, the counterculture—toward all of which the Democrats seemed to be too accommodating.

For many whites who had been Democrats—less affluent Southerners and working-class Northerners—the answer was George Wallace. Wallace's appeal was an ideologically odd mixture, but it was no odder than the revolution he was reacting to. The issues of 1968, as all aspects of the year's troubles show, no longer revolved around the economy but around the culture and its deepest traditions and standards. On these issues the old New Deal Coalition, based on opposition to concentrated economic power and support of the federal government to promote the public interest, became irrelevant.

Ultimately, the beneficiary of the Democrats' discomfiture and infighting in these times of revolution was not Wallace but the Republican Party. Erstwhile Southern Democrats, hostile to the black movement, the antiwar movement, and the taint of cultural liberalism in the national party, supported Wallace only as a way-station on the road to a permanent realignment with the Republicans, at least as far as presidential politics were concerned. On the other hand, after New Left militancy collapsed, the liberal sentiment that mobilized around the antiwar movement mushroomed within the Democratic party, giving George McGovern the presidential nomination just four years after the failure of Eugene McCarthy. This, of course, did not save the New Deal Coalition or win the election. The country had entered a long phase of ideological conservatism and Republican domination of the presidency, relieved only by the Watergate crisis that ended Nixon's rule and the one-term presidency of the indefinable Jimmy Carter.

Even twenty years later the politics of 1968 still scrambled much of America's political thinking and allegiances. Because the Democratic party and the philosophy of liberalism had become identified in many minds with the excesses of social radicalism of 1968, it proved difficult if not impossible for Democratic leaders to uphold the old economic liberalism of Franklin Roosevelt and Lyndon Johnson. A brief binge of revolution in an anxious modern democracy can have long-lasting antirevolutionary consequences.

5

Memphis and Washington

3 P.M., THURSDAY, APRIL 4. The Reverend Martin Luther King, Jr., is talking with his younger brother "A. D." (Alfred Daniel) in his room at the black-owned Lorraine Motel downtown on Mulberry Street in Memphis, Tennessee. They are waiting anxiously for Chauncey Eskridge and Andrew Young—one the counsel to King's Southern Christian Leadership Conference (SCLC), the other a veteran SCLC organizer (later a congressman, U.N. ambassador, and Atlanta mayor) —to report on their effort to persuade Federal District Judge Bailey Brown to modify his order banning a march in support of the striking Memphis sanitation workers. Together with his second-in-command, Reverend Ralph Abernathy, King is due to leave at 6 P.M. for dinner with the SCLC Memphis leader, Reverend Samuel "Billy" Kyles.

The sanitation strike has brought King repeatedly to Memphis to try to mobilize public sympathy for the strikers. To King's chagrin, an earlier demonstration on March 28 has broken down in violence between angry black youths and the police. A black who was thought to be looting was shot to death by the police, and this experience has caused Judge Brown to enjoin further marches by King's people. King has just flown back to Memphis 24 hours ago (the flight having been delayed by a bomb threat). He has been agonizing over his young followers' urge to resort to force, and the black-white polarization that he senses is a threat to his own life.

Along with its mobile tactical units posted around the city on account of the strike, the Memphis Police Department has assigned a uniformed security detail to meet King at the airport and to remain with him during his stay. They are withdrawn later on, however, leaving only two black plainclothesmen who take turns surreptitiously watching the Lorraine Motel from their post in the fire station diagonally across Mulberry Street. The two black firemen at the station are temporarily reassigned to other companies to forestall their betraying the surveillance of the Lorraine.

In the evening of April 3, King leaves the motel to address a mass rally at the Masonic Temple. He delivers one of the most extraordinary orations of his career—the unforgettable "mountaintop" speech. He seems to utter his own obituary:

> We've got some difficult days ahead. But it really doesn't matter with me now, because I've been to the mountaintop. And I don't mind. Like anybody, I would like to live a long life. Longevity has its place. But I'm not concerned about that now. I just want to do God's will. And He's allowed me to go up to the mountain, and I've looked over, and I've seen the promised land. I may not get there with you. But I want you to know tonight, that we, as a people, will get to the promised land. And so I'm happy tonight. I'm not worried about anything. I'm not fearing any man. Mine eyes have seen the glory of the coming of the Lord.[1]

While King is waiting at the Lorraine for the court's decision, on the other side of the block across from the motel, just to the north of the fire station, a clean-cut white man in his 30s drives up in a 1966 white Mustang with Alabama license plates. He checks into Bessie Brewer's tenement-style rooming house at $422\frac{1}{2}$ South Main Street, giving the name John Willard. Paying a week's rent in advance, he declines the first room offered him and takes one toward the back, from which it is possible to see the Lorraine Motel on the other side of Mulberry Street. He brings in a long object wrapped in a cloth.

John Willard is really James Earl Ray, a 39-year-old habitual criminal and escaped convict who was serving time for bank robbery in Missouri. The object he has carried into the rooming house is a 30.06 Remington deer rifle with a telescopic sight, which he purchased in Birmingham a few days back. Although he shares the antiblack prejudice still so common in this era, he is probably a killer for hire, though his motive and the conspiracy that led to his act may never be conclusively proven. Circumstantial evidence compiled by the Congressional Committee on Assassinations years later points to "the existence of a St. Louis-based conspiracy to finance the assassination of Dr. King." Ray, "a financially motivated killer," has apparently made a deal with a group of virulent George Wallace supporters who put a price on King's head.[2] In any case, Ray has been stalking King for several weeks, from Los Angeles to Atlanta. He has driven to Memphis upon hearing the public announcement of King's April 3rd trip, stopping along the way for some target practice with his new weapon. He seems to have advance information of the exact location of King's lodgings at the Lorraine—room 306 on the second story facing Mulberry Street—and anticipates the direct line-of-sight from the back of the Brewer rooming house to that point, for he takes the room without any previous opportunity to determine this fact. Deciding that he needs binoculars to spot his intended target, he goes out at about 4 P.M. to buy a pair at a gun store. When he returns, he locks himself in the communal bathroom at the back end of the rooming house and waits for the opportunity that he seems to know is coming.

At about 5 P.M., Young and Eskridge arrive at the Lorraine Motel with the good news that Judge Brown has agreed to modify his order and allow the march, set for the following Monday, April 8, to proceed under restrictions to prevent a recurrence of violence. Relieved, King and Abernathy repair to King's room so that King can change for dinner. Their car arrives and Reverend Kyles comes to the room to tell King that everyone is ready to go. Waiting a moment for Abernathy, King and Kyles step out on the small balcony to chat with the group of aides, including the headstrong young minister Jesse Jackson, waiting at the car in the parking lot below.

At this instant, just moments after 6 P.M., Ray levels his rifle on the windowsill of the bathroom in the rooming house across the way. He observes King with his binoculars, finds him in his scope at a range of about 70 yards, and fires one shot.

The assassin's bullet strikes King on the right side of his jaw as he is leaning over the balcony rail and traverses his neck, severing the spinal column. The impact throws him to the floor, fatally wounded. Abernathy and a local King supporter (actually, an undercover police officer) attempt to administer first aid. From his lookout post at the fire station, detective Willis Richmond sees King get hit and fall, while the dozen men of the police tactical unit who happen to be taking a short break there rush out on hearing the shot to investigate and secure the area. An ambulance arrives shortly; King is stretchered into it and Abernathy rides with him to St. Joseph's Hospital. His state is hopeless. At 7:05 P.M., the emergency room physicians pronounce Martin Luther King, Jr., dead.

Immediately upon shooting King, Ray rushes out of the bathroom, past two surprised residents of the rooming house, down the stairs to the street, and to the left toward his parked car. The storekeeper next door is startled to see someone drop a bundle in his doorway and run on. An instant later, before the police have reached this side of the block, Ray jumps into his white Mustang and speeds away. When the police do arrive at the rooming house, they find the unmistakable signs of the crime: an empty cartridge case in the bathroom, and the murder weapon and the binoculars in the bundle next door. The police radio an alert. A cruiser spots the getaway car and gives chase, only to lose it when Ray speeds up to 100 mph. He drives all night back to Atlanta, abandons the car, and, for the time being, disappears.

News of the tragedy is instantly flashed around the country. President Johnson goes on radio and TV to express the nation's grief and condemn "blind violence." He cancels a planned trip to Hawaii for a conference on the prosecution of the Vietnam War, and proclaims Sunday, April 7, a day of national mourning. King's closest lieutenants plead for his followers to uphold his principle of nonviolence despite their leader's terrible end. Moderate black leaders—Roy Wilkins of the NAACP, Whitney Young of the National Urban League, and James Farmer, ousted director of the Congress of Racial Equality (CORE)—call for restraint and the peaceful continuation of the cause. Even Hosea Williams, one of King's most militant staffers, calls the *Atlanta Constitution* to warn, "We have people on our staff who question nonviolence as a means of bringing about change. . . . We must—we must—maintain and advocate and promote the philosophy of nonviolence."[3] But the time for dignified grief and guilt has run out. Floyd McKissick, the new militant head of the more radical CORE, proclaims, "Dr. Martin Luther King was the last prince of nonviolence. . . . Nonviolence is a dead philosophy, and it was not the Black people that killed it."[4]

The angry rejection of nonviolence is not confined to theory. The tide of black militancy abruptly overflows in direct, violent action. Black ghettos in a series of big cities—mainly those that had escaped serious violence in the long hot summer of riots the year before—erupt in a spasm of rioting and looting. First and hardest hit of all is the nation's capital.

The trouble in Washington begins within minutes after the announcement of King's death at about 8:20 P.M. Eastern time. On hearing the radio bulletin, Stokely Carmichael, the militant former chairman of the Student Nonviolent Coordinating Committee, rushes to headquarters of King's SCLC at 14th and U Streets, N.W., in Washington's principal black business district to phone Memphis and confirm the tragedy. The Trinidad-born Carmichael, author of the slogan "Black Power," has become a leading advocate of direct action to address racial inequity, to which end he has set up a new "Black United Front" in Washington. "Now that they've taken Dr. King off," he announces to the crowd in the office, "it's time to end this non-violence bullshit."[5]

Leaving the SCLC office, Carmichael hurries through the usual evening crowd to the SNCC office at 14th and W. He debates with the movement workers there whether to call a black strike and ask the local stores to close in mourning for King. "They took our leader off, so, out of respect, we're gonna ask all these stores to close down until Martin Luther King is laid to rest. If Kennedy had been killed, they'd have done it. So why not for Dr. King?"[6] With his followers close behind, Carmichael starts down 14th Street, calling on every store, restaurant, and barbershop along the way to close its doors. He gathers a crowd of young black men as he moves along.

It is about 9:30 P.M. when a teenager in the crowd smashes the glass door of a movie theater. Carmichael remonstrates with him. Then someone smashes the window of the People's Drug Store at 14th and U Streets. Shouting antiwhite obscenities, the crowd goes out of control, despite the efforts of Carmichael and his fellow SNCC workers to restrain irrational violence. "If you mean business," Carmichael shouts at one would-be looter, "you should have a gun. You're not ready for the 'thing.' Go home."[7] But up and down 14th Street, store windows are being broken, and everyone begins looting the exposed merchandise—TVs, jewelry, cooking pots, clothing, whatever. It starts to rain, but this does not dampen the exuberance of the rioters. Shortly after 10:30 P.M., Carmichael, fearing arrest, flees the scene.

Up to this point, on the advice of Reverend Walter Fauntroy, vice chairman of the Washington City Council (and later the District's delegate in Congress), the police have kept a low profile. Now they move in, but the looting spreads faster than they can contain it. When a car full of white youths stops at a gas station on 14th Street, it is attacked by blacks; one of the whites is stabbed and dies before they can reach a hospital—the first fatality of the King riots.

Shortly after midnight, fires break out in two looted grocery stores on 14th Street. The crowd hurls stones and debris at the firemen, and the police respond with tear gas. Other outbreaks occur further downtown, even on Pennsylvania Avenue, "less than ten blocks from the White House," as Ben Gilbert of the *Washington Post* points out.[8] By now all three shifts of the city police force are mobilized. Mayor Walter Washington (black) and Public Safety Director Patrick Murphy (white) together set up an emergency command post at the nearby precinct station on 16th Street, from which they monitor the most troubled areas. The police seal off the riot area but adhere to Murphy's orders not to use excessive force or shoot looters, for fear of fanning the flames even more. Finally, near daylight on Friday the 5th, after nearly two hundred arrests, the rioting quiets down. The respite proves to be a brief one. As a precaution, Murphy confers in the predawn hours with the Army Operations Center at the Pentagon. Army units at Fort Meyer and other nearby posts are alerted, and the District of Columbia National Guard is advised of possible duty Friday evening.

The spirit of black rebellion unleashed Thursday night quickly spreads to the very young. The schools become the key to preserving order or losing control, so every effort is made to keep them open, but black youths nonetheless flock into the streets. Stokely Carmichael appears again at SNCC headquarters to hold a press conference: "When white America killed Dr. King last night, she declared war on us. We have to retaliate for the deaths of our leaders. . . . The only way to survive is to get some guns. . . . We are going to stand up on our feet and die like men. If that's our only act of manhood, then goddammit, we're going to die."[9] Carmichael then joins a rally at Howard University, the premier black educational institution a few blocks to the east. All the speakers there reject nonviolence, an ironic way to honor the apostle of nonviolence.

By Friday afternoon looting and burning begin again, this time not only along 14th Street but also in many other quarters of the predominantly black city. Some of the looters later admit to the press that the King assassination was only the signal, not the reason for their behavior; their underlying motives included a general antiwhite hatred, specific resentment of white storeowners (often expressed in anti-Semitic terms), and the sheer adventure of the moment. Example is more persuasive than principle: "The death of Martin Luther King had nothing to do with what happened," a black city employee cynically charges. "It was an excuse to be destructive or to clean up. Ever since the Watts riot, this has been picking up."[10] One arsonist later tells the press that he worked with an organized hit squad, but neither this fact nor the responsibility for it are ever clearly established.

The police, caught off guard while many of the force are home making up for lost sleep, have all they can do to protect the firefighters, and looters run wild, seizing piles of merchandise they cannot possibly use. Two teenage looters are trapped in a burning store and die. Black plainclothesmen acting as counterrioters are helpless to dissuade the growing mobs. Downtown stores close for safety's sake; the phone system is overloaded; and hordes of private sector and federal employees leave their jobs and head for home, only to create a monumental traffic jam.

By mid-afternoon, after drafting a proclamation for President Johnson, Deputy Attorney General Warren Christopher drives into the riot area with Public Safety Director Murphy and General Ralph Haines, assistant chief of staff of the army, to verify the need for federal troops to restore order. Losing an hour in the traffic before he can find a pay phone that hasn't been vandalized, Christopher calls the White House to start the Army and the District of Columbia National Guard officially moving. A pall of smoke hangs over the city.

In white, far North-West Washington, life remains oddly normal. Many residents become aware of the riots only when they see clouds of smoke billowing up downtown or hear of them through the media. One woman does not learn of the trouble until her parents telephone from France, where they have heard frightening news bulletins, and call to find out if she and her family are safe. But white Washington soon gets an eery sense of the enemy at the gates.

About 5 P.M., troops begin to arrive in the city, starting with the ceremonial guard units of the 3rd Infantry from Fort Meyer, across the Potomac in Arlington. They immediately throw up precautionary defenses around the Capitol and the White House, complete with machine guns. From the opposite direction the 6th Armored Cavalry of Fort Meade, Maryland, moves in to sweep the worst streets of the riot area, breaking up crowds with clouds of tear gas and making it possible for the police to arrest individual looters. Mayor Washington proclaims a state of emergency and imposes a 5:30 P.M. curfew as well as a ban on the sale of liquor and inflammable substances. By midnight more than 6,000 troops—racially integrated units specially trained in riot control following the 1967 riots elsewhere in the country—have enforced the curfew and restored some semblance of order. Cyrus Vance, who had quit the government over the Vietnam issue and returned to his New York law firm, is called in as a special riot-control advisor as he was the year before. He checks everywhere with the military and police authorities to make sure that the lessons he drew from the Detroit riots are applied—restraint in the use of force and nonresort to firearms except to save life, but liberal use of tear gas. The troops are even under orders not to load their rifles except in life-threatening situations. The adult blacks often try to cooperate with the troops and scold the unruly youths. One MP sergeant recalls, "Only the teenagers harassed us. And that really didn't seem to be racial, just against authority."[11] There is a marked contrast with the Maryland police across the District line, itching to use their weaponry but never given the chance.

By Saturday morning, Washington is quieting down under virtual military occupation by upwards of 13,000 federal troops and National Guardsmen. The worst riot zones—14th Street and 7th Street, N.W., and H Street, N.E.—are secured, though the looting and burning continue to break out in peripheral areas. Hordes of curious sightseers often get in the way of the police and firefighters. Nevertheless, by Sunday the city is basically calm, and there are only sporadic disturbances thereafter. On Wednesday, April 10, the major league baseball season opens at D. C. Stadium, two days late because of King's funeral, but otherwise as if nothing had happened. Vice President Humphrey, standing in for the brooding president at all ceremonial occasions these days, throws out the first ball; and the Senators lose to the Twins 3–0. The curfew is gradually shortened and then finally dropped on Friday the 12th, as the Army begins to pull out. On Monday, April 15, Mayor Washington officially declares an end to the state of emergency, and on the following day the last of the occupying troops depart for their bases.

It is estimated that some 20,000 individuals have participated in the rioting, overwhelmingly young black males in their teens or early 20s. Approximately 7,600 people have been arrested, the majority for curfew violations, and about 2,000 are charged with looting or disorderly conduct. Twelve deaths are attributed to the rioting, of which seven are victims trapped in fires. Around 1,000 people are treated for injuries, mostly smoke inhalation or tear-gas irritations. About 100 men among the forces of law and order are reported injured. Total property damage is estimated at $25 million.[12] But ordinary crime is conspicuous by its rarity during the occupation.

For Washington's blacks the rioting is a source of perverse pride. A psychiatrist who surveys the riot area describes "a spirit of euphoria." A black government worker writes, "The Black people in this city were really happy for three days. They have been kicked so long, and this is the one high spot in their life."[13]

Following the example set by Washington's rioters, angry blacks go on the rampage in Chicago, Baltimore, and Kansas City, as well as in many smaller cities. On April 5 and 6, Chicago is a replica of Washington, as federal troops come in to assist the police and National Guard in containing the looting and arson. Here there are almost 3,000 arrests and 11 rioters are killed, some of them shot while looting. In contrast to the policy followed in Washington, Chicago Mayor Daley shocks other officials around the country by ordering the police to "shoot to kill" arsonists and "shoot to maim or cripple" looters. He asserts, "If anyone doesn't think this was a conspiracy, I don't understand."[14]

Similarly, Baltimore erupts in riots on April 6, and the National Guard and federal troops are poured in to quell the trouble. Governor Spiro Agnew blames Stokely Carmichael and "local Black Power advocates and known criminals," but the Washington rule against shooting is observed. Nevertheless, there are six riot-related deaths as well as 5,000 arrests.

Kansas City is calm until April 9, when unnerved police try to disperse demonstrators protesting the decision to keep city schools open on the day of King's funeral. Although the disturbances of the next two days are not massive, there are incidents of sniper fire and Molotov cocktails. This is the most serious resort to force by blacks anywhere in the country. Six blacks are killed, most of them caught in the line of sniper fire.

In other major cities, there are only localized outbreaks of racial trouble. In San Francisco, blacks invade the hippy quarter and break every store window on Haight Street. In Memphis, thirty people are injured and a few fires are set; Governor Buford Ellington sends in the National Guard and Mayor Henry Loeb sets in motion a settlement of the sanitation strike. The march King planned is allowed to take place as scheduled on April 8, one day before his funeral.

Echoes of King's assassination travel around the world, wherever Americans are living or fighting. In Vietnam, writes John M. G. Brown, "Black GIs throughout the services suddenly went cold as stone and drew together. It was as if the assassination was a symbolic act that left the Blacks with no choice but to turn from non-violence to militant confrontation."[15] Michael Herr reports that the news sets off "a number of small, scattered riots, one or two stabbings, all of it denied officially."[16]

Tuesday, April 9, is the day of King's funeral in Atlanta. The list of mourners at Ebenezer Baptist Church, the parish of Martin Luther King, Senior, is a who's who of American politics, testimony to the moral authority King has won and the new significance of the black vote. Hubert Humphrey, not yet officially a candidate himself, is there to represent the lame-duck president. Richard Nixon is there, and Eugene McCarthy, and Jacqueline Kennedy (soon to be Onassis). Bobby Kennedy not only attends but provides the chartered plane to fly King's remains from Memphis back to Atlanta. George Wallace and Georgia Governor Lester Maddox of axe-handle fame are conspicuously absent. As many as 100,000 mourners crowd around the church to hear the proceedings on loudspeakers, and 50,000 march behind the symbolic cortege of a farm wagon pulled by a pair of mules. King's old professor Benjamin Mays delivers the eulogy at Morehouse College, with a note of bitterness: "Make no mistake, the American people are in part responsible for Martin Luther King Jr.'s death."[17]

It is not surprising that the black civil rights movement erupted into outright violence, but only that it took so long to happen. Every step of the black effort since Emancipation to achieve equality of the races within American democracy had been met by white violence, sporadic in the North, systemic in the South. In the face of this resistance, culminating as it did in the murder of the movement's leader, Martin Luther King's affirmation of the philosophy of nonviolence was an extraordinary feat of Gandhian forbearance. King's approach ultimately worked, but at a tragic personal price. It was his martyrdom, far more than the defiant rhetoric of the black power radicals, that ultimately did most to discredit the presumptions of racism in American public life.

Prior to the Sixties Revolution, racial inequality and segregation were among the most deeply ingrained features of American culture, although with different Northern and Southern variants. Together with the antiwar movement's rejection of patriotic virtue and the counterculture's rejection of the Puritan ethic, the black movement's defiance of white supremacy was one of the great psychological challenges of the era to the complacent mentality of the American status quo. It called into question premises of American society that had held sway ever since the founding of the Republic. Most extraordinary is the extent to which these deeply resisted movements, along with the campaign for women's rights that was beginning to gather momentum, eventually did change the mind and face of America.

The movement led by King to win equal rights or citizenship for blacks in America began in Montgomery, Alabama, on 1 December

1955, when Rosa Parks, a black seamstress, was arrested for refusing to move out of her seat in the front row of the black section of a city bus to make room for an overflow of white passengers. The black community responded with a boycott of the Montgomery buses for more than a year, until the U.S. Supreme Court ordered the integration of the system. This confirmed the revolutionary role of the judiciary initiated in 1954 by the Supreme Court's landmark school desegregation decision —a victory for the old, legal-oriented NAACP—in bringing the powers of the federal government and the principles implied in the Constitution into the struggle for racial equality.

It was in the course of the Montgomery bus boycott that Martin Luther King, Jr., then a 27-year-old Baptist minister fresh out of Boston University Divinity School, gained national recognition as the undisputed moral leader of the black struggle for equality. Coming from the black middle class, which took the lead in rejecting their segregated fate, King crystallized his philosophy of nonviolent resistance with elements of Gandhi, Thoreau, and the black pacifist Bayard Rustin. When his Montgomery home was bombed in January 1956, climaxing a white campaign of threats and harassment against the boycott organizers, King found in his faith words to calm his enraged followers: "We cannot solve this problem through retaliatory violence.... Remember the words of Jesus: 'He who lives by the sword will perish by the sword'.... We must meet hate with love."[18]

In 1957, King created an organizational form for his new role by setting up the Southern Christian Leadership Conference, an umbrella organization of black churches and other groups committed to the philosophy of nonviolence and the campaign for equal voting rights. As King gained national prominence, SCLC took its cause to Washington. Adroit aid by Senate Majority Leader Lyndon Johnson helped win passage of the first civil rights bill to be adopted since Reconstruction—a modest measure providing for federal injunctions against the obstruction of voting rights. Another form of federal civil rights action was brought to bear soon after in the Little Rock school integration case, when federal troops were sent in—again for the first time since Reconstruction—to impose the orders of the federal courts on Arkansas Governor Orval Faubus and the white mobs.

The civil rights movement escalated in 1960 with the memorable sit-in campaign, initiated by black college students at a white-only lunch counter in a Woolworth's store in Greensboro, North Carolina. To direct this new effort, SCLC spun off the Student Non-Violent Coordinating Committee, to fight for the integration of stores and restaurants throughout the South in the face of rising white resistance. In the course of this effort, King himself was arrested in Atlanta and briefly jailed, until John Kennedy, still just a presidential candidate, successfully interceded—with strategic benefit to his campaign.

At this point, a new force moved to the center of the civil rights effort—the Congress of Racial Equality, a northern-based, secular, half-white group that contrasted with King's movement in almost every respect. Under its new leader, the socialist-pacifist James Farmer, CORE adopted the course of militant confrontation, specifically to compel observance of the Supreme Court decision of December 1960 that overruled segregation in terminals serving interstate travel. CORE's method was the celebrated "freedom rides" of 1961, in which teams of white and black student volunteers (including the young Stokely Carmichael) rode buses throughout the South to demand compliance with the new rule. Alabama again became the center of violent white resistance, prompting the Kennedy administration to send in three hundred U.S. marshals to quell a riot against the riders in Montgomery. But the outcome was an outright ban by the Interstate Commerce Commission on segregation in interstate travel facilities. Kennedy's New Frontier manifested distinctly more sympathy to the black cause than had the Eisenhower administration, though its mandate in Congress was not clear-cut. Bobby Kennedy visited the South during his first year as attorney general to speak strongly for civil rights at the University of Georgia—a first for any incumbent of that office.

The most successful early effort in desegregation came in higher education, beginning in graduate and professional schools where it was impossible to argue rationally that separate is equal. In 1956, the Supreme Court ruled against segregation in tax-supported educational institutions at any level. Meanwhile, states of the border region and Upper South were peacefully and even voluntarily allowing at least token black enrollment in state universities. In the Deep South, however, state governments abetted by mob action used every conceivable device to block or delay desegregation. Georgia succumbed to federal court orders in 1961 after threatening to close its own state university system. Mississippi was worse—when black Air Force veteran James Meredith, armed with a federal court order, entered the University of Mississippi in 1962, violent white rioting had to be put down by federal troops. A sequel took place at the University of Alabama the following year, when George Wallace, newly elected governor, vowed to "stand in the school house door" to block the court-ordered admission of two black students. President Kennedy took the unprecedented step of federalizing the Alabama National Guard and using it to enforce the Supreme Court's decision. "We face . . . a moral crisis as a country and a people," he warned the nation on television (11 June 1963). "It is a time to act in the Congress, in your state and local legislative body, and above all, in all our daily lives."

Federal enforcement of civil rights was complicated by the ill-concealed antipathy of FBI Chief J. Edgar Hoover to the black movement. Minimally complying with his investigative responsibilities when federal law was broken, he used his agency at every opportunity virtually as a weapon of civil war. It is ironic that King, the moderate, attracted as much ire of counterrevolutionaries like Hoover as did the black radicals who actually encouraged violence. Apparently King roused Hoover's dander as early as 1962, when he complained that civil rights investigations were left in the hands of unenthusiastic Southern white agents.

Ignoring the almost total collapse of the Communist party in the 1950s, Hoover became obsessed with the possibility that any black civil rights organization might be a conduit for Communist influence. To be sure, King did take on one key advisor, New York lawyer and businessman Stanley Levison, who had, as David Garrow rather convincingly shows, been an active Communist until the mid-1950s.[19] Despite the lack of any evidence of Communist connections or sympathies on Levison's part after that time, his past was Hoover's excuse to get Attorney General Robert Kennedy's approval in 1963 of electronic surveillance of King (an enterprise whose focus soon shifted when it uncovered King's compulsive sexual habits). A lesser King assistant, Jack O'Dell, a black recommended by Levison, proved to have been a Communist until the late 1950s.[20] (O'Dell reappeared as a foreign-policy aide in Jesse Jackson's 1988 presidential campaign.) On the strength of these associations, King was placed on the FBI's list of potential subversives to be rounded up if a national emergency were declared (along with Norman Mailer and a host of other critics of the Establishment).

Despite Hoover's harassment, King was ready by 1963 to take his movement on a general offensive, focusing on the city of Birmingham, Alabama. His chief antagonist was Police Chief Eugene "Bull" Connor, who achieved national infamy when he ordered his men to disperse peaceful demonstrators with clubs and attack dogs. Despite mass arrests and jailings, including King himself, the tactics of nonviolent resistance won the broad desegregation of public facilities in Birmingham, and a sympathetic reaction all over the country. Similar successes were achieved in a number of other Southern cities, though violent white reprisals escalated: the NAACP's Mississippi field secretary, Medgar Evars, was murdered, and four black girls were killed when their church was bombed in Birmingham.

In August 1963 King brought the creed of nonviolent protest to Washington, in the great march of a quarter million people demanding equal justice for all. This extraordinary biracial assemblage, brainchild of the black elder statesman A. Philip Randolph of the Brotherhood of Sleeping Car Porters and the Negro American Labor Council, and co-sponsored by King's SCLC, SNCC, NAACP, and the National Urban League, represented the high water mark of liberal integrationist black reformism. It was the occasion of King's most famous words, the "I Have a Dream" speech that he delivered at the Lincoln Memorial:

> I have a dream that one day this Nation will rise up, live out the true meaning of its creed: "We hold these truths to be self-evident that all men are created equal".... I have a dream.... I have a dream that my four little children will one day live in a nation where they will not be judged by the color of their skin but by the content of their character....
>
> When we let freedom ring, when we let it ring from every village and hamlet, from every state and every city, we will be able to speed up that day when all of God's children, black men and white men, Jews and Gentiles, Protestant and Catholics, will be able to join hands and sing in the words of that old Negro spiritual: "Free at last! Free at last! Thank God Almighty, we are free at last!"[21]

The following year, King's dream and his patient commitment to non-violence won him world recognition with the award of the Nobel Peace Prize.

King's efforts, abetted by the national trauma of the Kennedy assassination and the powerful commitment of Lyndon Johnson to the civil rights cause, bore rich fruit at the federal level. Early in 1964, the Twenty-Fourth Amendment to the United States Constitution, overriding poll tax requirements in federal elections, achieved ratification by three-fourths of the states. This success was quickly followed by the Civil Rights Act of 1964, affirming the right to vote and barring segregation in hotels and restaurants. These victories sparked a broad campaign, beginning with the Freedom Summer of 1964, to enforce voting rights and get blacks registered in the Southern states. Hundreds of student volunteers from all over the country (and older militants like Allard Lowenstein) joined in. The effort was punctuated by more white mob action and the murder of three civil rights workers (two of them white) in Mississippi.

Memphis and Washington

J. Edgar Hoover pursued his own rearguard action, moving from surveillance to dirty tricks that ranged from attempts to disrupt SCLC meeting plans and foundation grants to false leaks about King to foreign governments. The worst ploy was the infamous anonymous tape sent to Coretta King in November 1964, with the patent suggestion that King commit suicide to avert scandal. But Hoover went too far when, after King received the Nobel Peace Prize, he publicly charged in a press conference that the black leader was "the most notorious liar . . . , one of the lowest characters in the country."[22] This was the point when Hoover's mesmerizing hold over the American mind finally began to come loose.

The year 1965 saw King's most celebrated use of nonviolent defiance, his civil rights march from Selma, Alabama, to Montgomery. The procession was turned back twice by state police but finally reached its destination despite still more murders of white civil rights volunteers (Viola Liuzzo of Detroit and the Unitarian minister James Reeb of Boston). Again President Johnson and the Congress responded, this time with the Voting Rights Act of 1965, the key legislation with federal teeth that finally broke the back of Southern resistance to political equality for blacks.

Political success, however, did not slacken the drive for full racial equality—it only whetted potential radical impatience. Starting with the staggering Watts riot in Los Angeles in August 1965—only one week after Johnson signed the Voting Rights Act—the civil rights movement spilled over the limits of nonviolence that King was trying to maintain. King himself shifted his target to de facto segregation in the North, focusing on Chicago, one of the nation's most completely segregated cities in terms of housing. Serious riots broke out in the black ghettos of Chicago and Cleveland in July 1966, taking the familiar form of confrontations with the police followed by rock-throwing, looting, burning, and occasional gunfire. As in the South, whites in Chicago attacked black protesters, and stoned King himself in August 1966.

As passions rose on both sides over the civil rights struggle, King was drawn to broader issues of poverty and exploitation. He plunged into the growing debate over the Vietnam War, above all in his April 1967 New York address when he protested the drain of war expenditures upon social programs needed by the poor. Unfortunately but not surprisingly, King's support of the antiwar movement precipitated a break with the president. Johnson suddenly found FBI allegations of King's subversive connections much more interesting, and began to lose his enthusiasm for the black cause as a whole.

King's extension of his fight to a national scale and to national issues did not prevent radical blacks from outrunning him in their strident calls for militancy. The turning point was James Meredith's voter registration march from Memphis to Jackson, Mississippi, in June 1966. When Meredith was shot and wounded, King tried to reaffirm the response of nonviolence. However, he found himself repudiated by SNCC—now led by Stokely Carmichael after a coup of dubious legality that ousted the moderate (and later congressman) John Lewis—and by the formerly biracial CORE, where the moderate leader James Farmer had been replaced by the hardline lawyer Floyd McKissick. Carmichael chose this moment to put forth the slogan of "Black Power"—"so strong that we will bring them to their knees every time they mess with us."[23] "Black Power," SNCC proclaimed, with the symbol of the black panther, "means: where you are in a majority . . . you run things; where you don't have a majority you take your share of control. Nobody pushes you around. Hope, and a reason to live."[24] Meanwhile, CORE officially rejected the goal of integration in favor of Black Power, an ironic new twist to "separate but equal."

King's response to this radical challenge came at the Atlanta Convention of SCLC in August 1967. Reaffirming nonviolence, he called for "restructuring the whole of American society" to attack the injustice of poverty. "Let us be dissatisfied," he reiterated, about slums and despair and segregation. "Let us be dissatisfied until that day when nobody will shout 'White Power!'—when nobody will shout 'Black Power!'—but everybody will talk about God's power and human power."[25] Targeting economic inequality, King set in motion the Poor People's Campaign that took him fatefully to Memphis in April 1968, and brought his people to Washington during the sad summer that followed. Early on he had shocked the FBI by calling himself a "Marxist," and at the beginning of 1968 he declared, "The Black Revolution . . . is exposing evils that are rooted deeply in the whole structure of our society. . . . We are engaged in the class struggle."[26] His last sermon, delivered at the Washington Cathedral on 31 March 1968, was a plea for economic justice for the race that alone in America had been victimized by generations of slavery.

Meanwhile theories and sermons were being bypassed by reality in the long hot summers of 1966 and 1967, when riots on the Watts model brought the reality of black discontent to the major cities of the North. The worst cases occurred in July 1967, in Newark, New Jersey, leaving twenty-five people dead, and in Detroit, where forty-three fatalities were attributed to the riots. King and the moderate blacks of the

NAACP and the Urban League deplored the violence, and the Johnson administration tried to respond constructively. The president issued an Executive Order on 27 July 1967, creating the National Advisory Commission on Civil Disorders, the famous Kerner Commission chaired by Illinois governor Otto Kerner, to study the racial crisis and recommend possible remedies for it.

In its makeup, the Kerner Commission was a political paragon of ticket-balancing: a Democratic governor as chair, a Republican mayor (John Lindsay of New York) as vice-chair; a Democratic senator, Fred Harris of Oklahoma, and a Republican, Edward Brooke of Massachusetts (also a black); a liberal Democratic congressman, James Corman of California, and a conservative Republican, William McCulloch of Ohio; business (Charles Thorton, chairman of Litton Industries) and labor (I. W. Abel of the Steel Workers); Roy Wilkins of the NAACP; a token woman, also representing state government (Katherine Graham Peden, former commerce commissioner in Kentucky); and finally local law enforcement (Atlanta Police Chief Herbert Jenkins). Appointed executive director of the Commission's large staff was David Ginsburg, a Washington lawyer with experience in successive Democratic administrations. (He subsequently worked in the Humphrey campaign.)

One of the Commission's first steps was to interview J. Edgar Hoover about the riots. Hoover assured them that the troubles were not the result of some revolutionary master plan. This admission did not restrain him from launching a secret "Black-Nationalist Hate-Group Cointelpro" (that is, a counterintelligence program of infiltration, provocations, burglaries, and disinformation) aimed at everyone from SCLC and the Poor People's Campaign through various black student and economic organizations to the Black Panthers and the truly radical Republic of New Africa. Hoover instructed the agents working in Cointelpro, "Ensure the targeted group is disrupted, ridiculed, or discredited."[27] As he advised the bureau early in 1968, he wanted particularly to "prevent the coalition of militant black nationalist groups" and to "prevent the rise of a 'messiah' "—whether King or Carmichael—"who could unify and electrify the militant black nationalist movement."[28] All of this was brought to light by the congressional investigations of the late 1970s conducted after Hoover's death. According to the House Committee on Assassinations, the FBI "grossly abused and exceeded its legal authority," and bore some of the responsibility for the atmosphere of hatred that led to King's murder.[29] The Senate committee found that the "chief investigative branch of the Federal Government, which was charged by law with investigating crimes and preventing criminal conduct, itself engaged in lawless tactics and responded to deep-seated social problems by fomenting violence and unrest."[30]

Fired up by the national sense of urgency, the Kerner Commission brought in its final report in late February 1968, four months ahead of its assigned deadline: "We believe that to wait until midsummer to present our findings and recommendations may be to forfeit whatever opportunity exists for this report to affect, this year, the dangerous climate of tension and apprehension that pervades our cities."[31] The report is an extraordinarily perceptive document. Although its oft-quoted conclusion—"Our Nation is moving toward two societies, one black, one white, separate and unequal"—glossed over the fact that the nation always had been so divided, the report offered a brilliant socio-logical analysis of both the macro-process of ghetto formation and the micro-process of riot outbreak. Underscoring the desperation of unem-ployed or underemployed young blacks in the midst of the affluent society that they saw on television, the report warned, "Segregation and poverty have created in the racial ghetto a destructive environment totally unknown to most white Americans."[32] King read the report as "a physician's warning of approaching death with a prescription to life."[33] Yet the remedies that the report proposed were mainly just to escalate the Great Society's spending programs—for jobs, education, welfare, and housing—at a time when the combination of war spending and mainstream disenchantment with the blacks had made it politically impossible even to sustain the level that Great Society commitments had reached in the mid-1960s.

The Martin Luther King riots in Washington and elsewhere closely fit the Kerner Report's analysis of the 1967 riots. In both series of distur-bances, major trouble was confined to a few large cities, usually where the ghetto population was underrepresented in government or mis-treated by the police. The active rioters were mainly young black males, economically and psychologically alienated from society. Contrary to widespread belief in the Congress and among the public, but as Hoover conceded, the violence was not the product of a grand conspiracy, though black militants abetted it. Typically, it was some incident in the evening—in Washington, the news of King's death—that set off unruly crowds, first to throw rocks and bottles, then to break store windows, then to commence looting and burning. Reading the report, one must constantly be reminded that it came out before, not after, the 1968 series of riots.

Unfortunately, the Kerner Report appeared just when the Johnson administration was tearing itself apart over the reassessment of the

Vietnam War. The president, angered by King's alignment with the antiwar movement and increasingly irritated by the black radicals, allowed his devotion to the civil rights cause to weaken. Even when he formed the Kerner Commission in the summer of 1967, he had objected to the newly formed Urban Coalition of city governments and its call for massive increases in federal aid to the cities; he even tried to pressure the president of the Mayor's Conference to scotch the movement. According to Hugh Sidey, Johnson was further miffed because he felt the Kerner Report failed to give enough credit either to his Great Society efforts or to federal actions to combat violent crime.[34] He did not even comment on the report until questioned at his next press conference, when he damned it with faint praise and noted that some of its conclusions were already policy while the others could not be funded. As he later pointed out in his memoirs, he could scarcely get Congress to sustain his existing Great Society programs, let alone pay for the Commission's new recommendations, and he didn't like being put on the spot. "President Johnson didn't thank us for our conclusions," Roy Wilkins recalled. "LBJ seemed to take the conclusions as a personal rebuke and affront. He did not accept and act on it. As a matter of fact, he refused to receive us when the work was done."[35] The *New York Times* reported (March 5), "The White House is said to be not completely satisfied because the report did not commend the Administration for its efforts to help the disadvantaged"; Johnson's silence showed "his annoyance with the Commission's lack of mention of his programs to aid Negroes."

The more committed members of the Kerner Commission soon realized that the report would just gather dust unless the Commission itself took some action. Fred Harris spoke out first, and then John Lindsay called for the group to reconvene on an emergency basis to propose steps to implement its recommendations. Lindsay invited all presidential aspirants to take a stand on the report, and they did. McCarthy and Kennedy criticized Johnson's inaction, and the *Times* speculated after Bobby threw his hat in the ring that the Kerner Report issue had contributed to his decision.[36] "This means," Kennedy reportedly commented, "that he's not going to do anything about the war and he's not going to do anything about the cities either."[37] Nixon and Wallace faulted the report for blaming the whole of white society and underplaying the role of black troublemakers. From the Left it was dismissed as a hasty and preconceived bundle of "solemn platitudes."[38] Humphrey, a potential candidate only in retrospect, said the report showed "the need for a massive program of rehabilitation and social action,"[39] but his endorsement so enraged Johnson that the vice president had to retreat behind the old excuse that he had been misquoted.

In the face of all the uproar, Kerner, apparently getting his signals from Johnson, temporized. The president's answer to the report came only in June—the creation of a brand-new commission on "Violence in America" to search out the cause of the national state of crisis. Repudiation of the Kerner Commission could not have been clearer in the conservative make-up of the new one chaired by Milton Eisenhower. Only one member of the earlier commission was carried over, the conservative Congressman McCulloch. Not a single person listed on the staff of the Kerner Commission was employed by the new body. In contrast to the Kerner group, the Eisenhower Commission took its time, received an extension from President Nixon, and issued its report only in December 1969—"To Establish Justice, to Insure Domestic Tranquility." This time the sharp issues were honed down in what amounted to a series of historical and sociological essays, interesting academically but too brief, vague, and hortatory to have any policy impact (with the signal exception of a strong, though ultimately futile, endorsement of gun control).

The black civil rights movement that Martin Luther King came to personify was a revolution in microcosm. It is a classic example of the protest movement that originates as a liberal reform effort, escalates in compass and intensity as it mobilizes both its following and its opposition, splits at the point of success into moderate and radical wings, loses its political momentum in the face of rising resistance, and falls back to a level of achievement somewhere between its point of departure and its climax. Of all the components of the Sixties Revolution, the civil rights movement most clearly fits the classic model of the revolutionary process.

Obviously the movement did not carry out revolution in the sense of overthrowing the government, even though some of the Black Power enthusiasts seemed to speak in those terms. On the local level a good deal of black political behavior in 1967 and 1968 was indeed revolutionary in the literal sense, though without direct success. On the national plane, it was rather as the force for a transformation in American values and expectations about the relationship between the races that the civil rights movement was most truly revolutionary.

Like the classic revolutions of history, the civil rights movement was generated not by worsened oppression but by progress and rising expectations. It was particularly the impact of World War II and the great migration of blacks from the rural South to the urban North, as well as into the growing cities of the South (not unlike the migrations of Russian peasants to the cities around the turn of the century) that made blacks aware that they could mobilize as a force for political and social change. As in the typical prelude to revolution, the American system of segregation and discrimination had been delegitimized by ideas and events. Two landmarks were the publication of Gunnar Myrdal's *An American Dilemma* in 1944, and the civil rights fight led by Hubert Humphrey at the 1948 Democratic Convention (at the cost of Strom Thurmond's Dixiecrat secession). The 1954 school segregation decision was particularly decisive in invoking basic constitutional principles and the powers of the judicial branch of government against race-based inequality.

In the classic pattern of revolution the civil rights movement gathered momentum slowly, within the channels of moderate, legal opposition as far as they were available. The NAACP represented this philosophy, taking the cause to the courtroom rather than to the barricades. Martin Luther King went further, with a much more sweeping, programmatic, and confrontational approach in his attack on the Old Regime, though he remained moderate in his methods of nonviolence. Then, as in every revolution, entered the true radicals, the ideologues of Black Power and the advocates of violent action. These hot heads were egged on rather than appeased by the authorities' reforms—in this case, the civil rights legislation and economic programs of President Johnson's Great Society. Inevitably, the challenge of the radicals caused a series of shocks— to whites who sympathized with the black movement, to those who resisted it, and to the black movement itself. As in every revolutionary experience, the emergence of the radicals in the riots and the Black Power agitation of 1968 splintered the movement and polarized the whole political field. Radicalism forced the question into the terms: seizure of power or collapse of the movement. Since, in the case of the Black Revolution, the movement was confined to one sector of a larger society, seizure of power in the last analysis was out of the question. Collapse, retreat, and disillusionment were inevitable. The remarkable thing is that the movement afterward sustained its gains as much as it did in the consciousness and legal practices of the nation as a whole.

The rise of black radicalism and the shift from religious nonviolence to revolutionary direct action were directly linked with the expansion of the civil rights effort from the South to the Northern ghettos. Here all the classic factors in a revolutionary movement were to be found—the change from the tradition-bound rural environment to the pressures of congested urban life, the discrepancy between hope and fulfillment in the migration to the North, rising expectations and relative deprivation, social pathology and family disintegration among the young ghetto-born generation. The ghetto was fertile ground for the sprouting of revolutionary leaders and the cultivation of revolutionary followers. Nathan Caplan writes of "a new ghetto man: a black militant who is committed to the removal of traditional racial restraints by open confrontation and, if necessary, by violence."[40]

As black political consciousness crystallized in the ghettos, it embraced "Black Power" as its unifying slogan. However, Black Power was understood among the radicals in two different senses, explained by the Los Angeles black leader James H. Hargett as "complete separation" versus "the affirmation of America being a pluralist society."[41] For many, the Black Power talk boiled down to some form of empowerment of blacks to control their own destiny within the one larger community. Stokely Carmichael defined Black Power in one of his less provocative moments as "a call for Black people to define their own goals, to lead their own organizations and to support those organizations."[42] Some of the radicals viewed blacks as a colonized people within white American society, akin to a Third World colony, whose only recourse was to fight for national liberation. In either variant, black radicalism meant giving up on King's dream of true racial integration. To others, black power meant an assault on the whole capitalist system, and some form of political independence for blacks in America.

Black separatism found its first serious expression in the black Muslims, organized in the Nation of Islam by the Detroit preacher W. D. Ford under the name Elijah Muhammad. Muhammad had a falling-out in the early 1960s with his most famous follower, the charismatic Malcolm X (Malcolm Little, a converted drug dealer and ex-convict), who took the avowedly political position of black political separatism and economic independence. "No, I'm not an American," Malcolm X asserted shortly before he was assassinated by unidentified enemies early in 1965, "I'm one of the twenty-two million black people who are the victims of Americanism."[43] The year before, he had broken with Elijah Muhammad and created his own Organization of Afro-American Unity. His ideas had a direct impact on the more political branch of the civil rights movement represented by SNCC and CORE, reflected in the turn to the Left in both organizations in 1966.

The most militant of the black radical organizations had its origin in yet another venture launched by Stokely Carmichael. Following his

116

1966 break with King, Carmichael set up the Lowndes County Freedom Party in Alabama, using the black panther as its symbol. From this came the name—the Black Panther Party. A variety of groups bearing the Black Panther name sprang up around the country, but the one that won national fame as the embodiment of black militancy was the organization launched in California at the end of 1966 by two young Oakland blacks, Bobby Seale and Huey Newton. Seale and Newton were deeply influenced by Malcolm X and by the Martinique-born revolutionary writer Franz Fanon, who used the experience of Algeria's war of independence against the French in the 1950s to formulate a theory of racial revolution in the Third World. In this vein the two black radicals formed a "Black Panther Party for Self-Defense," and called for a ghetto-based movement of armed resistance. Their ideologist was the California ex-convict-turned-writer Eldridge Cleaver, another follower of Malcolm X, who won national note with the publication (almost simultaneously with the Kerner Report) of his prison memoir, *Soul on Ice*.

Like any classic revolution, and like the American counterculture, the black radicalism of the late 1960s had its intellectual preparation. Franz Fanon, Malcolm X, the novelist James Baldwin, and the playwright Le Roi Jones were among the main progenitors of the new Northern ghetto-based black revolutionary consciousness, so different in its mental outlook from the religious inspiration of King's Southern-based movement and the early SNCC. All of the Panther leaders had steeped themselves in the angry antiwhite rhetoric of these writers and were thereby fortified in the rightness of their convictions.

From the start, the California Panthers attracted systematic provocation and harassment by the local police, including Mayor Alioto's San Francisco Tactical Squad. However, the resulting publicity only multiplied support for the movement around the country. Thanks to the jailing of Newton on murder charges after a shoot-out with Oakland police in November 1967 (while Seale was in prison for disrupting the California Legislature), Cleaver became de facto leader of the movement. He leaned more toward an interracial socialist revolution than to black nationalism, and reached out for allies wherever he could find them. To this end, in January 1968, Cleaver brought in Stokely Carmichael (as "Honorary Prime Minister") and the rump of SNCC with James Forman as "Minister of Foreign Affairs" and H. Rap Brown as "Minister of Justice." Brown was the Louisiana-born militant who succeeded Carmichael as chairman of SNCC and proclaimed during the 1967 riots, "Violence is as American as cherry pie."[44] Pursuing his

eclectic dream of a revolutionary coalition, Cleaver even dallied with
the Yippee group of Jerry Rubin and Abbie Hoffman: "The hippies, the
yippies, and all the unnamed dropouts from the white man's burden,
are our allies in this cause."[45]

The high point of black revolutionary unity was the series of "Free
Huey Newton" rallies held in California in February 1968. To an audience of 5,000 in Oakland on the 17th, Cleaver proclaimed the merger
of the Black Panther Party and SNCC, but Carmichael stole the show
and embarrassed his new comrades with his contemptuous rejection of
white allies and "white ideologies" such as socialism and Communism.
Rap Brown showed up in violation of travel restrictions in his bail status,
and exposed himself to arrest soon afterward. But SNCC was torn apart
internally over the merger with the Panthers, which its board never
formally approved, and the FBI planted anonymous threats to cultivate
all the factional hostilities it detected.

In May, SNCC's nominal chairman Brown was convicted and sentenced on the rather technical charge of carrying a firearm on an interstate plane while under indictment for his role in the 1967 riots in the
city of Cambridge, Maryland. SNCC replaced him with a more moderate collective leadership, expelled Carmichael from its ranks, and in July
formally broke off the alliance with the Panthers. But these moves did
not prevent SNCC activists from falling away or wasting their efforts in
fruitless struggles for control of a dwindling movement. "What remained," writes Clayborne Carson, "was a withering institution waiting
to be picked clean by the urban black militants seeking to expand their
influence, by police agents and informers seeking to undermine black
militancy, and by staff members more concerned with institutional
control than with the painstaking work of building mass struggles out of
black discontent."[46] By 1973, the ghost of SNCC was so insubstantial
that the FBI closed that file.

Meanwhile, the King riots signaled a violent crackdown on the
Panthers by California police. Cleaver was wounded and arrested in a
police assault on his Oakland home, and a young associate was shot to
death. In Los Angeles, arrests as well as purges of suspected police
informers virtually eliminated the Panther organization there. In addition, the Panthers were challenged by an even more violent-sounding
group, the U.S. Organization headed by Ron Karenga, in a rivalry (encouraged by the FBI) that led early in 1969 to the shooting deaths of two
Panthers at the hands of Karenga people on the UCLA campus.

By the summer of 1968, Cleaver, again out on bail, was steering the
Panthers to the tactic of electoral coalitions. He concluded an alliance

with the white radical Peace and Freedom party of California, and in August accepted nomination as the presidential candidate of the Panther-PFP ticket. The match quickly broke down over its domination by the Panthers, and Cleaver's opponents seceded in October to proclaim the black comedian Dick Gregory their "Freedom and Peace" presidential candidate. On his own, Cleaver garnered about 200,000 votes in the November election, while the Panther congressional and legislative candidates running in black districts in California were easily defeated by black moderates. From then on it was downhill for the Panthers, as they lost themselves in the sectarian squabbles of the white Left and drove the real black nationalists—particularly Carmichael and Brown—off in disillusionment.

Apart from the direct-action Panthers who would ally with any white revolutionaries, the Black Power movement continued for a time to assert the separatist line. A "National Black Government" conference was held in Detroit in April 1968 to set up the "Republic of New Africa," an outgrowth of the "Revolutionary Action Movement" of Robert Williams, a fugitive in Cuba since 1963. At the end of August, Karenga's group put on a "Third National Black Power Conference" in Philadelphia, from which it went so far as to bar white reporters. CORE met soon afterward to call for black nationalism and "autonomous" white and black societies in America. But the fire was going out; within a couple of years, separatism was forgotten.

After the climax of 1968, the black radicals went the most diverse ways. Several fled the country and made their way to Africa. Carmichael broke with the Panthers in 1969 and went to Guinea, where he still lives. Cleaver jumped bail and fled to Cuba, moving on later to Algeria, where he remained for nearly a decade before returning to the United States as a born-again Christian. Bobby Seale distinguished himself in the protest demonstrations at the Chicago Democratic Convention and then by his defiant conduct in the trial of the "Chicago Eight" in 1969, which prompted Judge Julius Hoffman to order him bound and gagged. He went through two more trials for conspiracy and abetting a murder, without conviction, and then eased into the American mainstream. By 1974, President Nixon was including him in the special advisory commission on undercounting of minorities by the census. Others persisted in their violent defiance of the system. Newton's murder trial in the summer of 1968, and his eventual sentence for manslaughter, made him a national hero of the New Left. He remained in jail until 1972, was arrested again for murder in connection with a brawl, fled to Cuba and then to Canada, was extradited and acquitted in 1979, entered the University of California, was arrested for DWI in 1980, and then became an underground fugitive until he surrendered in 1986. Brown, free while appealing his May 1968 sentence, jumped bail, only to be arrested in a 1971 shoot-out and convicted of robbery and assault; he was finally paroled in 1976. At the other end of the spectrum, James Farmer became assistant secretary of Health, Education and Welfare in the Nixon administration.

Just as revolutionary opportunity evokes radical fervor, so do manifestations of radicalism provoke counterrevolutionary responses. The Black Revolution in America was no exception to this proposition. White backlash against the civil rights movement in general and its violent vanguard in particular was reflected in George Wallace's political campaign. But the most destructive force for counterrevolution, offsetting judicial support for the movement, was embodied in the nation's own law-enforcement agencies, not only Southern but Northern, and not only local but federal, specifically the Federal Bureau of Investigation. "The unexpressed major premise" of Hoover's harassment program, the Senate assassinations investigation concluded, "was that a law enforcement agency has the duty to do whatever is necessary to combat perceived threats to the existing social and political order."[47]

The tragic denouement of Cointelpro in King's assassination did not slow down the bureau's antiblack efforts in the least. The Poor People's encampment in Washington was infiltrated and subjected to disruptive rumors and the provocation of violence. The Black Moslems were targeted, to the extent that a heavyweight match featuring Muhammad Ali was sabotaged for fear that he might contribute his winnings to the Nation of Islam. Finally, in the summer and fall of 1968, Cointelpro zeroed in on the Black Panther Party. Hoover, mistaking rhetoric for reality, described them as "the greatest threat to the nation's internal security,"[48] even though they were already being severely harassed by the local authorities in California. He kept up the campaign against the Panthers for more than a year, until the tragedy of December 1969, when Panther leaders Fred Hampton and Mark Clark were gunned down in an FBI-instigated raid on their Chicago apartment.

Given Hoover's view of the civil rights movement, it is not surprising that his first response to King's murder was to distance the FBI from the whole matter on the grounds that the crime was not a federal offense. Once President Johnson ordered him to act, putting the bureau's professional reputation at stake, it was a different matter. Despite the FBI's obsession with alleged radicals and the sexual habits of political figures, when it came to the technical side of crime-solving it had no peer. The bureau took just fifteen days to identify James Earl Ray as the killer. Early in May an indictment was handed down in Tennessee.

Ray had fled immediately from Atlanta to Detroit by bus, and thence to Canada, obtained a Canadian passport, and flew to London. On a tip from a former co-prisoner about Ray's past in Canada, the FBI alerted the Mounties, who were able to identify Ray's passport application and plane ticket in the name of Ramon Sneyd. They alerted Scotland Yard, and British agents arrested Ray on June 8 as he was about to board a plane for the Continent. Following extradition, Ray was arraigned in Memphis, and after some months of legal maneuvers and a change of lawyers, pleaded guilty. He was sentenced to ninety-nine years in prison, where he remains. Ray always denied any broader conspiracy, and the Justice Department let the matter drop, a decision that congressional investigators sharply criticized after the probe of the late 1970s.[49] According to the House Committee on Assassinations, the FBI "failed to investigate adequately the possibility of conspiracy," and the government missed its chance to go after the presumptive plotters who had bankrolled Ray or promised to pay him off.[50]

While the hunt for the assassin was underway, King's associates strove to carry on the plans he had left unfinished, most immediately the Poor People's March on Washington. The Reverend Ralph Abernathy took over as president of SCLC and personally led the march. To dramatize the plight of the black poor, some of his followers arrived in Washington by wagon and mule team. Beginning on May 13, the protesters encamped in the Mall with a permit from the National Park Service to set up their "Resurrection City" of tents and shacks, intended to confront Congress and the American public with the issue of economic deprivation. Jesse Jackson assisted as camp manager, for the first couple of weeks, until he was dropped because of complaints of a budding cult of personality. Abernathy stayed in a motel.

Resurrection City was less than spectacularly successful. Sympathy for the poor was already on the retrograde in Congress, and the riots had polarized opinion about further concessions to blacks. Meanwhile the rains came, and Resurrection City sank into a sorry morass of mud and petty crime, aggravated by government provocateurs and brought nightly to the TV audience along with the endless fighting in Vietnam. Late in June, when the permit for Resurrection City expired, campers began to be arrested for refusing to leave. Resistance by a dwindling minority dragged on until Abernathy called the whole show off in mid-July. Moderate black protest, no less than radical defiance, was running out of steam.

In all fairness to President Johnson, he had not given up on his Great Society despite his preoccupation with Vietnam and his antipathy toward Martin Luther King. Nevertheless, the push for reform from above, like the movements of protest from below, was weakening. Republican gains in the congressional elections of 1966 put the old Republican–Southern Democratic coalition back in the driver's seat, legislatively speaking, and the issue of the federal deficit brought on by spending for the war had given the conservatives a hammerlock on the budget—intimations of the 1980s. An international gold crisis and fears for the stability of the U.S. dollar gave more ammunition to the enemies of social spending. Contrary to the common belief that he thought he could have both the war and the Great Society without raising taxes, the president in his 1968 State of the Union speech called for an income tax surcharge. However, the powerful House Ways and Means Chairman Wilbur Mills of Arkansas would not let the measure budge until $6 billion was cut from the domestic spending request. Late in June, a 10 percent tax surcharge passed on Mills' terms, meaning that the Vietnam War had shunted the Great Society aside as the nation's economic priority. Far from a creative implementation of the Kerner Commission's urgings, the War on Poverty was turning into a last-ditch holding action.

Some of Johnson's key people in the antipoverty effort were giving up on it. Following McNamara, the talented HEW secretary John Gardner resigned in March, to be replaced by his deputy Wilbur Cohen, the New Deal architect of Social Security and more recently of Medicare. Sargent Shriver, the Kennedy brother-in-law, left the Office of Economic Opportunity to become ambassador in Paris.

Propelled by the Kerner Commission report, progress did continue in the civil rights area. The day before the New Hampshire primary, the Senate passed yet another in the Johnson era's epochal series of civil rights bills, this one directed against discrimination in housing and the intimidation of civil rights workers. A couple of weeks later, a jury reform bill was passed to ban discriminatory tactics against minorities. But the growing climate of racial violence expressed in the riots of the summer of 1967, intensified by the King riots and the clashes of black radicals with the police, turned the public mood from justice to law and order. Congress passed a new crime control bill in June 1968 that limited the "Miranda" ruling on advising suspects of their rights and expanded the legal use of wiretaps. A rider ironically attached to the new Civil Rights Act made it a federal crime to cross state lines with the intent to incite a riot. This "Rap Brown" law, as it became known, was the legal tool used to charge the Chicago Seven for their role in the disturbances at the convention as well as to prosecute sundry other violence-prone radicals of both races.

The black movement was the centerpiece of the whole American revolutionary experience of the 1960s. Although it crested in 1968 along with most other elements of social protest—student, countercultural, antiwar—it was the earliest to take on serious proportions, going back to the late 1950s. It exhibited by far the most violent behavior of the era. In its duration, complexity, and trajectory, it came nearest of all the new rebellious tendencies in America to replicating in microcosm the classic revolutionary process of moderate protest, radical revolt, utopian splintering, disillusioned reaction, and pragmatic consolidation. In retrospect, black protest was the most successful aspect of the Sixties Revolution, in accomplishing the reversal of what had passed as acceptable public attitudes and discourse about race relations in the United States.

The victory of the civil rights movement was neither immediate nor uncontested, nor was it complete, but as it was consolidated over the years that followed, the magnitude of its implications became increasingly obvious. In many respects, blacks won their lasting gains not so much through the assertion of the legislative power (like the classic revolutions of the seventeenth and eighteenth centuries) or through the favor of the executive branch of government (like the reforms of the New Deal), but through the judiciary—ultimately, through the United States Supreme Court. In essence, the Black Revolution was consolidated and legitimized by a new revolutionary recourse to the documents of a revolution almost two hundred years before, which had justified itself with an appeal to universal principles of equality whose fullest extension it never contemplated.

The significance of the judicial center of the revolution was underscored by political controversy then and since. In June 1968, Earl Warren, the racists' bête noire since the 1954 school desegregation decision, announced that he planned to retire as chief justice. To succeed him, President Johnson put forth the name of his liberal friend Abe Fortas, an associate justice since 1964. The nomination was bitterly fought by Southern senators, who not only blocked Fortas for chief justice by dredging up old charges of financial improprieties, but with the threat of impeachment even forced his resignation from the court altogether

123

the following year. Warren meanwhile held on until 1970, when President Nixon replaced him with Warren Burger. Rearguard actions by closet racists over the borderline issues of busing to integrate schools and affirmative action in employment continued through the 1970s and 1980s. However, the ultimate change in the public climate was underscored by the controversy over President Reagan's nomination of Robert Bork to the Supreme Court, pitting liberal senators (including Southern Democrats now dependent on the black vote) against the conservative judicial candidate who rejected the twentieth-century broadening of an eighteenth-century constitution.

A symbol of the gains and limits of the Black Revolution is the national martyrdom accorded Martin Luther King, Jr., culminating in the establishment of his birthday, January 15, as a national holiday on a par with the combined birthdays of Presidents Lincoln and Washington. King, as his biographers point out, was mythologized and de-radicalized in retrospect, to make him a figure of national unity based on the principle of legal equality, rather than the divisive radical he actually became over issues of economic injustice that the 1970s and 1980s preferred to soft-pedal. Indeed, the great shortcoming of the Sixties Revolution was its failure to reengage the unfinished economic aims of the New Deal era, even though Lyndon Johnson had tried to reopen this agenda with his Great Society. Blacks won political rights and freedom from public humiliation, and some blacks gained access to the social pyramid—that is, the same advances that the English and American and French revolutions won for middle-class whites. For the poor of both races, none of these revolutions made much difference.

For America, the black movement was a major element—perhaps even the leading element—in the Sixties Revolution. In its immediate impact, shaking the conscience of white society, it had a key influence along with the Vietnam War in establishing the country's mood of protest. In its more radical aspect, it served as a direct tactical inspiration to white students and the New Left. In the longer view, the black movement was by far the most successful aspect of this New American Revolution in the gains it scored and the paths it laid down for future change. Race, in its social and legal aspects if not the economic, was one area in which the revolution for personal equality proved substantially victorious.

Connections of the black movement with the revolution overseas are more difficult to pursue. By its nature, the black movement was limited to one segment of society. The colonial analogy is not really applicable, because in this case we have not a separate oppressed society but only a racial community scattered through the dominant society and distinguished more by the past experience of slavery and discrimination than by a separate national identity. For the same reason, comparison with East European defiance of Soviet domination fails. The black movement was more like youth protest, a manifestation of unrest among a certain category in a single broader society. What it did have in common with the other movements of the 1960s was the expression, in one form or another, of protest against every form of coercive dominance by one person over another.

6

Morningside Heights

TUESDAY, APRIL 23, noon on a windy spring day. Upwards of five hundred students have gathered at the sundial in the center of Columbia University's upper-Manhattan campus to hear the new leader of the local chapter of Students for a Democratic Society, Mark Rudd, denounce the university administration and press the organization's demands. Rudd is a 20-year-old junior enamored of Castro's Cuba and romantically committed to the cause of revolution. Tom Hayden, one of the early shapers of the national SDS, describes Rudd in retrospect as "sarcastic and smugly dogmatic," and "absolutely committed to an impossible yet galvanizing dream: that of transforming the entire student movement, through this particular student revolt, into a successful effort to bring down the system."[1]

The immediate aims of the Columbia University SDS reflect the national turmoil over the Vietnam War and race relations. They include abandonment of a gymnasium project under construction in Morningside Park because it symbolizes disdain for the nearby Harlem ghetto; a break with the Institute for Defense Analysis that does weapons research and counterinsurgency studies for the Pentagon; reinstatement of six students suspended for demonstrating against the IDA inside a university building; and reform of the autocratic system of disciplining students. To accomplish these demands, the SDSers aim, with the aid of the small but radical contingent of campus blacks of the Student Afro-American Society, to invade the domed Low Library where University

127

president Grayson Kirk and other administrators have their offices. However, on approaching the building, they learn that it is locked and guarded by a counterdemonstration of jocks who call themselves Students for a Free Campus, and the SDS rebels lose some of their resolve. One of them calls for a march to the gymnasium, and half the crowd heads over there to tear down the fence surrounding the construction site. Rudd, still an unseasoned revolutionary, rushes to keep up with his followers. To forestall a loss of momentum, he leads them to the unguarded office of undergraduate dean Henry Coleman in Hamilton Hall on nearby Amsterdam Avenue. In announced retaliation for the arrest of one black student at the gym site, some five hundred students take over the building and make the dean a hostage in his own office. Posters of Lenin, Malcolm X, and Che Guevara go up in the corridors. Rudd forms a ten-member steering committee of five whites and five blacks.

As the occupation of Hamilton Hall drags on through the evening in defiance of warnings by university vice president David Truman and other administrators, the black students are reinforced by Harlem militants mobilized by CORE and SNCC, reportedly with guns, and grow disquieted over what they regard as a lack of revolutionary decisiveness on the part of the whites. The steering committee splits, and the blacks, about seventy-five in number, take a separate floor of the building for the sleep-in. At 5:00 A.M., faced with the evident black intent on a violent confrontation and fearful of alienating the university's faculty, Rudd tells his followers, "The blacks have asked us to leave the building, and I think we should. . . . We should . . . go and find our own building to make a stand in."[2] Throughout, the white students are overawed by their image of the blacks as superior revolutionaries. Rudd comments afterward, "In struggle after struggle on campuses and in shops, the blacks have been taking the initial and even vanguard role."[3]

Without much premeditation, two hundred humbled SDSers of the "action faction" move across the campus in the early morning rain and smash their way through a basement door into the Low Library. They take over the president's office by the same means and rip through his files. Vice President Truman decides that it is time to call the New York police.

The arrival of the police at Low Library causes most of the occupiers to scramble out through the windows, but the police fail to secure the building and as soon as they depart the SDSers resume their occupation. The administration hesitates to take firm action for fear of provoking a chain reaction all the way to Harlem, and possible bloodshed, but President Kirk firmly rejects any relaxation of university discipline involving suspension or expulsion of the leaders of the revolt. While nonradical students conduct a counterdemonstration to protest the disruption on campus, the faculty meets to debate measures of conciliation, but it too rejects immediate granting of the protesters' demands. The blacks in Hamilton Hall are encouraged by every black organization and political figure in the city, from CORE to Manhattan Borough President Percy Sutton. They release Dean Coleman and stock up food for a siege. Meanwhile, Rudd fails to get the bulk of the SDSers to commit themselves to anything more radical than a strike, and in disgust he threatens to resign as chairman.

Other students are ready to take more direct action. Architecture students, electrified by the Hamilton Hall and Low Library takeovers, refuse to leave their building, Avery Hall, in the northeast section of the campus, when the order goes out to close it for the night. Their example is followed after midnight by radical graduate students, who take over nearby Fayerweather Hall. The uprisings threaten to become a true student revolution, and President Kirk orders the campus closed. Yet he also announces that he will ask the trustees to halt work on the gym and to confer with Mayor Lindsay about its future—a late concession on the issue that originally sparked the trouble.

Throughout the day on Thursday, April 25, there is no further yielding by either the administration or the protesters. Liberal professors, frustrated by their seeming impotence in the crisis, form an Ad Hoc Faculty Group to try to press a compromise whereby the students will end the occupation and the faculty will represent their demands; they are stalled off or rebuffed by the rebels. Tension rises in the evening when the student athletes, annoyed by the administration's indulgence toward black demonstrators, decide to take matters into their own hands and lay siege to some of the occupied buildings; professors try to cool them with academic reasoning.

Shortly after midnight on Friday the 26th, while the Ad Hoc Faculty Group is still debating what to do, the uprising spreads even further as students in the Low Library and Fayerweather Hall sally out and take over Mathematics Hall on the Broadway side of the campus. This is too much for the administration; Vice President Truman and Dean Coleman meet with the faculty group to announce that they have asked the police to clear the buildings. They are loudly booed by the professors, who hasten to distribute themselves around the occupied buildings in the hope of preventing the police action. Tom Hayden appears on campus to assume leadership in Mathematics Hall, while Professor Alan Westin, a civil liberties expert, leads a team of faculty negotiators

129

into the newly seized building through a window to parlay with Rudd. The talks prove fruitless.

At 3:00 A.M., plainclothes police concentrated in the crowd at the basement entrance to Low Library finally attack. But the faculty strategy works; faced with the possible spectacle of their professors being bloodied in the police charge, Kirk and Truman decide to call off the assault. They confirm that work on the gym will stop, but leave the students' demands about discipline unmet. (The IDA issue fades as the protesters pursue the power struggle.) All sides settle in for a long weekend standoff. In the "liberated" buildings, students form revolutionary communes, with incessant guitar music, debates, and speechmaking. There is even an impromptu wedding in Fayerweather Hall. SDS sets up a regular strike headquarters in the offices of the student Citizenship Council and tries to prevent defections among the non-SDS strikers.

Friday afternoon, the black students are visited by two illustrious black leaders—the ubiquitous Stokely Carmichael and his successor at SNCC, H. Rap Brown—but on this occasion the pair uncharacteristically avoid inflaming the situation further. More police move onto the campus to guard the unoccupied buildings and to bar outsiders from further access to the university.

Throughout Friday evening and Saturday, despite desperate faculty efforts to mediate, both the protesters and the administration harden their positions, particularly after the trustees reaffirm the principle of discipline. Kirk believes he has a responsibility to all American higher education to hold the line on this point. At the opposite extreme, the Strike Coordinating Committee declares, "The administration is illegitimate and must be forced to *de facto* declare itself illegitimate by granting amnesty before really substantive structural changes can occur." "Now the Man is desperate," the blacks tell their Harlem following. "Now we ask you to support us with a real show of physical support as well as moral support."[4]

Working throughout Saturday night, a steering committee of the Ad Hoc Faculty Group chaired by Professor Westin formulates its final compromise—a "bitter pill," someone dubs it—and resolves to support whichever side accepts the proposal. But an official meeting of the senior faculty on Sunday morning instead endorses overwhelmingly a pro-administration statement, thus repudiating the efforts of the Ad Hoc Faculty Group. That afternoon, the self-styled "Majority Coalition" of conservative students decides to take matters into its own hands and blockade the Low Library in order to cut off food to its occupiers.

Tension builds as the conservatives repulse efforts by sit-in sympathizers to break the blockade, while a cordon of professors strives to keep the uneasy peace. President Kirk orders the university kept closed and classes suspended until "normal operations" can resume.

On Monday the 29th, the day the Poor People's encampment opens in Washington, the Columbia University administration finally begins to bend. President Kirk agrees to recommend to the Trustees the Ad Hoc Faculty Group's proposal to put discipline in the hands of a faculty-student-administration board, as well as to discuss a permanent alternative to the construction of the gym. The Faculty Group cannot agree whether this meets the terms of the "bitter pill." Even the famous labor negotiator Theodore Kheel cannot find anything on which the students and the administration can agree. He notes, "This was unlike a labor dispute in that it was in the interest of one of the disputants, SDS, *not* to settle."[5] At 6:00 P.M., the protesters reject the faculty compromise *in toto*. Police action is expected in a matter of hours. In fact, President Kirk gives the word that evening and by midnight one thousand officers from precincts all over the city, many from the Tactical Patrol Force, are deployed around the edges of the campus.

Shortly after 2:00 A.M. on Tuesday the 30th, the bust begins. Surprisingly, the blacks in Hamilton Hall, who have been thought the most militant of the protesters, allow themselves to be arrested without resistance. Elsewhere, their warnings ignored, the police charge the protesters gathered outside building entrances, clubbing anyone who stands in their way, even professors and deans who have been trying to prevent violence. Avery Hall—the architecture students—proves easy; Fayerweather Hall opposite it is the scene of mayhem. At Low Library officers smash their way through the barricades at President Kirk's office and arrest the occupiers. Mathematics Hall offers the most resistance of all, but the students there are also overpowered as they shout defiance. Then a crowd of onlookers in the middle of the campus, jeering the police, is attacked in turn. More indiscriminate clubbing. Altogether over seven hundred students are arrested and carted off in paddy wagons to be booked; there are nearly one hundred fifty recorded injuries, and one hundred twenty complaints of police brutality are lodged.[6] Mark Rudd has judiciously taken up a position outside the campus gates to avoid arrest. It seems that the police believe they have been ordered to clear the campus, but this is denied by the administration. There are charges of theft and willful damage by police in the reoccupied buildings.

The police action quells the onrush of the revolution at Columbia.

Compared to the first heroic week, all else is anticlimatic as the revolutionary commitment proves to have exhausted itself. Yet its effects are lasting—Columbia University will never be quite the same and the nationwide student movement has gained a heroic benchmark.

The uprising at Columbia University was only part of a chain reaction of student protest on American college campuses, beginning with the "Free Speech" movement at Berkeley in 1964 and extending through the tragic antiwar demonstration in 1970 at Kent State University in Ohio. A movement such as this, erupting in the kind of passion and commitment exhibited at Columbia, obviously must have deep roots. First, it reflected widespread malaise over the authoritarian governance and regulations, academic and social, that prevailed at most institutions of higher learning. Feuer would call it the conflict of generations, the endemic tension between old and young, between those who have established themselves in life and those who are just beginning to make their way in it. In Freudian terms, there is always "the will to revolt against the de-authoritized father." "Student movements," Feuer argues, "arise whenever social and historical circumstances combine to cause a crisis in loss of generational confidence."[7] In other words, public misfortunes or conflicts, above all the Vietnam War and the black civil rights struggle in this instance, "de-authoritize" the elders and activate youthful rebellion. Reflected at Columbia in the issues of the Institute for Defense Analysis and the new gym, the war and racial oppression made all authority seem suspect and immoral. To radical youth, the stain of these transgressions legitimized the most violent and obscene defiance of the powers of the older generation as embodied in traditional university discipline and the public agencies of law and order.

The student revolt was closely linked to the civil rights campaign, even though the social bases of the two movements—the one drawing on the social conscience of the most successful stratum of society, the other based on the most oppressed—were diametrically opposite. One commentary describes white student involvement in the heroic and dangerous civil rights battles, from the "Freedom Rides" of 1961 to the "Mississippi Summer" of 1964, as an effort to achieve "freedom from guilt over one's privilege."[8] Most of the student leaders who distinguished themselves in the mid- to late 1960s, including Mario Savio of the Berkeley Free Speech Movement and Tom Hayden of SDS, learned their radicalism at the hands of Southern mobs and sheriffs.

The event that first lit up the dark sky of political apathy hanging over American student life in the 1950s and early 1960s was the celebrated

Free Speech Movement at the University of California. The trouble began in the fall of 1964 over the University's abrupt ban on political activity on a stretch of sidewalk—the so-called "strip"—between the campus and the Berkeley business district that the students had long considered the public domain. Savio, just back from the summer in Mississippi with SNCC, perceived the same kind of systemic repression that the blacks suffered, and he succeeded in turning the "strip" issue into a mass student protest. The upshot was mob confrontations with the police and a takeover of the administration building that ended only in a major police action. Declared Savio to a thousand followers preparing for the sit-in, "There is a time when the operation of the machine becomes so odious, makes you so sick at heart, that you can't take part. . . . You've got to put your bodies upon the gears and upon the wheels, upon the levers, upon all the apparatus and you've got to make it stop."[9]

Berkeley thus set the pattern for all of the student rebellions to follow: incidents fanned into flame by determined leadership, the resort to police force by stubborn university administrators, and the consequent radicalization of much larger numbers of students. "In the last analysis," writes Klaus Mehnert, an observer of the era's student troubles on five continents, "campus problems as such did not stand in the foreground of the conflict, either at Berkeley or in other universities. The true enemy was 'society'—whatever that might mean for the individual—the university simply being that segment of society with which the students happened to be confronted."[10]

The student protest movement of the 1960s was almost coterminous with what came to be known as the New Left. Although growingly radical in its philosophy and confrontationist in its tactics, the New Left bore sharp distinctions from the Old Left—Socialist, Communist, Trotskyist—that had its heyday in America in the years between the world wars. Wrote Seymour Martin Lipset in the midst of the events, "The New Left youth groups reject almost all political parties. For them, the political parties of the Left, both Socialist and Communist, are parties of the parliamentary establishment. They see no adult organizations that are genuinely revolutionary or resistant to the major trends of the society that they oppose."[11]

Most New Left activists (like most extremists of the counterculture) came from liberal (and often nonreligious) Jewish or WASP families. They usually suffered little generational conflict; a good many were "red diaper babies," offspring of radical parents. "Young people raised in this kind of family setting," wrote Richard Flacks, an SDS theorist and later sociology professor who personally illustrated the point, "are likely to be particularly sensitized to acts of arbitrary authority, to unexamined allegiance to conventional values, to instances of institutional practices which conflict with professed ideals."[12]

But the New Left was revolutionary in a different sense from the Old, partly as a result of widespread disillusionment with the Soviet experiment since World War II, partly out of revulsion from the mood of consumerism, personal success, and national self-congratulation that had prevailed in America since that time. "New Leftists," writes Maurice Isserman, "repudiated dogmas they never shared and then turned with the passionate intensity of the newly converted to building a movement based on what was left to them: personal morality, ethics, and sincerity."[13] Flacks defines the New Left as "a particular segment of young activists who were self-consciously radical ideologically, but disaffected from all 'established radicalisms,' and who self-consciously sought to provide political direction, theoretical coherence, and organizational continuity to the student movement."[14]

The New Left drew its philosophical inspiration not from Marx and Lenin but from a series of more recent radical writers, American and European, addressing the unfreedom of the individual in the modern bureaucratic culture. The first to stir the budding young radicals of the early 1960s was the sociologist C. Wright Mills, who challenged the domestic and international orthodoxies of the 1950s in a series of trenchant books, most notably *The Power Elite* (1956) and *The Origins of World War III* (1958). Next, and most famous, was the German-born American philosophy professor Herbert Marcuse, whose combination of Marxism and cultural radicalism, especially in *One-Dimensional Man* (1962), powerfully articulated the younger generation's sense of alienation from an oppressively permissive Establishment. A bit later came the French political writer Regis Debray, who idealized Che Guevara and advanced a model for worldwide guerrilla warfare in *Revolution in the Revolution* (1967). Yet despite an abundance of theoretical inspiration, the American New Left remained by European standards remarkably loose and casual in its ideology. "The New Left," writes Allen Matusow, "intended to let its ideology emerge from action and chose men of action, not mere thinkers, as its early heroes."[15] Emotion took the place of program; outrage substituted for reason. "The link between feeling and action was a short fuse," recalled Todd Gitlin, Hayden's successor as SDS president in the mid-1960s. "It was the immediate experience that counted most."[16] The Port Huron Statement dismissed ideology as "statementism." As the Columbia University takeovers began on 23 April 1968, an SDSer was heard to say, "We've got something going here and now we've just got to find out what it is."[17]

134

The new radicalism gave comparatively little heed to institutional changes in the economic order. On the other hand, it went much deeper than the Old Left ever had in its repudiation of the cultural legacy of earlier generations and in its rejection of the fruits of material progress (coinciding here with the nonpolitical counterculture). The New Left parted fundamentally both from the labor movement of the past and from the black movement of the present, each of which aimed with some eventual success at a fairer division of a growing economic pie. But the students did have something in common with the simultaneous Cultural Revolution in China: their rejection of anything old, hierarchical, or sacred in the social order. Both movements went out of their way to humiliate authority figures who had stood behind the shield of office and dignity.

As a social and cultural revolt aimed toward freedom and equality in realms where no one had yet tried to carry them, the New Left had much in common with the counterculture. To an extent the two currents of youthful protest overlapped, but the distinction always remained clear at the extremes: the countercultural purists of the communes and the Haight-Ashburys refused to take the political process seriously, whereas the New Left disdained the drug-induced personal withdrawal of the countercultural fringe. There were rare attempts to combine the two fully, notably in the "Yippee" movement of Jerry Rubin and Abbie Hoffman.

Organizationally the New Left became virtually synonymous with Students for a Democratic Society. SDS was originally formed as a youth arm of the Norman Thomas Socialist Party, under the name Student League for Industrial Democracy. In 1960, SDS severed this connection and moved in a steadily more radical direction, rejecting the Socialists' anti-Communist stance. The Cold War with the Soviet Union seemed to SDS a distraction from the real struggle to end imperialism and change American society. A benchmark in this evolution was the Port Huron Statement of 1962 (named for the locale of the SDS convention that year), mainly authored by Tom Hayden. Hayden, a recent graduate of the University of Michigan and the SNCC school of politics in the South, and an accomplished student journalist, served as SDS president in 1962–1963 and became the main theoretician of the organization. His Port Huron document was not particularly radical in the Old Left sense. It bemoaned the apathetic loss of hope and ideals in these years and posited the goal of "a democracy of individual participation"[18]—a theme that would soon mark the radicalism of youth all over the world.

The term "participatory democracy" appears to have been coined by

Hayden's University of Michigan philosophy professor Arnold Kaufman, who also baptized the antiwar teach-in movement later on. Kaufman had in mind not the anarchistic repudiation of representative government that participatory democracy later came to connote at the hands of the radicals, but rather an amplification of the representative process that would enhance "direct responsibility for decisions" and "the development of human powers of thought, feeling, and action."[19] At Hayden's hands in the Port Huron Statement, participatory democracy still sounded vague and romantic. James Miller notes the "elasticity" and "instability" of the term, allowing the emergence of a radical, anarchist vision of "the experimental commune."[20] The radical historian Staughton Lynd construed it as "parallel structures" and "the spirit of community," leading to "a brotherly way of life in the jaws of the Leviathan."[21] Thus, participatory democracy was not just a political means but an end in itself, though fuzzy and indefinite, a guiding inspiration in the New Left's disdain for formal organization.

In many respects—civil rights, the War on Poverty—Port Huron anticipated Lyndon Johnson's Great Society. Its strongest words were reserved for the military-industrial complex, the Cold War, and paranoid anti-Communism, suggesting the ready basis for disaffection when the Vietnam War intruded on the scene a little later. The most original notion in the Port Huron Statement was the proposition that the universities were the main repository of the skills and influence to launch "a new left" and to "start controversy across the land," provided that "an alliance of students and faculty" could "wrest control of the educational process from the administrative bureaucracy."[22]

In 1963, to put participatory democracy into practice and give its members a post-college future, SDS launched an "Economic Research and Action Project" (ERAP) to organize the urban poor, black and white alike. Cleveland, Chicago, and Newark, New Jersey, were the main sites of this effort, led nationally by Rennie Davis. Reminiscent of the Russian Populists' "Going to the People" movement of the 1870s, ERAP encountered almost insuperable difficulties. It was hard to get the target population to respond and to overcome suspicions of the students' communitarian life-style, even though the project coincided with the Great Society antipoverty program and in some places even took it over for a time. Although ERAP fell apart as a nationally coordinated effort as early as 1965, it did help pave the way for the new National Welfare Rights Organization. Tom Hayden made Newark his personal cause and kept the program there going longer than most, until the riot of July 1967 put an end to his effectiveness. By then he had become almost totally absorbed in the antiwar movement.

136

All this was only prelude. It took the onset of serious American involvement in the Vietnam War in 1964 to fan the sparks of student radicalism into a mass movement. In the theoretical respect, the war was a glaring manifestation of just that militaristic nationalism that Port Huron had inveighed against. Hayden went to Hanoi in November 1965 with the radical historians Staughton Lynd and Herbert Apteker and returned to sing the praises of anticolonial guerrillas. On the practical side, the war threatened students with military service in the combat zone, if not immediately, then after their deferments expired. (Students ranking in the bottom half of their class became subject to the draft in 1966, and graduate students regardless of their skills or promise in 1968.) In terms of the conflict of generations, Vietnam was the decisive circumstance delegitimizing the ruling age-group of the parents. Like so many other revolutionary occasions in history, an unpopular war—unpopular at least with the student segment of society—was the event that turned the potential of rebellion into actuality. SDS membership, only 1,000 in 1961 and 2,500 in 1964, burgeoned by 1968 to 100,000 in more than 300 chapters. Members of SDS played a key part in launching the antiwar crusade, by initiating the teach-in movement and organizing the April 1965 protest demonstrations.

Some extra flavoring of cultural radicalism was added to SDS in New York by the Lower East Side group of artistic anarchists (including Marcuse's stepson) who called themselves "Up Against the Wall, Motherfucker," (from a line by LeRoi Jones), and proclaimed themselves an SDS chapter. The Motherfuckers specialized in disrupting any somber activity, whether by dumping garbage at Lincoln Center during the New York sanitation strike of February 1968, or disrupting ideological debates at SDS national meetings. "Acid-fueled fanatics," Martin Lee and Bruce Shlain called them, who "prefigured the paramilitary fad that engulfed the New Left as the decade drew to a close."[23] Their antics amplified by the underground press, the Motherfuckers were instrumental in popularizing the tactics of trashing and ridicule that took hold at Columbia and spread to other campus radicals all over the United States during the next two years. Inevitably, they showed up to add spice to the Columbia uprising; "The freewheeling Motherfuckers dazzled Rudd," recalls Todd Gitlin.[24]

Of all the components of the American Revolution of the 1960s, the student upheaval had most in common with contemporary disturbances around the globe. As events in France were to dramatize only a few days after the Columbia University uprising, disaffection of the student generation from what they considered the manipulative hierarchies of modern society was intensifying throughout the industrialized world. Unsupported by the traditional Left, student radicals were already involved in violent confrontation with the authorities in Germany, Italy, and Japan. The agitation was also spreading to Latin America, where it soon erupted into mass defiance in Mexico and urban guerrilla warfare in Uruguay.

It is far easier to describe the international student revolt than to explain its upsurge in so many diverse places at the same time. Europe and Japan lacked the directly "de-authoritizing" experiences such as Vietnam and the civil rights movement were for America, although Vietnam did sharpen the spirit of anti-imperialism among youth elsewhere. As a common denominator, Klaus Mehnert falls back on "the restlessness of the epoch" and the nervous tension and doubts generated by the excesses of technological society.[25] The British oral historian Ronald Fraser points to "the uneven development of post-war Western societies in which the actual and ideological authority structures were out of synchronization with the rising expectations seemingly afforded by rapid economic growth."[26] This discrepancy was particularly true in universities around the world, where values of independence encouraged by liberal parents and the culture at large collided with tradition-bound bureaucracies. In most places—although not at Columbia and the Ivy League because of their fixed enrollments—educational administrators were swamped by the combination of the post–World War II demographic boom and escalating aspirations to higher education in the affluent society. Typically, their first response to the new student culture was intransigence, which only fueled the rebellion.

The problem with these explanations is that, apart from authoritarianism in university life, none of the underlying evils of modernity attacked by the student New Left have been significantly alleviated since then. Nevertheless, the youthful rebellion soon collapsed into apathy and routine or sank into the pursuit of small causes. Nowhere did the New Left make itself a lasting force either organizationally or ideologically. Maurice Isserman notes its failure to understand "the need for a patient, long-term approach to building movements."[27] Its pale reflection shows only in idealistic currents within the political system, such as the Greens in Europe or the Rainbow Coalition and the Ralph Nader Public Interest Research Groups in America. To be sure, student politics are circumscribed by the ordinary fact that students grow up and cease to be students, but the New Left of the 1960s failed either to carry its spirit effectively into adult life or to replicate itself among succeeding student generations. The history of the campus revolt is another example of the law that revolutionary action is inherently a transitory phenomenon, a passing wave that will not be felt again until new times and new circumstances bring society to some new and different point of crisis.

The various movements of student protest around the world in the 1960s were akin in their ideology or in the loudly vented emotions that passed for such. They hated the established social order—governments that hid behind the democratic façade, corporate bureaucracies that smothered humanity with their technologies, and all forms of coercion of the powerless—minorities, family members, and small nations. They were antiauthoritarian but intolerant, alienated but antiachievement, communitarian but antifamily. Infused with what Fraser calls "the culture of insubordination," they sought self-realization in revolutionary action and approached politics as "theater and confrontation."[28]

A signal difference between the two shores of the Atlantic was the Europeans' deep involvement in formal doctrines derived from the Old Left—Trotskyism, anarchism, council communism—contrasting with the Americans' rejection of intellectual creeds and historical thinking in favor of their own largely negative sloganeering. Compared with the French, the Americans met with far less resonance on the part of the general public; they were both distracted and compromised by their links with the counterculture and the drug scene. The spirit of the movement was international, but the Americans broke more deeply with precedent, in the repudiation of their country's tradition of national virtue implied by the civil rights and antiwar movements. The New American Revolution, remarked Jean-François Revel, is "the only revolution that involves radical, moral, and practical opposition to the spirit of nationalism."[29] In the 1970s, this mood spilled over into the teaching of American history and the writing of history textbooks, prompting Frances Fitzgerald, a historian of the Vietnam War, to write about the phenomenon in *America Revised: History Schoolbooks in the Twentieth Century* (1979).

The antinationalist spirit of the American New Left, disavowing everything that traditional authority stood for, went hand in hand with renunciation of the West's role in the world and an idealization of Third World revolutionary movements, sentiments that American radicals shared with their European counterparts. Moralistically rejecting their own governments' records of imperialistic ventures, past or present, they all extended what the British political scientist Nigel Young terms "a political blank cheque for any anti-imperialist movement that happened along."[30] Under the influence of Guevara, Franz Fanon, and

Regis Debray, spokesmen like Carl Oglesby (SDS president in 1965–1966 and a leader in the organization's subsequent radicalization) hailed Third World guerrilla warfare. This and the ghetto uprisings at home they viewed as manifestations of a new struggle of the worldwide nonwhite peasantry against the white urban civilization of the West. Oglesby called the National Liberation Front in Vietnam (that is, the Vietcong) "as honest a revolution as you can find anywhere in history."[31] The hatred of one's own society, where revolution could not really get off the ground, led to what SDSer James Weinstein called "self-repudiation" and "the implicit idea of redemption through identification with one of the true, or key revolutionary agents," among whom he listed "ghetto-blacks, freaks, youth-as-a-class (students), industrial workers or colonial-revolutionaries."[32]

An early inspiration for the Third World orientation of SDS came from Castro's revolution in Cuba, whither many SDS leaders journeyed in the early 1960s to breathe in the atmosphere of anti-imperialist solidarity. The influence was renewed by the Havana "cultural congress" in July 1967, joined in by a host of American New Left figures. Che Guevara quickly came to symbolize the "heroic guerrilla," and then achieved international martyrdom when he was killed while trying to kindle a peasant revolutionary movement in Bolivia in October 1967.

A far greater impact, of course, came with the Vietnam War. In Europe, the war conveniently brought together radicalism and anti-Americanism, and figured prominently in every student uprising of the late 1960s. In their own way, American radicals also used the war in Vietnam to justify repudiation of their own society. The pacifist David McReynolds wrote, "The New Left is profoundly alienated from this country. It is anti-American with a bitterness that is new."[33] This was the context for all the provocative demonstration tactics—the Vietcong flags, the chant "Ho, Ho, Ho Chi Minh"—and the conviction that the war was "the American war against the Vietnamese peasants"—a David-and-Goliath encounter between the technological might of the West and the virtuous villagers of the East.

Against the background of the student movement, which was relatively innocuous up to that time apart from its rhetoric, the sit-in at Columbia University during April and May of 1968 stands out as an abrupt turning point toward confrontational violence. The local SDS chapter at Columbia was already moving to the Left, drawn in that direction by the increasingly radical mood of the national leadership. Originally, direction of the organization at Columbia had been in the hands of the self-styled "praxis axis" of campus intellectuals, wedded (as student journalists described them) to "a relatively sedate tactical approach" of political persuasion.[34] By the time of the uprising, the "praxis-axis" had been upstaged by the newcomers of the "action faction," though they remained a restraining element whenever there was time for deliberation in the Columbia SDS leadership. Rudd's group was more in tune with the national SDS, which had taken to agitating against universities in general as a hopeless component of the old society. Less than a week before the Columbia trouble broke out, one SDS publicist wrote in the organization's publication, *New Left Notes*, "The university itself is the enemy."[35] In December 1967, the SDS national leadership had called for a "spring offensive," though in practical terms they could only suggest "educational programs, joint actions and demonstrations" aimed at getting the anticorporate and anti-imperialist message to nonstudents.[36]

SDS started up comparatively late at Columbia University—in 1966 —and only as a product of the antiwar movement. Still, there were a number of obvious reasons why Columbia should become a critical focus of student protest in 1968. First, it was large, diffuse, and impersonal, but had quite a small undergraduate body (less than 3,000) among whom discontent could be mobilized quickly. Also, the Columbia tradition was particularly autocratic, where not even the faculty, much less the students, had much voice vis-à-vis the administration and the trustees (who were easy to identify with the corporate Establishment). Finally, Columbia existed in a congested urban environment exposing it both to new currents of radicalism and to the social problems of its black neighbors in Harlem.

First and foremost, the student movement became radicalized where it intersected with the black civil rights movement. Black students, organized on many campuses as the Black Students Union and at Columbia as the Student Afro-American Society, proved highly sensitive to the freshening currents of black nationalism. By 1968, they were expressing the new mood in demands for separate facilities, admissions quotas, and autonomous black studies programs. An early link between the radical wing of the black movement and the incipient student upsurge of 1968 was the May 1967 student riot at Jackson State College in Mississippi (in which one student was killed by police gunfire), followed by the killings at Orangeburg State College in South Carolina. This clash triggered a brief takeover of the administration building at all-black Howard University in March 1968 by protesters demanding student control over curricular and student life matters. Although the

Howard University incident was compromised without resort to the police, white radicals at Columbia and elsewhere had come to feel deferential to the blacks as revolutionary role models.

Rudd and the action faction in the Columbia SDS drew up a position paper in December 1967 outlining the use of the war issue to provoke a student strike and thereby revolutionize the whole student body. Additionally, Rudd was able to cast the university administration in the role of racists by using the growing controversy over the institution's relations with the Harlem ghetto—or lack thereof—and the specific issue of the gymnasium in Morningside Park. Students demonstrating against the gym and trying to block the ground-clearing operations had already clashed with police in February, with a number of arrests resulting; the demonstrators were backed up by resolutions of the faculty in several divisions of the university.

The pot was brought near the boiling point at Columbia in March, when the action faction took over the leadership of the SDS chapter. It was this event that put Mark Rudd in the presidency of the organization. (Shortly before, Rudd had made himself a hero to the student body by shoving a lemon meringue pie in the face of a visiting colonel from Selective Service.) According to Tom Hayden, the Rudd group "sought the impossible: the university's surrender," by calling for "a provisional government of the university run by students, employees, and Harlem citizens."[37]

Rudd capitalized on three primary issues to set up his confrontation with the university. One was Harlem and the gym. Another was a derivative of the antiwar movement—the campaign against Columbia's participation in the Institute of Defense Analysis. A third, relating to Columbia's structural sclerosis, was the question of student discipline and student participation in this sensitive area of university governance. The university administration had made the latter issue particularly acute by decreeing probation for the leaders of an SDS demonstration against IDA in the Low library on March 27 that violated the rule against such activities inside university buildings. To President Kirk, the signs of student radicalism indicated only "a turbulent and inchoate nihilism whose sole objectives are destruction."[38] Rudd replied by circulating an open letter on April 22, the day before the uprising started, accusing Kirk of running a racist and imperialist institution of corporate manipulation. The generation gap lamented by Kirk was "a real conflict between those who run things now—you, Grayson Kirk—and those who feel oppressed by, and disgusted with, the society you rule—we, the young people." Therefore, "Up against the wall, motherfucker, this is a stick-up."[39]

Predictably, the police action at Columbia in the early hours of April 30 radicalized hundreds more students and many of the faculty. The protesters then invoked their last weapon, a student strike, demanding now the resignations of Kirk and Truman as well as protesting the police action. They announced a boycott of classes to begin the following week when the university was supposed to reopen. Rudd was determined to sustain the radicalism of his movement, and led a protest on May 1 against the continuing police presence on campus. This ended in some nasty fighting (even though the police this time were not authorized to take such action).

To assure the success of the strike, Rudd compromised with the more moderate elements of the student body and threw the membership of the Strike Coordinating Committee wide open. More than 4,000 students took part in choosing delegates, but the core element of the Committee came from the "communes," the students who had achieved a special solidarity, building by building, by participating in the sit-in. They added to their previous demands a new one—"that the administration recognize our right to participate in the restructuring of the University" and particularly "to break the confines of the traditional 'lecturer and passive audience' mold."[40] A "liberation school" of impromptu courses appropriate to the revolutionary mood was proposed. Increasingly wider circles of the faculty endorsed restructuring and democratization of the university, and a new Executive Committee of the faculty was formed to carry their case to the administration and trustees. In turn, the Executive Committee initiated a study of the violence, chaired by Archibald Cox of the Harvard Law School (former U.S. solicitor general, subsequently made more famous as a victim of the "Saturday Night Massacre" in 1973 when he was fired as the Watergate special prosecutor).[41] The Grateful Dead arrived to put on a free rock concert for the rebels.

On May 6, the Columbia student strike became a more serious matter as the university endeavored to reopen classes. Pickets deterred most students who tried from entering classroom buildings, but the point of the strike was blunted when the undergraduate faculty voted to cancel classes for the rest of the semester and rely on individual study to complete courses. Moderates on the Strike Committee became increasingly impatient with the radicals' insistence on using the campus confrontation to revolutionize students' attitudes toward society at large. On May 15, the moderates walked out and formed their own group, "Students for a Restructured University," to focus on campus issues. Two days later, Rudd led another confrontational action, to occupy a university-owned tenement near the campus. Police action quickly ensued and over a hundred people were arrested, about half of them students, this time including Rudd himself, for once.

Meanwhile, the Columbia administration persisted in its efforts to discipline the leaders of the uprising, going back to the IDA affair in March. The accused, including Rudd, called a new protest demonstration for Tuesday afternoon, May 21, and once again the militants occupied Hamilton Hall where the undergraduate dean's office was located, this time with network television on the scene. An ultimatum issued by the administration only attracted more demonstrators. But in this instance Columbia officials were more resolute; the police Tactical Patrol Force moved into Hamilton Hall at 2:30 A.M. and arrested the occupiers, again including Rudd. Minor clashes and fires around the university did not change the outcome, but President Kirk overreacted and again called on the police to clear the entire campus, with the now-familiar pattern of indiscriminate police violence resulting. Although the behavior of some students was provocative and repellent, according to the Cox report, "The police engaged in acts of individual and group brutality for which a layman can see no justification unless it be that the way to restore order in a riot is to terrorize civilians." The basic trouble was "the mutual desire of the Administration and SDS for a further confrontation."[42] Kirk remained unrepentant, and summarily suspended nearly seventy-five students, with notification to the draft boards of the leaders that this action made them eligible for military service.

The Columbia radicals had one more shot when Kirk tried to hold commencement-as-usual in June. Nearly three hundred students staged a walkout from the exercises in St. John's Cathedral and held their own countercommencement on the steps of Low Library. Everyone expected more trouble in the fall, only to be surprised by an unexpected student victory: on August 23, the unyielding but exhausted Grayson Kirk resigned as president of the University, and his successor, acting president Andrew Cordier, immediately requested the city to drop trespass charges pending against students arrested in the sit-ins. There were still some minor attempts at campus disruptions by the radicals, but the response in the student body was meager. The revolution had spent its force. Columbia, at least, was on its way back to normal.

Columbia commanded national attention on student unrest as the summer riots of 1967 and the King riots of 1968 had done for the blacks. The Establishment was thrown into a state of panic. Presidential candidate Nixon, campaigning in Oregon on May 15, called the Columbia uprising "the first major skirmish in a revolutionary struggle to seize the universities of this country and transform them into sanctuaries for radicals and vehicles for revolutionary politics and social goals." He perhaps reflected SDS hopes more than the reality. J. Edgar Hoover inevitably appeared before a congressional committee to call SDS a security threat, infiltrated by the Communist Party. Academics everywhere bemoaned student anti-intellectualism and the danger to academic freedom. Congress voted to cut off federal grants and loans to students guilty of illegal disruptions.

None of these threats and warnings deterred the spread of the Columbia example to other campuses, even when Columbia itself was quieting down in a state of postrevolutionary fatigue. Paraphrasing Che Guevara, Tom Hayden urged "two, three, many Columbias."[43] Some two hundred student demonstrations occurred around the country before the end of the spring semester of 1968.[44] The big event of the fall was the student strike at San Francisco State College, started early in November by black militants protesting the firing of a Black Panther instructor. Acting President S. I. Hayakawa, a noted linguist and future senator from California, achieved national note when he faced down demonstrators and brought in the police to reopen the campus. It was Columbia all over again. But the worst was yet to come—the following year violent SDS and black radical sit-ins struck such stalwart Ivy-League institutions as Harvard and Cornell as well as Berkeley again. Nationally, however, the wave of radical sentiment had passed, leaving a growing gap between the moderate majority of students and a dwindling but ever more extreme movement of uncompromising revolutionaries.

This trend was reflected in the fate of SDS. From its beginnings, SDS prided itself on its organizational openness and ideological fluidity. It sought to avoid the classic fate of protest movements predicted long ago by Roberto Michels in *Political Parties,* to become bureaucratic and conservative with success. But because SDS resisted developing the bureaucracy, it could not handle its own surge into a mass movement, stimulated among other things by the Columbia battles. Overwhelmed by numbers, the national leadership of SDS lost touch with its chapters, and vice versa. It could not address the growing turnover in the membership or check the organization's rapid decline in total numbers from 1969 on.

At the same time, what there was of a national organization to SDS could not stave off infiltration and takeover by more disciplined and more ideological groupings. SDS had already opened the door to this trouble at its national convention in 1965 when, in its anti–Cold War

145

spirit, it dropped the explicit exclusion of Communists and other totalitarians from its membership. The very next year, the disciplinarian and pro-Chinese Progressive Labor party (PLP), which formed in 1962 as a split-off from the CP-USA, joined SDS en masse, all one thousand of them. They proved to be a highly indigestable accretion, quickly asserting their new presence and threatening by the time of the June 1968 SDS convention in East Lansing, Michigan, to take over the whole organization. It was all as if to validate J. Edgar Hoover's worst fears.

The national leadership of SDS stood off the PLP for a time by taking a position scarcely less radical and enlisting such figures as Rudd and the future terrorist Bernadine Dohrn, who declared, "I consider myself a revolutionary communist."[45] They idealized Vietnam rather than China and came to the view that the future would be determined by the revolutionary struggle of the Third World and American blacks against U.S. imperialism, in which white students would only be an auxiliary force. Most of the early national leaders of SDS, including Hayden, felt repudiated by the new trend in the organization and gave up on it altogether. At the same time, the centrifugal force of radical sectarianism could not be contained. The Motherfuckers distinguished themselves by aimless campaigns of vandalism in the academic ghettos of Cambridge, Massachusetts, and Berkeley. In December, National Secretary Michael Klonsky called on SDS to convert itself into a Revolutionary Youth Movement (RYM), to combat the PLP and extol students as the leading revolutionary class.

In June 1969 in Chicago, SDS held what proved to be its last convention. Bernadine Dohrn led a walkout of the enemies of the PLP to organize the separate RYM. But within months, this fragment split as well. One branch, "RYM I" led by Rudd and Dohrn, begot the terrorist Weathermen, who took their name (a bit illogically) from a line by Bob Dylan: "You don't need a weatherman to know which way the wind blows."[46] "Revolutionary violence is the only way," said Bernadine Dohrn, citing as her ideal the new urban guerrillas of Uruguay: "Now we are adopting the guerrilla strategy of the Tupamaros."[47] Klonsky's faction, "RYM II," held to more conventional radicalism. But none of these groups had any future. The RYM, like the rump of SDS under PLP aegis, had become a hollow shell by the end of 1969. Only the Weathermen held together as a small, communal, bomb-planting organization until the early 1970s, when arrests or the need to go underground rendered them futile.

Mark Rudd finally surfaced and surrendered in 1977, only to be put on probation, and went into teaching and writing. Bernadine Dohrn

146

followed suit three years later, and received the same lenient treatment; other Weather Undergrounders got jail sentences for their terroristic exploits. Tom Hayden, for his part, moved back into mainstream politics, married the actress Jane Fonda (who had achieved note herself for supporting North Vietnam), ran unsuccessfully for the U.S. Senate, and then won a seat in the California State legislature.

Within two years of its peak in membership and national influence, SDS was dead. Its failure, writes Nigel Young, was the consequence of "its inability to relate to the hundreds of thousands of young people who, aware of the organization's name and tradition, were searching for a humane and libertarian radicalism."[48] When the occasion for the largest and most spontaneous wave of student protests came in May 1970 over the shooting of four students by National Guardsmen at Kent State University, there was no national student political organization left to sustain the momentum. Stanley Rothman and Robert Lichter call Kent State, appropriately, "a coda of the 1960s."[49]

In part, the collapse of American student radicalism was a product of its success, to the extent that it helped win concessions at the federal level—"Vietnamization" of the war, curtailment of the draft, and the 18-year-old vote—and stimulated broader student concern and dissent. Universities everywhere hastened to reform their rules and curricula lest violence resume or spread to them. David Westby refers to "ideological diffusion accompanied by organizational demise," and cites the rule, "as the constituency grows, militancy of tactics subsides."[50] Many writers concur that student radicalism never developed a coherent ideology that made sense in the American context. Physical repression or the threat of it kept large numbers of students away from overtly violent forms of defiance. Many gave up on political radicalism and turned to more concrete endeavors such as the environmental movement and consumer protection. Others, in considerable numbers, withdrew into the counterculture and the drug scene. For all these reasons and perhaps out of sheer fatigue as well, the rule seems to be affirmed that radical protest movements cannot sustain themselves for more than a few years, especially if they do not solidify themselves with governmental power.

7

Paris

EARLY AFTERNOON, Friday, May 3, a nice, sunny day for demonstrations. Today American and North Vietnamese representatives in Laos agree on Paris as the site of their future peace talks. A crowd of several hundred students gathers in the central courtyard of the vast neobaroque building of the Sorbonne, housing the Faculty of Arts of the University of Paris in the Latin Quarter on Paris's Left Bank. The Latin Quarter—so named in the Middle Ages because its academic residents spoke Latin—is an area defined only by tradition. It encompasses university faculties and student rooming houses in an area of ancient, narrow streets roughly six or eight blocks to a side in the Fifth Arrondissement of Paris east of the Boulevard St-Michel and south of the Boulevard St-Germain. With the Sorbonne at its heart, the Latin Quarter accounts for about the same area and population as Haight-Ashbury.

The occasion of this particular student meeting is to protest the closing of the satellite campus in the western industrial suburb of Nanterre as well as the disciplinary proceedings initiated against six leaders of a rebellion at Nanterre over the ban by the Ministry of Education on heterosexual visits in dormitory rooms. One of the accused *enragés* is Daniel Cohn-Bendit, "Danny the Red," son of German-Jewish refugees, soon to win international fame as the leader of the French student revolution.

The courtyard gathering turns tense with rumors that it may be attacked by the neo-fascist force of right-wing students and ex-paratroopers called Occident. Meanwhile, more students cluster in the streets and squares around the Sorbonne to see what is going to happen. At this juncture, University rector Jean Roche, a biochemist, not a politician, appears to panic; this gives President de Gaulle's education minister, Alain Peyrefitte, the chance to take direct action, while Premier Georges Pompidou, who might have taken a more adroit course, is away on a diplomatic visit to Iran. Peyrefitte, a slick young bureaucrat, is convinced that the protest is the work of "a handful of trouble-makers."[1] He directs the rector to take the extraordinary step of calling the police into the traditionally privileged academic sanctuary.

Near 5 P.M., the police move in. These forces and those employed throughout the May troubles are for the most part not ordinary city officers but the Compagnies Republicaines de Securité (CRS), paramilitary riot police under the control of the Ministry of the Interior. They are already hated by students and workers alike. Pouring into the courtyard of the Sorbonne, the CRS hustle the retreating students out through the archways into those distinctive black police vans. Then, spontaneously, with cries of "Down with repression!" "Free our comrades!" and "CRS equals SS!" the crowd in the streets outside the Sorbonne attacks the police vans with fists, rocks, and here and there barricades of over-turned cars. The police respond with truncheons and tear gas, which only magnifies the protest. As described by British journalists Patrick Seale and Maureen McConville, "The immediate effect of the authorities' crude display of strength was to unite the mass of uncommitted students—and their teachers—behind the *enragés*. In a few minutes a mass movement was created."[2]

Organized reaction comes even before the police, clubbing students and bystanders alike, finish clearing the last knots of outraged protesters out of the narrow streets of the Latin Quarter. The leaders of the students' and lecturers' unions proclaim nationwide strikes for Monday. (This is a revolution that usually takes weekends off.) Rector Roche, urged on by the ministry, takes the unprecedented step of ordering the Sorbonne closed, and the police seal it off. This event, writes *New York Times* correspondent Lloyd Garrison, is "a major tactical victory for the New Left student-power movement."[3] Five hundred demonstrators are given suspended sentences and released the next day, while four of them are sentenced to two months in jail, giving the student multitude a new ongoing grievance.

"Bloody Monday," May 6, begins with a gathering of five thousand students marching along the boulevards and quais around the Latin

Quarter. Leadership of the movement has been assumed by a medley of ultrarevolutionaries who run the ideological gamut from Trotskyist to Maoist to Anarchist. They are backed up by the national leadership of the students' union and the instructors' union. But the orthodox Communists are conspicuous in their distaste for the student agitation. They call these radical scions of the bourgeoisie "fils de papa" ("daddy's boys").[4]

When the growing crowd approaches the Sorbonne in midafternoon, the police suddenly charge—after someone throws a stone, according to one report. Again, it is a scene of truncheons and grenades against paving stones and makeshift barricades all over the Latin Quarter. Fighting goes on through the afternoon and evening, as the demonstrators yield to police charges, regroup on unguarded streets, and throw up new barricades. Student hatred for the police is matched by the fury of the forces of law and order, but the police are meeting an intensity of resistance—even counterattacks—for which they are tactically and psychologically unprepared. There is a certain inhibition among the authorities in France in using physical repression against the rebellious children of the ruling class, but the police are contemptuous of these softies until they prove their mettle behind the barricades. "I have rarely seen demonstrations so brutal and violent," says the Paris chief of police.[5] It is the worst street fighting in Paris since its liberation from the Germans in 1944, but looting and ordinary crime are totally absent despite shattered shop windows.

The fighting quiets down over the next three days, and student demonstrations remain peaceful though growing steadily larger. The more mainstream National Union of French Students (UNEF) temporarily takes charge in Paris, while sympathy demonstrations spread around the country and among Parisian high-school students. As President Charles de Gaulle speaks out to warn against further violence, some twenty thousand students march without major incident to the Arc de Triomphe at the head of the Champs-Elysées, the heart of Right-Bank, right-wing Paris, to show their determination. By Thursday, May 9, the rector is ready to reopen the Sorbonne, but the minister, with ultimate authority over the universities, overrules him. On Thursday evening, the Trotskyists of the Revolutionary Communist Youth hold a mass meeting featuring Cohn-Bendit, who proposes the grandiose idea of turning student defiance into a socialist revolution. A giant demonstration of all factions is scheduled for Friday evening starting at the Place Denfert-Rochereau, uphill from the Latin Quarter.

Friday evening the student throng assembles, fifteen thousand strong, and hears various factional leaders who climb up on the Lion of Belfort monument to debate where to march. The students are informed that acting premier Louis Joxe is willing to withdraw the police and reopen the Sorbonne, but they shout for their third demand—"Libérez nos camarades." Since the Latin Quarter is still sealed off, they march toward the Sainte Prison to the east to protest the arrests, and then move north toward the Seine through a working-class district hoping to rouse popular support. They turn west on the Boulevard St-Germain, past the Sorbonne, but are blocked at the Boulevard St-Michel and must turn south again, this time into the heart of the Latin Quarter. It appears that the police strategy is to draw them into a pocket where they can be contained until they get tired and cold and decide to go home. The demonstration swells to perhaps fifty thousand.

Late in the evening, as new negotiations with Rector Roche about reopening the Sorbonne reach an impasse, word spreads through the milling crowd that they should take over the area. Spontaneously, by most accounts, or on the initiative of small groups, the students start building a new set of barricades throughout the district east of St-Michel and opposite the Luxembourg Gardens. In all, over fifty barricades go up. The most imposing are constructed on the Rue Gay-Lussac that angles uphill off of St-Michel. Gisela Mandel, a Trotskyist, describes the process:

> With the help of a megaphone and a city map, the students divided up the mass of demonstrators into companies of a few thousand each. The cobble-stones were loosened in professional style with picks, grubbing hoes, and shovels provided by people living in the area. At every barricade four to six lines, each including about fifty people, passed cobblestones from the work sites and up onto the barricades.
>
> This work was carried on to the singing of the "Internationale." Street signs were used to reinforce the barricades and as guideposts. Eight-foot paving stones formed the foundation of every barricade. On top of these were piled cars, gasoline-soaked wood, branches of trees to block the CRS view into the street, and as much wire as could be found.[6]

Around midnight, Cohn-Bendit and the leaders of the students' union parlay again with the rector and his aides at the Sorbonne, but to no avail—the university authorities are willing to withdraw the police and reopen the Sorbonne but have no power to release the four jailed student leaders. Cohn-Bendit tells the crowd, "We told the rector that what is happening in the street tonight is a whole generation rising against a certain sort of society. We told him blood would flow if the police did not leave the Latin Quarter. We know the demonstrators will stay behind the barricades until our three demands have been met."[7] The vice-rector tells the media, "We have tried to negotiate. We have tried by all possible means to avoid the use of force, but the situation is now out of our control. We have failed."[8]

Shortly after 2 A.M. on Saturday, May 11, anxious to do President de Gaulle's will and clear the streets in time for the morning traffic, the Cabinet overrides the rector's advice and orders the police to storm the barricades.

Thus begins the unforgettable "Night of the Barricades." The CRS forces hope to drive the students off with tear gas and smoke bombs, but the rebels hold their own tenaciously, aided by residents of the streets who pour water from upper-story windows to put the gas down. Police respond by firing gas grenades into the open windows. The epicenter of the fighting is the Rue Gay-Lussac, where two huge barricades are manned by as many as two hundred defenders. Balked in their first assault along Gay-Lussac, the CRS resort to stronger gas, by some accounts chlorine—the first poison gas used in the trenches in World War I.[9] The students set fire to their first barricade and retreat to the second, overturning parked cars along the way as supplementary obstacles. They hold out on their second line of defense until daybreak, when they are overcome by police firing gas grenades from adjacent rooftops.

The same story is told on dozens of other side streets in the Latin Quarter. Police brutality, particularly in searching out students who have taken refuge in houses along the path of attack, scarcely knows any bounds. Red Cross workers try to reach wounded students and get them to ambulances but are beaten off by police. By 5:30 A.M., when Cohn-Bendit directs the students to cease resistance and disperse, nearly 500 of them have been arrested. The police claim 367 of their men wounded, without tallying the many times greater number of injured on the student side. Despite the carnage, write Patrick Seale and Maureen McConville, "In that first unforgetable week the most striking quality of the student explosion was joy. Later the revolt was to degenerate into pathos and squalor."[10]

Unlike Americans' constant exposure, month after month, to nightly violence on the TV news, the state-controlled radio and television in France virtually black out news of the disorders in Paris. Only two commercial radio stations, Europe I and Radio Luxembourg, carry live reports of the riots, but the public hears enough to be shocked by the conduct of the police. With opinion on the Left half of the spectrum swinging heavily to the side of the student rebels, the nation goes into a state of crisis and its government stands on the brink of disgrace.

During the weekend respite, the political situation changes abruptly. Premier Pompidou finally returns from his trip to the Middle East and sets in motion a shift in the government's strategy to conciliate the rebels and the nation. He announces that the Sorbonne will be re-opened the following Monday and that the courts will consider leniency for the students who have been jailed. At the same time, Pompidou is confronted with a call for a general strike issued by the country's main labor organizations—the Communist-run CGT, the Catholic-Socialist CFDT, and the independent teachers' organization FEN. The Communists have decided that the student revolt is too serious to go on without their pro forma support. On Sunday the 12th, the two big labor organizations sit down to plan the Monday affair with the student leaders, whom they feel they have to include on their own terms. This means that Cohn-Bendit and the UNEF leader, Jacques Sauvageot, will be at the head of the march, with the Communist and Socialist party leaders behind.

On Monday the 13th—the same day that Averell Harriman and Xuan Thuy finally begin their truce talks—nearly a million unionists throng the boulevards of Paris to demonstrate their support for the student rebels. It is the biggest demonstration France has seen since the Liberation. Nevertheless, Pompidou follows through with his resolve and grants the students all their demands—release of their jailed comrades, withdrawal of the police from the Latin Quarter, and reopening of the Sorbonne.

Revolutions, however, are not so easily ended by redress of the originally articulated grievances that started the process rolling. The students answer the opening of the Sorbonne by occupying the building themselves, hoisting the red flag of revolution, and making the university center their insurrectionary headquarters and debating forum, day and night, for the next month. The government abandons the Latin Quarter to the student rebels so totally that they even take on responsibility for directing traffic. At the same time the workers, dragging their reluctant Communist leaders along, jump at the chance to express class defiance of the Gaullist government, and by Tuesday France is in the grip of a spontaneous general strike. President de Gaulle takes it upon himself now, of all times, to leave on a four-day diplomatic trip to Romania. His desperate premier is left to face the National Assembly and defend the government's bankrupt policies, first too strong and then too weak. It appears that the country is on the verge of the revolution that the student radicals have been talking about for months.

Paris

The troubles of 1968 in France began at one of the newest, freest, and most "American" of French institutions of higher education. This was the branch of the University of Paris recently established in the suburb of Nanterre as a gesture of decentralization and democratization, complete with campus and dormitories (albeit depressingly designed). Nanterre had become a hot bed of ultra-Left ideologies and agitation for total university democratization and "student power," concentrated particularly in its Department of Sociology. The irony of the locale bears out again de Tocqueville's thesis that it is attempted reform, rather than unyielding repression, that most directly begets revolution.

The issue that sparked defiance at Nanterre had a comic-opera quality to it. Coming on top of more general grievances about university bureaucracy and the Vietnam War, this was the so-called "bedroom revolt" against the university rule barring male and female students from visiting each others' rooms. The issue gave the opportunity for leadership to the most radical students, the *enragés*, who took their name from the farthest Left faction in the French Revolution. A confrontation over the matter occurred in January 1968, when the minister of youth and sport came to Nanterre to open a fancy new swimming pool and gave the opening for national fame to the man destined to lead the May uprising, Daniel Cohn-Bendit. "Mr. Minister," said Cohn-Bendit, "you've drawn up a report on French youth six hundred pages long. But there isn't a word in it about our sexual problems. Why not?" "If you have sexual problems, I suggest you jump in the pool." To which Cohn-Bendit retorted, "That's what the Hitler youth used to say."[11]

Two weeks later, rumors of disciplinary action against Cohn-Bendit (in fact wrong) gave the Nanterre *enragés* the excuse to demonstrate and provoke the dean to call the police. This immediately radicalized the mass of Nanterre students. Unrest broke out again in February, when the National Vietnam Committee (CVN) organized protest demonstrations following the German example. When half a dozen student members of the CVN were arrested, the *enragés* led by Cohn-Bendit occupied the administration building at Nanterre and proclaimed the "March 22 Movement" to commemorate this date. Cohn-Bendit's movement quickly drew in Trotskyists, Maoists, and independent Marxists, all seeking an opportunity for revolutionary leadership. Their base was significantly broadened when UNEF, the National Student Union, moving to the Left under its militant acting president Jacques Sauvageot, joined the protest and declared a national anti-Vietnam campaign for late March. Signally missing from the revolutionary lineup were the orthodox Communists, regarded by all the radical youth (including the party's own student organizations) as a stuffy part of the bourgeois Establishment.

By late April, the radical leaders of the various factions were conferring regularly on advancing the revolutionary cause. According to Seale and McConville:

> Student extremists detonated the May Revolution. . . . [However] it would be a mistake to consider this command a tightly knit revolutionary apparatus. It was not. These men were agreed on long-term political objectives, rather than on immediate tactics. They were held together by ideology, not by organization or planning. This gave them the guerrilla-like flexibility to hold their own against the state in the insurrection which was about to burst upon them and unfold with breakneck speed.[12]

Nanterre had to be closed again on May 2, when students violently protested faculty efforts to restore security and pursue disciplinary measures against the six student leaders arrested in March. The fuse was lit for the explosion in Paris.

Premier Pompidou's policy of conciliating the students after eight days of ferocious rioting proved again the Tocqueville effect of revolutionary response to gestures of reform. The radicals' answer was to move back into the Sorbonne and organize a revolutionary commune. Upwards of twenty thousand students packed into the building and camped in its classrooms and offices. The occupiers threw the Sorbonne open to anyone, and drew a broad cross-section of the curious and the committed, as well as plainclothes police and an aggressive group of veterans and drop-outs called the Katangais (playing an ambiguous role like the Hell's Angels in Haight-Ashbury). Committees drafted vast plans of reform while revolutionary portraits and posters, turned out by the students occupying the School of Fine Arts, went up everywhere. Such eminent writers as Jean-Paul Sartre came in to lecture on revolution. Che Guevara was the rebels' special hero, and a statue to him was erected in the Sorbonne courtyard.

Practicing the purest form of direct democracy, the students held a general assembly every evening in the courtyard, and doing the Athenians one better, elected an executive committee for exactly one day at a time. Inevitably the general assembly broke down in endless debating. Moderates were mainly interested in reforming the university, while the true revolutionaries thought they were going to overturn the entire social order, and seized every opportunity to bring on confrontations with the police outside the Sorbonne building. In the end, the story was the familiar one of revolutionary disintegration—the radical leaders moved out and the hippies and crazies moved in. When the police finally got orders to clear the Sorbonne in mid-June—on a weekend—there were only a few hundred occupiers left and they offered hardly any resistance.

Meanwhile, the more serious response to the government's gestures of conciliation surged up among the French workers. The containment plan of the trade union leadership misfired. Far from satisfying the rank and file of labor, the demonstration of May 13 only proved to be the transition to spontaneous actions. The next day, a wave of wildcat sit-down strikes broke out all over the country. This was the most amazing and unique side of the French revolt. Everywhere else the New Left pumped up its pipe dreams of leading the working class to revolution. Only in France did the workers actually respond positively to the students' challenge, in contrast to the United States and China where workers were often a force at the disposal of countermovements. "What distinguished the French situation from that of other countries," write Seale and McConnelle, "is that here the students' example was immediately and massively copied, carrying the crisis to a new level of gravity. . . . For the first time in recent history intellectuals and manual workers seemed to be marching side by side to revolution."[13] The worker response in France was all the more surprising because it largely took place against the will of the workers' own paramount leadership institutionalized in the trade unions and the Communist party. Throughout the crisis the Communists saw the ultra-leftist challenge as the main danger for their own bureaucratic structure and cautious strategy. Moscow inveighed against the New Left rebels for trying to "confuse and divide" the working class.[14] Peking offset this cold shoulder by organizing great demonstrations in sympathy with the French students and by denouncing the vacillating role of the Moscow-oriented French Communists.

The truth is that many rank-and-file workers had been aroused as they had not been for years by the defiant example of the students of the Latin Quarter during the Night of the Barricades. They had deep-seated grievances in this most bureaucratized and hierarchical society in the West. French workers had old anarchist and syndicalist traditions, and the revolutionary situation stirred up talk of "worker power."[15] The CFDT, more openly sympathetic to the students than the Communist leadership, found that the youthful rebels "pose a fundamental challenge to the rigid and stifling class structure of a society in which they can assume no responsibility."[16] The workers' revolt in France thus shared with all the other movements of the 1960s the basic drive to achieve equality and humanity in face-to-face social relationships.

During the week of May 13, the strike wave spread and intensified. Teams of young workers drove from one plant to the next, all over the country, to spread the revolutionary gospel. "The aim is now the overthrow of the regime," Cohn-Bendit told Sartre in an interview, leaving the decision up to the unions.[17] "Action Committees," reminiscent of the Jacobin "Sections" of 1792, were formed all over Paris to handle strike logistics and bring the revolutionary message to their neighborhoods. By Saturday the 18th, when de Gaulle finally returned from his trip to Romania, the country was virtually in the grip of a general strike throughout the manufacturing, mining, and transport sectors. Utilities were seized as well, though service was allowed to continue. There were runs on banks and gas stations. The movement peaked the following week as it spread to textiles, department stores, and the teachers. Artists, actors, architects, civil servants, atomic energy workers, and even some physicians joined in or expressed sympathy. By May 22, nine million workers were counted on strike.[18] The government of President de Gaulle and Premier Pompidou appeared to be on the verge of collapse, and the parties of the Left, spearheaded by the Socialists with the Communists uneasily in tow, tried to push it over the brink by introducing a no-confidence motion in the National Assembly. The move was beaten back by a party-line vote of the Gaullists and their conservative allies. The government tried (unsuccessfully) to bar Cohn-Bendit from the country as an "undesirable," and demonstrators and strikers chanted, "We are all undesirables, we are all German Jews."[19]

At this point de Gaulle finally realized that he could not bide his time any longer. Friday evening the 24th he went on television to demand order, to promise reform, and, gambling on a conservative majority's revulsion against the turmoil, to propose a nationwide referendum on his leadership. For once, de Gaulle had lost his charm as France's great communicator, and the Council of State, guardian of constitutionality, ruled his referendum out of bounds. The speech did nothing to stop the re-escalating tension between students and police in the Latin Quarter from erupting into another violent riot, the "Second Night of the Barricades." This time the trouble spread to the Right Bank, with many young workers joining the students. The fighting was as bad as earlier in the month: an estimated 1,500 demonstrators were wounded, one was killed, and 800 were arrested.[20] Cohn-Bendit thought in retrospect that this would have been the time to occupy the ministries and the radio stations and to turn the revolt into a real revolution; he blamed all the established parties of the Left for not following through.[21] Evidently nobody really had the revolutionary will. Nevertheless, faced with unending turmoil, the government entered into nationwide negotiations with the employers' associations and the trade-union leadership. On Monday the 27th, they achieved an accord, the "Grenelle Agreements," so called from the Rue de Grenelle, near the Eiffel Tower, where the Ministry of Social Affairs, site of the talks, is located. Whopping increases in wage scales and fringe benefits were to be granted the workers, along with half pay for strike time. The union leadership was delighted with the deal, which seemed to undercut the ultra-Left.

Then, to everyone's surprise, rank-and-file workers all over the country, led by the huge Renault auto plant at Boulogne-Billancourt just outside Paris, rejected the agreement. The government seemed totally discredited, as the general strike continued. The city of Nantes on the Atlantic coast, pointing the way, was run for a week by a revolutionary soviet. Every politician of the Left spoke out to demand a change of leadership. François Mitterand, de Gaulle's defeated opponent of 1965, even called for a "provisional government" under a popular figure like Pierre Mendès-France after the anticipated defeat of "Le Grand Charles" in the promised referendum. Amid the general crisis, de Gaulle turned on Premier Pompidou to blame him for the mess, and made up his mind to handle matters his own way.

On Wednesday morning the 29th, de Gaulle disappeared. Officially, he had departed for his country retreat at Colombey-lès-deux-Églises in eastern France, but he did not directly arrive there. Actually, he flew on to the army headquarters for eastern France and then to the headquarters of the French forces in West Germany, commanded by General Jacques Massu, a key figure in de Gaulle's 1958 takeover of the government. Only after conferring with military chiefs at both locations did he return to Colombey. In the face of the near-revolutionary situation in the streets and the prospect of a Mendès-France government uniting all the disparate elements of the Left, de Gaulle was preparing a new military coup—the method by which he had come to power ten years before.

His first step on returning to Paris the following day was to address the nation briefly and bluntly on radio. This time he was firmly in charge; he assured his listeners that he had no intention of giving up the presidency, and announced the dissolution of the National Assembly and new parliamentary elections in lieu of the referendum idea. He then went on, inappropriately but effectively, to blame the Communists for the crisis and to accuse them of planning a totalitarian dictatorship. In the face of this alleged threat, de Gaulle concluded, "The Republic will not abdicate."[22] This assurance was immediately backed up by massive conservative demonstrations organized by de Gaulle's party, and by ostentatious troop movements. In the face of this firmness, the incipient revolution collapsed.

Following de Gaulle's national address, the revolutionary mood in France dissipated steadily. The strike wave subsided and the students grew discouraged, while the Right was emboldened to assert itself, often in armed attacks on Leftists. The Communist union leaders pushed the back-to-work movement and the government nibbled away with further economic concessions to certain workers on top of the Grenelle Agreements. Direct action proved premature, however, when police tried to break the strike at the Renault plant at Flins west of Paris during the second week in June; with the aid of eager students, the workers succeeded in frustrating the operation. In a similar effort at the Peugeot plant at Sochaux near the Swiss border, two workers were killed, and the government backed off. Still, de Gaulle felt confident enough to issue an order on June 12 to ban further demonstrations for the duration of the election campaign and to outlaw the organizations of the ultra-Left. That night the story of fighting between police and protesters was reenacted one last time, with futile results for the Left. Four days later, on June 16, the central symbol of the students' new society—the occupied Sorbonne—fell with hardly a whimper. Two days after this, the citadel of the general strike, the Renault plant at Boulogne-Billancourt, finally ran up the white flag.

On Sunday the 23rd came the first of the two rounds of parliamentary voting. It was a referendum of fear. President de Gaulle scored a smashing triumph over an opposition coalition suffering from association with violence and disruption. By the time the distribution of National Assembly seats was settled in the runoff a week later, the Gaullist party—the Union for the Defense of the Republic—registered its greatest triumph ever, winning an absolute majority even without counting its conservative allies. Ten days afterward, the General settled his last score: he fired the valiant Pompidou. The counterrevolution was in full swing.

A year later, de Gaulle overreached, threatening to resign if his constitutional proposals were rejected by the voters. They were, and he did. Pompidou scored a triumphant comeback, winning the presidency himself as the Gaullist candidate and ushering in the long period of France's consolidation under Gaullism without de Gaulle. Danny the Red was finally shipped back to his native Germany, where he joined the radical ecologists of the Green Party and even tried to run—unsuccessfully—for mayor of Frankfurt.

160

Paris

The student upheaval in Paris was only one of a whole string of youthful revolts all over the world. Students everywhere—from California to France to Eastern Europe and Japan, in Latin America and even in China—protested, demonstrated, rioted, went on strike, and occupied university buildings, in an international chain reaction. Their grievances ranged from dormitory conditions to the war in Vietnam to authoritarian arrangements in society as a whole. If the universities in America had become bureaucratic, in Europe they were positively archaic, in physical facilities as well as in their organizational structure revolving around the autocratic power of superannuated senior professors (the "mandarins"). Against this heritage, universities throughout Western Europe were undergoing a revolution of democratization as enrollments multiplied, a transformation with which the old system could never effectively deal. Higher learning was frequently perceived as being "industrialized."[23] The ultra-Left politics of Trotskyism and Anarchism, as well as Marx's doctrine of alienation under capitalist and bureaucratic regimes, provided theoretical articulation and amplification of student grievances.

Yet these circumstances do not explain why revolution should have come everywhere at once or in the particular year 1968. A wave of simultaneous revolutionary behavior such as students worldwide manifested in 1968 is virtually without precedent. To find a historical analogy it is necessary to go back to the revolutions of 1848, when practically all the European continent west of the Russian border experienced violent protest and upheaval, much of it initiated by students. Like 1968, most of the hopes of 1848 ended in counterrevolution and disillusionment. But neither revolutionary wave, with their simultaneous confluence of protests in different countries and under different circumstances, is easy to explain. Somehow an outburst in one country inspires another somewhere else; if the conditions are ripe, the force of example is irresistible. "This is our Berlin," a French militant was heard to exclaim as the May protests were getting underway.[24]

Germany was indeed the earliest focus of Europe's student troubles in 1968. The background there was explicitly ideological, as youth groups previously affiliated with the Social-Democratic party broke away and took up revolutionary defiance of the status quo, from standpoints ranging from Trotskyism to Maoism. Most influential was the organization known as the SDS, standing for "Socialist German Student League," not to be confused with its American counterpart. Out of the SDS emerged Rudi Dutschke, an East German-born graduate student at the Free University of Berlin, who like Cohn-Bendit became a remarkably charismatic leader of generational revolt. The Free University, with its American-style freedom, egalitarianism, and student representation, was an exception to the authoritarianism of German tradition. Founded in 1947, it had become by the 1960s a hotbed of student radicalism. West Berlin, a mecca for the alienated and disaffected of all sorts, was, in the words of Italian sociologist Gianni Statera, "the laboratory where the utopia of protest was polished, revised, and developed until its final failure."[25]

Under the prodding of the SDS and others, widespread student demonstrations broke out in February 1968, concentrated in West Berlin. A favored target was the Springer Press, the right-wing chain of popular newspapers and publishing outlets. Berliners, fearful of provoking the Communists surrounding their city, met the students with widespread hostility, a mood that translated into violent action in April when an unemployed artist shot at Dutschke and grievously wounded him. This event set off a new wave of mass student demonstrations, again focused on Springer enterprises in Berlin.

As happens all too often, the violent acts of the radical minority only prompted reaction and repression by the conservative majority. The Bonn government enacted a set of emergency laws allowing the suspension of constitutional rights at times of crisis (shades of the Weimar Republic). This step, coinciding with the upheaval in Paris, provoked more radical student action, including sit-ins at several institutions in Berlin. But these responses proved futile. By the fall of 1968, the bulk of German students were lapsing back into normalcy, while the radicals splintered and splintered again. The SDS fell apart and dissolved. The Maoists split over the apparent retreat from the Cultural Revolution in China. One serious consequence remained—the emergence of ultra-radical groups committed to terrorism in the name of revolution and anti-imperialism. Into the early 1970s, Germany continued to be agitated by the bombings and assassination attempts committed by the Baader-Meinhof Gang and the "Red Army Faction."

For a time, Italy seemed to be in as serious trouble as Germany, if not more so. Anticipatory student takeovers, inspired by Dutschke's preaching and revulsion over the traditional university authoritarianism, took place at Trent and Turin in the fall of 1967. Then, the German example of February 1968 triggered a wave of student sit-ins at universities all over the country. Most serious was the clash of students and police at the University of Rome on March 1, followed by fighting between Left- and Right-wing students. Two hundred fifty rioters were arrested, hundreds more were injured, and the press and public opinion were shaken out of their usual support for law and order, much more so than in Germany. In May and June, there was another upsurge of protests, starting in Rome and spreading to Turin and Milan, in response to the events in Paris. The last sit-in ended in Milan in July. (It is hard to sustain a student revolution anywhere when summer vacation rolls around.) Meanwhile, the Italian government, more sensitive than most to the complex balance of public opinion, hastened to promise reform of the antiquated and authoritarian organization of the universities. By fall, the wave of rebellion had passed and university life was getting back to normal, leaving, as in Germany, only a few ultra-Left sectarians to find their way into terrorism with the Red Brigades.

In Eastern Europe, even though student agitation had a very different target under the Communist bureaucracies, the cycle of rebellions tracked closely with the West. In Czechoslovakia, student action was instrumental in precipitating the fall of the Novotný dictatorship and in supporting the reforms of the Prague Spring, not to mention the protests against the Soviet occupation after August 20. In Poland, student outbreaks came in March, and though they were not immediately effective, they did represent the beginning of the end of the conservative Communist leader Gomulka. A major outbreak, French and American style, took place in Yugoslavia in June when students clashed with the police and occupied the University of Belgrade. Surprisingly for a Communist government, Marshal Tito responded with sympathy and promises of reform, while wages were raised to make sure that the trouble did not spread to the workers. But Tito needed all the national solidarity he could muster in the face of the crisis with the Soviet Union brewing over Czechoslovakia.

On the surface, the motives of the New Left revolt in Europe are hard to fathom. Unlike past revolutions it was not particularly aimed at privilege, nor were its participants particularly underprivileged, any more than their American counterparts. To be sure, radical Old Left doctrines—notably Trotskyism—lent their traditions and their vocabularies to some of the rebel leadership, far more than in America, but the issues were novel. As described by Jean-Jacques Servan-Schreiber, the noted liberal editor of *L'Express*:

> This was not a "socialist" movement as the term is applied traditionally and so dogmatically in Eastern Europe. . . . What it dared to question was not the legitimacy of property, which was treated as a secondary problem, but above all, power and authority. It made no attempt to seize the means of production, but rather the centers of command.[26]

There was really more relevance in the example of the China of the Cultural Revolution, with its remarkable influence among students who considered themselves Maoists.

The paramount intellectual influences in the background of the upheaval were the writings of the young Marx on alienation, a recent philosophical fashion, and the works of Herbert Marcuse on the "repressive tolerance" of even the most liberal bourgeois society. Antiauthoritarianism was at the root of the movement, with everything that the term implies—rejection of the state, the technocratic structure of society, and bureaucracy and hierarchy whether they appeared under capitalism or under Soviet-style Communism. For some, the whole achievement-oriented social system—the "rat race" of personal success, in American parlance—was the enemy.

Dutschke, an enemy of all authoritarian systems East and West, wrote of alienation as "an acute feeling of powerlessness in relation to the established system, neuroticized to such a degree that the individual internalizes the belief in his own absolute impotence . . . , thus making him useful and exploitable according to the needs of capital."[27] Anything that smacked of manipulation by the people in power, from the politics of the old parties to the consumerism of the new prosperity, came under condemnation. "The revolution which is beginning will call in question not only capitalist society but industrial society," proclaimed a wordy placard when the Sorbonne was occupied. "The consumer's society must perish of a violent death. The society of alienation must disappear from history. We are inventing a new and original world. Imagination is power."[28] Commented Stephen Spender as an eyewitness: "They equate revolution with spontaneity, participation, communication, imagination, love, youth."[29]

Rebels need to find an alternative in some existing society, past or present, to measure their hopes by. For the European New Left the model was the Third World in general and North Vietnam in particular, apotheosized in the name of anti-imperialism. In turn, anti-imperialism enabled the rebels to blame everything wrong in the rest of the world on the misbehavior of the West. Che Guevara was often the idol, with his doctrine of guerrilla struggle everywhere against imperialism. (The rebels remained blissfully unaware that after Guevara's death in Bolivia the year before, Castro was swinging Cuba quickly toward the cynical Soviet line in foreign policy and the bureaucratic Soviet model domestically.)

Most quixotic was the rebels' sense of the tactics that would bring about the radical reconstruction of society. Suspicious of all parties, Left,

Right, or Center, they preferred to operate as an "extra-parliamentary opposition," whose use of confrontation and violence, without waiting for the approval of the masses, could discredit Establishment institutions and values and thereby radicalize the majority. They wanted everything to happen spontaneously, with a maximum of direct democracy and debate and a minimum of preconceived plan and organization. Gianni Statera applies Karl Mannheim's theory of utopia to the student movement and finds it the

> "chiliastic utopian type" . . . a form of irrationalism . . . based on "absolute presentness," on the inversion of the traditional relation between means and ends, on the idea of revolution as something to be carried out "here and now," on the striving toward individual liberation through direct, immediate action."[30]

Rebels carried away by such a faith do not reckon with the innate conservatism of that majority who, faced with the choice, inevitably opt for the forces of order. The students thought they could appeal to the workers. In France for a time they appeared to be succeeding, much more than in America where the workers (except for blacks) were substantially better integrated socially and economically into the system. In the spirit of the *Communist Manifesto*, Cohn-Bendit thought he could erase the division of labor: "To start with we must reject the distinction between student and worker."[31] Nevertheless, the workers' leadership never accepted the New Left, and the rank-and-file workers, rankled as they were by France's vast inequalities of income, were readily weaned away by economic concessions. "Workers' control" and "self-management" were popular slogans among the students but of lower priority among actual workers' concerns. Some New Left theorists concluded, in Europe as they did in America, that while the class struggle was still a fact, the real revolutionary class was now not the workers but the students or the youth per se.

What student rebels everywhere truly wanted was a Socialist-anarchist utopia. They achieved this goal only briefly and locally in the communes they created in occupied university buildings. The uprising was a romantic protest against the realities of modern life. Momentarily it lit up political skies around the world like a brilliant rocket, but then burned out and left nothing except its legend.

8

Peking

SATURDAY, JULY 27, mid-morning on a hot summer day. A throng of some 30,000 factory workers, organized by the local military command, approaches the American-style campus of the Tsinghua Technical University situated in the northwest part of Peking adjacent to Peking University. Marching in military columns and brandishing their copies of the "Little Red Book" of Quotations from Chairman Mao, the workers hope to stop the fighting that has been going on for months at the paralyzed school between two rival factions of students, each considering itself the legitimate representative of the celebrated Red Guard movement.

The underdog faction of students, known as the "Fours," greet the arriving force as liberators, admit them to the Science Building, which they have turned into a fortress, and agree to be disarmed. The Fours are evacuated from the campus, leaving their arsenal of guns, hand grenades, and booby traps in the hands of their rescuers.

Next, the worker columns surround the buildings held by the more militant rival faction, the "Chingkangshan Regiment," so-called from the Communists' legendary guerrilla base where Mao Tse-tung began his rise in the late 1920s. The "Regiment" has been led ever since the beginning of the Cultural Revolution in 1966 by K'uai Ta-fu, a 21-year-old chemistry student of peasant origin.* All this time K'uai has

* On the spelling of Chinese names, I have generally followed the old Wade-Giles transcription used by most of the works in English on this period. The main peculiarity is that *p* without an apostrophe is pronounced *b*; similarly, *t* = *d*, *k* = *g*, *ch* = *j*. More recent

167

been identified with the most ultra-Left leaders of this extraordinary revolution within the revolution. Running his group of nearly a thousand activists at Tsinghua through a hard core of toughs called "rods" (from their slogan, "staunch, hard-core iron-rod rebels"),[1] he fancies himself a military commander, and has been providing leadership by telephone to student radicals all over the country. K'uai's people regard their student opponents as traitors to the revolution because they accept the efforts of moderates in the government, especially Premier Chou En-lai and the military, to turn Mao back in the direction of order and authority after two years of virtual anarchy. The antielitist frenzy of the radicals runs closely parallel to New Left thinking in the West despite the vast difference in China's circumstances.

K'uai's first impulse when the force of workers arrives at Tsinghua is to start shooting at the besiegers, but his lieutenants persuade him simply to order his units to defend themselves. Then K'uai slips away from the campus unobserved and drives to meet with the Municipal Revolutionary Committee to protest the invasion of his territory. The committee tells him to submit to the workers, but instead he phones the campus to tell his followers that the workers are supposed to pull out. Activists demand that the workers leave, but they refuse, shouting, "Use reason, not violence!"[2]

At 3:00 P.M., the Regiment launches a counterattack, shooting nuts and bolts with slingshots from their dormitory windows at the besiegers, who are armed only with their Little Red Books. Then they charge out to attack the surrounding throng with spears, rocks, and homemade hand grenades. They actually capture several of the army officers who are leading the pacification march and subject them to beating and all-night interrogation.

The fighting is dampened down, literally, by a late afternoon rain shower. Then more clashes occur as the fanatics of the Regiment throw themselves at the overwhelming numbers of besiegers. In all, three workers are killed by spears or hand grenades, but the commanders of the worker force exhort their followers to observe the "Five Won'ts" of controversy, including not hitting back and not cursing back. During the night, K'uai and the Regiment agree to a truce and order their forces to withdraw from the campus, but not before one last student assault on a worker-occupied building takes the lives of two more visitors. Altogether almost a thousand workers have been wounded or beaten.

---

sources use the new official transcription, pinyin, which has different peculiarities: $zh = j$, $z = dz$, $c = ts$, $q = ch$, $x = sh$. Thus, formerly Mao Tse-tung, now Mao Zedong; Teng Hsiao-p'ing, now Deng Xiaoping; Chou En-lai, now Zhou Enlai; Chiang Ch'ing, now Zhang Qing; Peking, now Beijing.

Peking

In the early morning hours of July 28, Mao Tse-tung personally calls in K'uai and other prominent Peking student leaders to meet with the Central Cultural Revolution Group.[3] K'uai arrives late, to endure with the other students stern lecturing by the Communist chieftains for the errors of divorcing themselves from the masses and distrusting the worker-soldier pacification effort. When K'uai voices his suspicion of a counterrevolutionary plot, Mao replies, "If you want to seize the 'black hand,' it's me. . . . We told the workers to go and do propaganda work. . . . The workers were unarmed but you refused to allow them to do so, ending up killing and injuring some of them." He makes it clear that from now on the workers are the leading class; the students and intellectuals must submit to worker discipline and supervision. In the version reported from Peking by Stanley Karnow, Mao tearfully tells the students, "You have let me down and, moreover, you have disappointed the workers, peasants, and soldiers of China."[4] Mao has reluctantly decided that he must disavow the student Red Guards whom he had put so much trust in two years before to set China on the right revolutionary course: the self-defeating disorder is too much to tolerate.

During the day on the 28th, in line with Mao's wishes, members of the propaganda team at Tsinghua attempt to persuade the students of both factions to return peacefully to the campus and reconcile their differences, meanwhile collecting weapons and seeing to the exchange of prisoners. The inventory of captured armament comes out as follows:

5 semiautomatic rifles	1,435 spears
57 rifles	380 short knives
31 pistols	9 steel whips (made of fine chain)
12 homemade rifles	25 cannon shells
5 small-bore rifles	2 type-59 semiautomatic rifles
5 air guns	1 type-56 assault-gun (tommy-gun)
1,038 bullets	16 packages of dynamite
688 hand grenades	2 homemade tanks (tractors with
52 homemade cannon	armored plate)
9 explosive satchels (for antitank use)	50 bottles of poisonous gas
168 homemade mines	185 bottles of acid and other
15 big knives and bayonets	corrosive chemicals[5]

Having accomplished their mission, the hordes of workers withdraw from the Tsinghua campus but leave a permanent Propaganda Team of workers and soldiers to talk restraint into the student radicals. For days on end they conduct constant meetings, study groups, and negotiating sessions to elicit agreement between the two campus factions on the basis of mutual self-criticism. Similar occupations of campuses are carried out at Peking University and all over the country, sometimes with much more violent resistance than Tsinghua manifests after July 28.

At this point occurs one of the most bizarre episodes of this whole strange era. Mao Tse-tung receives a basket of mangoes as a gift from a visiting Pakistani delegation, and decides to send it to the Tsinghua Propaganda Team as a token of his appreciation. In turn, the team distributes individual mangoes to the factories that its members represent. William Hinton describes the response at Tsinghua on the basis of the interviews he was able to conduct four years later:

> The gift of mangoes and this statement of support had a profound effect. Few people slept at all that night. Everyone wanted to see and touch the mangoes that came directly from Chairman Mao, and everyone wanted to discuss this extraordinary idea that the propaganda teams, far from being a temporary, emergency expedient, were a form of permanent supervision over higher education. . . .[6]

So awed are the printers by this offering that they stay up late at night to find a chemical with which they can embalm their mango, already rotting in the summer heat, to preserve this physical symbol of the Great Helmsman's approbation. Hinton continues:

> The original mangoes were preserved, put in glass cases, and displayed in the reception rooms of key factories. Later numerous models of these mangoes were made and displayed by all the other factories that had taken part in the pacification of Tsinghua. A veritable cult arose around these mangoes, as if they were some religious relic—a hair of the Buddha, a nail from Christ's cross.[7]

Nevertheless, the sustained fervor of the Mao cult cannot conceal the decisive downturn suffered by the ardent and often spontaneous movement of youthful radicals that has made the Cultural Revolution a unique experience for a Communist country. Up to this point, China has in a most extraordinary way run parallel with the Western New Left and its repudiation of all authority in social relationships and cultural standards, no less than in political affairs. From here on it begins the tortuous path of recovery from the revolutionary adventure.

The Great Proletarian Cultural Revolution is usually dated from May 1966. In its origin it appears to be just one in a series of attempts ever since the late 1950s by China's enigmatic Communist leader Mao Tse-tung to revitalize his revolution. For the first decade after their victory in the Chinese Civil War and the establishment of the People's Republic in 1949, the Communists had been content to follow the Soviet model of government and economy, which meant bureaucratic centralism and planning. Many of the Chinese leaders acquired a vested interest in the new social hierarchy of officeholders that they were creating, but Mao himself soon became concerned that this was a slippery path toward the betrayal of true revolutionary values. Moreover, he had a political falling-out with the Soviets over a combination of issues, including what he regarded as insufficient Soviet support in his confrontation with United States "imperialism" over Chiang Kai-shek's Nationalists on Taiwan. In addition Nikita Khrushchev had upstaged him ideologically by unilaterally undertaking the de-Stalinization campaign of 1956. Mao's pique was accentuated by underlying historical and racial antipathies between the Chinese and the Russians.

By the late 1950s, Mao had rejected what he called the "capitalist road" of the Soviet Union (that is, the bureaucratic model) in favor of a new mass-based revolutionary campaign. At first he thought he had the force for this drive in the peasants, through whom he had risen to power in the first place. In 1958, he launched a new double-barrelled revolution from above, with the "Great Leap Forward" of do-it-yourself rural industrialization and the reorganization of the peasant cooperatives into large communes. These were allegedly closer to the Marxist ideal of communism than anything the Soviets had achieved. However, the Great Leap was a failure, and Mao had to defer to the bureaucratic orientation in his party represented by his number-two man, President Liu Shao-ch'i. Biding his time, Mao looked around for a new force that he could unleash against his own Communist bureaucrats; he found them, he thought, in the young generation of students. Through the youth, he tried to do the same thing to his society from the top down that French and American students were attempting from the bottom up. There ensued one of the most extraordinary episodes of mass hysteria in all of modern history.

After preliminary denunciations of various high party intellectuals, Mao launched his unusual new revolutionary campaign on 7 May 1966. The occasion was a letter he wrote to the civil war hero and defense minister General Lin Piao, about the need for a new revolution in China's educational system with a practical base in manual work. Lin was a devoted follower of Mao who had already begun to repoliticize the army, abolishing military ranks in 1965 and asserting the human factor over the power of weaponry. The date May 7 was later taken as the name for the "May 7 Cadre Schools," to which bureaucrats and intellectuals were sent to be "reeducated." Organizationally, the movement began to take shape a week later with the formation of the "Central Cultural Revolution Group," headed by Mao's secretary Ch'en

171

Po-ta and his wife Chiang Ch'ing (a former actress and the last of a string of wives). Action commenced at Peking University with wall posters denouncing the university president for suppressing the masses. The country was electrified on June 1 when Mao himself endorsed this unprecedented event and invoked the memory of the revolutionary Paris Commune of 1871.

Students at Peking University, Tsinghua University, and elsewhere rose to the occasion by sacking faculty apartments and marching professors around their campuses in dunce caps. It was during this commotion that K'uai Ta-fu emerged at Tsinghua as a militant, single-minded leader of the radical upsurge, loudly denouncing moderate students who were children of privileged officials. This radicalism was fueled by a reaction against the most fundamental principles of American and Soviet education on which the Chinese system had been modeled: "the whole idea of 'expertise in command,' " as William Hinton expressed it. "As the system had developed through the 1950s and 1960s, the sole measure of merit had become grades. Education, it was held, had no class character; everyone was equal before grades."[8] Peasant youth, in particular, were quite unprepared for this style of rigorous academics.

Faced with the student uproar, the Communist party apparatus guided by President Liu Shao-ch'i tried to maintain order by setting up so-called "Work Teams" in the universities, ostensibly to help fight counterrevolution but actually to restore discipline. This was far from what Mao wanted. To counter the party conservatives, he ordered that the Work Teams be dissolved, and gave the nod to the formation of an independent movement of youth. This was the origin of the famous Red Guards, encouraged from above but drawing extraordinary energy from below. One of the earliest units was formed at the high school attached to Tsinghua University.

Mao formalized the new radicalism at a session of the party's Central Committee in August, when he promulgated the "sixteen points" to serve as the guidelines for the Cultural Revolution:

> Our objective is to struggle against and crush those persons in authority who are taking the capitalist road, to criticize and repudiate the reactionary bourgeois academic 'authorities' and the ideology of the bourgeoisie and all other exploiting classes and to transform education, literature and art. . . . Trust the masses, rely on them and respect their initiative. Cast out fear. Don't be afraid of disorder . . . , firmly rely on the revolutionary Left. . . . Hold aloft the great red banner of Mao Tse-tung's thought. . . .[9]

Immediately afterward, on August 18, at a huge rally in Peking's Tienanmen Square fronting the Forbidden City, Mao gave his formal endorsement to the Red Guard movement and called on the hysterical crowd of youth to "spread disorder."[10]

Mao does not himself appear to have spoken formally on this crucial occasion or any other during the Cultural Revolution, leaving public statements to intermediaries until the party congress that ended the radical phase of the Cultural Revolution in 1969. This reticence naturally invites speculation about Mao's actual condition and role in these years. Rumors at the time about his health were allayed by the official report of his endurance swim in the Yangtze River in July 1966—a super-Olympic feat, if the story was not exaggerated.

In the frenetic spirit set by the Tienanmen rally, the Red Guard craze spread throughout the country. To facilitate a "link-up" within the movement, Mao directed that Red Guard youth be granted free rail passage so that they could come to Peking or other major centers to steep themselves in the new fervor or fan out to carry the revolutionary message to the provinces—provided, of course, that the trains moved at all. Red Guards were even allowed to mail in their complaints to Peking postage-free. The million or more urban youth who had been involuntarily resettled in villages took advantage of the opportunity to flock back to the cities. At Tsinghua, K'uai Ta-fu was riding high; he mobilized the bulk of the student body in the "Tsinghua University Chingkangshan United Regiment," adjudged by William Hinton to be "the most famous and the most prestigious Red Guard detachment in the whole of China."[11] He took over effective control of the campus from the old administration and was even able to draw funds from the State Bank to support his followers.

Early on in the Cultural Revolution, the Red Guard movement divided more or less into two tendencies, which underlay much of the factional fighting that marked the subsequent upheaval, including the climax at Tsinghua University in 1968. The basis of this division was the social origin of university students, who at this date had naturally been born before the Communist government was set up over the whole of China in 1949. Those of "bourgeois" or intelligentsia (that is, "bad class") background seemed to outdo themselves in their Maoist ardor so as to prove their personal revolutionary virtue. In contrast, the children of workers or peasants or old Communist functionaries, secure about their class origin, were concerned mainly to purge elitism out of the educational system. Otherwise they were more inclined to support whatever appeared to be the party of order. The cleavage calls to mind the hostility in American life at the same time between pampered young revolutionaries and blue-collar enemies of change and disorder.

Mao's radical drive using the Red Guards virtually immobilized the regular party organization that had managed the country ever since the takeover of 1949. The more extremist Red Guards, in the ascendancy with Mao's blessing by the fall of 1966, assumed the power to assault and arrest "counterrevolutionaries" and "evil elements," parading their enemies in dunce caps along the streets. Pursuing a campaign to "Destroy the Four Olds"—old ideology, old culture, old habits, and old customs—they plundered the homes of people of "bad class" background, especially teachers and other intellectuals. Terror spread through the ranks of officialdom and among the survivors of the old educated class, as the unrestrained Red Guards—mostly teenagers—subjected them to beatings, jail, and interrogations under torture. Knowledge of foreign languages was considered a sure mark of a counterrevolutionary. A leading official in international finance who had graduated from the London School of Economics "before liberation" was put under house arrest in his office and kept there for three years. Not surprisingly, chaos spread throughout the country's administrative structure. Any manifestation of Western cultural influence—even the performing of Beethoven—was forcibly attacked. This was the development that most alerted the attention of the West itself—and of the Soviet Union, already alienated from China since the late 1950s by the clash of national interest between the two governments. "What kind of a cultural revolution is it that is against all culture?" commented a Soviet engineer to this writer.

High on Mao's agenda was a shake-up in the country's leadership. He demoted (and ultimately ousted and jailed) both President Liu Shao-ch'i and party general secretary Teng Hsiao-p'ing (the same Teng—or Deng in the revised spelling—who took over after Mao's death) for resisting his disruptive campaign against the bureaucracy. Mao's adversaries were harrassed and vilified. The students at Tsinghua went so far as to seize Liu Shao-chi's wife and children (one of them a Tsinghua student herself) and force them to denounce the country's nominal president, whom the radicals called the "Chinese Khrushchev." Lin Piao, appointed national commander of the Red Guard, evidently won Mao's confidence by plumping for the radical line; Mao made him his deputy and heir apparent. Ultra-leftists were installed in all the key positions in the media to provide constant justification for the radical line, along with the "big character posters" with which the Red Guards advertised their sentiments everywhere. In between the fanatics of the Left and the "capitalist roaders" of the Right was Premier Chou En-lai, a political survivor who managed to keep his job throughout the era of the Cultural Revolution while trying as much as he could to be a moderating force.

Peking

By the end of 1966, Mao and his Red Guards were ready to turn their movement into a real revolution against the old power structure. The new phase began early in January in Shanghai, the most ardent center of radicalism, with a literal coup d'état: radicals, here including workers, seized government buildings and arrested the city administration. Mao thought this was a reincarnation of the Paris Commune of 1871. Radicals in other cities tried to follow suit, with the encouragement of representatives of the Tsinghua Chingkangshan Regiment. Their success varied, as the party Establishment mobilized workers and students of the elite high schools to fight back. Severe fighting ensued around the country, complete with torture of prisoners.

At this juncture, in February 1967, Mao ordered the army to step in on the side of the radicals, but instead it did what it could to contain them and restore order. Then Mao himself was persuaded by Chou En-lai that the Red Guards had gotten out of hand. Blaming the anarchy on the "individualism" and "bourgeois" education of the students, Mao ordered them to adopt the Chou compromise by entering into "revolutionary committees" and form "triple alliances" with the party and the army. Ostensibly guardians of the Cultural Revolution, the revolutionary committees really served as a new version of the old system, acting to bring the forces of revolution under control. However, it was not easy to repair the shattered structure of authority—only Mao's charisma or the projection of his charismatic image gave the country any coherence. Both the Cultural Revolution and the defense of the conventional Communist order depended heavily on local strength and initiative from one province to another. If there was any functioning national institution it was the army, which therefore became the paramount element in the new revolutionary committees as they were slowly established in one center after another.

Yet this by no means eliminated the Red Guards as a political force, particularly on the campuses. Liu Shao-ch'i and other senior officials continued to be vilified, and Liu's wife was hauled before a student court at Tsinghua and subjected to a marathon interrogation. Students and young workers armed themselves and clashed with older workers and military personnel in many places. Mao continued to vacillate between restraining the stormy forces of youth that he had unleashed and restraining the restrainers. But in the summer of 1967, when he ordered the army not to hold the radicals back, he was openly defied by local commanders. The garrison at Wuhan in central China actually mutinied. Although the Wuhan trouble was contained, the military threat to the revolutionary line provoked a new radical outburst. By August, between the uncontrolled forces of the revolution and the military, the country was again approaching anarchy. Youth by the hundreds of thousands camped out in the streets of Peking, with banners, loud-speakers, and cooking fires, to keep up the campaign against Liu Shao-ch'i, with radical and not-quite-so-radical factions vying to do Mao's will. Mobs attacked foreign diplomatic missions, setting fire to the British Embassy and ransacking the Soviet consular office. Factional feuding in the provinces sometimes grew so chaotic that it was impossible to identify radicals and conservatives. Once again Mao was compelled to order the army to try to restore order, and even his wife and the other Cultural Revolution chieftains had to call on the Red Guards to restrain themselves. In some places the army cracked down vigorously on the radicals, with arrests and even executions, but it was to take many months before normal public order was restored.

Under this tension the disparate tendencies among the Red Guards turned into warring factions. At Tsinghua University those willing to accept the new moderate line from above broke away from K'uai Ta-fu's Regiment and organized as the Tsinghua Chingkangshan April 14 Regiment (named for the date of their founding caucus, in Chinese "four-one-four," hence their nickname, the "Fours"). K'uai's radicals, many of whom came from a "bad" (that is, bourgeois or intelligentsia) social background and thus had less at stake in the conventional Communist system, remained convinced that the new moderation was a falsification of Mao. Thus the battle lines were drawn for the violent struggle that broke out between the two factions the following year, each believing that the other was "the Kuomintang of today" of which Mao had warned.[12] The violence of the animosities among these student factions all over the country went far beyond the largely theoretical differences among Western youth factions—perhaps because China had had a more extreme experience of radical behavior and more emotional splintering of the radical movement, perhaps because the role of Mao as a cult figure had given the whole phenomenon a special emotional intensity.

As 1968 opened, the keynote for the last crusade of the Cultural Revolution was sounded by a group in Hunan Province, Mao's home ground, calling itself the "Hunan Provincial Proletarian Revolutionaries Great Alliance Committee," or Sheng Wu Lien. They published a manifesto called "Whither China," in which they assailed the restoration of bureaucracy under the recent line and called for a return to the Shanghai Commune as the model for revolutionary China. "Society needs a more thorough change—overthrow of the rule of the new bureaucratic bourgeoisie, thorough smashing of the old state machinery, realization of social revolution, realization of a redistribution of assets, and establishment of a new society, 'People's Commune of China' "—all this directed against the people who wanted to hang onto a *Communist* system. On the new revolutionary committees the Shen Wu Lien was quite blunt: "The fruit of victory of both the January revolution and the August storm has been basically usurped by the bourgeoisie . . . , and the 'end' of the first Great Cultural Revolution has not been reached."[13] For its pains, the Sheng Wu Lien was soon suppressed by the military and police authorities as "anarchist" and "Trotskyist."

In the early months of 1968, the restoration of postrevolutionary normalcy proceeded apace with the extension of the system of revolutionary committees around the country. Mao's wife led a rearguard action to keep the spirit of revolution alive and hold off the conservative military leaders, and was evidently responsible for a major shakeup in the army in March. Army chief of staff Yang Ch'eng-wu, an enemy of revolutionary disorder, was suddenly removed with a number of other like-minded officers, and the share of the enthusiasts of the Cultural Revolution ("representatives of the masses") on the revolutionary committees was ordered increased from 20 to 30 percent. But preeminence on the committees was now accorded, for the first time since mid-1966, to the bureaucrats of the party. The only place where the radical movement could still seriously express itself was in the universities. As Maurice Meissner observes, "The last battles of the Cultural Revolution were fought where the struggle had begun two years ago before: on university campuses in Peking."[14]

The new campus outbreak had a deliberate purpose. K'uai Ta-fu, by this time a national figure of some renown, was unmollified by his inclusion as a vice chairman on the Peking Revolutionary Committee. He conceived a new offensive strategy—to seize total power in the major universities, put down any student supporters of the new moderate line, and pressure the pro–Cultural Revolution leaders in Peking to revive the revolutionary effort. Picking up a comment by Mao on the Communists' old adversaries, Chiang Kai-shek's Nationalists, K'uai charged, "The Kuomintang of today are the Fours and those like them. If they have protectors in high places, we shall be glad to see them intervene so that we can unmask them and fight them in the open at last."[15]

Fighting broke out at Peking University ("Peita," in the popular abbreviation) late in March, where the Chingkangshan radicals were opposed by a pro-government group called the "New Peita Commune." New Peita was formed, oddly enough, around the woman who had launched the original attack on authority two years before, Nieh Yuan-tzu, now a member of the new Peking Revolutionary Committee. After the radicals attacked the New Peita headquarters and took several of the leaders hostage, the head of the Peking Revolutionary Committee, followed by a military contingent and Nieh Yuan-tzu herself, came to the university to calm the rebels down. The students took this as a provocation and attacked the visitors; Nieh was stabbed, though not fatally. Six hundred troops had to be sent into the campus to restore order even temporarily, while the two contending student factions fortified their respective positions in university buildings.

Late in April, K'uai Ta-fu renewed his revolutionary offensive at Tsinghua University. His people began by kidnapping several leaders of the Fours and torturing them into confessing a nonexistent counterrevolutionary plot. The Fours countered by seizing a leader of the Regiment, to which the Regiment responded with an ultimatum. This prompted the Fours to fortify the science building and to seize another militant from the Regiment who approached too close. Linking his adversaries with the recently ousted army commanders, K'uai mobilized his own people to attack. This action, on April 23, opened what came to be known as the "Hundred Day War," not to end until the carnage of July 27 and the intervention of the army and the workers.

In the first rush, the forces of the Regiment captured two buildings lightly held by the Fours. Spears were the main weapon. Further clashes occurred during the next few days, while the two sides labored to turn the buildings they held into fortresses. One student died when a truck was overturned on him. On May 30, K'aui launched what was intended to be his knock-out attack, starting with an assault on the bathhouse held by the Fours. His forces were repulsed in bloody fighting, with several dead, until they set fire to the bathhouse and made prisoners of the defenders. The Regiment then laid siege to the Fours' main stronghold in the Science Building, with the aim of starving them out.

As the contest settled into a war of attrition, both sides availed themselves of the technological resources of the university to fashion firearms and explosives for the fray. Several of the Fours were killed by gunfire as the Regiment enforced its siege. In protest, a delegation from the Fours demonstrated at the City Hall against K'uai's "Fascist atrocities."[16] One of the Regiment's adherents later explained their fervor: "Anything could be done to the class enemy and we were fighting class enemies! We saw ourselves as only one front in a much larger national struggle, a struggle between two headquarters on the Central Committee, but we thought we were the focal point of this struggle."[17]

Peking

Factional fighting paralleling the Tsinghua trouble broke out again in many places around the country. At Peita the entrenched factions stood on their respective rooftops wearing homemade straw helmets, and bombarded their adversaries with bricks, tiles, and any other available missiles. They even devised medieval-style catapults. This exchange was accompanied by denunciatory propaganda blared by each side at the other through loudspeakers. Simultaneously, bad clashes among Red Guard factions broke out in Canton and the southern region, especially in the province of Kwangsi, where the army undertook a regular military campaign followed by thousands of executions, in the name of restoring order.

By July, the Communist authorities had had enough of the turmoil, and issued definitive orders that it be stopped—essentially, by the army. For the schools and universities, "Mao Tse-tung Thought Propaganda Teams" were devised to go in and curb all contending factions. This was the mission of the 30,000 workers with military leadership—hardly a mere "team"—who entered the Tsinghua campus on July 27.

Mao's repudiation of the student Red Guards did not mean the immediate end of the Cultural Revolution. Denunciations of "counterrevolutionaries" and "capitalist roaders" continued apace, whether the targets were really conservatives or ultra-leftists, whether the motives were purely ideological or crudely personal. The campaign against the official devil Liu Shao-ch'i, long since under house arrest, culminated in October 1968, when the Central Committee of the party (meeting for the first time since the opening of the Cultural Revolution) lifted his party membership and formally removed him as President of the Republic. He died in 1969, of pneumonia, it is said, while being transported from one prison to another. All this time the cult of Chairman Mao reigned undiminished, and the top Cultural Revolution leaders around Madame Mao hastened to attach themselves to the new line of order.

The big turnabout of July and August 1968 was to dethrone the students from their premier place in the revolutionary program in favor of the real masses. As the French diplomat Jean Daubier describes it, "The dispatch of the workers into the universities . . . was the curious reversal of the opening stages of the Cultural Revolution, which had begun with the students moving into the factories. . . . What was involved was nothing less than *doing away with students as a faction, a separate social entity*."[18]

Official expression of the new priorities came in an August 25 article by the major theoretician of the Cultural Revolution, Yao Wen-yuan

179

(later one of the "Gang of Four"), in the party's ideological organ *Red Flag*. Yao made it clear to the radical youth that they must recognize the superior political virtue of the working class and, for the sake of completing the revolution, bow to worker takeover of education. A directive from Mao about the same time called for the worker-soldier teams that had taken over the universities to "stay permanently."[19] For rural areas the new faith in the masses was carried to the extreme of inviting peasants to take over the management of local schools. To assure the proletarianization of the universities as they geared up to resume their disrupted work, admission exams were abolished in favor of a general requirement of three years manual labor before enrollment in an institution of higher learning.

To drive home the new doctrine and forestall any recurrence of factional fighting among students, the national leadership revived the program of "sending down"—that is, shipping young Red Guards off to remote villages where they would presumably spend the rest of their days. Any former bureaucrats and intellectuals who could still be found in the cities were also "sent down"; for example, an accomplished interpreter was sent out of Peking to run the motor pool in a rural district. The stories of functionaries turned into pig farmers are legion. Stanley Karnow reports that as many as twenty million people were compelled to leave their urban amenities and move to villages and border areas during the winter months of 1968–1969—"the biggest and most intensive migration scheme in human history."[20] The less fortunate among the transplants found themselves committed to May 7 Cadre Schools for forced labor and indoctrination. Some professionals committed suicide rather than submit to a rural fate; some young students in their resentment turned to banditry.

By the end of the year 1968, the radical revolution was in full retreat. A symptomatic move in January 1969 was the formal establishment of a revolutionary committee at Tsinghua University, with student representatives a distinct minority. By 1970, professors who had been arrested in 1966 were allowed to return to work, and the university began functioning again on a normal basis, though it started out with scarcely one-fifth of its pre-1966 enrollment.

A major step toward regularizing the national political scene was the convening of a Communist Party Congress in April 1969, the first in thirteen years. It was a different sort of party now, with new working-class blood in the rank and file and a strong infusion of the military at the leadership level. But the signal given by the congress was that the party organization, with its hierarchy of committees and secretaries copied from the Soviet pattern, would resume its former primacy in the nation's power structure. The Cultural Revolution had clearly come to an end.

There remained many more aftershocks of the Cultural Revolution still to be undergone. As Mao more and more obviously went into the decline of advanced years—he had turned 75 in December 1968—a bitter behind-the-scenes struggle developed around the personage of his designated successor, General Lin Piao. Later on (1980) the authorities permitted the dissident writer Liu Guokai to publish an account calling the period of Lin's preeminence a time of "fascistic rule" under a "military junta," all in Mao's name.[21] Lin's fate in 1971 has never been fully explained: he was killed in a plane crash in Outer Mongolia while ostensibly fleeing to the Soviet Union after a failed attempt to seize power. In any case, his demise widened the opportunity for Premier Chou En-lai to move the country toward a course of pragmatic moderation and modernization. Ch'en Po-ta, the original mastermind of the Cultural Revolution Group, had already slipped and fallen when the moderates were trying to get at Lin between 1969 and 1971; by 1973, this oracle of the ultra-Left was being denounced as "a Kuomintang anti-Communist, a Trotskyist renegade, and a revisionist secret agent."[22] At the same time Teng Hsiao-P'ing, the party's general secretary before the Cultural Revolution, reappeared in the leadership and provided a rallying point for the moderates when Chou fell terminally ill. There were still Mao's wife and the other top figures of the Cultural Revolution Group to be reckoned with, and upon Chou's death in January 1976, they moved in to assume power with the alleged sanction of the dying Mao. Once again Teng was cut out of the deal. A dramatic moment was the giant popular demonstration in honor of Chou in Tienanmen Square in April 1976, broken up by the police on the orders of the new leftist leadership.

The ghost of the Cultural Revolution, briefly ascendant again, could not withstand the death of Mao when it finally came in September. Just as the Left grasped for power, they were foiled by a military coup. They were arrested, vilified, brought to trial, and condemned to prison as the nefarious "Gang of Four," including Mao's wife Chiang Ching, Chang Ch'un-ch'iao of Shanghai Commune fame, the ideologist Yao Wen-yuan, and Wang Hung-wen, a young Shanghai activist and protegé of Chiang Ch'ing who had risen meteorically during the Cultural Revolution. With the Gang of Four out of the way, the path was now clear for Teng and the pragmatists to resume the movement begun by Chou En-lai to repudiate the Cultural Revolution altogether. Along with them returned untold numbers of functionaries and intellectuals from their rural exile, to resume their old occupations and help bring China into the modern world.

Like the contemporary waves of youthful protest in most Western countries, the Cultural Revolution in China was an affair in which the emotional intensity of conflict seemed to outdistance by far the material issues that divided people. This was particularly true of the fighting among rival factions of Red Guards as the Cultural Revolution was winding down. Perhaps it is the sense of the waiting dustbin of history that intensifies the struggle to control a waning movement. Here the Red Guards' fighting reminds one of the infighting among dwindling radical sects in the American student and black movements.

Among all the protest movements of the 1960s, the Chinese Cultural Revolution was unique as a revolution within an ostensibly revolutionary country. It had no analogue among other Communist states, save possibly revolutionary Cambodia a decade later. Comparisons of the Cultural Revolution with Stalin's purges of the 1930s are wholly misplaced, and it had nothing in common with the Prague Spring except coincidental timing and its anti-Soviet sentiment. To be sure, China's postrevolutionary circumstances ran parallel to the Soviet bloc. The key difference was Mao Tse-tung and his genuinely revolutionary convictions.

Both Mao and the young radicals he unleashed were perturbed by the trend toward a new social inequality after they—or their parents—had fought to establish the classless society. What was happening in China was the same thing that innumerable critics of the Soviet Union have observed: the postrevolutionary emergence of a new form of social stratification that was not based on heredity or property as under the old order, but on function, expertise, and political status. In other words, China, like the Soviet Union and the Communist states of Eastern Europe, was experiencing the rise of the "New Class," in the term popularized by the Yugoslav dissident Milovan Djilas. The administrators, experts, technicians, and above all Communist party officials, by virtue of their education, experience, and political favor, were becoming the decisive social stratum, in effect the new ruling class in all those countries that were trying to modernize without relying on capitalist enterprise. It was against all this, in a romantic assertion of political will against economic reality, that Mao and the Cultural Revolution Group together with their hordes of young followers were rebelling. Liu Shao-ch'i was made the living symbol of this hated reality.

However, the social issues in China were not altogether different from those in the industrialized West. As many political writers have noted, beginning with James Burnham in *The Managerial Revolution* (1941) and C. Wright Mills in *White Collar* (1951), Western societies have quietly shifted, without overt revolution, away from the hierarchy based on property and toward the hierarchy based on bureaucratic or expert function, corporate as well as governmental. It was this new reality, with its premium on the educational ladder to success, that the New Left was rebelling against. Thus, despite the vast difference in their circumstances, there was a basic parallel in the motivation of radical protest in China and in the West.

A major difference between the two antibureaucratic movements was proximity to the seats of power. The Cultural Revolution, after all, was sponsored by the two most powerful men in China, Mao Tse-tung and Lin Piao, and it continued to have the favor of a major faction in the governmental leadership until 1976. It was as though Lyndon Johnson had hailed the Columbia University sit-in and the Chicago demonstration and urged everyone to copy them, or as though General de Gaulle had personally organized the March 22 Movement as a way of getting at his own bureaucrats. Thanks in part to its patronage from the top, revolt in China had the widest, deepest, and most violent manifestations of any to occur in this epoch. Nevertheless, the Cultural Revolution went far beyond a mere contrivance of feuding factions in the leadership. Unqualified encouragement from above lasted only for the first six months, until the Shanghai Commune; from then on, Mao vacillated between the factions, and the Cultural Revolution persisted on its own momentum among the youth.

The leaders of China during the Cultural Revolution readily recognized their affinity with the New Left elsewhere in the world. High-level resolutions and editorials hailed the student disorders in Europe and the United States. Twenty million people were mobilized to demonstrate in sympathy with the French student rebels. Mao commented self-righteously on the assassination of Martin Luther King and the racial troubles in the United States:

> The U.S. imperialists . . . used counterrevolutionary violence and killed him in cold blood. This has taught the broad masses of the black people in the United States a profound lesson. It has touched off a new storm in their struggle against violence, a storm which has swept well over 100 cities in the United States such as has never taken place before in the history of that country. . . . The struggle of the black people in the U.S. for emancipation is a component part of the general struggle of all the people of the world against U.S. imperialism, a component part of the contemporary world revolution.[23]

A certain naive exaggeration characterized Peking's whole perception of the West during these years; reported *The People's Daily* (May 27), "The revolutionary masses in Europe and North America dared to look down on the law and bayonet of the reactionary ruling cliques, showed no fear of suppression, persisted in their heroic struggle, and demonstrated a lively, revolutionary spirit."[24] All of which presumably spelled the doom of capitalism and imperialism.

The feeling of affinity was reciprocated by the Western New Left, by all in a general way, and by the small Maoist sects in a very dogmatic way. But all were responding quite unrealistically to the image that the Cultural Revolution created in its first few months, the image that China continued to show to the outside world. Meanwhile Peking returned to practices that were much more authoritarian than any forms of the New Left (except, perhaps, for the remarkably disciplined Progressive Labor Party in the United States).

In keeping with the deepening hostility between Peking and Moscow, the leaders of the Cultural Revolution dismissed all pro-Soviet Communist governments and parties with contempt, an attitude enthusiastically shared by the most radical New Left elements. When the French Communist party demurred at the violent behavior of the ultra-Left students in the May uprising, it offered the Chinese a perfect target for their verbal abuse. Although Czechoslovakia was a harder case to classify because the Prague Spring was patently revisionist on the Chinese ideological scale, it was easy for the Chinese leadership to condemn Soviet intervention as a blatant example of Russian imperialism and "hegemonism."

Was the Cultural Revolution really a revolution, any more than the protest movements in the West? They all manifested the typical phases of the revolutionary process—an upsurge of defiance, a peak of anarchistic confusion, crises and splits in the movement, and the relapse of society as a whole into a mood of conservative consolidation. If they differed, it was more in degree than in kind, with China representing the case nearest the classic revolutionary model. The eyewitnesses David and Nancy Milton write:

> For more than two years, China had experienced that extraordinary level of popular participation in politics always associated with the great revolutions of history. The Chinese people had experimented with new popular forms of government, while exposing a whole society and its institutions to merciless inspection and criticism.[25]

Further, this new Chinese Revolution implanted its own distinctive values:

Peking

The Chinese Cultural Revolution of the Sixties extended the concept of equality, first spread by the American and French revolutions and noted by de Tocqueville as an irreversible idea, to the vision of wiping out the age-old differences between mental and manual labor, town and country, leaders and led.[26]

The Cultural Revolution was closely akin to the Western New Left as a protest movement of the young. Unlike most of the great revolutions of the past, made by youngish men in their 30s, the Cultural Revolution relied on students and workers in their teens. It was, in some cases literally, a revolt of children against their parents, a true example of Lewis Feuer's "conflict of generations." What Anita Chan says of the "self-deception" of the young Red Guards, though controversial, might apply to the Sixties Revolution everywhere:

> They were able to sublimate their less noble impulses . . . , frenzied drives to persecute the weak. The helpless and stigmatized . . . deceiv[ed] themselves in the belief that they were dedicated to a charismatic leader and a greater cause without ulterior motives.[27]

The Chinese Cultural Revolution remains one of the most difficult events of recent history to grasp. In some respects it was unique, occurring in a unique country under unique circumstances and inspired by a unique leader. In other respects, it was clearly part of the worldwide movement against interpersonal dominance based on job or expertise, a parallel recognized both in China and in the West. The Red Guards and the Western New Left alike were rebelling against the convergent drift toward systems of ranks and commands that was taking place in all modern and modernizing societies.

In China the revolt went much further than anywhere else thanks to its initial sponsorship by the supreme leader. Ultimately it failed much more completely than anywhere else because of the extremeness of its original surge and the later loss of top-level sponsorship. Everywhere, the most radical excrescences of the 1960s rebellion tended to self-destruct. In China they had risen higher, and fell harder.

9

Prague

10 P.M., Tuesday, August 20, a misty, moonless night. Czechoslovakian radar is being heavily jammed, as well as NATO radar along the West German border, but NATO intelligence assumes that this is Soviet maneuvers again. An unscheduled Aeroflot airliner approaches the Ruzyně* Airport in the western outskirts of Prague. It is given permission to land because of a reported fuel emergency, but it parks on a taxiway instead of approaching the terminal. It is, in fact, a Soviet mobile air traffic control station.

An hour later another unscheduled Soviet commercial plane lands and discharges a group of passengers in civilian clothes. They are actually a special Soviet Army command group headed by General Ivan Pavlovsky, commander of all Soviet ground forces. They are waved through customs and passport control by Czech Interior Ministry officials as instructed by the pro-Soviet chief of the STB security police, Viliam Šalgovič, at a secret meeting that afternoon. (Šalgovič, typifying the collaborationists through whom the Soviets control the secret police in their satellites, has received his marching orders from KGB officials

---

* On the spelling of Czech names: ě is pronounced *ye*; č = *ch*; š = *sh*; ž = *zh* or French *j*; ř = *r* + ž; c = *ts*; ch = hard *h*; j = *y*. The stress is always on the first syllable, even on the *l* and *r* when they serve as vowels. The acute accent is to lengthen a vowel, not to mark stress.

who flew into Prague a couple of days before.) Cars from the Prague Aeroflot office are waiting to whisk the Russians off to the Soviet Embassy in the northern suburbs of the capital.

Shortly after midnight, three Antonov-12 troop-carrying planes land and discharge a company of paratroopers with two tanks. While a unit in civilian clothes from the earlier landing secures the airport control tower, the troops charge the terminal building, and the nervous tank gunners shoot out all the glass in this brand-new structure. Some of the unanticipated visitors stop to loot the duty-free shop, while others go about their assignment of clearing all tourists and employees from the terminal so it can be used as a command post. The evacuees are forced to wait until nearly 5:30 A.M., when they are ordered to walk the five miles back into town. "Our armies also must march a great many miles on foot," explains a Soviet officer in justification.[1]

The Soviet advance party is followed by a steady stream of Antonov-12s that come in from the east, drone over the city, and land at Ruzyně at one-minute intervals. By dawn, a whole airborne division complete with tanks has disembarked at the airport and headed downtown. They rendezvous at the Circle of the October Revolution, not far from the Soviet Embassy and just north of Hradčany Castle (an impressive medieval landmark rising high over the left bank of the Moldau that serves as the official residence of President Ludvik Svoboda and the ceremonial center of government). Then Soviet units fan out across Prague with detailed instructions to secure key points and arrest all the top figures in Czechoslovakia's Communist leadership. One of their earliest objectives is to throw a guard around Western embassies and those of the independent-minded Yugoslav and Romanian governments, to prevent their quarry from seeking asylum or else to apprehend them in the effort. Another is to block all the bridges across the Moldau, effectively cutting Prague in two.

While the preemptive airborne strike at the Czech seat of government is in progress, massive mechanized forces of the Warsaw Pact, mostly Soviet with token units of Poles, Hungarians, Bulgarians, and—to the particular disgust of the nation being occupied—East Germans, cross Czechoslovakia's borders without resistance and drive toward Prague and all other important centers. There are at least 200,000 troops in the first wave, followed by an equal or larger number, 90 percent Soviet, to secure the occupation. All of this takes place in the name of defending the freedom-hungry Czechoslovaks against the menace of "imperialism."

Prague

At 11 P.M., simultaneously with the ground invasion, the Soviet Ambassador to Prague, Stepan Chervonenko, drives to Hradčany Castle to inform President Svoboda. The white-haired retired general is waked up to receive the news that his Warsaw Pact allies have entered the country to save it from "anti-Socialist" and "counterrevolutionary" dangers. Soon afterward—on whose initiative it is never made clear—the pro-Soviet party secretary Alois Indra calls on Svoboda to propose a new cabinet with himself as prime minister. Svoboda throws him out of the office and hastens to the headquarters of the Czechoslovak Communist Party, an imposing riverbank building on the other side of the Moldau.

There, Alexander Dubček, first secretary of the Communist party and the leader of the country's newly-born reform movement, is chairing a meeting of the party's policy-making presidium. The subject of discussion is the Soviets' most recent demand to suppress "anti-Communist propaganda," as the expressions of Czechoslovakia's new freedom appear in Moscow. Prime Minister Oldřich Černik has just relayed to the presidium the telephone message he has received from Defense Minister Martin Dzur about the invasion. "This is a tragedy, I didn't expect this to happen," says the stunned and tearful Dubček. "That they should have done this to me, after I have dedicated my whole life to cooperation with the Soviet Union, is the great tragedy of my life."[2]

At the direction of the presidium, Svoboda issues an order to the Czech armed forces not to resist, which, in any case, in the face of overwhelming Soviet might, they are not attempting. The presidium agrees on a proclamation to the citizens, drafted by Ideological Secretary Zdeněk Mlynář, denouncing the invasion as "contrary to the fundamental principles of relations between socialist states and a denial of the basic norms of international law."[3] It is read over Prague radio beginning at 1:30 A.M. The conservative, pro-Soviet minority of the party presidium is evidently as surprised as anyone else by the invasion, but four of them nonetheless vote against the proclamation. Pro-Soviet officials cut off the main radio transmission for a time, but broadcasting of the proclamation resumes at 5 A.M. A counterbroadcast on "Radio Vltava" out of East Germany alleges that the invasion is only "assistance," at the "request" of "Party and Government leaders of the Czechoslovak Socialist Republic."[4] The heavy German accent makes the broadcast not only a travesty but an affront. In fact, no such "leaders" are ever identified, not even among the conservatives.

While the presidium is still in session, the Communist party chief for the city of Prague, Bohumil Šimon, presents Dubček with propositions for action: call an emergency meeting of the delegates, largely reformist, who have been elected to the forthcoming national congress of the party; launch a general strike; and issue an appeal to the Communist parties of the world. Dubček apparently agrees to the first idea, and Šimon immediately sets the wheels in motion for the congress to meet the following day, August 22. But Dubček is reluctant to provoke the Soviets with a strike and instead issues an appeal to the citizenry to remain calm and go about their normal work. This is broadcast by the still unfettered radio along with reports on the Soviet occupation.

Dubček's forbearance is not rewarded. His prime minister, Černik, soon after reaching his government office adjacent to Hradčany Castle to try to organize an emergency cabinet meeting, is arrested when paratroopers break into the building. They confiscate everyone's wristwatches and march Černik off at bayonet point. A little later, about 4:30 A.M., Soviet forces surround the party headquarters where Dubček and most of the presidium are still holding forth. Soviet officers, guided by Czech agents under orders from the Stalinists in the STB, find the presidium and place Dubček, National Assembly president Josef Smrkovský, František Kriegel, chairman of the "National Front," and party secretary Josef Spaček under detention in the building. They know who the potential collaborators are, to be left to go free—Indra, Slovak party chief Vasil Bilak, and Drahomir Kolder, an ostensible reformer who chaired the party commission that prepared the "Action Program" of April, the basic document of the Prague Spring. With others of their ilk, these favored individuals hurry to the Soviet Embassy to confer with Ambassador Chervonenko and General Pavlovsky. Svoboda has meanwhile returned to his residence at the castle, but it is soon sealed off by Soviet troops and he is, in effect, under house arrest. It is not until the afternoon that the Soviets decide what to do with Dubček and the others. They are painfully bound and taken in a Soviet armored car to the airport, whence they are flown (with Prime Minister Černik as well) to eastern Slovakia and then driven into the Soviet Union, treated like criminals all the way.

Meanwhile, by daybreak, crowds of Czech civilians alerted by the radio broadcasts or phone calls from friends and relatives pour into the streets of downtown Prague, shouting defiance at the occupiers who are now reinforced by heavy tanks that have driven the fifty miles from East Germany. The first shooting takes place as early as 5 A.M., when a crowd of protesters gathers in front of party headquarters where

Dubček is being held. Two youths trying to enter the premises are killed by automatic rifle fire and a third is crushed by a tank. Elsewhere crowds shout "Dubček, Dubček," and "Russians go home." Some Russian-speakers try to argue with the tank crews: "Why did you come? After all you are our friends. And friends do not come visiting armed."[5] The Soviet troops believe they have been invited, or think they are on maneuvers, or have the impression that they are occupying Nazi Germany. Others cannot answer at all because they do not understand Russian—they are Georgians from the Caucasus, or Central Asian Turks.

The occupying troops appear to be under great tension, and there is a good deal of nervous machine-gun fire by the tank crews. Perhaps fearing personal contact, the Soviets are trying to control the streets mainly with armor, without adequate infantry support, and the tanks are vulnerable to close-in crowd tactics, both psychological and physical. By and large the protesters are made up of the same kind of people —educated youth—who are rebelling against the Establishment both in the West and in China. They daub swastikas on the tanks, while graffiti go up everywhere: "We Condemn Soviet Fascism," "USSR = SS," "Russian Circus in Town! Do Not Feed the Animals!" "Make Love, Not War!" "We Shall Overcome."[6] Even the slogans recall the New Left in the West. But the Soviets are not just Paris or New York police: they respond to all this sporadically but brutally. Here and there even children who shake their fists are shot down by the tank gunners.

The confrontation becomes particularly serious around 7:30 A.M., when the Soviets figure out the location of Radio Prague on Vinohradská Street near the neo-baroque National Museum that stands at the head of Wenceslas Square. They send tanks there to stop the broadcasts. The crowd quickly fashions a barricade around an overturned bus. A tank rams the bus, which explodes, and the fire stops all the tanks. At this, youths rush the vehicles, shove burning paper into their exhaust pipes and through holes punched in their outside gas tanks, and set four or five of them on fire. Soviet paratroopers arrive in armored personnel carriers, firing wildly. All this is heard and reported on the still-functioning radio. When a tank antenna hits a trolley wire and sets off sparks, the whole company of tanks opens fire with its heavy guns at the National Museum, believing this totally peaceful monument to be the source of an attack. Altogether about thirty Czech civilians are killed during the day by the occupation forces, some in acts of resistance and others totally innocent bystanders. Hundreds of injured are taken to the city's hospitals. The extent of the dead and wounded among the invaders is not tabulated, but at least four Soviet soldiers are reported to have committed suicide out of chagrin for the situation they find themselves in.

Not until 11 A.M., against no military resistance whatever, are the occupation forces able to penetrate the radio building and stop the broadcasting. But by then the radio staff has arranged for stations in other cities to carry on national programming. Before long broadcasting is resumed in Prague from secret locations as the crews move around to avoid detection. The signal is picked up in West Germany and rebroadcast to the world on shortwave: "Vy poslouchajte legalní, svobodný, československý rozhlas" ("You are listening to the legal, free, Czechoslovakian Radio").

The invasion of Czechoslovakia is condemned all over the world, by Communist governments no less than non-Communist. All of the Communist regimes that are not Soviet puppets—Yugoslavia, Romania, Albania, and above all China—denounce the intervention, fearing a precedent that might be applied to themselves. Most of the Communist parties in democratic countries, particularly the powerful parties in Italy and France, condemn the action; the Stalinist remnant who make up the CP–USA stand out as apologists for it. Soviet dissidents are as angered by their country's action in Czechoslovakia as any foreign critics. Eighty-eight prominent writers sign a letter of protest: "Freedom today is being stifled not only in Czechoslovakia but in our country also."[7] Other than the governments directly involved in the intervention, only the North Koreans, the North Vietnamese, and the Cubans approve it. The Cuban case is significant because it testifies to the effectiveness of Soviet trade subsidies in pulling Castro out of the orbit of Peking and the insurrectionary Left that he has been flirting with.

In Washington, at 7 P.M. EDT on August 20, an hour after the ground invasion of Czechoslovakia has begun, the White House receives a phone call from Soviet Ambassador Anatoly Dobrynin asking for an immediate appointment. President Johnson is just about to accept a Soviet invitation to a summit meeting in Moscow in October to pursue nuclear arms talks. This is all scuttled when Dobrynin arrives at 8 P.M. to present the official Soviet story that Czechoslovakia "approached the allied states, the Soviet Union among them, with a request of rendering direct assistance."[8] Johnson calls an emergency meeting of the National Security Council for midnight, but nothing is decided, except to issue (in the words of *New York Times* correspondent Tad Szulc) "pious expressions of regret and condemnation."[9] Preoccupied militarily and politically with the war in Vietnam, Washington is holding its breath lest the Soviets move into Romania and Yugoslavia and create a real crisis.

The UN Security Council meets in emergency session the following day to debate the Czech crisis. A resolution condemning the Warsaw Pact action comes up for action on August 23, and wins ten votes against two (the Soviet Union and Hungary), with three Third-World abstentions (Algeria, India, and Pakistan). But the Soviet veto—their 105th—kills the legal effect of the resolution, which, in any case, is purely formal. Other than verbal expressions of outrage and token cutbacks in the cultural exchanges with the Soviets, the West does nothing. Czechoslovakia is clearly conceded to be part of the Soviet sphere of influence.

Despite the shock of the invasion and Prague's isolation from any effective international support, the decapitated Czech leadership tries to regroup. At 10 A.M., the presidium of the National Assembly convenes in emergency session with First Deputy Chairman Josef Valo presiding in place of Smrkovský, who has been arrested along with Dubček. The presidium calls a special meeting of the full assembly, issues a protest to the five occupying governments demanding an end to the occupation, and sends a delegation to the Soviet Embassy with this message. The Prague city committee of the Communist party meets to assume the functions of nationwide leadership now that the party's national headquarters building has been occupied, and pushes plans to convene the national party congress the next day. The leaders of the artistic unions —writers, artists, and musicians—meet and call for a two-minute protest strike at noon. Radio Prague immediately broadcasts the appeal, and at 12 o'clock all work and all movement in the city come to a halt, a response that conveys to the occupiers better than any words the unanimity of national resistance.

Shortly afterward, the cabinet manages to convene at Hradčany with the minister of consumer goods industry, Mme. Božena Machočová, in the chair in place of Černik. They back the proclamation of the assembly presidium and call the occupation "an illegal act, contrary to international law and the principles of socialist internationalism."[10] The foreign ministry cables its ambassadors in the Warsaw Pact capitals to present formal protests and to demand withdrawal of all troops. About the same time, over one hundred National Assembly deputies meet in response to the presidium's call and vote unanimously to affirm the position of their leadership against the occupation and to prepare the country for a general strike. From the political standpoint, the occupation has totally failed to break up the normal operation of the Czech government or to silence it as a national voice of resistance. More pleading than decreeing, the Soviet commander for the Prague region calls for a 10-to-5 curfew, a ban on public meetings, and censorship of all media.

In the evening, under the eyes of Soviet officers, a rump meeting of conservative members of the Communist Party Central Committee is held at the Praha Hotel. None appears willing to take responsibility for forming a quisling government despite prodding from Moscow on a direct phone line.

By the second day of the invasion, Thursday the 22nd, the Czechs have settled down to quiet defiance, while the occupiers continue to seek out and occupy newspaper offices and district party headquarters. They fail to prevent or even detect the convocation of the Extraordinary Fourteenth Congress of the Czechoslovak Communist Party, held in a factory in Prague's eastern industrial suburb of Vysočany. Over a thousand delegates, two-thirds of the total elected, are able to get to Prague and enter the meeting site disguised in ordinary workers' clothes. But only a half-dozen delegates from Slovakia are able to get through, which crimps the congress's national legitimacy. Working feverishly throughout the day, fearful of detection and dispersal at any moment, the congress issues a proclamation to the people denying any counter-revolution; adopts an appeal to the international Communist movement; draws up a letter of support to Dubček; and elects a new party presidium and Central Committee that exclude all known collaborators.

At noontime, a crowd of 20,000 mass in Wencelas Square (it is actually a boulevard, leading up to the National Museum). They stage a mass sit-down demonstration as whistles and horns throughout the city signal the beginning of an hour-long protest strike. For the moment, Prague is completely shut down in a manifestation of national solidarity against the occupiers.

Despite their political isolation, the Soviets keep trying to form a new government. All day at the Soviet Embassy, they negotiate inconclusively with the conservatives in the Czechoslovak Communist leadership, while the one liberal with the group, Mlynář, discovers that he can use Ambassador Chervonenko's private phone to keep the Vysočany congress informed of the proceedings. Finally, Chervonenko and conservative party presidium member Jan Piller go to President Svoboda to get his approval of a new "troika" of Indra, Bilak, and Kolder. Svoboda refuses even to discuss the matter until Dubček, Černik, and the others

194

are freed, and proposes a meeting of government chiefs. The Soviet leadership sees no alternative but to agree, and Svoboda takes off for Moscow Friday morning the 23rd, accompanied by the leading quisling candidates for power.

In the Soviet capital, Svoboda receives a ceremonial welcome, but he faces down General Secretary Brezhnev and Prime Minister Kosygin, refusing to deal until Dubček and the others are released. He even threatens to commit suicide. At midnight, Brezhnev backs down and agrees to allow the interned leaders to join in the talks and then return to Prague to their posts. The price he demands in return is acceptance of a permanent Soviet garrison in Czechoslovakia and a rollback of the Prague Spring reforms.

In the meantime, national resolve in Czechoslovakia stiffens even more. This time the noon protest strike, called by the secret party congress, extends nationwide. To confuse the enemy, road signs are taken down all over the country; in Prague, street names and even house numbers are removed or painted over. Occupation units lack adequate maps and often cannot find their assigned objectives. The cabinet meets under Deputy Prime Minister Lubomir Strougal and takes the amazing step of ousting the traitorous security chief Šalgovič. The loyal interior minister Josef Pavel comes out of hiding to take charge of the police, and orders the dismissal of all security officers who collaborated with the invasion.

Negotiations between the Soviets and the full Czech leadership begin in Moscow on Saturday the 24th and continue through Monday. Svoboda and Dubček are hamstrung by the presence of the Czech conservatives and a blackout on news from home. It is brinkmanship on both sides as Brezhnev bluntly warns that Prague will be bombarded if the Czechs do not submit to his demands. This is no idle threat, in view of the Hungarian precedent of 1956 and the 70,000 Soviet troops with hundreds of tanks and heavy artillery pieces concentrated in Prague itself, plus nearly a quarter million elsewhere in the country (soon to reach a half million). What Brezhnev wants above all is for the Czech leaders to agree that Prague's policies will be changed to accord with the Soviet type of dictatorial socialism and to declare that "there was a counterrevolution," along with the reimposition of censorship and the ouster of the most anti-Soviet ministers.[11]

Unbeknownst to the Czech negotiators, while the confrontation is in progress a small group of courageous Soviet dissidents (including Pavel Litvinov, grandson of the long-time Soviet foreign commissar) attempt to stage a protest demonstration in Red Square. They recognize the affinity of the Prague Spring with their own hopes for reform. So do the Soviet authorities: KGB agents swoop in, beat up the protesters, and take them away for trial and Siberia. The episode ushers in a new stage of repression in the Soviet Union.

Inside the Kremlin, Svoboda does the best he can in a game where he has no cards save world opinion. He refuses to concede on "counter-revolution" and persuades the Soviets to agree to remove their security agents as well as their troops when "normalization" has been completed. Otherwise, undermined by the "realists," like the Slovak deputy prime minister Gustav Husak, who want to keep their jobs, Svoboda caves in. The Soviet demands are glossed over in a joint communiqué that the Czechs have to sign, testifying to "a free, comradely discussion."[12] It is left to Moscow to determine what "normalization" means before withdrawing its forces.

Early in the morning on Tuesday the 27th, the Czech leaders take off from Moscow, physically and emotionally wrung out. At the last minute, the Soviets try to keep Kriegel as a hostage—Brezhnev particularly hates him because he is Jewish—and Svoboda refuses to leave until Kriegel is released to depart with them. They arrive at Ruzyně at 6 A.M. Czech time, just as Soviet tanks are withdrawing their most obtrusive presence around government buildings in Prague. The Czech leaders are back to resume the posts from which they were so rudely snatched less than a week before, but in reality they are still prisoners, even though the walls of their jail have been widened to include the whole country. The long, agonizing, disheartening, and demoralizing process of Soviet-style "normalization" is about to begin.

Czechoslovakia, a land of flowering nationhood during the Middle Ages, has had a tragic history of the foreigner's heavy heel ever since the Thirty Years' War. Independence from the Austrians, finally gained with Woodrow Wilson's blessing in 1918, gave way in a few short years to betrayal at Munich and the Nazi occupation. Liberation in 1945— mainly by the Red Army with assists from General Patton's army in the west and from the German-sponsored corps of anti-Communist Russians near Prague who tried to change sides at the end—was followed all too quickly by the Communist coup of 1948. This tragedy ushered in a one-party Stalinist police state under Klement Gottwald, which went so far as to purge the idealists in the Communist party's own ranks. Among those arrested in 1951 were the future Prague Spring president

Svoboda and the turncoat who took over after Dubček, Gustav Husak. The following year, Prague was the scene of the notorious show trial in which the fallen Communist party boss Rudolf Slánský and a host of other party and government officials were found guilty of a Zionist-CIA conspiracy, and hanged.

The Stalinist regime in Prague, once cemented in place by the purges, survived all the turmoil of the 1950s that afflicted other Soviet satellites, above all Hungary and Poland, as well as Khrushchev's Russia. Gottwald, dead in 1953 soon after Stalin himself, was replaced by Antonin Novotný, a one-time mechanic and career Communist bureaucrat. Until 1964, Novotný ruled the abject nation without major incident. Nevertheless, the winds of de-Stalinization were felt a bit in Czechoslovakia, as the surviving victims of the purges of the early 1950s were released and rehabilitated. In 1962, as a sop to public feeling, Novotný ordered the demolition of the huge statue of Stalin in the Letna Park overlooking the Moldau—the world's largest Stalin monument. In 1963, an investigation of the Slánský trial (conducted by the same Drahomir Kolder who turned pro-Moscow in 1968) officially determined that the purge was based on a frame-up, and Novotný felt compelled to weed the worst Stalinists out of the Communist leadership. One beneficiary of the shakeup was Dubček, the Soviet-educated son of a Communist family who had risen as a career party functionary showing no taint of liberalism. He became head of the party in Slovakia and effectively the number-three man in the country. The economy, suffering from Soviet-style centralization and the heavy-industry complex, actually went into decline.

Along with the political echoes of de-Stalinization in Czechoslovakia, a modest relaxation in party control allowed the nation's irrepressively creative intellectuals—always in the vanguard of reform in Communist countries—to put truth ahead of dogma. After 1962, the academic disciplines began a remarkable recovery; the writers got permission to read Kafka and the historians got permission to read Trotsky. The Writers' Union became a solid force for reform, culminating in the congress of June 1967, when Milan Kundera and other illustrious authors openly called for full freedom to publish. Like the Western New Left, Czechoslovak philosophers went back to the young Marx as a source of inspiration, and from him and Kafka developed the proposition that bureaucratic social organization could be responsible for a sense of alienation even under socialism.

And alienation was exactly what was afflicting Czechoslovak youth and students. Their protest through apathy, reflected in their precipitous abandonment of the official youth organization in the mid-1960s, recalled American university students in the 1950s. The Western youth culture complete with jazz and blue jeans invaded Czechoslovakia with a rush. Even Prague officials came to refer to the students as a class in themselves. By October 1964, students were rioting against Communism in Wenceslas Square.

Novotný's fatal mistake came a few days later. Alerted by early reports of Khrushchev's troubles in Moscow, he got his signals wrong and rushed a telegram off in support of the man who was just being deposed. Brezhnev never forgave him.

From this point on, with Novotný's authority weakening, a broad, snowballing reform movement got underway among the younger officials of the party, abetted by the restless intellectuals. The situation—politically, economically, and intellectually—was remarkably similar to the Soviet Union in the last years of Brezhnev two decades later, and the outcome had its parallel there as well. Ota Šik, head of the party's Economic Commission, worked out plans for a "New Economic Model" on the Yugoslav lines of marketizing and decentralizing the Stalin-style planned economy. Mlynář, a lawyer who had been Mikhail Gorbachev's roommate at Moscow State University, took charge of the Academy of Sciences' "New Political Model Commission," and reported that economic reform required political reform as well as intellectual freedom.

Novotný began to lose his personal grip when, in June 1967, he enthusiastically joined the Soviet bloc's break with Israel over the Six-Day War. His stance was widely unpopular in Czechoslovakia and was immediately challenged by the Writers' Union. Shortly afterward, the Writers' Congress heard charges that Stalinism had set the nation's development back as seriously as the Nazi occupation, and listened to a reading of Alexander Solzhenitsyns's unpublished letter denouncing censorship in the Soviet Union. Speakers openly attacked the mediocrity and narrow-mindedness of the Novotný regime. Novotný struck back by purging the leadership of the Writers' Union, firing pro-reform editors, and expelling his chief intellectual critics from the party, but he was unable to stop the growing strength and boldness of the dissenters. Meanwhile, bureaucratic resistance to Šik's reform aggravated the country's economic slump.

In the fall, Novotný's political position rapidly deteriorated. The Slovaks were being alienated by his centralist disdain for their national sensitivities, and this primed Slovak chief Dubček to take the lead in the anti-Novotný forces at an acrimonious meeting of the party Central Committee in October.

Like so much of the turmoil around the world during these times, it was a student movement that precipitated the final crisis of the Novotný regime. On the evening of October 31, a power failure in the dorms of the Czech Technical College in the Strahov district west of Hradčany Castle prompted the students there to protest the chronic failures of heat and electricity in their buildings. They poured out onto the streets and started to march downhill toward the Moldau bridges and the center of town. They had not gone far, however, when the police attacked them and, as police so often did these days in the West as well, went wild with their clubs and tear gas. The clash set off an escalating spiral of university protests and sit-ins, as well as open debate about individual rights. By December, Novotný was ready to back down and accede to the students' demands, but his regime had been fundamentally delegitimized. It did not save itself by giving permission for Prague's first big rock music festival, held just before Christmas with all the lights and accouterments of San Francisco.

Ambassador Chervonenko became so concerned by this time over the political corner into which Novotný had painted himself that he got Brezhnev to come in person to Prague to resolve the crisis. For the Soviet leader this was an opportunity to settle the old scores with Novotný that had rankled him ever since they had clashed over Khrushchev three years before. He pulled the political rug out from under Novotný and tacitly endorsed Dubček as the next Czechoslovak leader.

Anticipating dismissal by the Central Committee after Brezhnev's intervention, Novotný actually laid plans for a military coup. Unfortunately for him, word leaked out, the plot failed, and the anti-Novotný forces were stiffened all the more. After two more weeks of confrontation and maneuver in the party presidium, the body voted on 4 January 1968 to remove Novotný as first secretary of the party in favor of Alexander Dubček. The revolution had begun.

Or so it became clear in retrospect, though the upheaval in Czechoslovakia's life made possible by the fall of Novotný began quite imperceptibly. Czechoslovakia was still a one-party state, and although the Communist party's top leadership in the party presidium and Central Committee was now more collective than individual, those bodies were still full of Stalinist conservatives prone to look on any fundamental change with great trepidation. Novotný himself was kept on for the time being as titular president. Nevertheless, liberal writers and journalists responded to the Novotný ouster with a call to end the censorship, and reformers among the party leadership began to speak out for democratization of the country's political life.

Dubček was an enigmatic personality, idealistic and naive but at heart a compromiser, who had nonetheless successfully worked his way up the Communist party hierarchy all through the Stalinist era. Shocked by further evidence of the Stalinist repressions of the 1950s that he had never seen until he reached the pinnacle of power, he acceded to all the demands of the reformers. As early as February 1, he announced that the new "Action Program" for the party, promised at the time he was elevated to the leadership, would be ready shortly. A draft of the Action Program, prepared by reformist theoreticians in the party, was approved by the presidium on February 19 and circulated for public discussion.

This fifty-page policy guide was an extraordinary document, considering the brief time in which it was drawn up and sold to the party leadership.[13] Reading like a manifesto of democracy, the program called for guarantees of freedom of speech, press, assembly, and travel, and rejected the long-standing Communist proposition that the party should keep firm control of all other institutions in society. It proposed restrictions on the secret police, complete cultural freedom, and economic reform based on the "socialist market" and autonomy of enterprises, with democratic workers' councils in charge of each unit (similar to Yugoslavia's heretical brand of Communism). All in all, the Action Program was a head-on repudiation of the Soviet pattern of central command in politics, economics, and everything else, though it promised to observe Czechoslovakia's alliance with the Soviet Union in the spirit of "anti-imperialist" unity. It prefigured everything in the Soviet reform campaign under Gorbachev two decades later.

The response to the Action Program was an outpouring of debate, letters, and resolutions. As realization soaked in of the new and broader scope that the Dubček regime was allowing in speech and press, a true public opinion began to take shape. Mlynář recalls:

There was a growing sense of a national resurgence, of a national destiny . . . , the sudden joy at the end of a long period of despair, at the end of oppression, and the feeling of a new beginning. . . . A new and powerful factor appeared on the scene of the Prague Spring: the feeling that the nation as a whole was involved. . . . It was a huge public forum of hopes and desires, in which private and political hopes merged and gave rise to a kind of festive atmosphere. . . .[14]

From this time on the public mood moved ahead of the political leadership. Reform acquired a momentum of its own that proved impossible to control once the old methods of repression were abandoned.

Just as this new political ferment was beginning to brew, the party conservatives were rocked by a scandal. Novotný's plan of the previous autumn to stage a military coup was made public, and his key party agent in the defense ministry, General Jan Šejna, defected to the West. (In the United States, Sejna became a major intelligence source on Communist bloc espionage operations and later published a sensationalist book, *We Will Bury You*.) These events served as the signal for a more uninhibited implementation of reform by the new leadership. Conservative officials, particularly in security and cultural jobs, were replaced, and the National Assembly came back to life as a real legislative forum instead of its previous rubber-stamp role typical of Communist regimes. More victims of the Stalinist era were rehabilitated, dead or alive. The founder of the Czechoslovak Republic, Thomas Masaryk, was revived as a national hero, and inquiry was undertaken into the circumstances of the alleged suicide of his son, Foreign Minister Jan Masaryk, at the time of the Communist coup in 1948. Climaxing this phase was Novotný's resignation from the titular presidency in late March, and his replacement by the former defense minister and onetime purge victim, General Svoboda. (Svoboda was confirmed by the National Assembly on March 30 in a truly contested vote, 288 to 282—something unprecedented in a Communist country.)

On March 28, the full 150-member Central Committee of the Czechoslovak Communist Party convened for the first time since Dubček took over, meeting (as was the custom) in the ornate seventeenth-century Spanish Hall in Hradčany Castle. The week-long session proved to be a decisive event. Dubček chose this opportunity to announce the publication of the final version of the Action Program, in a speech on April 1 that was as rousing as his habitual Marxist jargon would permit. "The . . . deeper sense of the program," he declaimed, "lies in the fact that it opens scope for basic structural changes in our society and for the creation of a new dynamic of socialism."[15] "Socialism with a human face," it would soon be called.

In addition to adopting the Action Program officially, the Central

Committee took concrete steps to bring the party and government into line with the new political winds. It voted a major revamping of the party's guiding bodies, the presidium and the secretariat, removing Novotný and some of his adherents and promoting pro-Dubček liberals, Smrkovský and Kriegel among them. Central Committee recommendations were reflected a few days later in a corresponding reorganization of the government, when the incumbent prime minister and many cabinet members had to resign in favor of the new reformist prime minister Černik and other fresh faces, including Smrkovský as president of the revitalized National Assembly. These steps put in place the key leadership of the Prague Spring. Unfortunately, the reform forces were not yet strong enough to eliminate all their enemies from the party and governmental leadership, and left the conservatives still in a position to undercut Dubček and play the quisling when the time came to stand up to the Soviets. But it was truly an inexplicable blunder that Dubček allowed the appointment of Šalgovič, known in the inner circle as a Soviet agent ever since World War II, to be deputy interior minister and chief of the secret police.

Czechoslovakia's revolution in 1968 was a unique affair, truly revolutionary in the changes that took place in public values and in the basis of authority, but carried through without a hint of civic disorder or violence. Like the movements of a considerably more disruptive and confrontational character upsetting the nations of the West and China as well, it was above all a youth revolution, spearheaded by the student generation and young intellectuals thirsting for political and cultural freedom. The passion that the Prague Spring brought out among youth, and the fervor of their support for their hero Dubček, strikingly resembled the hope and excitement that simultaneously stirred Americans of the same age group about Bobby Kennedy and Gene McCarthy. Prague night-life took on a zest that almost rivaled Greenwich Village and San Francisco. The official Czechoslovakian Union of Youth finally collapsed and independent student organizations filled part of the vacuum, though the younger age group often turned out to be skeptical of any organization whatsoever. The Prague Spring was thus sociologically akin to the Western New Left, even though in the political and ideological realm it settled for those bourgeois liberties of conscience and expression that New Left radicals were in the habit of disparaging.

The connection between the Prague Spring and antiauthoritarian movements in the West and in China was more a coincidental parallel than a direct tie. The Czechoslovaks were fighting for rights well established in the West—individual freedom and real national independence—that their country had not enjoyed since before World War II (except for the false hopes of the first postwar years). Nor was there any anarchic revolution within the revolution as in China. On the other hand, the original push for reform leading up to the Prague Spring came from the same kind of people who supported the New Left in the West—not the workers, but the students and the bolder intellectuals, those who felt most keenly that the existing system was a sell-out. On the eve of 1968, writes Z. A. B. Zeman, "Young people found it hard to understand the moral turpitude of their elders. They felt that something incredible, discreditable, was going on in the world of authority."[16]

Their focus on the more conventional understanding of freedom perhaps accounts for the fact that the young Czechoslovak revolutionaries enjoyed broad sympathy and solidarity among ordinary people, in contrast to the alienation that set their Western counterparts apart from the masses most of the time. To be sure, workers and farmers at first reacted to Dubček more slowly and more skeptically, until they began to realize that the reform philosophy meant more voice over their own destiny in the enterprises and on the collective farms. May Day, 1968, saw a great burst of spontaneous enthusiasm for the new regime. Brief strikes, still technically illegal, became common, and sometimes they were even supported by reformist party organizations against the still stodgy state managers. Older workers, veterans of the Workers' Militia who had backed up the Communist coup twenty years before, remained more skeptical, and the Stalinist conservatives were always able to find some support there.

The major development affecting industrial labor was the workers' councils movement, sketched out in the Action Program and endorsed in principle by the cabinet in June, despite foot-dragging by the old official trade-unions who saw their power threatened. Prior to the Soviet intervention, actual councils were formed at the Škoda works in Pilsen and a few other large enterprises, though they had no legally defined role. Interestingly enough, the intervention did not stop the spread of the council movement up until early 1969, when the government actually published a draft law on enterprise autonomy empowering enterprise councils to elect the director and approve plans and policies. This was the high-water mark. The new law was never put in force, and Soviet-style "normalization" soon crushed this experiment in industrial democracy.

One of the most welcome aspects of the Prague Spring was the revival it permitted of all the normal civic organizations and movements—religious, professional, cultural, political—that had been caught in the party's grip and turned into the transmission belts of totalitarian rule. Czechoslovakia had been unique among Communist countries in its policy of controlling and paying for the churches rather than trying to suppress them outright. Under the new freedom, the churches, above all the majority Catholics, were permitted to express their resentment of governmental restraints. The Dubček leadership responded with promises of "respect for freedom of religion, profession and conviction,"[17] but this reform also came to grief after intervention and normalization. The unions of writers and journalists, of course, had already been hotbeds of reform agitation well before Novotný's fall. They stood in the forefront of the reform movement all through 1968, and gave the reformers overwhelming dominance of the country's media once they were allowed free rein. Non-Communist political parties had survived ever since 1948—the Socialists and the Catholic Czech People's Party, plus two Slovak parties—but only as dummies controlled by the Communists and assigned a few parliamentary seats as members of the so-called National Front in single-slate elections. Now—a decisive sign of emergent political pluralism—the non-Communists revived and began to talk about freeing the National Front from unilateral Communist direction, as long as everybody abided by the principles of socialism. Even former prison camp inmates formed their own autonomous association, "Club 231," from the number of the 1948 law authorizing political prosecutions. Needless to say, all these developments put the Communist conservatives in fear of the collapse of everything they had devoted their lives to; worse, the new movements even made many Communist reformers nervous.

Was the Prague Spring really a part of the worldwide Sixties Revolution or only a side issue, an effort by beleaguered subjects of Soviet imperialism to recover some of the same bourgeois values that the young radicals of the West and the Far East hoped to overthrow? It was both at the same time. It was certainly no spectacle of countercultural defiance against national tradition, though it did—like moderates of the stripe of Martin Luther King—try to hold the powers that be to the best principles in their own espoused lexicon. Timewise, the Prague Spring happened to fall in the middle of a closely linked sequence of youthful protest movements that rocked Western Europe, America, and the Far

East during the late 1960s. There was an affinity of spirit even though the ideologies of protest varied tremendously from one country to another—from the war- and race-based protest of the Americans, to the ultra-Left antielitism of the Europeans and the Chinese, to the pathetic quest for democratic freedoms in the Soviet satellites of Eastern Europe. Polish students, stirred by the two-fold example of the West German student disruptions and political reform in Czechoslovakia, rioted in Warsaw in March and took over the university; the Gomulka government cracked down with thousands of police and workers' militia and blamed the entire trouble on "Zionism." Yugoslav students in Belgrade and Zagreb, as noted in chapter 7, kicked over the traces in June, and met with what was for the time being a much kinder response; Tito, worried more about the Soviet threat to his independence than about domestic rebels, promised reforms and proceeded with a real decentralization of power among the country's constituent republics. Without prejudice to its own values, the Prague Spring was part of an extraordinary international process.

As the Prague Spring unfolded with the new foliage of the season, outside as well as inside the government, the oligarchs in Moscow began to realize that the leadership shake-up in Czechoslovakia they had condoned in January was getting out of hand. As early as February, the Soviet defense ministry started making contingency plans for a possible military intervention. Novotný's resignation from the Czech presidency on March 22 sounded an urgent alarm, and the Soviets, responding to entreaties from the nervous East German and Polish governments, decided that Dubček had to be called back from his dangerous experiment with freedom. The very next day, March 23, Dubček was summoned along with his top associates to a meeting in Dresden in East Germany with the Warsaw Pact leaders, the same infamous five— Brezhnev of the Soviet Union, Ulbricht of the GDR, Gomulka of Poland, Kadar of Hungary, and Zhivkov of Bulgaria—who collaborated in the August invasion. Romania's Ceauşescu, a maverick in his foreign policy for the past four years, was not invited.

"The decision to call the Dresden meeting," observes the international affairs analyst Karen Dawisha, "marked the real beginning of the crisis."[18] Dubček was put on trial before his nominal allies to defend himself against the charge that "negative processes" and "anti-socialist tendencies" were endangering Communist party control in Czechoslovakia.[19] The Soviets warned him of "developments that could lead to a counterrevolutionary coup." Ulbricht bluntly stated what all the bloc leaders feared: "If the January line is continued in Czechoslovakia, all of us here will be running into great danger. We may all find ourselves kicked out."[20] Although the communiqué issued by this bloc summit papered over the cracks with "confidence" in "the further development of socialist construction in the country," Dubček had received a clear warning of the limits that his neighbors would tolerate. From this early moment, the whole Prague Spring was darkened by the ominous cloud of potential Soviet interference.

As the leadership shake-ups, reforms, and energized public opinion of the Dubček era continued to gather momentum, the Politburo in Moscow decided to take demonstrative action while still keeping its ultimate options open. Marshal Ivan Yakubovsky, the Soviet commander of all Warsaw Pact forces, turned up in Prague late in April to propose combined maneuvers of bloc military forces in Czechoslovakia. Early in May, Dubček was summoned to Moscow on only a few hours notice to account for himself again. "We realized they weren't interested in the facts," Smrkovský recalled, "but were looking for pretexts to oppose us."[21] Nevertheless, reporting to the National Assembly on the mission, Smrkovský asserted that "no force, whether international or domestic" would stop the creation in Czechoslovakia of a "humanist, democratic, and socialist society."[22] But the conservative Slovak leader Bilak, also a member of the delegation to Moscow, afterward expressed the Soviet concern in the sharpest terms: "To permit Czechoslovakia to fall out of the socialist [Communist] camp would mean the betrayal of socialism and the annulling of the results of the second world war . . . , and this they could not *permit* even at the cost of a third world war."[23]

In mid-May, while the Dresden Five met in Moscow without the Czechs, a Soviet military delegation followed by Premier Kosygin and Defense Minister Marshal Grechko came to Prague to firm up arrangements for the Warsaw Pact maneuvers. Kosygin's conciliatory stance persuaded the Czech leaders to agree to the maneuvers, starting May 30 and continuing for a month. But Kosygin was in a minority against the hawks of the Politburo. Showing their disdain for the niceties of agreements, the Soviet visitors came ahead of time—simultaneously with the next meeting of the Czech Central Committee—and left late. The operation was supposed to be a "staff exercise," but the Soviets brought in 15,000 troops, laden with communications gear and accompanied by tanks and aircraft, which the Czechs had not expected. The twin objectives of political pressure and reconnoitering for the intervention were more than obvious, and to make the message even clearer, the Soviets and their subservient allies concentrated as many as 300,000 troops on Czechoslovakia's borders. Undeterred, the Czech Communist Central Committee met in Prague to advance the reform agenda by suspending Novotný from the party and calling an emergency party congress for September, when presumably it would deal with the conservatives still entrenched in the party leadership. The National Assembly formally repealed the censorship law.

Then, on the 27th of June came the step that inflamed the Soviets beyond the point of no return. This event, brandishing the red flag to the Muscovite bull, was the publication of a manifesto by the writer Ludvik Vaculik on behalf of his scientific friends, which soon became known as the "Two Thousand Words." The document was a concise denunciation of the record of Communist rule in Czechoslovakia, described as "very attractive . . . to egotists avid for rule, calculating cowards, and unprincipled people." It concluded with a skeptical appraisal of the Dubček reforms and an assertion that the nation was ready to fight for its government if "foreign forces . . . interfere with our development," as the country continued to cleanse itself of "people who have misused their power."[24]

Moscow immediately took the "Two Thousand Words" as a challenge to the "leading role" of the Communist party in Czechoslovakia and "a platform for further activization of counterrevolutionary actions."[25] Within minutes after Czech newspapers came out with the manifesto, an enraged Brezhnev personally telephoned Dubček to demand an explanation, and reached him before he had even read the text himself. Pressured at his own end by the conservatives still in the party leadership, Dubček gave in and allowed the party presidium to condemn the "Two Thousand Words" as a "clear threat to the entire democratization process"[26]—at the very moment that the "Two Thousand Words" was attracting thousands of signatures and mobilizing unprecedented public enthusiasm for the Dubček government. "If anything," writes Karen Dawisha, "the party's heavy-handed reaction probably increased popular sympathy for the manifesto," and stimulated the election of pro-reform delegates to the forthcoming party congress.[27] From this point on, the prospects were dim that either side would turn back. Before the "Two Thousand Words" appeared, the position of the Soviets was that they *might* have to intervene if in their view the situation in Czechoslovakia worsened; after the "Two Thousand Words," they were *certain* they would have to intervene unless the situation improved.

While the Soviet forces in Czechoslovakia dragged out their scheduled June 30 withdrawal after the maneuvers, Moscow called another summit of the Warsaw Pact leadership. This time Dubček turned bold; he refused to attend or even to bring the Czech leadership to a bilateral meeting with the Soviets. The pact members warned the Czechs more ominously than ever:

> The offensive of the reactionary forces . . . threatens to push your country off the road of socialism and thus jeopardizes the interests of the entire socialist system. . . . A decisive rebuff to the forces of anti-Communism and decisive efforts to preserve the socialist system in Czechoslovakia are not only your task but ours too.[28]

The Soviet Central Committee was called together immediately to ratify the hard line on Czechoslovakia, and on July 20–21 (according to the circumstantial evidence assembled by Dawisha), the Politburo approved preparations for a full-scale invasion if Dubček did not reverse his course. As a test of his intentions, Ambassador Chervonenko was instructed to demand the permanent stationing of Soviet troops on Czech territory.[29] The "Brezhnev Doctrine," as it later came to be known in the West, was by now fully formulated.

Perhaps to satisfy the Kremlin skeptics, including Kosygin and chief ideologist Mikhail Suslov, perhaps to give Dubček one last chance (even though he had evaded the troop question), Brezhnev agreed in late July to bring the Politburo to Czechoslovakia. The two sides met on July 29, in the little Slovakian town of Čierna nad Tisou, just over the border from the Soviet-ruled Carpatho-Ukraine. The exchanges between them for the next four days were anything but amicable, as harsh Soviet charges were met by stubborn Czech defenses. Finally, Dubček backed down again, assuring his Big Brothers that he would preserve Communist party rule and curb anti-Soviet statements in the Czechoslovak press.

Superficially, the Čierna agreement was sufficient to justify yet another Warsaw Pact Summit, this time within Czechoslovakia itself, in Bratislava. At this point—on August 3—the bloc appeared to give ground, desisting from their charges of counterrevolution and the open threat to intervene, although they alluded again to "the common international duty of all the socialist countries."[30] In all probability the Soviet leaders had already made up their minds (while conferring during the Čierna talks when they withdrew to Soviet territory each night) that Dubček and his supporters would not really get into line and that intervention had become a necessity. This position was apparently confirmed at a formal Politburo meeting on August 6, immediately after the Soviet leaders returned to Moscow from Čierna.[31] Thus, Bratislava and the days that followed represented a tactic of dissimulation intended to encourage the Czechs to relax while the Soviets waited for the most appropriate moment to move.

The moment came sooner, perhaps, than Moscow expected. To a tumultuous welcome, Marshal Tito of Yugoslavia arrived in Prague on August 9 for a two-day state visit to manifest his support for Czechoslovakia's reform and independence. That and the impending visit of Romania's President Ceauşescu, also to show solidarity with Czechoslovakia's resistance to Moscow, were too much for the Soviets, who saw the prospect of losing the whole southern side of their East European defense system to a bloc of independent Communist neutrals. On August 17, despite last-minute efforts at mediation by Hungary's Janos Kadar and an agreement to restrain the reformers that he wrung out of Dubček, the Politburo put the plan in motion to invade on August 20.[32]

When word of the Soviet intervention was flashed around the world on August 21, the reaction was one of outrage all across the political spectrum. Governments from the beleaguered Johnson administration in Washington to the Maoist utopians in Peking condemned the act as naked Soviet imperialism. Practically every Communist government and party not directly under the Kremlin's thumb joined the chorus of criticism. Soviet ideological secretary Suslov was proven correct in his fear that intervention would ultimately result in a net loss to Soviet international influence. Yet for all the moral condemnation of the Soviet move from so many different quarters, no one was prepared to risk triggering World War III over the opportunity to roll back the Soviet empire just a little bit.

Within Czechoslovakia itself the immediate aftermath of the Soviet intervention was an unprecedented paradox. Czechoslovakia was an occupied country, yet the authority of its reform government and the popular loyalty it commanded were undiminished. The unanimous support for Dubček and the hesitation of the Czech conservatives to present themselves as an alternative government spelled the failure, for the time being, of the Soviet plan to create a puppet regime.

Could the Soviets have lived with this anomalous situation, now that the presence of their troops took care of any real security concerns they might have had? Or were the subsequent "salami tactics," to cut up Czechoslovakia's reform regime a little at a time, the inevitable outcome of Soviet military dominance? Immediately after returning from Moscow, Dubček and his associates resumed their domestic agenda of reform. Some of the Czech participants in the invasion conspiracy were actually demoted or fired from their jobs, and the new Communist Central Committee chosen at the underground party congress elected a strongly liberal presidium. On the other hand, the Soviets secured the removal of the economic reformer Šik and some of the liberals in the media, and began cultivating possible compromisers in the Dubček regime, particularly Prime Minister Černik and the new chief of the party in Slovakia, Husak. These Soviet moves were capped by an article in *Pravda* on September 26 making the "Brezhnev Doctrine" official:

> The weakening of any of the links in the world system of socialism directly affects all the socialist countries, which cannot look indifferently upon this. . . . The Communists of the fraternal countries [sic] could not allow the socialist states to be inactive in the name of an abstractly understood sovereignty, when they saw that the country stood in peril of antisocialist degeneration.[33]

In plainer language, no country still within the Soviet sphere of influence would be allowed to work its way free of the Stalinist kind of life and rule that the Kremlin felt necessary to be secure in its control of the region.

Subjected to incessant Soviet pressure, coupled with the dangling carrot of a Soviet troop withdrawal, Dubček gave in bit by bit to the demands of Moscow and the Czech conservatives. He allowed the Central Committee plenum in November to authorize a new "Executive Committee" of eight men within the party presidium, thereby isolating himself in a group dominated by the conservatives and the compromisers. Meanwhile, popular resentment of the Soviets erupted more and more frequently into open demonstrations. It was, in fact, impossible for Dubček to satisfy both Moscow and his own people. The end of his rule under the occupation was only a matter of time.

The last crisis began in January 1969, when a Czech student by the name of Jan Palach burned himself to death like a Vietnamese monk in Wencelas Square. The resulting manifestation of mass outrage was like August 1968 all over again. Then, on the 28th of March came the last straw. The Czech national hockey team beat the Soviets 4–3, and the crowd went on a nationalist rampage, burning Soviet vehicles and sacking the Aeroflot office in Prague. The Soviets responded with naked threats of intervention and successfully demanded the restoration of censorship and rigorous crowd control. Then, in mid-April, Moscow threw its backing to Husak to get Dubček out of office. On April 17, Dubček handed in his resignation as general secretary of the party and Husak immediately claimed the position.

From this point on the liquidation of the Prague Spring was a sad but inexorable saga of crackdowns on the reformers. Liberals were removed one after another from the party leadership, from the government, and from the media, often to be replaced by officials straight out of the Novotný regime. Late in 1969, Dubček was deprived of his Central Committee seat and given the consolation post of ambassador to Turkey. Shortly afterward, the vacillating Černik was rewarded for his contribution to "normalization" by removal from the post of prime minister. In May 1970, Dubček was recalled from Turkey, expelled from the Communist party altogether, and assigned to a clerical job in a Slovakian factory. Czechoslovakia's version of the new worldwide experiment in idealistic freedom against power and fear had finally come to a close. All that can be said for the gloomy outcome is that there were no more trials and hangings.

10

Chicago

1:00 P.M., WEDNESDAY, AUGUST 28, a hot sunny afternoon. It is the day after Dubček was allowed to return from Moscow to pick up the nominal reins of government in Czechoslovakia, and the third day of the Democratic National Convention. Down at the Chicago stockyards five miles south of the Loop, the more than three thousand delegates and hundreds of alternates are gathering for this crucial session of the conclave. They have to queue up to get past the machines that check their credential cards and admit them into the huge International Amphitheater where the formal convention proceedings take place. The security ordered by Mayor Richard Daley and the Convention Arrangements Committee, with guards everywhere and masses of police and barbed wire outside the hall, makes the place seem more like a concentration camp than a forum of national deliberation. David Brinkley comments, "You have a great cumbersome machine set down here in the middle of Chicago's stockyards, 5000-odd delegates invited here to take part in the Party's most serious ritual, and then nobody would allow them to say anything. They were treated as if they had been led over here from one of those sheep pens."[1] With the aid of a public transportation and taxi strike, the Amphitheater has been sealed off from downtown Chicago; no protest demonstrations are allowed anywhere near the neighborhood and delegates can only get to the convention on the official buses from their hotels. Daley's personnel have little sense of humor—when the New Hampshire McCarthy leader David Hoeh demonstrates that his Dartmouth ID card will work the credential machines, they beat him up. Dan Rather and other eminent press representatives experience the same treatment when they incur the ire of the forces of law and order.

Seating of states in the hall has been arranged in direct relation to each delegation's loyalty to Mayor Daley and the Johnson-Humphrey administration. Illinois, Texas, and Minnesota are prominently in front; New York and California with their unreconstructed McCarthy and Kennedy partisans are in the rear. Dissidence on the floor is thereby concentrated.

After an evening and a day of ceremony and credentials wrangling, the convention is getting down to its main business of adopting the platform this afternoon, and of balloting on the presidential nominee during prime time in the evening. A boomlet for Teddy Kennedy, the last of the dynasty, has risen and collapsed, and Senator McCarthy has conceded that he cannot make it himself, so there is little for the anti-Johnson forces to rally round except the matter of the party platform, specifically the Vietnam plank. The Vietnam debate, with alternating speakers on each side, runs all afternoon. The Kennedy people argue that the war must be ended because of its cost to American society. Arguments for the pro-Johnson majority version range from support of our forces in the field to disparagement of the demonstrators in downtown Chicago. The floor vote on Vietnam, a foregone conclusion, presages the outcome of the evening ballot—1,567¾ for the majority plank, 1,041¼ for the minority. As the convention is adjourning for a meal, a tumult erupts at the New York and California center of floor opposition, when the delegates in the back of the hall join in singing "We Shall Overcome."

Meanwhile, more serious trouble is developing among the protesters assembling in Grant Park across Michigan Avenue from the candidates' convention headquarters in the Conrad Hilton and Blackstone hotels. This is the culmination of a series of confrontations that have taken place between the Chicago police and the several thousand antiwar youth who have congregated in Chicago's lakefront parks since the weekend before the convention under the loose aegis of the National Mobilization Committee to End the War in Vietnam. These are the same people, led by the Quaker pacifist David Dellinger, who organized the march on the Pentagon one year before, now teamed up with Rennie Davis and Tom Hayden of SDS. The Mobilization leaders are troubled by the Yippees—the "Youth International Party" of Jerry Rubin and Abbie Hoffman—who have come in from New York in search of opportunity to provoke the authorities with taunts and pranks. Hoffman is missing because he has just been arrested for having an obscenity painted on his forehead. As one young convention page puts it, "They want to overthrow the government by farce."[2]

At 3:00 P.M., still debating whether to attempt to march to the convention hall in defiance of the city's ban on such a move, the Mobilization begins its one legally permitted rally at the Grant Park bandshell, near the lakeshore and a bit south of the Conrad Hilton. There are perhaps 10,000 people in the crowd, both hippies and straights. Red, black, and Vietcong flags are visible everywhere. The police are also there in force, backed up by an MP battalion of the Illinois National Guard.

About 3:30 P.M., amidst the speeches (featuring Dick Gregory and Norman Mailer, among other luminaries), someone hauls down the American flag flying from a nearby pole, and a police detail moves in under a rain of thrown debris and bags of urine to arrest the perpetrator of this sacrilege. Other demonstrators raise some sort of red cloth on the pole (a provocation by plainclothesmen, according to some reports).[3] This prompts further police intervention.

Mobilization marshals try to contain the crowd, but the police interpret their movements as another provocation. A flying wedge of officers attacks the multitude in what is later described at the Chicago Seven trial as a "punitive assault."[4] There is no tactical purpose to the attack save the ventilation of rage, as the police club everyone within reach and zero in on the hapless individuals who have fallen under their feet. Rennie Davis, trying to restrain his followers, is recognized by police and beaten unconscious to the cry of "Get Davis!"[5] (The police invade the hospital where he is taken and try to arrest him despite his concussion. He only escapes because the staff smuggle him out to go and stay with friends.) Tom Hayden urges the protesters to disperse and start lots of little demonstrations—"Let us make sure that if blood is going to flow let it flow all over this city . . . , that if the police are going to run wild, let them run wild all over this city and not over us."[6] Other speakers are calmer; the poet Alan Ginsburg has the crowd chanting the Hindu mantra "Om" together. The Yippees, pursuing their adolescent satire of the system, nominate a pig for president, a real pig that they name "Pigasus," and hold it up for the crowd to cheer. "If elected," declaims Jerry Rubin, "pig will run the country on the same principles that have always guided our government's existence—garbage."[7]

Dellinger tries to keep the focus of the rally on the nonviolent march to the Amphitheater, but police loudspeakers warn of mass arrests and the crowd filters away toward Michigan Avenue. This is actually the strategy that Tom Hayden has been advocating, to slip away from the police in small groups and regroup in front of the hotels so that if there are mass arrests, they will take place in front of television cameras.

Nervous guardsmen repeatedly fire tear gas in a vain effort to contain the movement, but the lake breeze blows it back into the hotels and the streets of the Loop. Three young women plant stink bombs inside the Hilton, pervading the lobbies with the smell of vomit.

While Dellinger and his aides parlay with the police about marching to the convention, up at Jackson Drive adjacent to the Chicago Art Institute the crowd—now really a leaderless mob—finds an open bridge over the Illinois Central tracks and pours through toward Michigan Avenue. At this moment the Reverend Ralph Abernathy happens along, leading a mule-and-wagon detachment of the Poor People's Campaign down the avenue with a legal parade permit. The antiwar demonstrators mass around him to march down to the Hilton and the batteries of TV cameras. Hemmed in by police lines that keep them away from the Hilton, the crowd of two to three thousand jams the intersection of Michigan Avenue and Balbo Drive. Where groups of protesters break away and get onto other streets there is sporadic violence perpetrated by both protesters and police. Chants go up—"Dump the Hump," "Ho Ho Ho Chi Minh," and much worse. Police with loudspeakers try to get the main crowd to move back into Grant Park; they are met with shouted obscenities and spat at, and some demonstrators sit down in the street. Police make occasional arrests; here and there, so they claim, they are pelted with debris.[8] Then comes the collision that makes Chicago go down in the history of riots.

At about 8:00 P.M., as night is falling, a strong force of police suddenly moves out of Balbo Drive and attacks the crowd on Michigan Avenue with clubs. The crush of people makes it impossible for those facing the police charge to retreat fast enough. Once club swinging begins, the rage the police have been storing up in their confrontations with the demonstrators boils over. Outdoing the crowd in the homicidal obscenities they shout, the officers of law and order beat their victims unmercifully—male and female, elderly as well as youthful, those lying wounded on the pavement and those still trying to run, active protesters and hapless onlookers. Murray Kempton, himself a McCarthy convention delegate from New York, observes from his own experience of arrest that police conduct varies: some mean, some professional, depending on the personality. He sees a sort of official "permissiveness" that allows individual cops to behave as they please.[9] In any case, police command appears to break down completely. Favored targets of the more aggressive officers are anyone including medics who are trying to shield injured demonstrators, and also the press. Reporters and photographers are treated as though it is a crime to report the melee. Two hundred people caught on the sidewalk between the police barricade and the Hilton building are viciously attacked with clubs and mace. Before long they are literally pushed through the plate glass window into the hotel's Haymarket Restaurant. British journalists Chester, Hodgson, and Page quote from the notes of one of their reporters:

> The kids screamed and were beaten to the ground by cops who had completely lost their cool. Some tried to surrender by putting their hands on their heads. As they were marched to vans to be arrested, they were rapped in the genitals by the cops' swinging billies. I saw one girl, surrounded by cops, screaming, "Please God, help me. Help me." A young man who tried to help got his head bloodied by a flailing club. Some of the demonstrators were thrown against a window of the hotel and pushed through it. The cops were using Mace indiscriminately. But then there was no discrimination about any of it. One policeman I overheard said with a delighted smile, "They're really getting scared now." It was a sadistic romp.[10]

All this is recorded on TV film in gory detail for the worldwide viewing public. The investigation for the federal Commission on Violence later calls it a "police riot."

By 8:30 P.M. the drama has passed, though sporadic clashes occur for the next couple of hours. The bulk of the demonstrators are herded back into Grant Park across from the Hilton. More National Guard troops come up from their assembly point at Soldier Field and form security cordons on both sides of Michigan Avenue, in front of the Hilton and along the edge of Grant Park. Nearly two hundred arrests are tallied in the evening troubles, including Jerry Rubin, Dellinger's Mobilization deputy Sidney Peck, and at least a half dozen convention delegates. Says Rubin, "We wanted exactly what happened. . . . The message of the week was of an America ruled by force. That was a big victory."[11]

Once again, the events at the Hilton illustrate the power of the electronic media to focus on the high spots of violence at any time of crisis, and provoke a revolutionary polarization of responses among their audiences. Great numbers of people favorably disposed to protest, especially the young, are thereby radicalized, but many other viewers see only an exaggerated threat to the foundations of society and their own sense of security. In a modern society where most people sense they have more to lose than to gain from radical social change, the concentrated spectacle of violent defiance of authority drives the majority to the Right.

Simultaneously with the climax of radical protest at the Hilton comes the climax of the political process at the Amphitheater. The delegates reassemble at 7 P.M. for the ritual of nominating speeches and demonstrations, to be followed by the presidential ballot itself. By this point the arrogant egoism of the Daley organization passes all bounds. City employees pack the galleries, ousting people carrying official guest credentials with the threat of calling the police; they post Humphrey placards everywhere and display a huge banner, "We Love Mayor Daley." Since the nominations, are considered in the alphabetical order of the states proposing them, Humphrey taps California to get at the head of the line. Of all people, and on this of all nights, he picks San Francisco Mayor Alioto to make the nominating speech. (Alioto is one of the few California delegates chosen apart from the primary that Kennedy won.)

When Connecticut is called, Senator Abraham Ribicoff takes the podium to offer the last-ditch candidacy of South Dakota's Senator George McGovern, around whom some of the fragmented Kennedy forces have tried to rally. By this time, pictures of the events at the Hilton have reached the TV monitors in the corridors of the Amphitheater—an hour late because a telephone strike forces the television crews downtown to rely on film rather than transmit their pictures live by cable and microwave. The scenes of police beating demonstrators, or just word of them, create profound revulsion among the anti-Humphrey delegates. Ribicoff changes his script to assert, "With George McGovern we wouldn't have Gestapo tactics on the streets of Chicago." Chester, Hodgson, and Page describe the response:

> Stunned silence. Then pandemonium. The television cameras focused on Daley, purple with rage and mouthing an expletive that looked to millions of lip-reading television viewers like an expression he was said never to use. The semantic riddle has never been satisfactorily solved, but the sentiment was unmistakable. Ribicoff stuck to his guns. Staring down at the Mayor, less than twenty feet away, he repeated, "How hard it is to accept the truth. How hard it is."[12]

Faced with the crisis in the city and the futility of their cause in the convention, the peace forces repeatedly move to adjourn. The chairman, House Speaker Carl Albert, gavels them down in good old Sam Rayburn style, and at 11:20 P.M. orders the ballot to begin. There are no surprises: Humphrey goes over the top when Pennsylvania casts the preponderance of its vote for him, and racks up a total of 1,760¼ out of the 2,622 full votes at the convention. McCarthy holds his forces together and gets 601 votes. McGovern gets only 146½, primarily from California, while the District of Columbia's black favorite son, the Rev. Channing Phillips, gets 67½, North Carolina's favorite son Governor Dan More 17½, and Teddy Kennedy 12¾ diehards. Fourteen abstain. Humphrey's victory reflects the power of organization over voters according to the old unreformed rules, plus the swing of the South and many Kennedy regulars into the Humphrey column.

With the ballot concluded near midnight, Illinois moves according to the old custom to make the nomination unanimous. Albert, without taking any vote, has the bad grace to declare the motion passed. Pandemonium in the hall again, as the assemblage is adjourned for the anticlimax the following day.

Outraged McCarthy and Kennedy delegates, refusing to leave the Amphitheater, move to a smaller hall to discuss how to protest the carnage both in the streets and on the convention floor. Candles, procured in anticipation of trouble by Richard Goodwin and Allard Lowenstein, are distributed to the upwards of five hundred delegates and alternates for fear the electricity in the Amphitheater may be turned off. They raise bail money for arrested demonstrators and talk of running someone to challenge Humphrey's choice for vice president—Governor Philip Hoff of Vermont is mentioned, but he demurs the following day because he does not want to stand in the way of fellow New Englander Edmund Muskie. Finally, since the delegate buses have left, the assemblage resolves to march on foot to the Hilton, using the candles to light their way, on a route that conveniently takes them past the home of Mayor Daley. Then, as the group forms up in the parking lot, buses appear as if miraculously and the delegates ride to the Loop.

Debarking one load after another at the corner of Michigan Avenue and Randolph Street, next to the Art Institute, the delegates light their candles and march solemnly in column of twos along the Michigan Avenue sidewalk between the demonstrators in the park and the cordon of National Guardsmen with their fixed bayonets, down to the Hilton. There, at 3:30 A.M., they break up and join the demonstrators (who are thrilled at this manifestation of solidarity) to hear speeches and folksingers. Chicago, say the demonstrators as the crowd finally thins out, has become "Prague West."

The assassination of Bobby Kennedy left the Democratic presidential nomination virtually a foregone conclusion. The Kennedy forces were left angrily floundering, while the enigmatic McCarthy, instead of pushing into the vacuum, slacked off his presidential drive, often failing to pursue opportunities to woo potential supporters of influence. One Kennedy staffer opined, "We regarded Gene as a dangerous man. . . . He raised enthusiasms without following through. We much preferred Humphrey. Maybe even Nixon."[13] Even McCarthy aides, frustrated over his diffidence about the customary delegate vote-gathering, doubted his commitment to the presidency: "I think he was schizophrenic about whether he really wanted it," said one.[14] In any case, there had been so much bad blood between the two antiadministration camps that with a few individual exceptions they were incapable of combining forces.

This division meant a missed opportunity, because the end of the Kennedy challenge drained support away from the Humphrey cause. Much of the vice president's fund-raising proved to have been more anti-Kennedy than pro-Humphrey. President Johnson, no longer needing Humphrey to stop Kennedy, allowed his fixations about Vietnam once again to move ahead of partisan political advantage. It was just six weeks after Kennedy was assassinated that he met President Thieu of South Vietnam and rejected the negotiating compromise that Averell Harriman had sent from Paris in the hope of saving Humphrey and stopping Nixon. Despite Humphrey's abject loyalty to him, the conclusion is hard to escape that Johnson had become more concerned with vindicating himself by victory in the war than with promoting a Democratic victory at home.

Following Robert Kennedy's death there were efforts to get Humphrey to declare his independence of the Johnson war policy and pull the leaderless Kennedy forces under his wing. Governors Hoff of Vermont and Curtis of Maine, the only two Democratic state executives to endorse Kennedy, flew to Washington to urge Humphrey to resign the vice presidency in order to make himself a free agent for the campaign and speak his real feelings about the war and the peace negotiations. Humphrey heard them out, as was his nature, but still declined their advice out of loyalty to Johnson[15]—a loyalty greater than the president reciprocated. Hoff thereupon switched to McCarthy, one of two Democratic governors (along with Harold Hughes of Iowa) to declare for him. Humphrey knew by this time that he had to say something about Vietnam to keep the antiwar people in the Democratic column in November and to show his independence of the president. He actually had such a speech prepared in late July, but he still lacked the temerity to confront Johnson with it and risk his own hold over organization delegates.

Another last minute alternative for the Kennedy forces was created by Senator George McGovern, one of the people whom McCarthy had failed to pursue. Following encouragement by some of the Kennedy people, the South Dakota Senator threw his hat in the ring on August 10, scarcely two weeks before the convention. Although he catered strongly to the McCarthy constituency when he did become the party's nominee in 1972, McGovern sounded at this point more like a moderate compromise. Yet there was no time to build momentum. When the balloting came, McGovern had only an insignificant scattering of delegate votes outside of California and his home state.

On the Republican side, the conservative partisans of Barry Goldwater had not given up their hope of gaining control of the party and the national government. The standard-bearer they found this time was the new governor of California, the former film actor and reader of ultra-conservative radio speeches, Ronald Reagan, propelled into office in 1966 by the early West Coast backlash against countercultural experiments in social mores and Great Society social cures. Within two weeks after his election as governor, Reagan was laying plans for a presidential run, with California and Goldwater's southern bloc as his base. Led by Goldwater's own campaign chief F. Clifton White, Reagan's advisors began a nation-wide effort to organize "Citizens for Reagan" groups, despite the new governor's pledge to serve out his four-year term in Sacramento. However, the plan was thrown off cadence, as Theodore White recounts it, by a homosexual scandal among Reagan's staff.[16] Reagan did not seriously return to the quest for delegates until after Robert Kennedy had been shot and Nelson Rockefeller had reannounced.

Although Reagan did not formalize his candidacy until the actual opening of the Miami Convention, he undertook to build a grand Sun-belt coalition, starting with his big favorite-son base in California and reaching into the South with Goldwater's appeal of ultra-conservatism and implicit opposition to the civil rights movement. Yet for the Southerners the practical politics of leverage within the party and national victory prevailed over outright ideology. Here the key figure was Senator Strom Thurmond of South Carolina, the Dixiecrat third party presidential candidate of 1948, who had since been elected to the Senate as a Republican, spearheading the new swing of Deep South segregationists to the GOP. Satisfied by Nixon's assurance of support for the Southern position on civil rights, defense, and the vice presidency, Thurmond made a deal and threw the Southern balance of power his way. That move denied Reagan his main hope as a national contender. In the end, the only states where he had a majority of Republican convention delegates were California and North Carolina.

On the other flank of the party, Nelson Rockefeller's campaign never got seriously rolling again after the spring hiatus. Although he ran better against Humphrey in the polls than Nixon did, Rockefeller's liberalism made him anathema to most Republican power-brokers outside the Northeast, who had not yet reconciled themselves to Roosevelt's New Deal let alone the Sixties Revolution. Apart from southern New England and his own state of New York, Rockefeller won only a scattering of delegates.

Between Rockefeller and Reagan, Nixon was the favored though unexciting representative of the Republican Center. If he failed of a first ballot nomination, however, there was no predicting the outcome. It was touch and go between him and Reagan for control of the Southern delegates, all the way to the actual balloting in Miami in the early hours of Thursday, August 8. The contest was not decided until the roll call reached Wisconsin; Nixon managed to eke out a first ballot victory with the scant margin of twenty-five votes over the combined forces of his more ideological challengers and scattered favorite sons.

The Democratic race was much more one-sided, with Humphrey's sweep of delegates from the nonprimary states. Events in the State of New York, where local delegates were chosen by primary and at-large delegates by the State Democratic Committee, typified what was happening. McCarthy won the primary, the last, on June 18, but the State Committee gave the bulk of the at-large delegates to Humphrey, at the price of bitter rancor between liberals and regulars. It was not that the organization people liked Humphrey that much, but at least he was an insider to the system; the McCarthyites, in most states mainly outsiders, were intolerable. By July, nothing short of a political earthquake could deny the vice president the nomination.

Antiwar Democrats, frustrated over the choice of candidates, shifted their efforts to the preparation of the party platform. The Democratic Platform Committee met in Washington during the week of August 19 to finalize the document it would put before the convention. In the chair was Representative Hale Boggs of Louisiana, a solid Johnson man who worked in close touch with the White House. The president was willing to let the committee write a platform that was as liberal as it pleased, but on one plank he was adamant—the Vietnam War; here he insisted on unconditional endorsement of his hardline policy. McCarthy, who perhaps should have been an analyst of politics rather than a practitioner, later commented at his perspicacious best:

> Johnson and the people who controlled the Convention were set on making no concession. Rather curious, the whole Johnson role, from the time of his withdrawal in March when he said he was going to withdraw so that he wouldn't be accused of political motivation in what he might do.
>
> The only base upon which that would have made much sense was that he was going to end the war somehow. But instead of that he persisted in conducting or trying to force whoever followed him to conduct the same kind of war. And I think in his own way he'd figured this out, that if he'd stayed in he could have been nominated but he would have had to admit that the war policy was wrong, and by pulling out he could really control who would be his successor, I think. Either it could have been Nixon or Humphrey. So whoever succeeded, he was going to see it would be a person who would have to, in office, carry on the Johnson policies.[17]

In fact, it went beyond this: Johnson was controlling every significant decision about the convention. Carl Solberg writes, "Watching and wirepulling from his Texas ranch was the unabdicated Johnson. The president dictated the city, the date, the officers, the program of the Convention. His control of its arrangements was so complete that Humphrey's son-in-law had to line up every morning for tickets for members of the Humphrey family."[18] He brushed off Humphrey's wise suggestion—concurred in by the media because of costs and the electricians' strike in Chicago—to move the convention site to Miami.

The president's inflexibility finally pushed the McCarthy and Kennedy people together to present a united resistance to the administration on the platform. Given the state of public opinion by now, the challenge was serious, and through David Ginsburg, the erstwhile executive director of the Kerner Commission, the administration negotiated gingerly with the opposition about a compromise plank.

All this collapsed with the Soviet intervention in Czechoslovakia on August 20, which seemed in many minds to vindicate Johnson's hard line. McCarthy's immediate response to the Czech situation only made matters worse; he brushed it off as "not a major world crisis," and criticized President Johnson's emergency convening of the National Security Council as "out of proportion."[19] The damage was not undone when McCarthy tried to amend his judgment a couple of days later. Johnson was in a stronger position than ever when, at the last minute, he vetoed the final attempt at a Vietnam compromise that would have isolated McCarthy and his more unyielding supporters. Humphrey, though he was "upset and angry" over this "outrageous turn of events," gave in to Johnson once more.[20] His biographer Carl Solberg reasons that Humphrey had some sort of unresolved father-complex about Johnson; Humphrey himself later explained to his staff, "I had become like the oldest son—and I couldn't make the break."[21] Ex-Governor John Connally, Johnson's man from Texas, encouraged the rumors that the president might reenter the race and seek a convention draft at the last minute, although Larry O'Brien considered this pure bluff.[22]

Thanks to the president's stand, the platform committee was compelled to submit to the convention a majority and a minority plank on Vietnam. The difference, mainly in their language about the bombing, was not great: "Stop all bombing of North Vietnam when this action would not endanger the lives of our troops in the fields; this action should take into account the response from Hanoi" (majority), versus "an unconditional end to all bombings in North Vietnam" (minority).[23] But the political polarization embodied in these competing proposals

223

guaranteed a bitter-end platform fight by the opposition on the convention floor, if only to make Johnson and Humphrey pay a price for their intransigence.

The events of March 1968—the challenge of McCarthy and Kennedy and the withdrawal of Johnson—took much of the wind out of the sails of the radical wing of the antiwar movement. McCarthy was accomplishing exactly what he said—drawing alienated youth back to work within the system. To be sure, he did not attract everyone. Anti-draft leaders continued their direct-action campaign despite continuing prosecutions. The trial of Dr. Benjamin Spock and the Rev. William Sloane Coffin with the "Boston Five" for counseling draft evasion went on all winter and spring, ending in a guilty verdict in June. In the meantime, in April the Columbia University radicals organized a nationwide Student Strike for Peace (overshadowed by the time it took place by the violent uprising at Columbia). The stream of deserters and draft evaders fleeing to Canada and other countries increased in volume, to total ultimately more than 50,000 American fugitives from the war effort. The pacifists of the Catholic Left assumed a prominent role in antiwar protests and prompted the beginning of domestic spying by military counter-intelligence. On May 17, nine Catholic pacifists led by the Jesuit Berrigan brothers Daniel and Philip raided a draft board office in the Baltimore suburb of Catonsville, Maryland, made away with hundreds of draft files, and burned them in the street with napalm. Philip Berrigan had meanwhile been put on trial for an October 1967 foray into a Baltimore draft office to pour blood over the records, for which the "Baltimore Four" were eventually convicted in October 1968, just as the trial of the "Catonsville Nine" with its equally foreordained outcome was commencing. Both the Berrigans went into hiding and were not found by the FBI until 1970.

On the side of authority, the Mayor of Chicago, having been shaken by the King riots after the city kept order in 1967, showed his hand about demonstrations with his dramatic order, "Shoot to kill any arsonist . . . , shoot to maim or cripple anyone looting. . . ."[24] He loosened the strictures that reforming police superintendents had placed on the use of force, and let the police work out their authoritarian hatreds (equating any peace activity with Communism) in a vicious attack on Chicago's counterpart of the April 27 antiwar demonstrations. Moderate, naive, and truly nonviolent elements were both pulled and pushed away from a convention confrontation, leaving the demonstration idea to a dwindling corps of radicals.

Mayor Daley was above all afraid of another black uprising that

224

would disrupt the convention and make Chicago look bad while the whole nation was watching. With this in mind, he arranged the heavy security that so repelled the delegates at the International Amphitheater. But Daley also made up his mind that Chicago would not abet the white protesters by giving them a permit for a demonstration or march, and he stalled their requests for negotiations and permits almost to the very week of the convention. His excuse—that they were "outsiders" threatening to disrupt the city—overlooked the fact that the convention itself was a national gathering largely of outsiders and that any protest of its proceedings logically had to occur in Chicago. In effect, Daley was selectively denying the right of free assembly and thumbing his nose at the First Amendment.

Although the Mobilization to End the War was becoming radicalized in its dealings with Chicago, it remained tame compared with Rubin and Hoffman's Yippees. Rubin, a veteran of the Berkeley Free Speech Movement of 1964 and West Coast antiwar agitation, was the ideologist and planner: "I support everything which puts people into motion, which creates disruption and controversy, which creates chaos and rebirth," he declaimed.[25] Hoffman, a product of the civil rights effort and then of the hippie scene (he was especially impressed by the Haight-Ashbury Diggers), supplied the zany inspiration for the Yippees' antics; "street theater" and "monkey warfare" were his ideas of political tactics. Rubin and Hoffman's basic plan when they launched their organization (on New Year's Eve 1967, according to the legend, when they were all stoned) was to combine New-Left political radicalism and countercultural ridicule of all Establishment values. Typical was their "raid" on the New York Stock Exchange when they rained dollar bills from the gallery and gleefully watched the disruption of trading as the brokers scrambled to garner this unexpected manna from heaven. Hoffman believed that power came, not out of the barrel of a gun, as Mao Tse-tung put it, but out of "charisma, myth, and put-on—the triple-barreled YIP shotgun."[26]

Quite independently of the Mobe, the Yippees undertook to organize a "festival of life" to coincide with the "Death Convention." The program they proposed ranged from a "nude-in" in Lake Michigan to the injection of LSD into Chicago's water supply, a threat that the city's police took seriously despite its chemical infeasibility. Like the Mobe, the Yippees were set back in their organizing by the competition of the McCarthy and Kennedy campaigns and by Johnson's pullout. They were likewise stalled off by the City of Chicago in their quest for demonstration permits. Their Chicago affiliates, wary of official repression, dissociated themselves from the New Yorkers' schemes. The Yippees remained a minuscule group of only a few hundred crazies who attached themselves to the Mobe's demonstrations, to the embarrassment and ultimate regret of the more serious peace advocates.

After all the months of talk and preparation, only about five thousand young protesters braved the threats of the Daley administration and came to Chicago to demonstrate against the convention. They were joined by roughly an equal number of sympathizers from the Chicago area. Even at their peak, they remained fewer in absolute numbers than the well-armed police and military forces mobilized to contain them. No more than a few hundred of the protesters were of the Yippee persuasion, but this was enough to give the proceedings a constantly provocative edge. Sectarianism divided the effort: SDS and Old Left elements (mainly Trotskyists) rejected the Mobe plan because they considered it a front for McCarthy liberalism, and the Mobe declined to cooperate with Allard Lowenstein's "Coalition for an Open Convention" for the same reason. Lowenstein, the indefatigable one-man movement, thought he could build a bridge between the Kennedy and McCarthy forces but his idea collapsed when even he, a bona fide convention delegate, was denied a demonstration permit by the Chicago authorities. He found himself arrested on the floor of the convention for carrying a newspaper in alleged violation of the fire code.

The Yippees produced the earliest confrontations. They began arriving in Chicago on Thursday, August 22, and set up their headquarters in the southern part of Lincoln Park, on the lakeshore adjacent to the city's "Old Town" hippie district and about a mile north of the Michigan Avenue hotels. That night, in an incident not directly related to the protests, a hippie was shot and killed by police—the only fatality of the convention episode, as it turned out.

After repeated clashes and the selective arrests that ensued, including their first demonstration with the pig-nominee, the Yippees decided on Sunday the 25th to defy the park curfew and stage a mass sleep-in. After midnight, the police moved in to clear the park and broke into the indiscriminate clubbing (including reporters and photographers) that was already familiar in Chicago and was soon to become a national spectacle. Venomous and sexually crude epithets were shouted by both sides: "Kill the pigs" and "Get those commies" were among the mildest. Hayden, there with the Mobe marshals to lend support, was arrested; soon out on bail, he appeared thereafter only in disguise. Monday night, as the convention opened and went into its first round of credentials challenges, the story was repeated in Lincoln Park, this time with an impromptu barricade of picnic tables thrown up to slow the police down. As before, once the police began swinging, they seemed to go berserk, unmercifully attacking isolated or wounded individuals or those trying to retreat.

Tuesday evening the crowd gathered once again in Lincoln Park and was treated to an address by Bobby Seale, just in from California to bring the Black Panther message of revolution. Later on, the police once again cleared the park with clubs and tear gas to enforce the curfew. But this time, oddly enough, they let other protesters, mostly Mobe and McCarthy sympathizers numbering several thousand, spend the night in Grant Park opposite the convention hotels. All this set the stage for the Wednesday night confrontation that gave the week of the convention its most enduring image.

The commotion inside the convention and the violence outside it did not end with the events of Wednesday evening. Demonstrations continued the next day in Grant Park and on nearby streets without serious confrontation, until Dick Gregory made yet another attempt to lead a march to the Amphitheater, which was literally beaten back by the National Guard with rifle butts and tear gas. Senator McCarthy spoke in Grant Park to dissociate himself from the Democratic ticket and to extol the demonstrators as "the government of the people in exile."[27]

Thursday was the final day of the convention, scheduled for the vice presidential ballot to confirm Humphrey's choice of Senator Ed Muskie, and the acceptance speeches of both. The only really dramatic moment was the showing of a film on the life of Robert Kennedy, triggering the most emotional demonstration of the week capped by seemingly endless singing of "The Battle Hymn of the Republic." Humphrey, his "politics of joy" rudely interrupted both on and off the convention floor, remained seemingly insensitive to these events that threatened to destroy the Democratic party or at the very least ruin its chances for victory in November. In his acceptance speech, he barely alluded to the violence that had shocked the nation. Theodore White observed:

After its days of turbulence and excitement, no speech could have pulled the Democratic convention together except a masterpiece devoting itself entirely to the meaning, the events, and the historic perspectives of the convention itself. But the old Hubert Humphrey who might have done just that was now too tired to reflect, and still felt only vaguely the terrible disturbance in the ranks on the floor. . . . The convention was treated to a standard political oration of the kind of prose which, in Chicago, on the night of August 29th, 1968, had been rendered archaic by the events of the previous twenty-four hours.[28]

227

In a television interview as the convention closed, Humphrey was still unyielding about the events on the streets:

> I think we ought to quit pretending that Mayor Daley did anything wrong. . . . These demonstrations . . . were planned, premeditated by certain people in this country that feel all they have to do is riot and they'll get their way. . . . The obscenity, the profanity, the filth that was uttered night after night in front of the hotels . . . , is it any wonder that the police had to take action?[29]

After the election he complained, "I was a victim of that convention. . . . I could've beaten the Republicans any time—but it's difficult to take on the Republicans and fight a guerrilla war in your own party at the same time. Chicago was a catastrophe."[30] In his memoirs, Humphrey ignored the Wednesday crisis completely.

Still the violence was not over. In the early morning hours of Friday, August 30, police stationed at the Hilton, believing they were being pelted by objects coming from the windows of Senator McCarthy's headquarters suite, raided the premises without warning or warrant. When they found numbers of young people there, it was the same spectacle of clubbing all over again. McCarthy, summoned to the scene, confronted the police himself: "Who's in charge here?"[31] No one was—a repetition of the frequent theme of the breakdown of police command. McCarthy postponed his departure from Chicago to assure the safe evacuation of his people from the city.

The events in Chicago underscored the uniqueness as well as the inherent weakness of the radical youth movement in America. As on the campuses nationwide, the Chicago confrontation with the Establishment was distinguished by a reliance on theatrics in place of ideology or program. Unlike the Europeans, the American protesters showed no capability either for offensive action or for sustained resistance in the face of police attacks. They behaved most of the time as an emotional but largely anarchic and fluid mob, for all the efforts of the Mobe to give them some deliberate leadership. The French student radicals really wanted to overthrow their government and had considerable popular following in this aim. The Americans could not think much beyond gestures to embarrass theirs, and were conspicuous in their inability to mobilize anything stronger than sympathy for the beating they took.

Mayor Daley lost no time in seeking retribution for the insult suffered by his city. While the House Un-American Activities Committee opened its inevitable inquiry into the putative role of Communists in the Chicago riots, Jerry Rubin and diverse marchers (including a number of convention delegates) were indicted and tried by the Cook County authorities, found guilty, and fined. But the big move was to invoke the new federal antiriot law against the demonstration leaders. At Daley's apparent instigation, a federal grand jury was impaneled in the Northern Illinois district (where the judges all owed their jobs to him) to investigate the disturbances as violations of this statute. It returned an indictment in March 1969 against eight men, the celebrated "Chicago Eight," soon to become the "Chicago Seven." They included Dellinger, Hayden, and Rennie Davis of the Mobe, together with two of their lesser-known assistants who seem to have been rather arbitrarily singled out: John Froines, a chemistry professor from Oregon, and Lee Weiner, a Northwestern graduate student in sociology and the straight man of the group. These were joined in the improbable charge of conspiracy by the Yippees' Hoffman and Rubin, and by the Panthers' Bobby Seale. (Rubin had meanwhile been a candidate for vice president of the United States on the ticket with Eldridge Cleaver for the rump of the Peace and Freedom Party.) Heading the defense was William Kunstler, veteran advocate for radical and civil rights causes and a believer in the revolutionary philosophy himself. Just to maintain appearances of evenhandedness, the Grand Jury managed to single out eight Chicago policemen for indictment for unnecessary roughness, while a few other officers were disciplined by suspension or dismissal.

Legal maneuvers consumed another six months, before the trial actually commenced in September 1969. The accused, or most of them, chose to make the trial yet another revolutionary forum, each in his own style of disruptive and confrontational tactics. The presiding judge, Julius Hoffman (no relation to Abbie, as both hastened to point out), hated protesters and was determined to maintain the dignity of his court; devoid of a sense of humor, he was doubtless the least qualified person imaginable to handle this bizarre trial. Court and defense vied in the exchange of denunciations of one another. Early in the proceedings, Bobby Seale proved to be so disruptive that Judge Hoffman ordered him brought into the courtroom bound and gagged; soon he was forced to separate Seale's case from the other seven altogether.

The trial dragged on until February 1970, with a jury that was sequestered most of this time because of an alleged Black Panther death threat. This marathon, punishing the jurors as much as the accused, exposed them to Judge Hoffman's pressure to vote for conviction so as to avoid a hung jury and the necessity of starting the trial all over again. The two factions of the jury—for conviction and acquittal, respectively —negotiated in their hotel rooms (a rule violation cited later by the Appeals Court) and agreed to acquit on the conspiracy charge while convicting five of the accused on charges of individual incitement to riot. Froines and Weiner were found completely innocent. But Judge Hoffman meanwhile sentenced all seven plus Kunstler to jail for contempt of court.

The conviction was naturally appealed. It took the Circuit Court of Appeals two and a half years to reach its decision—it overturned all the sentences as well as the contempt convictions because of Judge Hoffman's "demeanor," his handling of the jury, and the withholding of exculpatory information from the defense. At this late date, the Nixon Justice Department decided not to attempt a new trial, perhaps because it would have to reveal its electronic surveillance operations. So ended one of the most spectacular political trials in modern American history, and with it the revolution of Chicago.

Daley's regime was not destined to last much longer either. The mayor died in office in 1976, and his autocracy fell apart among warring personalities, while Chicago's growing black population made the possibility of a black mayor a reality in the 1980s. Across the nation, in fact, the demographics of black migration to the inner cities and white flight to the suburbs and to the Republican party cut the ground out from under the old big-city Democratic machines. There was little resistance to the reform of the presidential nominating process brought in by the McGovern Commission for the 1972 campaign, paving the way for McGovern's own ill-fated nomination and the last hurrah of the antiwar Democrats.

After the Democratic Convention had done its wrecking job, the events of the election campaign unfolded with relentless logic toward the anticlimax of November. Immediately after the convention, Humphrey headed down in the polls, reaching a low of 28 percent in late September against Nixon's 43 percent, with 21 percent for George Wallace.[32] Time was abnormally short to close the gap because the Democratic Convention had been scheduled unusually late on the original assumption that it would merely anoint Johnson for reelection. Still bearing the albatross of the Vietnam War, the Democrats could not regain their unity and recover their usual appeal fast enough. McCarthy, embittered by the whole Chicago experience, proved incapable either of supporting the ticket or of organizing any effective alternative; he withheld his endorsement of Humphrey almost to the last minute, meanwhile wandering off to Europe and then to the World Series as a journalist. It was not until October 29 that he gave Humphrey his formal endorsement, and that on a grudging lesser-evil basis. (Humphrey thought McCarthy never tried to swing a single vote to him.)[33] But McCarthy was not the only one to hang loose through

230

most of the campaign: Johnson made no campaign appearance on behalf of his vice president until the 10th of October.

Midway in the campaign, a desperate Humphrey, fifteen points behind Nixon and running out of funds, heeded Larry O'Brien's advice and took the step he should have made at least six weeks before—he finally cut himself loose from Johnson's war policy. Fortunately, the ground was shifting in Paris to facilitate the move; Harriman, with Soviet help behind the scenes, was getting the North Vietnamese close to the San Antonio Formula—a bombing halt in return at least for the implied promise of de-escalation. Through George Ball, now the former undersecretary of state, Harriman communicated his approval of Humphrey's move. This was not surprising, since Harriman had been trying since July to get President Johnson to ease his stand in order to advance the peace talks and the Democrats' chances. At the same time, Humphrey's patience with Johnson was reaching the breaking point. "That no-good son of a bitch," he blurted out to his physician and aide Edgar Berman after one of the president's threatening phone calls. "The way I've treated him—I must be a god-damned fool. . . . You'd think he'd at least respect my loyalty. But not a bit. I think I've had Lyndon Johnson around my neck just long enough."[34] And so Humphrey decided to commit his last ready cash to a nationally televised speech from Salt Lake City on September 30. Salt Lake City was remembered afterward as the turning point of the campaign: "As President," he announced, "I would be willing to stop the bombing of North Vietnam as an acceptable risk for peace."

The effect of this admittedly slight deviation from the administration position was immediate and electrifying. As the liberals returned to the fold, Humphrey's campaign came alive again and he started to close the gap with Nixon, while the much-feared breach with Johnson never materialized: the old curmudgeon respected resistance more than compliance. Wallace's challenge peaked and faltered when the Alabama governor highlighted his right-wing radicalism by designating the nuclear bombing enthusiast and retired chief of the Strategic Air Command, General Curtis LeMay, as his vice-presidential running mate. By November 5, Humphrey had recovered enough to make the election too close to call.

But not close enough to insure him from the vicissitudes of political chance. The outcome now depended more on events in Paris and Saigon than on anything the candidates did. In mid-October, Harriman achieved a breakthrough of sorts with the North Vietnamese, getting their implied agreement to the San Antonio Formula and to formal talks including South Vietnam at the bargaining table. Hanoi had no doubt begun to realize, especially after the Salt Lake City speech, that it would fare better under a Humphrey administration than with Nixon and that it ought to show some cooperativeness that would aid the Democrats. In any case, President Johnson accepted the opportunity and instructed Ambassador Bunker to get President Thieu's concurrence. Haggling went on over the shape of the negotiating table until Hanoi agreed to the two-sides formula, and then Johnson summoned General Abrams back from Vietnam to assure himself that the field commander had no reservations. On October 31, the president made his dramatic last-minute announcement that he had ordered the bombing of North Vietnam to cease.

But now Saigon held the cards and played them its own way. In response to hints relayed through the South Vietnamese Embassy by Mrs. Anna Chennault (widow of the famed World War II Flying Tiger chief and vice-chair of Women for Nixon-Agnew) that he would fare better under the Republicans, President Thieu backed out of the deal. President Johnson was informed of all this on the basis of FBI and NSA electronic intercepts, but it was too late to salvage the situation before Election Day. The four-party talks in Paris (counting the Vietcong separately from the North Vietnamese) could not begin, and the Democrats were denied their election-eve triumph. Without that, Humphrey could not do quite well enough. The Republicans squeaked in, and America went on to four more years of war, until Nixon and Kissinger accepted the tenuous Paris Accords of 1972 (again delayed by Saigon while the North was bombed one last time). As Senator Aiken was credited with suggesting long before, the United States declared victory and got out, only to witness in April 1975 the ignominious end of the client state for which so much blood, American and Asian, had been shed.

The 1968 presidential election proved to be one of the closest on record, so much had Humphrey closed the September gap in the time left to him. In popular vote, the official totals were 31,304,992 to 30,994,354, a scant 0.43 percentage points apart. As always, the electoral vote outcome was more lopsided: Nixon, 302; Humphrey, 191; Wallace, 45 (all in the Deep South). But even in the Electoral College it was closer than the totals suggest. If either California or Illinois (plus any small state decided by a couple of percentage points) had gone for Humphrey, Nixon would have been denied the required absolute majority in the Electoral College, and pursuant to the Constitution the election would have been thrown to the new House of Representatives, with each state delegation casting one vote. This was what George Wallace was striving to accomplish, though to what effective purpose it is not clear; the Democrats still held a comfortable state-by-state majority in the House, and if everyone voted on party lines Humphrey would have been in. But Mayor Daley failed to try as hard as he might have to deliver Illinois, or so the Humphrey people believed; he was no doubt miffed when Humphrey began late in the campaign to change his tune on the August riots as well as on the war: "Chicago last August was filled with pain."[35]

Many observers took the view after the debacle of 1968 that the Democratic party was disintegrating under the strain of the social revolution and the nation's unresolved dilemma about its international role. This is an exaggeration, though the party was badly torn by events and losing voters through its wounds. Its constituency, brought together as the New Deal coalition by the programs and benefits of the old economic liberalism, was badly divided over the new social liberalism of racial equality, youthful life-styles, and antinationalist protest. Shocked by the successive episodes of TV-magnified violence throughout the year, most of the American public was falling back from the movements of reform that had swirled in the streets and in the halls of Congress ever since Johnson became president. The South had already defected en masse to vote for Barry Goldwater, and Northern ethnic working-class voters, the most solid phalanx for liberal Democrats in the past, were drifting away as well. To both of these elements the Wallace candidacy, combining anti-elitist populism with racism and ardent nationalism, was powerfully attractive. However, thanks to the bias of the system against minor parties and Wallace's own vulnerability as an extremist, the American Independent party proved to be only a way-station in the realignment of major party strength. The rightward trend was partly offset by the gravitation into the ranks of the Democrats of two minorities—on the one hand the blacks and on the other affluent and better-educated whites (limousine liberals, if you will: the kind of people who had contributed to the moderate Republicanism of the Northeast). Contrary to past tradition, the Democrats became the party of choice for new college graduates. These trends brought new activists to the party and contributed to McGovern's nomination in 1972, but they could not compensate on a national scale for the party's losses on the right.

By November 1968, the combined strength of the Republicans and the Wallace defection was too much for the defending Democrats to withstand, even though they were partially recovering at the end. The result at the polls was indicative of the conservative backswing that the Sixties Revolution had finally provoked. This was only the beginning of a long new phase in American political life. Nixon's victory signaled the opening of a progressively deepening period of reaction, destined to last (with mild interruptions) for two decades. The counterrevolution had begun.

11

The World
Social Revolution

THE YEAR 1968 was the climax of the most sweeping upsurge of revolutionary feeling that the world had seen in half a century. From the Great Wall of China to the streets of Chicago young radicals appeared on the scene to sound the message of protest, often violently and in the face of violent responses by the forces of order. Everywhere, revolutionary movements came to a crescendo; everywhere, they faltered and collapsed.

The worldwide revolutionary wave of the 1960s had a common denominator that distinguishes it from the familiar revolutions of modern history. It took for granted, even deprecated, the old struggles for political rights and economic redistribution, and focused instead on issues of inequality and coercion in face-to-face human relationships. The driving force in these new movements was not the downtrodden masses but the disaffected youth of the privileged classes, induced by their education and often by their humanistic upbringing to reject any relationship based on power and subordination. "The social protest of the 1960s has very little to do with poverty," observed Herbert Gans of Columbia Teachers College even before 1968 came to a close. "The social protest of the 1960s has to do with *inequality*, with the pervasive inequities

235

remaining in American life," or that of any other country, he might have added.[1] It was not a revolution of interests but a revolution in values, not a struggle of classes but a struggle of generations.

The Sixties Revolution was novel in the magnitude of the challenges it posed and the changes it wrought without actually overthrowing governments. It was a revolution in minds more than in institutions; in America it relied much more on the courts and the amplification of old constitutional principles than on any seizure of power or legislative enactment. Although the accomplishments of the Sixties Revolution seem limited in the tangible sense, it left a mood everywhere of skepticism and even cynicism, a propensity to drop out or abjure social responsibility, that has had a corrosive effect on the fabric of modern society, particularly in the United States.

Even though the transformation of the 1960s was more mental than material, as a social phenomenon it followed the classic model of development manifested in the literal, institutional revolutions of the past. In this instance, as before, the process ran through a gradual accumulation of articulated discontent, the shift from liberal methods to radical ones, and the climax of violent emotions in conflict, followed by the splintering of the movement among various shades of radicalism, fatigue and disillusionment, retreat, and counterrevolutionary backlash. The pattern was manifest everywhere from the American ghettos and campuses to the streets of the Latin Quarter and the teeming cities of China.

Tactically, every episode of revolutionary defiance in the 1960s was distinguished by anarchic protest against organized authority. The powers that be, not seriously threatened as much as they were embarrassed, were as a matter of policy relatively restrained in the use of force, and usually desisted from deliberate killing and maiming, even in the Soviet occupation of Czechoslovakia. They were always aware at the command level that real casualties would work politically against the cause of order. In action, by contrast, the professional police forces employed in the United States and Western Europe—and the army in China—invariably were carried away by personal and perhaps class hatred for defiant youth. The rebels themselves varied widely in organized staying power and readiness to fight back, oddly enough showing these qualities most vigorously in Communist countries.

Yet force, except in relations among countries, rarely decides the outcome. Political conviction and its swings in response to events are more decisive. In an industrial democracy, the chances of igniting popular revolution by means of New Left–style confrontation are nil. Where the great majority have become reasonably well fixed in matters of creature comforts, they are much more likely to respond to disorders and provocations by turning to those leaders who claim to represent order and tradition—in other words, the Right. The French Communists were correct in trying to resist the wild tactics of the ultras and hold to the parliamentary path, though they could not escape being tainted and victimized by the spirit of revolution. Only where national identity or ethnic autonomy is at stake—as among the American blacks, the Czechoslovaks, or the Vietnamese—is mass support for the revolution a real likelihood.

The Sixties Revolution was the first to travel round the world by television. The electronic media have the capacity to zero in on the most dramatic or violent events, however atypical they may be, and make them seem the norm for the viewer or listener who has no benchmark in personal experience. It began with Vietnam, the first true media war and a milestone in the rise of the mass media, print as well as electronic, to become the decisive force in modern society. When Marshall McLuhan, the guru of contemporary communications theory, wrote in 1953, "The medium is the message," he could not have dreamed how decisively the medium-message would soon be able to shape minds and govern events, in the United States more than anywhere else. In Vietnam, every battle, every crisis, was raw material for the writers and the cameras. The news gatherers, in turn, focused the impact of every act of drama or violence for millions of viewers and readers. The audience was thereby drawn far more intimately into the experience of unique and remote events than ever had been the case in the past.

The same effect holds for all the other critical turning points in the axial year of 1968. Television coverage made every violent confrontation seem a crisis in the national or international order. The exceptional and sensational, carried by the air waves to every living room screen, came to seem like the norm. To be sure, there were special cases overseas. In France, governmental control of television slowed the impact of the student uprising, though it could not avert the national crisis. In Czechoslovakia, the printed word was the main tool for demanding and disseminating reform during the Prague Spring, and radio was the force that kept the nation united and inspired in the immediate aftermath of the Soviet occupation. China had its own unique form of revolutionary mass communication, the "big character posters," used by all factions to try to promote their respective causes. But everywhere the impact of every individual act of protest or defiance was magnified and generalized by the media. The typical American television viewer of 1968 may have personally witnessed more revolution than the average French-man of 1789 or the average Russian of 1917.

The revolutionary challenge of the 1960s was not confined to the United States, Western Europe, China, and the Soviet bloc, although these were the most spectacular instances of defiance of entrenched power. The entire Third World, nominally freed from imperial rule, was still in the throes of continuing anti-imperialist ferment. Southeast Asia, of course, was in the turmoil of battle, as a decades-old nationalist revolution in Vietnam endeavored to consummate its goal of national unity against the intervening power of the United States. Next door in Cambodia a revolution of even more extreme character was brewing among the Khmer Rouge guerrillas. Franz Fanon extolled the purgative virtue of violence in empowering the victims of social or national oppression to achieve faith in themselves.[2]

Revolution simmered all over Latin America, in this case driven more by the old issues of economic justice than by the social concerns of the New Left. In part it was inspired by Castro's Cuba, although Castro himself came to a parting of the ways with ultra-Left romanticism after the death of Che Guevara, and opted for the Soviet model of bureaucratic rule and the game of power politics. He showed his new hand by endorsing the Soviet occupation of Czechoslovakia when China and most European Communists were denouncing it. But the guerrilla ideal that Castro and Guevara had been touting was beginning to catch on, notably in the form of the Tupomaros in Uruguay. These student revolutionaries—disciples of Guevara's Argentine follower Abraham Guillén—launched an urban guerrilla action in 1968, ironically directed against Latin America's most stable democratic government. The outcome dramatized what happens when deliberate revolutionary activity is attempted without the necessary setting. It alienates most of the population and encourages right-wing coups, which in Uruguay ushered in one of the continent's most repressive military regimes after five years of indecisive struggle with the rebels. A comparable fate quickly befell the lesser-known urban guerrilla movement of Carlos Marighella in Brazil, which tried vainly to challenge the military dictatorship of that era.

A development of the opposite sort took place in Peru, where the military intervened in the fall of 1968, as they did so often in Latin American politics, to head off a democratic reform movement represented by the Aprista Party. The irony in this case was that the military government itself swung toward anti-imperialist socialism, nationalizing most large foreign business properties and promoting agricultural cooperatives for the Indian masses. The experiment ultimately came to grief in corruption and inflation, while rural radicalism became a source for the "Shining Path" terrorist movement that continued to disrupt the country into the 1980s.

Most dramatic of all the Latin American echoes of the Revolution of 1968 was the student uprising in Mexico. Demonstrations began in Mexico City over university autonomy and freedom for political prisoners. The police initially overreacted, as they did in so many other places, causing a prolonged series of clashes and huge student-led marches with as many as 300,000 participants. Fearful of disruption to the Olympic Games scheduled for Mexico City in the second half of October, the Mexican government sent troops to occupy the National University. Students protested en masse, and on October 2, ten thousand of them were demonstrating in Tlatelolco Plaza, the "Square of the Three Cultures," when troops and riot police attacked them, shooting wildly. No realistic count of the casualties was ever released, but the dead probably reached several hundred, while thousands were arrested and a number of student leaders "disappeared." Mexico City was the bloodiest disaster of the Sixties Revolution anywhere outside China. Nevertheless, "the events of 1968 constitute a phenomenon that had a tremendous impact on an entire generation, and they continue to have an impact," declared the new secretary general of Mexico's ruling party twenty years later. "They did not change the regime or its economic or social structure or political base. But they did affect the way that rising generations perceived the country's problems."[3] This well describes the ultimate meaning of 1968 all over the world.

Revolutionary protest in Latin America received new legitimation in 1968 from an unexpected quarter. A conference in August of the Roman Catholic bishops of Latin America in Medellín, Columbia, adopted an extraordinarily radical statement of social and economic doctrine. Thus was born the "theology of liberation," formulated by the Peruvian professor-priest Gustavo Gutiérrez, evoking the communitarian spirit of early Christianity and equating capitalism with idolatrous sin. "How do you say to the poor, the oppressed, the insignificant person, 'God loves you'?" questioned Gutiérrez.[4] The answer from thousands of rank-and-file priests and nuns was to throw themselves into the life of the poor and the fight for social justice, at great personal risk. Long identified with political immobility and economic privilege, the Latin American Church was moving at least in part to become a voice for radical change, a stance that has since made it a major player on the side of social justice in violence-torn Central America.

Africa and the Middle East were still in turmoil in the 1960s, following the achievement of national independence from European rule or domination (in the Middle East, after World War II; in Africa, abruptly in 1960 or the years just preceding). In Iraq in July 1968, six years after the fall of the British-sponsored monarchy, a coup by the Ba'ath party of "Arab Socialism" installed a radical military government and swung the country for the time being toward the Soviet camp. The pattern here was similar to Peru. In Africa, meanwhile, there were riots in Senegal (one of the few constitutionally governed states in the region) and a military coup in Mali on the Left-leaning Iraqi model. Most dramatic in the affairs of the continent was the eruption of a new nationalism within a nationalism, when the region known as Biafra in southeastern Nigeria endeavored to secede and form an independent state based on the Ibo-speaking people. Nigeria's authorities were no more disposed to grant the secessionists independence than the British and French had earlier been in regard to any colonial independence movement. With British backing, Nigerian forces invaded and blockaded Biafra in 1967, and crushed most Biafran resistance during 1968 even while negotiating with the rebels. The secession was finally liquidated in 1970.

Elsewhere in the Third World the 1960s were only a prelude to spectacular revolutionary developments during the first half of the following decade. Chile was the scene of a revolution by ballot in 1970, when the Socialist Salvador Allende was narrowly elected president, only to be toppled three years later by yet another typical Latin American military coup with United States encouragement. Guerrilla independence movements in Portugal's African colonies, the first and last West European empire, wore down the dictatorship in Lisbon to the point where it succumbed to a military coup in 1974 and an extraordinary revolution in microcosm that ran for a year and a half before democratic government was consolidated. Ethiopia was next to experience the now-familiar pattern of a left-wing military revolution, in 1975, swinging it into the Soviet orbit and subjecting the country to disastrous attempts at socialist organization. Also in 1975, Cambodia underwent the only foreign replica of the Chinese Cultural Revolution when the Khmer Rouge guerrilla forces took over the country in the wake of United States abandonment of Indo-China. They subjected Cambodia to a murderous version of China's antiurbanism and anti-intellectualism, until intervention by Vietnam four years later put an end to that experiment in utopian national suicide.

Another kind of revolutionary change was getting underway in 1968 across the northern boundary of the United States, in Canada. What was occurring here was another kind of movement for social justice, in this case a revolution for linguistic equality. The long-submerged French-speaking population of Quebec had, through the so-called "Quiet Revolution" of the 1960s, manifested a new ethnic self-assertion that threatened the unity of the Canadian federation. An answer was provided by the ruling Liberal party, after it underwent a major leadership struggle in the spring of 1968: the new prime minister, Pierre Elliott Trudeau, offered a bold program of Anglo-French bilingualism and biculturalism for the whole country, corresponding to the goals of racial equality and integration in the United States. Trudeau led his party to a sweeping electoral victory in June, but as so often happens, reform begets more radical demands. Liberal dissident René Levesque split off in October 1968 and founded the Parti Quebecois with an avowed program of independence for the province—the Canadian analogue of black nationalism. Eventually, a decade later, after brushes with terrorism, economic realities cut Quebec separatism down just as they had built up French self-confidence in the first place, while Trudeau's bilingual efforts staved off the day of reckoning. But the ultimate outcome was ironic, a solution based on a return to the "separate but equal" principle: Quebec opted for French monolingualism insofar as it could be enforced, and the rest of the country accepted this price to hold the nation together. Trudeau retired in 1984 with his integrationist philosophy about to be repudiated.

The paradox of 1968 was the quick collapse of all these movements of defiance, seemingly so deeply rooted in the character of modern or modernizing society. This year of revolutionary spectaculars actually represented not the upsurge of discontent but rather the peak and downturn of the process. As always in the revolutionary experience, the excesses of the zealots alienated governments and potential supporters and drove them to take refuge in some degree of conservatism. In the process, as in France and the United States, the majority often rejected the gradualist reformers who were never the favorite of the radicals either. At the same time, the extremists themselves broke up into feuding splinter groups, exemplified everywhere from the black nationalists to the Red Guards. There was no staying power.

The post-1968 counterrevolution was most pronounced in the United States, the country that had experienced the deepest and most varied challenge to its previously accepted values. It fit the pattern, noted by Arthur Schlesinger and many others, of political cycles in American history, as the country oscillated between liberal reform and conservative retrenchment.[5] Counterrevolution was, of course, symbolically rep-

241

resented by Richard Nixon's electoral success in November 1968, and the ostensible repudiation of the Great Society.

But movements of reaction, no more than revolutions, are not completed overnight. They unfold over a period of time, as leaders of the retreat are emboldened to accelerate the move backward. During his first term, Nixon, without any mandate from his razor-thin victory, played more the part of the pragmatic consolidator than the counter-revolutionary, halting further reform but leaving most of his predecessor's accomplishments in place. It is no accident that the real counter-revolutionaries of the 1980s have claimed no parentage from Nixon, but have lumped the years of his administration together with those of the Democrats before and after him as the era of "failed policies" when "government was the problem."

Whatever shift further to the right that Nixon may have been contemplating after his landslide reelection in 1972, the counterrevolutionary agenda was set back by the Watergate affair and the paralysis of the Nixon presidency. This paved the way for a prolongation of the nation's respite from counterrevolution under President Jimmy Carter. However, as the Reagan years attested, it did not eliminate the powerful emotions among much of the American electorate pressing to undo the Sixties Revolution.

Elsewhere in the world the momentum of the late 1960s was quickly lost, though the sense of shock lingered. Much of Europe and Japan were subjected to the anxieties of left-wing terrorism on the part of small groups of diehards—the Baader-Meinhof Gang in Germany, the Red Brigades in Italy, the "Red Army Faction" in Japan—complete with bombings, kidnappings, and assassinations. Yet the center held, attesting to the stability that democratic institutions had finally achieved in the industrialized world. China repudiated the radical 1960s completely, after the death of Mao Tse-tung in 1976 permitted a return to political rationality. The Soviet bloc, now including Cuba, settled down after the shock of 1968 to a self-protective bureaucratic immobilism for as long as the old ruling generation could sustain it.

Yet the collapse of radical protest did not leave the movement of 1968 without lasting impact. Everywhere, 1968 is recalled sometimes with horror, sometimes with nostalgia, but always with intensity. It is the intensity begotten by the social revolution, challenging the most personal aspects of life, that could not be ignored regardless which side of the barricades one chose.

The various components of the Sixties Revolution had very different outcomes after the climax of 1968, even in the United States taken by itself. Some elements—the politically oriented youth movement, agitating against the war and for campus revolution—flamed out quickly. Others—the black movement and certain aspects of the counterculture —established firm and remarkable changes in American public thinking. Still others—radical feminism and the movement for reproductive choice—became an arena for bitter controversy throughout the ensuing decades.

The antiwar movement continued unabated for the first couple of years of the Nixon administration. In fact, it reached its peak of numerical involvement in the spring of 1970 to protest the extension of the war to Cambodia. This was the setting for the demonstration at Kent State University in Ohio, when nervous National Guardsmen fired on the crowd and killed four students. While it triggered the greatest wave of student protests on record, the episode nevertheless sobered the younger generation as well as the government. The war and the opposition wound down together, until the Paris Accords of January 1973 ended direct American involvement in Vietnam. There followed the anticlimactic collapse of the Saigon government, confounding predictions both of falling dominoes all over Southeast Asia and of an outraged American backlash at home. To the contrary—America was gripped for the balance of the 1970s by the "post-Vietnam syndrome" of withdrawal from foreign entanglements. Although the Reagan years partly reversed this mood, the legacy of anti-interventionist feeling, exemplified by the case of Central America, did not cease to act as a political restraint on new overseas ventures.

Campus revolution was even shorter-lived. After a final series of flare-ups in 1969, with its leadership riven by destructive factionalism, the student movement rapidly lost momentum. Part of the reason was the alacrity with which universities responded to the most tangible of student demands, such as co-ed dorms, the abolition of *in loco parentis* controls, and the relaxation of course requirements. Little dent was made in the basic structure of universities, which grew more bureaucratic even while they were becoming more permissive, bearing out Marcuse's proposition about repressive tolerance.

Where the Sixties Revolution in America had its most remarkable success was in the gains registered by the black civil rights movement. Not only in matters of law and political rights but in most realms of public discourse and even mass entertainment, the old presumptions of racial inferiority were abruptly rejected and discredited. While the black nationalists and separatists collapsed, the way was finally opened to equal black participation in what remained a society of extreme inequalities. Probably the two most decisive things in shaming racism out of American public life were the achievement of equal voting rights and the martyrdom of Martin Luther King. A white backlash there was indeed, but it could only be expressed in oblique and coded ways, usually in opposition to measures (such as busing of schoolchildren and affirmative action in employment) designed to turn theoretical racial equality into a reality. However, highly visible openings of opportunity in education and jobs did not suffice to correct the disabilities of economic inequality for most blacks, as well as many whites. Despite all of the Great Society programs of welfare support and educational outreach that remained in place, poverty among blacks was as bad twenty years later as it was before the War on Poverty began.

In some respects, the Black Revolution cleared open a path for other groups that suffered discrimination and unequal social standing. Through the courts and the creative application of eighteenth-century constitutional rights and principles to the newly felt social needs of the mid-twentieth century, America achieved a new level of legal protection for every aggrieved interest against arbitrary power. Along with the law went a new standard for public attitudes—equal acceptance of every kind of personal difference. Everyone moved into the free air of equal rights—feminists, then champions of abortion rights, then the handicapped, then advocates for the retarded and the mentally ill, and eventually gay rights activists—everyone who had felt historically victimized by society's fear or disdain. This is why the issue of "original intent" of the framers of the American Constitution that swirled around President Reagan's nomination of Robert Bork to the Supreme Court in 1987 loomed so large: it was reasoning that would spike the legal artillery of the whole egalitarian movement spawned by the 1960s.

The rise of radical feminism and the transformation in the legal and social status of women, although stimulated by the Sixties Revolution and the black civil rights precedent, is a subject that goes beyond the bounds of a work on that era. The women's movement really began to gather momentum only when the country as a whole was already in a mood of reaction from the traumas of the 1960s. Moreover, its progress in altering the national consensus was much more difficult and controversial than the cause of the blacks after their breakthrough under King. Women's rights, above all legal abortion and the Equal Rights Amendment, remained through the 1980s the principal postrevolutionary battleground between those who wanted to advance the social revolution in this unconquered terrain and those would call a halt to the whole thing.

244

In the post-1960s legal climate warmed by the black movement and the women's movement, general personal rights vis-à-vis the power of the state were measurably enhanced. The doctrine of privacy established a new principle of protecting personal behavior, particularly sexual, from intrusions by the police power. Rights of criminal defendants were enhanced by a wide range of judicial decisions and liberalized corrections policies, much to the disgust and alarm of the general public. The year 1968 was the first year in American history when no one was executed. Legal Aid, a creature of the Great Society that survived subsequent conservative attacks, helped redress economic inequality in civil cases. Vietnam and Watergate bequeathed an openness-in-government movement, answering governmental surveillance and covert operations with the Freedom of Information Act and congressional investigations of the CIA and of the Kennedy and King assassinations.

Apart from these legal and attitudinal changes in the United States regarding personal freedom and nondiscrimination, the Sixties Revolution had little immediately to show for its efforts. The New Left and the student movements in America and Europe, enthralled by dreamlike visions of revolution and entangled in factional discord, failed like the American black separatists, though they did leave an imprint in university reform. The Red Guards in China ended by being totally repudiated along with the whole wild experience of the Cultural Revolution, when the country finally turned toward pragmatic modernization. The Czechoslovak reformers, the life crushed out of their resistance by Soviet boots, had only the satisfaction of seeing the principles of their reform—their Socialism with a Human Face—take life in the Soviet Union itself twenty years later. Bureaucratic and technocratic society weathered the challenge everywhere and became more and more entrenched as the basic form of modern life.

More influential than any direct challenge of the Sixties Revolution to the old order was the legacy of the counterculture in America. Most of the everyday features of the counterculture—drug use, mind-numbing music, linguistic degradation, the sexual revolution, and the propensity to drop out of the rat race—rippled through the entire youthful generation and showed no signs of abating throughout the long era of political reaction after 1968. So the revolution that succeeded most of all was not the organized revolution of social principles but the individual revolution of independence from the old norms of society. The pollster Daniel Yankelovich found the real cultural revolution in the ascendancy of the new ethic of "self-fulfillment."[6]

Unfortunately, as these features of the counterculture spread down through less educated and less philosophical strata of the Sixties Generation, their role shifted from the positive quest for self-realization to the negative escape from reality and responsibility. The shift was visible in Haight-Ashbury, for example, even during 1968. This is not to say that the counterculture of the 1960s was alone responsible for the galloping social pathology of the 1970s and 1980s—economic frustrations among the underclass were a major culprit—but the hippie example clearly pointed the way to the weakening of traditional social controls and institutions among disadvantaged segments of the American people. Advocates for every disfavored group abandoned the philosophy of responsibility that put the burden on the victim, and asserted the philosophy of entitlements that put the burden on society. In turn, the agonies of a liberal society fed the conservative reaction against the social revolution as a whole. The deepening of counterrevolution and the emergence of the New Right in the 1980s were only the last chapter in a thirty-year process of national upheaval and consolidation.

Rare is the movement in history that completes its agenda in its own time. The Sixties Revolution left more undone than done when it succumbed to the counterrevolutionary mood of the next two decades. Yet no counterrevolution can entirely suppress the needs and hopes that inspired revolution in the first place.

Could the social revolution resume? Could there be a new 1968? History never repeats itself exactly; old struggles recede from attention and new ones appear. Yet many of the real issues of 1968 persist in the dehumanizing structures of modern society, and the potential for the revolt of the young against the old is always present. The gains and traditions established by revolution are a sort of plateau for the next assault, like a new base camp set up by a team of mountain climbers to support the next leg of their advance.

Many of the unfinished tasks or revived concerns of the 1960s came into focus again by the end of the 1980s. Anti-imperialism stayed alive and well in American opposition to covert operations and the United States presence in Central America; the ghost of Vietnam can still be invoked. For the European Left, Israel is the imperialist villain and sympathy goes to the Palestinian Arabs. There are rumblings of renewed anti-Establishment radicalism directed against government, corporations, universities, even the whole tradition of Western culture, all in the spirit of antidiscrimination and cultural pluralism. Discrimination—or more accurately, lingering economic injustice for the former victims of discrimination, black, female, or other—certainly remains a major problem in American life. A greater challenge for future reformers and revolutionaries is the entire area of economic restructuring and economic fairness—the agenda of the 1930s and 1940s in America and Europe—that the rebels of the 1960s neglected or left in the realm of theory alone. In the Communist world, 1968 has already come back to life. The Gorbachev reforms in the Soviet Union appear as though they had been lifted in their entirety from the "socialism with a human face" of the Czechoslovak reformers. China is another matter, where the nation is pell-mell replicating the system and spirit that alienated the youth of the West and likely will again.

Along with the unfinished agenda inherited from the past, reformers of the next wave will encounter issues and aspirations that were at best dimly or marginally felt in the 1960s. Environmental concerns and doubts about the unqualified benefits of technological advance have become much more pressing. Students and professors are rebelling against instruction in the traditions of Western civilization. A pervasive nonconfidence in all manner of public institutions, exemplified by the steady decline in voter participation, has taken hold in the United States. Social pathology in the underclass, aggravated by the reluctance of both the Left and the Right to assert effective social controls, has assumed epidemic proportions and demands radical action.

Renewed revolution is not necessarily the answer to all this unfinished business. The realities of political life, however, point to a continuing cyclical swing between the evasion of problems and a radical furor over them—a furor that will generate its own excesses and its own undoing as new demands are advanced that society at large cannot assimilate. Perhaps the next worldwide generation of revolutionaries, presaged by the drug culture, will go beyond the social freedom of the individual to something else. If the vogue of the occult and the mystical and the self-expressive is any indication, the new aim could be a demand for freedom in personal mental life, a revolt against the whole modern tradition of rational and scientific thinking. This might be the last revolution.

NOTES

Chapter 1: The Spirit of '68

1. Tom Hayden, *Reunion: A Memoir* (New York: Random House, 1988), 283.
2. All income and population figures here and on p. 12 are from Bureau of the Census, *Statistical Abstract of the United States* (Washington, D.C.: Government Printing Office, 1960, 1968, and 1980).
3. David Burner and Thomas R. West, *The Torch Is Passed: The Kennedy Brothers and American Liberalism* (New York: Atheneum, 1984), 214.
4. Yuri Zhukov in *Pravda*, 30 May 1968.
5. Lewis S. Feuer, *The Conflict of Generations: The Character and Significance of Student Movements* (New York: Basic Books, 1969), 152, 529.

Chapter 2: Saigon

1. Quoted in Don Oberdorfer, *Tet!* (New York: Doubleday, 1971), 25.
2. Quoted in George C. Herring, *America's Longest War: The United States and Vietnam, 1950–1975*, 2nd ed. (Philadelphia: Temple University Press, 1986), 186.
3. Oberdorfer, *Tet!*, 34; William C. Westmoreland, *A Soldier Reports* (Garden City, N.Y.: Doubleday, 1976), 325.
4. NSA filing with U.S. District Court, Southern District of New York, 15 Oct. 1984, quoted in Bob Brewin and Sydney Shaw, *Vietnam on Trial: Westmoreland vs. CBS* (New York: Atheneum, 1987), 204.
5. Quoted in Don Kowet, *A Matter of Honor* (New York: Macmillan, 1984), 89.
6. Commander-in-Chief Pacific and Commander, U.S. Military Assistance Command, Vietnam, *Report on the War in Vietnam* (Washington, D.C.: Government Printing Office, 1968), 158.
7. Neil Sheehan, *A Bright Shining Lie: John Paul Vann and America in Vietnam* (New York: Random House, 1988), 715.
8. John M. G. Brown, *Rice Paddy Grunt: Unfading Memories of the Vietnam Generation* (Chicago: Regnery, 1986), 62–64.
9. Oral history interview, Johnson Papers, quoted in Herring, *America's Longest War*, 137.
10. Quoted in Oberdorfer, *Tet!*, 67.
11. Quoted ibid., 75.
12. CIA memo of 26 Feb. 1968, National Security Council files on Vietnam, quoted in Gabriel Kolko, *Anatomy of a War: Vietnam, the United States, and the Modern Historical Experience* (New York: Pantheon, 1985), 311.
13. *The Pentagon Papers: The Defense Department History of United States Decisionmaking on Vietnam*, Senator Gravel ed. (Boston: Beacon Press, 1971), IV, 546–47.
14. *The New York Times*, 14 March 1978.
15. Associated Press, 7 March 1968.
16. Quoted in Oberdorfer, *Tet!*, 184.

17. Ibid., 185.

18. Text in Patrick McGarvey, ed., *Visions of Victory: Selected Vietnamese Communist Military Writings, 1964–1968* (Stanford, Calif.: Hoover Institution Press, 1969), 252–53.

19. Quoted in Stanley Karnow, *Vietnam: A History* (New York: Viking, 1983), 544.

20. Michael Herr, *Dispatches* (New York: Knopf, 1977), 71.

21. Presidential press conference, 18 February 1982.

22. Quoted in Doris Kearns, *Lyndon Johnson and the American Dream* (New York: Harper & Row, 1976), 251–53.

23. *The New York Times*, 31 December 1967.

24. Quoted in Clark Dougan et al., *The Vietnam Experience: Nineteen Sixty-Eight* (Boston: Boston Publishing Co., 1983), 23.

25. Quoted in *The Pentagon Papers*, IV, 538–39.

26. Quoted in Henry Brandon, *Anatomy of Error: The Inside Story of the Asian War on the Potomac, 1954–1969* (Boston: Gambit, 1969), 119.

27. Herr, *Dispatches*, 47.

28. Lyndon Baines Johnson, *The Vantage Point: Perspectives of the Presidency, 1963–1969* (New York: Holt, Rinehart & Winston, 1971), 384.

29. Oriana Fallaci, *Interview with History* (Boston: Houghton-Mifflin, 1976), 82.

30. Karnow, *Vietnam*, 545.

31. Brandon, *Anatomy of Error*, 121.

32. Mark A. Stoler, "What Did He Really Say? The Aiken Formula for Vietnam Revisited," *Vermont History* 46, no. 2 (Spring 1978): 100–108.

33. Quoted in Nancy Zaroulis and Gerald Sullivan, *Who Spoke Up? American Protest Against the War in Vietnam, 1963–1975* (New York: Holt, Rinehart & Winston, 1984), 118.

34. Quoted in James Miller, *Democracy is in the Streets: From Port Huron to the Siege of Chicago* (New York: Simon & Schuster, 1987), 280.

35. Quoted in Zaroulis and Sullivan, *Who Spoke Up?* 131–32.

36. Norman Mailer, *The Armies of the Night* (New York: New American Library, 1968), 280, 288.

37. Oral history interview, Johnson Papers, quoted in Herring, *America's Longest War*, 192.

38. Brandon, *Anatomy of Error*, 121.

39. Quoted in Karnow, *Vietnam*, 541.

40. Quoted in Herbert Y. Schandler, *The Unmaking of a President: Lyndon Johnson and Vietnam* (Princeton: Princeton University Press, 1977), 95.

41. Interview, 16 Sept. 1973, quoted ibid., 97.

42. Quoted ibid., 98–99.

43. Quoted in *The New York Times*, 19 February 1968.

44. Schandler, *Unmaking of a President*, 115–16.

45. Michael Charlton and Anthony Moncrieff, *Many Reasons Why: The American Involvement in Vietnam* (New York: Hill & Wang, 1978), 146.

46. Lawrence J. Korb, *The Joint Chiefs of Staff: The First Twenty-five Years* (Bloomington, Ind.: Indiana University Press, 1976), 167.

47. Report of Chairman, JCS, on Situation in Vietnam and MACV Requirements, 27 Feb. 1968, *The Pentagon Papers*, New York Times ed. (New York: Quadrangle Books, 1971), 628–29.

48. Korb, *Joint Chiefs*, 166.

49. Johnson claimed that McNamara jumped overboard because of pressure from Robert Kennedy (Kearns, *Lyndon Johnson*, 321). According to Kennedy, McNamara said he was pushed (information from Arthur Schlesinger, Jr., cited in Karnow, *Vietnam*, 511).

50. Schandler, *Unmaking of a President*, 133–76; *The Pentagon Papers*, IV, 549–84.

51. *The Pentagon Papers*, IV, 558.

52. Ibid., IV, 562.

53. Ibid., IV, 564.

54. Interview in Schandler, *Unmaking of a President*, 162; cf. Clark Clifford, "A Vietnam Reappraisal: The Personal History of One Man's View and How it Evolved," *Foreign Affairs* 47, no. 5 (July 1969): 610–12.

55. Townsend Hoopes, *The Limits of Intervention: An Inside Account of How the Johnson Policy of Escalation in Vietnam was Reversed* (New York: McKay, 1969), 145–46.

56. *The Pentagon Papers*, IV, 574.

57. Johnson, *The Vantage Point*, 398.

58. Schandler, *Unmaking of a President*, 185.

59. Johnson, *The Vantage Point*, 399.

Chapter 3: Haight--Ashbury

1. Martin A. Lee and Bruce Shlain, *Acid Dreams: The CIA, LSD, and the Sixties Rebellion* (New York: Grove Press, 1985), 145.

2. Quoted in Leonard Wolf, *Voices from the Love Generation* (Boston: Little, Brown, 1968), xxxix.

3. *The Haight-Ashbury Maverick* 1, no. 2 (1967): 9–10.

4. Charles Perry, *The Haight-Ashbury: A History* (New York: Random House, 1984), 252.

5. L. H. Whittemore, *Cop* (New York: Holt, Rinehart & Winston, 1969), 247.

6. David E. Smith and John Luce, *Love Needs Care: A History of San Francisco's Haight-Ashbury Free Medical Clinic and its Role in Treating Drug Abuse Problems* (Boston: Little, Brown, 1971), 22.

7. Whittemore, *Cop*, 264–65.

8. Quoted by Hans Toch in "Last Word on the Hippies," in Herbert E. Robb and Raymond Sobel, eds., *From Left to Right: Readings on the Socio-Political Spectrum* (New York: Benziger, 1969), II, 95.

9. Smith and Luce, *Love Needs Care*, 22.

10. Ibid., 253.

11. Ibid., 254.

12. Alan Williams, quoted in *The New York Times*, 19 Feb. 1968.

13. *The Haight-Ashbury Maverick* 2, no. 3 (1968), 2.

14. Quoted in *The San Francisco Chronicle*, 21 Feb. 1968, p. 2.

15. Lee and Shlain, *Acid Dreams*, 141.

16. Henry David Thoreau, *Walden*, in *The Portable Thoreau* (New York: Viking, 1964), 264.

17. Ibid., 266.

18. Charles Reich, *The Greening of America* (New York: Random House, 1970), 10.

19. J. Milton Yinger, *Countercultures: The Promise and the Peril of a World Turned Upside Down* (New York: The Free Press, 1982), 23.

20. Theodore Roszak, *The Making of a Counter-Culture: Reflections on the Technocratic Society and its Youthful Opposition* (New York: Doubleday-Anchor, 1969), 186.

21. Richard Neville, *Play Power: Exploring the International Underground* (New York: Random House, 1970), 34.

22. Ibid.

23. Lewis Yablonsky, *The Hippie Trip* (New York: Pegasus, 1968), 36–7.

24. Robb and Sobel, *From Left to Right*, II, 83. Interpolation from the 1970 tract-by-tract census figures suggests a settled population of 6,000 to 7,000 in Haight-Ashbury.

25. Ross V. Speck, et al., *Youth, Communes, and the Politics of Drugs* (New York: Basic Books, 1972), 19.

26. Perry, *The Haight-Ashbury*, 106.

27. Wolf, *Voices*, xxxvi.

28. Quoted in Burton H. Wolfe, *The Hippies* (New York: New American Library, 1968), 169.

29. Wolf, *Voices*, xxxix.

30. Lee and Shlain, *Acid Dreams*, xx–xxi.

31. Timothy Leary, *The Politics of Ecstasy* (New York: Putnam's, 1968), 16, 18.

32. Quoted in Annie Gottlieb, *Do You Believe in Magic? The Second Coming of the Sixties Generation* (New York: Times Books, 1987), 173.

33. Lee and Shlain, *Acid Dreams*, 196.

34. Ibid., 159.

35. The Grateful Dead, "That's It for the Other One," in *Anthem of the Sun* (Burbank, Calif., and New York: Warner Bros., 1968).

36. Speck et al., *Youth*, 178.

37. Lee and Shlain, *Acid Dreams*, 184.

38. Robert G. Pielke, *You Say You Want a Revolution: Rock Music in American Culture* (Chicago: Nelson-Hall, 1986), 161–63.

39. Robert A. Rosenstone, " 'The Times They Are A-Changin': The Music of Protest," *Annals of the American Academy of Political and Social Science*, no. 382 (March 1969): 133.

40. The Beatles, *Sergeant Pepper's Lonely Hearts Club Band* (London: Northern Songs, Ltd., 1967).

41. Jefferson Airplane, "White Rabbit," in *Surrealistic Pillow* (New York: RCA, 1967).

42. Helen Swick Perry, *The Human Be-in* (New York: Basic Books, 1970), 76.

43. Lee and Shlain, *Acid Dreams*, 252–53.

44. Jonathan Eisen, ed., *The Age of Rock: Sounds of the American Cultural Revolution* (New York: Random House, 1969), xiii–xv.

45. Jefferson Airplane, "We Can Be Together," in *Volunteers* (New York: RCA, 1969).

46. Allan Bloom, *The Closing of the American Mind: How Higher Education has Failed Democracy and Impoverished the Souls of Today's Students* (New York: Simon & Schuster, 1987), 75, 79–81.

47. Pauline Kael, "Bonnie and Clyde," *The New Yorker*, 21 Oct. 1967, p. 171.

48. Myra Friedman, *Buried Alive: The Biography of Janis Joplin* (New York: Morrow, 1973), 172.

49. David Pichaske, *A Generation in Motion: Popular Music and Culture in the United States* (New York: Schirmer Books, 1979), 92–93.

50. Robb and Sobel, *From Left to Right*, II, 85.

51. Fred Davis, *On Youth Sub-Cultures: The Hippie Variant* (New York: General Learning, 1971), 14–15.

52. Robert Houriet, *Getting Back Together* (New York: Coward, McCann and Geoghegan, 1971), xiii, xv.

53. Keith Melville, *Communes in the Counter-Culture: Origins, Theories, Styles of Life* (New York: William Morrow, 1972), 80.

54. Quoted in Craig Canine and Michael McRae, "Paddling into the Mainstream: Where Have All the Homesteaders Gone?" *Harrowsmith* 2 (March–April 1987): 42.

55. John Rothchild and Susan Berns Wolf, *The Children of the Counter Culture* (Garden City, N.Y.: Doubleday, 1976), 196–97.

56. Reich, *Greening of America*, 225–29.

57. Nathan Adler, *The Underground Stream: New Life Styles and the Antinomian Personality* (New York: Harper & Row, 1972), 21, 35.

58. Quoted in David A. Noebel, "The Hippie Cultus—the New Pagans," in Robb and Sobel, *From Left to Right*, II, 103.

59. Ibid.

60. William L. Partridge, *The Hippie Ghetto: The Natural History of a Subculture* (New York: Holt, Rinehart & Winston, 1973), 52.

61. *The New York Times*, May 25, 1968.

Notes

62. William L. O'Neill, *Coming Apart: An Informal History of America in the 1960s* (New York: Times Books, 1971), 256.

63. Ibid., 255.

64. Gary Snyder, "Buddhism and the Coming Revolution," *The Berkeley Barb*, 15 Nov. 1968, p. 90.

65. Jefferson Airplane, "The Other Side of This Life," in *Bless Its Pointed Little Head* (New York: RCA, 1968).

66. Whittemore, *Cop*, 275.

67. Lee and Shlain, *Acid Dreams*, 195.

68. Jean-François Revel, *Without Marx or Jesus: The New American Revolution Has Begun* (Garden City, N.Y.: Doubleday, 1971), 242.

69. Neville, *Play Power*, 40.

70. Lee and Shlain, *Acid Dreams*, 208.

71. James F. Drane, *A New American Reformation: A Study of Youth Culture and Religion* (New York: Philosophical Library, 1973), 38.

72. The Beatles, *The White Album* (London: Northern Songs, Ltd., 1968).

73. Jerold M. Starr, ed., *Cultural Politics: Radical Movements in Modern History* (New York: Praeger, 1985), 244.

74. Lee and Shlain, *Acid Dreams*, 184.

Chapter 4: New Hampshire

1. Eugene J. McCarthy, *The Year of the People* (Garden City, N.Y.: Doubleday, 1969), 69.

2. Interview with Herbert Schandler, 13 Oct. 1975, quoted in Herbert Schandler, *The Unmaking of a President: Lyndon Johnson and Vietnam* (Princeton, NJ: Princeton University Press, 1977), 201.

3. *Newsweek*, 11 Mar. 1968.

4. Quoted in Jeremy Larner, *Nobody Knows: Reflections on the McCarthy Campaign of 1968* (New York: Macmillan, 1970), 41.

5. John Adler, "New Hampshire: 'A Youthful, Clean, Enthusiastic Volunteer,' " in Joseph Frank, ed., *The New Look in Politics: McCarthy's Campaign* (Albuquerque: University of New Mexico Press, 1968), 26.

6. Quoted in Theodore H. White, *The Making of the President: 1968* (New York: Atheneum, 1969), 187.

7. McCarthy, *Year of the People*, 89.

8. Quoted in *Time*, 22 Mar. 1968, p. 16.

9. Quoted in White, *Making of the President*, 103.

10. Quoted in Jules Archer, *1968: Year of Crisis* (New York: Messner, 1971), 82.

11. Ibid.

12. Ibid., 17.

13. Quoted in White, *Making of the President*, 84.

14. Ibid.

15. Michael Charlton and Anthony Moncrief, *Many Reasons Why: The American Involvement in Vietnam* (New York: Hill & Wang, 1979), 165.

16. Lewis Chester, Godfrey Hodgson, and Bruce Page, *An American Melodrama: The Presidential Campaign of 1968* (New York: Viking, 1969), 82.

17. McGovern interview of 16 July 1970, RFK Oral History Program, quoted in Arthur M. Schlesinger, Jr., *Robert Kennedy and His Times* (Boston: Houghton-Mifflin, 1978), 826.

18. Quoted in Arthur Herzog, *McCarthy for President* (New York: Viking, 1969), 32.

19. McCarthy, *Year of the People*, 265–67.

20. Quoted in Chester, Hodgson, and Page., *American Melodrama*, 90.

21. Hubert H. Humphrey, *The Education of a Public Man: My Life and Politics* (New York: Doubleday, 1986), 376.

22. Vanden Heuvel interview, in George Plimpton and Jean Stein, eds., *American Journey: The Times of Robert Kennedy* (New York: Harcourt Brace Jovanovich, 1970), 226.

23. Quoted in Chester, Hodgson, and Page, *American Melodrama*, 85.

24. Quoted in Richard Cummings, *The Pied Piper: Allard K. Lowenstein and the Liberal Dream* (New York: Grove Press, 1984), 352.

25. Galbraith interview, in Plimpton and Stein, *American Journey*, 225–26.

26. David Burner, *The Torch Is Passed: The Kennedy Brothers and American Liberalism* (New York: Atheneum, 1984), 212.

27. Eugene McCarthy, *Up Til Now: A Memoir* (New York: Harcourt Brace Jovanovich, 1987), 188–89.

28. Quoted in Herzog, *McCarthy*, 104.

29. Hugh Sidey, *A Very Personal Presidency: LBJ in the White House* (New York: Atheneum, 1968), 291.

30. Chester, Hodgson, and Page, *American Melodrama*, 119.

31. McGovern interview, in Plimpton and Stein, *American Journey*, 228.

32. Remarks of Nixon speechwriter Ray Price to Theodore White, in White, *Making of the President*, 147.

33. Lyndon B. Johnson, *The Vantage Point: Perspectives of the Presidency, 1963–1969* (New York: Holt, Rinehart & Winston, 1971), 537–38.

34. Quoted in Walter Isaacson and Evan Thomas, *The Wise Men: Six Friends and the World They Made* (New York: Simon & Schuster, 1986), 695.

35. *The New York Times*, 13 Feb. and 26 March, 1968.

36. Quoted in Townsend Hoopes, *The Limits of Intervention* (New York: McKay, 1969), 185.

37. Isaacson and Thomas, *The Wise Men*, 686.

38. Schlesinger, *Robert Kennedy*, 848.

39. Westmoreland interview of 23 Oct. 1972, quoted in Schandler, *Unmaking of a President*, 236.

40. Hoopes, *Limits of Intervention*, 210–11.

41. Quoted in Isaacson and Thomas, *The Wise Men*, 702.

42. Ibid., 700.

43. Stanley Karnow, *Vietnam: A History* (New York: Viking, 1983), 562.

44. Schandler, *Unmaking of a President*, 264.

45. Lawrence O'Brien, *No Final Victories: A Life in Politics from John F. Kennedy to Watergate* (Garden City, N.Y.: Doubleday, 1974) 228, 229.

46. Doris Kearns, *Lyndon Johnson and The American Dream* (New York: Harper & Row, 1976), 343.

47. Schandler, *Unmaking of a President*, 279.

48. Humphrey, *Education of a Public Man*, 358.

49. Carl Solberg, *Hubert Humphrey: A Biography* (New York: Norton, 1984), 322.

50. Humphrey, *Education of a Public Man*, 358.

51. Ibid., 359.

52. Kearns, *Lyndon Johnson*, 349.

53. Sam Houston Johnson, *My Brother, Lyndon* (New York: Cowles, 1969), 252.

54. Quoted in Schlesinger, *Robert Kennedy*, 868.

55. Johnson, *The Vantage Point*, 435.

56. Quoted in Archer, *1968*, 84.

57. Acheson to Harriman, 19 April 1968, quoted in Isaacson and Thomas, *The Wise Men*, 708.

58. Chester L. Cooper, *The Lost Crusade: America in Vietnam* (New York: Dodd, Mead, 1970), 401.

59. Interview with Harriman aide Dan Davidson, quoted in Isaacson and Thomas, *The Wise Men*, 706.

60. Clark Clifford interview, in Merle Miller, *Lyndon: An Oral History* (New York: Putnam's, 1980), 522.

61. Anonymous source, quoted in Allan E. Goodman, *The Lost Peace: America's Search for a Negotiated Settlement of the Vietnam War* (Stanford, Calif.: Hoover Institution Press, 1978), 69.

62. Quoted in Chester, Hodgson, and Page, *American Melodrama*, 280.

63. Edgar Berman, *Hubert: The Triumph and Tragedy of the Humphrey I Knew* (New York: Putnam's, 1979), 164.

64. Fred Harris, *Potomac Fever* (New York: Norton, 1977), 161–62.

65. Humphrey, *Education of a Public Man*, 370.

66. Quoted in Archer, *1968*, 94.

67. Humphrey, *Education of a Public Man*, 371.

68. *The Washington Post*, 5 April 1968.

69. See White, *Making of the President*, 160–61.

70. Quoted in Solberg, *Hubert Humphrey*, 328.

71. Sandy Vogelgesang, *The Long Dark Night of the Soul: The American Intellectual Left and the Vietnam War* (New York: Harper & Row, 1974), 144–45.

72. Schlesinger, *Robert Kennedy*, 905.

73. Interview with McCarthy aide Andreas Teuber, in Plimpton and Stein, *American Journey*, 312.

74. David Riesman, "McCarthy and Kennedy: Some Very Personal Reflections," *The New Republic*, 13 April 1968, p. 21.

75. William O'Neill, *Coming Apart: An Informal History of America in the 1960s* (New York: Times Books, 1971), 376.

76. Abigail McCarthy, *Private Faces/Public Places* (Garden City, N.Y.: Doubleday, 1972), 380.

77. Berman, *Hubert*, 156–57.

Chapter 5: Memphis and Washington

1. King Papers, quoted in David J. Garrow, *Bearing the Cross: Martin Luther King, Jr., and the Southern Christian Leadership Conference* (New York: Morrow, 1986), 621.

2. House Select Committee on Assassinations, *Final Report* (Washington, D.C.: GPO, 1979), 371–72.

3. Quoted in *The Washington Post*, 5 April 1968.

4. Quoted in Jules Archer, *1968: Year of Crisis* (New York: Messner, 1971), 44.

5. Quoted in Ben W. Gilbert and *The Washington Post* Staff, *Ten Blocks from the White House: Anatomy of the Washington Riots of 1968* (New York: Praeger, 1968), 16.

6. Ibid., 17.

7. Ibid., 22.

8. Ibid., 30.

9. Ibid., 61.

10. Ibid., 50.

11. Ibid., 106.

12. Ibid., 119, 148.

13. Ibid., 145, 154.

14. Quoted in Janet M. Knight, ed., *Three Assassinations* (New York: Facts on File, 1971), 140–41.

15. John M. G. Brown, *Rice Paddy Grunt: Unfading Memories of the Vietnam Generation* (Chicago: Regnery, 1986), 145.

16. Michael Herr, *Dispatches* (New York: Knopf, 1977), 158.

17. Quoted in David L. Lewis, *King: A Critical Biography* (New York: Praeger, 1970), 392.

18. Quoted in Thomas R. Brooks, *Walls Come Tumbling Down: A History of the Civil Rights Movement, 1940–1970* (Englewood Cliffs, N.J.: Prentice-Hall, 1974), 113.

19. David J. Garrow, *The FBI and Martin Luther King, Jr.: From "Solo" to Memphis* (New York: Norton, 1981), 42–43.

20. Ibid., 50.

21. "The Great March to Freedom," Gordy-Motown record no. 906, quoted in Garrow, *Bearing The Cross*, 283–84.

22. 18 November 1964; quoted in Richard G. Powers, *Secrecy and Power: The Life of J. Edgar Hoover* (New York; The Free Press, 1987), 418.

23. Quoted in Knight, *Three Assassinations*, 275.

24. "The Black Panther is Coming—What Is Black Power and Why Do We Need It?" (New York: SNCC, 1966); reprinted in Herbert E. Robb and Raymond Sobel, eds., *From Left to Right: Readings on the Socio-Political Spectrum*, vol. 1 (New York: Benziger, 1968), 26.

25. From "Where Do We Go from Here?" Text in James M. Washington, ed., *A Testament of Hope: The Essential Writings of Martin Luther King, Jr.* (San Francisco: Harper & Row, 1986), 250–51.

26. Quoted in Garrow, *The FBI and Martin Luther King*, 213–14.

27. Hoover to Special Agent in Charge, Albany, 25 August 1967, in Senate Select Committee, *Hearings*, 6, FBI, p. 383; quoted in Powers, *Secrecy*, 425.

28. Hoover to Special Agents in Charge, 4 March 1968, Senate Select Committee, *Final Report*, Book III, 180, quoted in Powers, *Secrecy*, 425.

29. House Select Committee, *Final Report*, 15.

30. Senate Select Committee, *Final Report*, Book III, 189, quoted in Powers, *Secrecy*, 426.

31. *Report of the National Advisory Commission on Civil Disorders* (Washington, D.C.: GPO, 1968), preface, 15.

32. Ibid., 1.

33. Quoted in Knight, *Three Assassinations*, 277.

34. Hugh Sidey, *A Very Personal Presidency: LBJ in the White House* (New York: Atheneum, 1968), 290.

35. Roy Wilkins with Tom Matthews, *Standing Fast: The Autobiography of Roy Wilkins* (New York: Viking, 1982), 328.

36. *The New York Times*, 8 March and 14 March 1968.

37. Quoted in Jules Witcover, *85 Days: The Last Campaign of Robert Kennedy* (New York: Putnam's, 1969), 53.

38. Andrew Kopkind, "White on Black: The Riot Commission and the Rhetoric of Reform," in David Boesel and Peter H. Rossi, eds., *Cities Under Siege: An Anatomy of the Ghetto Riots, 1964–1968* (New York: Basic Books, 1971), 226.

39. *The New York Times*, 2 March 1968.

40. Nathan Caplan, "The New Ghetto Man: A Review of Recent Empirical Studies," in Boesel and Rossi, *Cities Under Siege*, 343.

41. James H. Hargett, "Negroes and Leadership," *The Los Angeles Times*, 26 March 1966; quoted in Lewis M. Killian, *The Impossible Revolution? Black Power and the American Dream* (New York: Random House, 1975), 126.

42. Quoted in Milton Viorst, ed., *Fire in the Streets: America in the 1960s* (New York: Simon & Schuster, 1979), 375.

43. Malcolm X, "The Ballot or the Bullet," address to CORE, 3 April 1964; quoted in Judith C. Albert and Stewart E. Albert, eds., *The Sixties Papers: Documents of a Rebellious Decade* (New York: Praeger, 1984), 127.

44. See Clayborne Carson, *In Struggle: SNCC and the Black Awakening of the 1960s* (Cambridge, Mass.: Harvard University Press, 1981), 259–60.

45. Quoted in Martin A. Lee and Bruce Shlain, *Acid Dreams: The CIA, LSD, and the Sixties Rebellion* (New York: Grove Press, 1985), 209.

46. Carson, *In Struggle*, 285.

47. Senate Select Committee, *Final Report*, Book III, 3, 27; quoted in Garrow, *The FBI and Martin Luther King*, 211.

48. Quoted in Frank I. Donner, *The Age of Surveillance: The Aims and Methods of America's Political Intelligence System* (New York: Vintage, 1981), 221.

49. Report of the Department of Justice Task Force to Review the FBI Martin Luther King, Jr., Security and Assassination Investigations, 11 Jan. 1977 (Washington: Department of Justice, 1977), 101–4, 110–11.

50. House Select Committee, *Final Report*, 5, 371, 374.

Chapter 6: Morningside Heights

1. Tom Hayden, *Reunion: A Memoir* (New York: Random House, 1988), 275.

2. Quoted in Jerry L. Avorn, et al., *Up Against the Ivy Wall: A History of the Columbia Crisis* (New York: Atheneum, 1968), 63.

3. Mark Rudd, "Columbia," *Movement*, March 1969, reprinted in Immanuel Wallerstein and Paul Starr, eds., *The University Crisis Reader* (New York: Random House, 1971) II, 182.

4. Quoted in Avorn, *Up Against the Ivy Wall*, 150–51.

5. Quoted, ibid., 173.

6. Ibid., 196, 203.

7. Lewis S. Feuer, *The Conflict of Generations: The Character and Significance of Student Movements* (New York: Basic Books, 1969), 528–29.

8. Stanley Rothman and S. Robert Lichter, *Roots of Radicalism: Jews, Christians, and The New Left* (New York: Oxford University Press, 1982), 12.

9. Quoted in Max Heirich, *The Beginning: Berkeley 1964* (New York: Columbia University Press, 1971), 199–200.

10. Klaus Mehnert, *Twilight of the Young: The Radical Movements of the 1960s and Their Legacy* (New York: Holt, Rinehart & Winston, 1977), 29–30.

11. Seymour Martin Lipset, "The Possible Effects of Student Activism on International Politics," in Seymour Martin Lipset and Philip G. Altbach, eds., *Students in Revolt* (Boston: Houghton-Mifflin, 1969), 511–12.

12. Richard Flacks, "The Liberated Generation: An Exploration of the Roots of Student Protest," quoted in James Miller, *Democracy Is in the Streets: From Port Huron to the Siege of Chicago* (New York: Simon & Schuster, 1987), 185.

13. Maurice Isserman, *If I Had a Hammer: The Death of the Old Left and the Birth of the New Left* (New York: Basic Books, 1987), 214.

14. Richard Flacks, "The New Left and American Politics after Ten Years," *Journal of Social Issues* 27 (1971), 23–24.

15. Allen J. Matusow, *The Unraveling of America: A History of Liberalism in the 1960s* (New York: Harper & Row, 1984), 311.

16. Todd Gitlin, *The Sixties: Years of Hope, Days of Rage* (New York: Bantam Books, 1987), 286.

17. Quoted, ibid., 283.

18. Text in James Miller, *Democracy Is in the Streets*, 333.

19. Arnold Kaufman, "Human Nature and Participatory Democracy," in Carl J. Friedrich, ed., *Nomos III: Responsibility* (New York: Atherton, 1960), quoted in Miller, *Democracy Is in the Streets*, 94.

20. Miller, *Democracy Is in the Streets*, 142, 147.

21. Quoted in Wini Breines, *Community and Organization in the New Left, 1962–1968: The Great Refusal* (New York: Praeger, 1982), 58–59.

22. Miller, *Democracy Is in the Streets*, 373–74.

23. Martin A. Lee and Bruce Shlain, *Acid Dreams: The CIA, LSD, and the Sixties Rebellion* (New York: Grove Press, 1985), 227–28.

24. Gitlin, *The Sixties,* 307.

25. Mehnert, *Twilight of the Young,* 335.

26. Ronald Fraser et al., *1968: A Student Generation in Revolt* (New York: Pantheon, 1988), 354.

27. Isserman, *If I Had a Hammer,* 219.

28. Fraser, *1968,* 354, 359.

29. Jean-François Revel, *Without Marx or Jesus: The New American Revolution Has Begun* (Garden City, N.Y.: Doubleday, 1971), 242.

30. Nigel Young, *An Infantile Disorder? The Crisis and Decline of the New Left* (Boulder, Colo.: Westview Press, 1977), 185.

31. Quoted in Edward J. Bacciocco, Jr., *The New Left in America: Reform to Revolution, 1956 to 1970* (Stanford, Calif.: Hoover Institution Press, 1974), 169.

32. Quoted in Young, *Infantile Disorder,* 187.

33. Quoted, ibid., 182.

34. Avorn, *Up Against the Ivy Wall,* 30.

35. Quoted in Breines, *Community,* 118.

36. Text of resolution in Wallerstein and Starr, *University Crisis Reader,* II, 138–40.

37. Hayden, *Reunion,* 278.

38. Quoted in Avorn, *Up Against the Ivy Wall,* 25.

39. Text, ibid., 25–27.

40. Quoted, ibid., 226–27.

41. *Crisis at Columbia: Report of the Fact-Finding Commission Appointed to Investigate the Disturbances at Columbia University in April and May 1968* (New York: Random House, 1968).

42. Ibid., 182.

43. Tom Hayden in *Ramparts,* quoted in Gitlin, *The Sixties,* 308.

44. Rothman and Lichter, *Roots of Radicalism,* 36.

45. Quoted in Matusow, *Unravelling of America,* 336.

46. Fraser, *1968,* 308.

47. Quoted in Young, *Infantile Disorder,* 276.

48. Ibid., 203.

49. Rothman and Lichter, *Roots of Radicalism,* 390.

50. David L. Westby, *The Clouded Vision: The Student Movement in the United States in the 1960's* (Lewisburg, Pa.: Bucknell University Press, 1976), 172.

Chapter 7: Paris

1. Quoted in Daniel Singer, *Prelude to Revolution: France in May 1968* (New York: Hill & Wang, 1970), 117.

2. Patrick Seale and Maureen McConville, *Red Flag/Black Flag: French Revolution 1968* (New York: Putnam, 1968), 66.

3. Lloyd Garrison, *The New York Times,* 4 May 1968.

4. Quoted by Lloyd Garrison, *The New York Times,* 12 May 1968.

5. Quoted, ibid.

6. Gisela Mandel, "The Night of the Barricades," in *Revolt in France, May–June 1968: A Contemporary Record* (New York: Les Evans, 1968), 10.

7. Quoted in Seale and McConville, *Red Flag/Black Flag,* 83.

8. Ibid.

9. Mandel, "Night of the Barricades," 12.

10. Seale and McConville, *Red Flag/Black Flag,* 68–69.

Notes

11. Quoted, ibid., 29.

12. Ibid., 52, 59.

13. Ibid., 145–46.

14. Yuri Zhukov, "Werewolves," *Pravda*, 30 May 1968; translated in Klaus Mehnert, *Moscow and the New Left* (Berkeley: University of California Press, 1975), 149–50.

15. Quoted in Stanley Hoffman, "The French Psychodrama: De Gaulle's Anti-Communist Coup," *The New Republic*, 31 Aug. 1968.

16. Quoted in Seale and McConville, *Red Flag/Black Flag*, 150.

17. "Daniel Cohn-Bendit Interviewed by Jean-Paul Sartre," *Le Nouvel Observateur*, 20 May 1968; translated in Hervé Bourges, ed., *The French Student Revolt: The Leaders Speak* (New York: Hill & Wang, 1968), 73.

18. Seale and McConville, *Red Flag/Black Flag*, 152.

19. Quoted in Singer, *Prelude to Revolution*, 177.

20. Seale and McConville, *Red Flag/Black Flag*, 174.

21. Daniel Cohn-Bendit, *Obsolete Communism: The Left-Wing Alternative* (New York: McGraw-Hill, 1968), 70–73.

22. Quoted in Singer, *Prelude*, 201.

23. Alain Schnapp and Pierre Vidal-Naquet, *The French Student Uprising, November 1967–June 1968* (Boston: Beacon Press, 1971), 30–31.

24. Quoted in *The New York Times*, 7 May 1968.

25. Gianni Statera, *Death of a Utopia: The Development and Decline of Student Movements in Europe* (New York: Oxford University Press, 1975), 50.

26. J. J. Servan-Schreiber, *The Spirit of May* (New York: McGraw-Hill, 1969), 30.

27. R. Dutschke, "Contradictions of Late Capitalism, the Anti-authoritarian Students, and Their Relation to the Third World," quoted in Statera, *Death of a Utopia*, 85–86.

28. *The Times* [London], 17 May 1968; quoted in Theodore Roszak, *The Making of a Counter Culture: Reflections on the Technocratic Society and Its Youthful Opposition* (Garden City, N.Y.: Doubleday/Anchor, 1969), 22.

29. Stephen Spender, *The Year of the Young Rebels* (New York: Random House, 1969), 45.

30. Statera, *Death of a Utopia*, 96–97.

31. Quoted in Bourges, *The French Student Revolt*, 82–83.

Chapter 8: Peking

1. William Hinton, *Hundred Day War: The Cultural Revolution at Tsinghua University* (New York: Monthly Review Press, 1972), 111.

2. Quoted, ibid., 196.

3. Purported transcript published in Taiwan in 1973; reprinted in Harold C. Hinton, ed., *The People's Republic of China, 1949–1979: A Documentary Survey* (Wilmington, Del.: Scholarly Resources, 1980), IV, 2137–48.

4. *The Washington Post*, 28 August 1968; quoted in Stanley Karnow, *Mao and China: From Revolution to Revolution* (New York: Viking, 1972), 441.

5. Listed in William Hinton, *Hundred Day War*, 214–15.

6. Ibid., 227.

7. Ibid.

8. Ibid., 20.

9. Text in *Peking Review*, 12 August 1966, pp. 6–11.

10. Quoted in Karnow, *Mao and China*, 302.

11. William Hinton, *Hundred Day War*, 105.

12. Ibid., 111.

13. Text in Harold Hinton, *People's Republic*, IV, 1861.

14. Maurice Meissner, *Mao's China and After: A History of the People's Republic* (New York: Free Press, 1986), 362.

15. Quoted in K. S. Karol, *The Second Chinese Revolution* (New York: Hill & Wang, 1974), 331.

16. *The New York Times*, 8 July 1968.

17. Quoted in William Hinton, *Hundred Day War*, 167.

18. Jean Daubier, *A History of the Chinese Cultural Revolution* (New York: Vintage Books, 1974), 251.

19. *The New York Times*, 29 August 1968.

20. Karnow, *Mao and China*, 446.

21. Liu Guokai, *A Brief Analysis of the Cultural Revolution* (Armonk, N.Y.: M. E. Sharpe, 1987), 133.

22. Resolution of the Tenth Party Congress, August 1973; quoted in Jacques Guillermaz, *The Chinese Communist Party in Power, 1949–1976* (Boulder, Colo.: Westview Press, 1976), 461.

23. "Statement by Mao Tse-tung on the Death of Martin Luther King, 16 April 1968"; text in Harold Hinton, *People's Republic*, 2004–5.

24. Text, ibid., IV: 2092–93.

25. David Milton and Nancy Dall Milton, *The Wind Will Not Subside: Years in Revolutionary China, 1964–1969* (New York: Pantheon, 1976), 376.

26. Ibid.

27. Anita Chan, *Children of Mao: Personality Development and Political Activism in the Red Guard Generation* (Seattle, Wash.: University of Washington Press, 1986), 183–84.

Chapter 9: Prague

1. Quoted in Robert Littell, ed., *The Czech Black Book* [prepared by the Institute of History of the Czechoslovak Academy of Sciences] (New York: Praeger, 1969), 6.

2. Quoted, ibid., 16–17.

3. Proclamation "To All the People of the Czechoslovak Socialist Republic," 21 Aug. 1968, ibid., 11.

4. TASS statement broadcast by *Vltava*, 21 Aug. 1968, ibid., 23.

5. Ibid., 34.

6. Alan Levy, *Rowboat to Prague* (New York: Grossman, 1972), 334–35.

7. Quoted in Vojtech Mastny, ed., *Czechoslovakia: Crisis in World Communism* (New York: Facts on File, 1972), 87.

8. Quoted in Lyndon Johnson, *The Vantage Point: Perspectives of the Presidency, 1963–1969* (New York: Holt, Rinehart & Winston, 1971), 488.

9. Tad Szulc, *Czechoslovakia since World War II* (New York: Viking, 1971), 399.

10. Quoted, ibid., 396.

11. The list of Soviet demands was published in *The New York Times*, 8 Sept. 1968; quoted in Szulc, *Czechoslovakia*, 422–23.

12. Text in Robin A. Remington, ed., *Winter in Prague: Documents on Czechoslovak Communism in Crisis* (Cambridge, Mass.: MIT Press, 1969), 379–82.

13. Text, in *Czechoslovakia's Blueprint for "Freedom"* (Washington: Acropolis Books, 1968), 89–178.

14. Zdeněk Mlynář, *Nightfrost in Prague: The End of Humane Socialism* (New York: Karz, 1980), 116.

15. "Speech Delivered by Comrade Alexander Dubček at the Plenary Session of the Central Committee of the Communist Party of Czechoslovakia," 1 April 1968, *Czechoslovakia's Blueprint*, 78.

Notes

16. Z. A. B. Zeman, *Prague Spring: A Report on Czechoslovakia 1968* (New York: Penguin, 1969), 79.

17. Prime Minister Černik in April 1968; quoted in H. Gordon Skilling, *Czechoslovakia's Interrupted Revolution* (Princeton, N.J.: Princeton University Press, 1976), 601.

18. Karen Dawisha, *The Kremlin and the Prague Spring* (Berkeley: University of California Press, 1984), 37.

19. Ibid., 43.

20. Quoted in David Floyd, "The Czechoslovak Crisis of 1968," in *Brassey's Annual: The Armed Forces Yearbook, 1969* (London: Clowes, 1969), 39.

21. Josef Smrkovsky, *An Unfinished Conversation* (Sydney: Red Pen Publications, 1976), 11.

22. Quoted in Dawisha, *Kremlin*, 74–75.

23. Quoted, ibid., 76.

24. Text in Szulc, *Czechoslovakia*, 341–46.

25. *Pravda*, Editorial, 22 Aug. 1968.

26. William Shawcross, *Dubček* (New York: Simon & Schuster, 1970), 161–62.

27. Dawisha, *Kremlin*, 168.

28. Text in Remington, *Winter in Prague*, 224–25.

29. Dawisha, *Kremlin*, 239–42.

30. "Statement of the Communist and Workers' Parties of the Socialist Countries," *Pravda*, 4 Aug. 1968.

31. Dawisha, *Kremlin*, 272–73.

32. Ibid., 287–89.

33. S. Kovalev, "Sovereignty and International Duties of Socialist Countries," *Pravda*, 26 Sept. 1968 (translated in *The New York Times*, 26 Sept. 1968).

Chapter 10: Chicago

1. David Brinkley in an NBC network roundtable on the convention, 30 Aug. 1968; excerpts in Donald Myrus, ed., *Law and Disorder: The Chicago Convention and Its Aftermath* (Chicago: Donald Myrus and Burton Joseph, 1968), n.p.

2. Robert H. Daniels, personal comment, Aug. 1968.

3. Daniel Walker, *Rights in Conflict: Chicago's Seven Brutal Days* (New York: Grosset & Dunlap, 1968), 146.

4. Quoted in David Farber, *Chicago '68* (Chicago: University of Chicago Press, 1988), 196.

5. Walker, *Rights in Conflict*, 146.

6. Quoted in Farber, *Chicago '68*, 196–97.

7. Quoted in David Lewis Stein, *Living the Revolution: The Yippies in Chicago* (Indianapolis: Bobbs-Merrill, 1969), 113.

8. This testimony, recorded in the Walker Report (p. 166), is disputed. See John Schultz, *No One Was Killed—Documents and Meditations: Convention Week, Chicago, August 1968* (Chicago: Big Table, 1969), 190–91.

9. Murray Kempton, quoted in Myrus, *Law and Disorder*, n.p.

10. Lewis Chester, Godfrey Hodgson, and Bruce Page, *An American Melodrama: The Presidential Campaign of 1968* (New York: Viking, 1969), 582–83.

11. Quoted in Milton Viorst, *Fire in the Streets: America in the 1960s* (New York: Simon & Schuster, 1970), 458–59.

12. Chester, Hodgson, and Page, *American Melodrama*, 584–85.

13. Quoted in Arthur Herzog, *McCarthy for President* (New York: Viking, 1969), 214.

14. Quoted, ibid, 220.

15. Interview of Philip H. Hoff by Robert V. Daniels, 27 Aug. 1987.

16. Theodore H. White, *The Making of the President, 1968* (New York: Atheneum, 1969), 40–41.

17. Interview of 1977, in Michael Charlton and Anthony Moncrieff, *Many Reasons Why: The American Involvement in Vietnam* (New York: Hill & Wang, 1978), 166.

18. Carl Solberg, *Hubert Humphrey: A Biography* (New York: Norton, 1984), 357.

19. Quoted in Herzog, *McCarthy for President*, 236.

20. Hubert H. Humphrey, *The Education of a Public Man: My Life and Politics* (Garden City, N.Y.: Doubleday, 1976), 389.

21. Quoted in Solberg, *Hubert Humphrey*, 354.

22. Lawrence O'Brien, *No Final Victories: A Life in Politics from JFK to Watergate* (Garden City, N.Y.: Doubleday, 1974), 251.

23. Quoted in Chester, Hodgson, and Page, *American Melodrama*, 536, 534.

24. Quoted in Mike Royko, *Boss: Richard J. Daley of Chicago* (New York: New American Library, 1979), 168–69.

25. Jerry Rubin, statement made at a debate with Fred Halstead of the Socialist Workers' party, 29 Dec. 1967; published in *The East Village Other* as "Yippie! Revolution! What Is to Be Done?" and reprinted in Herbert E. Robb and Raymond Sobel, eds., *From Left to Right: Readings on the Socio-Political Spectrum*, vol. 3 (New York: Benziger, 1972), 144.

26. Quoted in Chester, Hodgson, and Page, *American Melodrama*, 515.

27. Quoted in Walker, *Rights in Conflict*, 341.

28. White, *Making of the President*, 356.

29. Quoted in Solberg, *Hubert Humphrey*, 370.

30. Quoted in White, *Making of the President*, 354.

31. Quoted in Solberg, *Hubert Humphrey*, 362.

32. Gallup Poll, released 26 Sept. 1968.

33. In his memoirs, McCarthy appears to ignore completely the turning point of September 30. Eugene J. McCarthy, *The Year of the People* (New York: Doubleday, 1969), 228–33.

34. Edgar Berman, *Hubert: The Triumph and Tragedy of the Humphrey I Knew* (New York: Putnam's, 1979), 210–11.

35. Quoted in Chester, Hodgson, and Page, *American Melodrama*, 761.

Chapter 11: The World Social Revolution

1. Herbert J. Gans, "The 'Equality' Revolution," *The New York Times Magazine*, 3 Nov. 1968.

2. See Franz Fanon, *The Wretched of the Earth* (New York: Grove Press, 1968).

3. Manuel Camacho Solis, quoted in *The New York Times*, 2 Oct. 1988.

4. Quoted in *The New York Times*, 27 July 1988.

5. See Arthur Schlesinger, Jr., *The Cycles of American History* (Boston: Houghton-Mifflin, 1986).

6. Daniel Yankelovich, *The New Morality: A Profile of American Youth in the '70s* (New York: McGraw-Hill, 1974), 3, 6.

BIBLIOGRAPHY

This listing covers only a fraction of the vast amount of material published on the events of the 1960s in general and of 1968 in particular. Included here are sources cited in this book as well as others that are particularly useful and those that readers may wish to consult on particular aspects of the epoch.

I. General Works

Albert, Judith C., and Stewart E. Albert, eds. *The Sixties Papers: Documents of a Rebellious Decade.* New York: Praeger, 1984.

Annals of the American Academy of Political and Social Science. "Protest in the 60s," vol. 382 (March 1969).

Archer, Jules. *1968: Year of Crisis.* New York: Messner, 1971.

Aja, Roderick, and Norman Miller. *The New American Revolution.* New York: The Free Press, 1971.

Caute, David. *Year of the Barricades.* New York: Harper & Row, 1988.

Daniels, Robert V. "The Sixties: How Near Was Revolution?" *Journal of the Institute of Socio-Economic Studies* 4 (Winter 1979): 46–57.

Gans, Herbert J. "The Equality Revolution." *New York Times Magazine,* 3 November 1968, pp. 36ff.

Graham, Hugh D., and Ted R. Gurr. *Violence in America: Historical and Comparative Perspective.* New York: New American Library, 1969.

Hayden, Tom. *Reunion: A Memoir.* New York: Random House, 1988.

Horowitz, David, Michael Lerner, and Craig Pyes, eds. *Counterculture and Revolution.* New York: Random House, 1972.

Howard, Gerald, ed. *The Sixties.* New York: Washington Square Press, 1982.

Kearns, Doris. *Lyndon Johnson and the American Dream.* New York: Harper & Row, 1976.

Lifton, Robert Jay. "The Young and the Old: Notes on a New History," *Atlantic Monthly* 224:47–54 (September 1969), 83–88 (October 1969).

Matusow, Allen J. *The Unraveling of America: A History of Liberalism in the 1960s.* New York: Harper & Row, 1984.

Mehnert, Klaus. *Twilight of the Young: The Radical Movements of the 1960s and Their Legacy.* New York: Holt, Rinehart & Winston, 1978.

O'Neill, William. *Coming Apart: An Informal History of America in the 1960s.* New York: Times Books, 1971.

Revel, Jean-François. *Without Marx or Jesus: The New American Revolution Has Begun.* New York: Doubleday, 1971.

Robb, Herbert E., and Raymond Sobel, eds. *From Left to Right: Readings on the Socio-Political Spectrum,* 3 vols. New York: Benziger, 1969.

Sidey, Hugh. *A Very Personal Presidency: Lyndon B. Johnson in the White House.* New York: Atheneum, 1968.

Spender, Stephen. *The Year of the Young Rebels.* New York: Random House, 1969.

Statera, Gianni. *Death of a Utopia: The Development and Decline of Student Movements in Europe.* New York: Oxford University Press, 1975.

Tariq, Ali. *1968 and After.* London: Blond & Briggs, 1978.

Viorst, Milton, ed. *Fire in the Streets: America in the 1960s.* New York: Simon & Schuster, 1979.

Wofford, Harris. *Of Kennedys and Kings: Making Sense of the 60s.* New York: Farrar, Strauss & Giroux, 1980.

II. *The Vietnam War*

Adler, Renata. *Reckless Disregard: Westmoreland v. CBS et al., Sharon v. Time.* New York: Knopf, 1986.

Baskir, Lawrence M., and William A. Strauss. *Chance and Circumstance: The War and the Vietnam Generation.* New York: Knopf, 1978.

Braestrup, Peter, and Burns Roper. *Big Story: How the American Press and Television Reported and Interpreted the Crisis of Tet 1968 in Vietnam and Washington.* Boulder, Colo.: Westview Press, 1977.

Brandon, Henry. *Anatomy of Error: The Inside Story of the Asian War on the Potomac, 1954–1969.* Boston: Gambit, 1968.

Brewin, Robert, and Sidney Shaw. *Vietnam on Trial.* New York: Atheneum, 1987.

Brown, John M. G. *Rice Paddy Grunt: Unfading Memories of the Vietnam Generation.* Chicago: Regnery, 1986.

Charlton, Michael, and Anthony Moncrieff. *Many Reasons Why: The American Involvement in Vietnam.* New York: Hill & Wang, 1979.

Clifford, Clark. "A Vietnam Reappraisal: The Personal History of One Man's View and How it Evolved." *Foreign Affairs* 47 (July 1969): 601–22.

Cooper, Chester L. *The Lost Crusade: America in Vietnam.* New York: Dodd, Mead, 1970.

Dougan, Clark, Stephen Weiss, and the Editors of Boston Publishing Co., eds. *The Vietnam Experience: 1968.* Boston: Boston Publishing Company, 1983.

Fallaci, Oriana. *Interview with History.* Boston: Houghton-Mifflin, 1976.

Gelb, Leslie, and Richard K. Betts. *The Irony of Vietnam: The System Worked.* Washington, D.C.: Brookings Institution, 1979.

Goodman, Allen. *The Lost Peace: America's Search for a Negotiated Settlement of the Vietnam War.* Stanford, Calif.: Hoover Institution Press, 1978.

Herr, Michael. *Dispatches.* New York: Knopf, 1977.

Herring, George C. *America's Longest War: The United States and Vietnam, 1950–1975.* New York: Wiley, 1979.

Hersh, Seymour. *My Lai 4: A Report on the Massacre and Its Aftermath.* New York: Random House, 1970.

Hoopes, Townsend. *The Limits of Intervention: An Inside Account of How the Johnson Policy of Escalation in Vietnam was Reversed.* New York: McKay, 1969.

Johnson, Lyndon B. *The Johnson Presidential Press Conferences* (2 vols.). New York: Coleman, 1978.

Johnson, Lyndon B. *The Vantage Point: Perspectives of the Presidency, 1963–1969.* New York: Holt, Rinehart & Winston, 1971.

Karnow, Stanley. *Vietnam: A History.* New York: Viking, 1983.

Kendrick, Alexander. *The Wound Within: America in the Vietnam Years, 1945–1974.* Boston: Little, Brown, 1974.

264

Bibliography

Kolko, Gabriel. *Anatomy of a War: Vietnam, the United States, and the Modern Historical Experience.* New York: Pantheon, 1985.

Korb, Lawrence J. *The Joint Chiefs of Staff: The First Twenty-five Years.* Bloomington, Ind.: Indiana University Press, 1976.

Kowet, Don. *A Matter of Honor.* New York: Macmillan, 1984.

McGarvey, Patrick, ed. *Visions of Victory: Selected Vietnamese Communist Military Writings, 1964-68.* Stanford, Calif.: Hoover Institution Press, 1969.

Mailer, Norman. *The Armies of the Night.* New York: New American Library, 1968.

Oberdorfer, Don. *Tet!* Garden City, N.Y.: Doubleday, 1971.

The Pentagon Papers, vol. 1 [New York Times ed.]. New York: Quadrangle, 1971; vol. 4 ["Senator Gravel" ed.] Boston: Beacon Press, 1971.

Pisor, Robert. *The End of the Line: The Siege of Khe Sanh,* New York: Norton, 1982.

Report on the War in Vietnam. Washington, D.C.: Government Printing Office, 1968.

Schandler, Herbert. *The Unmaking of a President: Lyndon Johnson and Vietnam.* Princeton, N.J.: Princeton University Press, 1977.

Sheenan, Neil. *A Bright Shining Lie: John Paul Vann and America in Vietnam,* New York: Random House, 1988.

Stoler, Mark A. "What Did He *Really* Say? The Aiken Formula for Vietnam Revisited." *Vermont History* 46 (Spring 1978): 100-108.

Taylor, Maxwell. *Swords and Ploughshares.* New York: Norton, 1972.

Thompson, Robert. *No Exit from Vietnam.* New York: McKay, 1969.

Vogelgesang, Sandy. *The Long Dark Night of the Soul: The American Intellectual Left and the Vietnam War.* New York: Harper & Row, 1974.

Westmoreland, William C. *A Soldier Reports.* New York: Doubleday, 1976.

Zaroulis, Nancy, and Gerald Sullivan. *Who Spoke Up? American Protest Against the War in Vietnam, 1963-75.* New York: Holt, Rinehart & Winston, 1984.

III. The Counterculture

Adler, Nathan. *The Underground Stream: New Life Styles and the Antinomian Personality.* New York: Harper Torchbooks, 1972.

Bryant, Beth. *The West Coast on $5 & $10 a Day.* New York: A. Frommer, 1968.

Burt, Robert, and Patsy North. *West Coast Story.* Secaucus, N.J.: Chartwell Books, 1977.

Canine, Craig, and Michael McRae. "Paddling into the Mainstream: Where Have All the Homesteaders Gone?" *Harrowsmith* 2 (March-April 1987): 42-57.

Cavan, Sherri. *Hippies of the Haight.* St. Louis: New Critics Press, 1972.

Davis, Fred. *On Youth Subcultures: The Hippie Variant.* New York: General Learning Corporation, 1971.

Drane, James F. *A New American Reformation: A Study of Youth Culture and Religion.* Totowa, N.J.: Littlefield, Adams, 1974.

Eisen, Jonathan, ed. *The Age of Rock: Sounds of the American Cultural Revolution.* New York: Vintage Books, 1969.

Friedman, Myra. *Buried Alive: The Biography of Janis Joplin.* New York: Morrow, 1973.

Gleason, Ralph J. *The Jefferson Airplane and the San Francisco Sound.* New York: Ballantine Books, 1969.

Gottlieb, Annie. *Do You Believe in Magic? The Second Coming of the Sixties Generation.* New York: Times Books, 1987.

Grogan, Emmett. *Ringolevio: A Life Played for Keeps.* London: Heinemann, 1972.

Houriet, Robert. *Getting Back Together.* New York: Coward, McCann and Geoghegan, 1971.

Kael, Pauline. "Bonnie and Clyde." *The New Yorker,* 21 October 1967.

Leary, Timothy. *The Politics of Ecstasy.* New York: Putnam's, 1968.

Lee, Martin A., and Bruce Shlain. *Acid Dreams: The CIA, LSD, and the Sixties Rebellion.* New York: Grove Press, 1985.

Melville, Keith. *Communes in the Counter Culture: Origins, Theories, Styles of Life.* New York: Morrow, 1972.

Neville, Richard. *Play Power: Exploring the International Underground.* New York: Random House, 1970.

Partridge, William L. *The Hippie Ghetto: The Natural History of a Subculture.* New York: Holt, Rinehart & Winston, 1973.

Perry, Charles. *The Haight-Ashbury: A History.* New York: Random House, 1984.

Perry, Helen S. *The Human Be-in.* New York: Basic Books, 1970.

Pichaske, David. *A Generation in Motion: Popular Music and Culture in the Sixties.* New York: Schirmer Books, 1979.

Pielke, Robert G. *You Say You Want a Revolution: Rock Music in American Culture.* Chicago: Nelson-Hall, 1986.

Reich, Charles. *The Greening of America.* New York: Random House, 1970.

Rosenstone, Robert A. " 'The Times They Are a-Changin': The Music of Protest." *Annals of the American Academy of Political and Social Science* 382 (March 1969): 131–44.

Roszak, Theodore. *The Making of a Counter-Culture.* New York: Doubleday, 1969.

Rothchild, John, and Susan B. Wolf. *The Children of the Counter-Culture.* New York: Doubleday, 1976.

Smith, David E., and John Luce. *Love Needs Care: A History of San Francisco's Haight-Ashbury Free Medical Clinic and Its Pioneer Role in Treating Drug Abuse Problems.* Boston: Little, Brown, 1971.

Snyder, Gary. "Buddhism and the Coming Revolution." *The Berkeley Barb,* 15 November 1968.

Spates, James L., and Jack Levin. "Beats, Hippies, the Hip Generation and the American Middle Class: An Analysis of Values." *International Social Science Journal* 24 (1972): 326–53.

Speck, Ross V., et al. *The New Families: Youth, Communes, and the Politics of Drugs.* New York: Basic Books, 1972.

Starr, Jerold M., ed. *Cultural Politics: Radical Movements in Modern History.* New York: Praeger, 1985.

Whittemore, L. H. *Cop.* New York: Holt, Rinehart & Winston, 1969.

Wolf, Leonard. *Voices from the Love Generation.* Boston: Little, Brown, 1968.

Wolfe, Burton H. *The Hippies.* New York: New American Library, 1968.

Wolfe, Tom. *The Electric Kool-Aid Acid Test.* New York: Farrar, Strauss & Giroux, 1968.

Yablonsky, Lewis. *The Hippie Trip.* New York: Pegasus, 1968.

Yinger, J. Milton. *Counterculture: The Promise and the Peril of a World Turned Upside Down.* New York: The Free Press, 1982.

IV. *The Presidential Campaign*

Berman, Edgar, M. D. *Hubert: The Triumph and Tragedy of the Humphrey I Knew.* New York: Putnam's, 1979.

Burner, David. *The Torch Is Passed: The Kennedy Brothers and American Liberalism.* New York: Atheneum, 1984.

Chester, Lewis, Godfrey Hodgson, and Bruce Page. *An American Melodrama: The Presidential Campaign of 1968.* New York: Viking, 1969.

Cummings, Richard. *The Pied Piper: Allard K. Lowenstein and the Liberal Dream.* New York: Grove Press, 1984.

Bibliography

Frank, Joseph, ed. *The New Look in Politics: McCarthy's Campaign*. Albuquerque: University of New Mexico Press, 1968.

Harris, Fred R. *Potomac Fever*. New York: Norton, 1977.

Herzog, Arthur. *McCarthy for President*. New York: Viking, 1969.

Humphrey, Hubert H. *The Education of a Public Man: My Life and Politics*. Garden City, N.Y.: Doubleday, 1976.

Isaacson, Walter, and Evan Thomas. *The Wise Men: Six Friends and the World They Made*. New York: Simon & Schuster, 1986.

Johnson, Sam Houston. *My Brother, Lyndon*. New York: Cowles, 1970.

Kopkind, Andrew. "The McCarthy Campaign." *Ramparts* 6 (March 1968): 50–55.

Larner, Jeremy. *Nobody Knows: Reflections on the McCarthy Campaign of 1968*. New York: Macmillan, 1970.

McCarthy, Abigail. *Private Faces/Public Places*. Garden City, N.Y.: Doubleday, 1972.

McCarthy, Eugene. *Up Til Now: A Memoir*. New York: Harcourt Brace Jovanovich, 1987.

McCarthy, Eugene. *The Year of the People*. New York: Doubleday, 1969.

Miller, Merle. *Lyndon: An Oral Biography*. New York: Putnam's, 1980.

O'Brien, Lawrence. *No Final Victories: A Life in Politics from JFK to Watergate*. Garden City, N.Y.: Doubleday, 1974.

Plimpton, George, and Jean Stein. *American Journey: The Times of Robert Kennedy*. New York: Harcourt Brace Jovanovich, 1970.

Riesman, David. "McCarthy and Kennedy: Some Very Personal Reflections." *The New Republic*, 13 April 1968.

Schlesinger, Arthur M., Jr. *Robert Kennedy and His Times*. Boston: Houghton-Mifflin, 1978.

Solberg, Carl. *Hubert Humphrey: A Biography*. New York: Norton, 1984.

Stavis, Ben. *We Were the Campaign: New Hampshire to Chicago for McCarthy*. Boston: Beacon Press, 1969.

White, Theodore H. *The Making of the President: 1968*. New York: Atheneum, 1969.

Witcover, Jules. *85 Days: The Last Campaign of Robert Kennedy*. New York: Putnam's, 1969.

V. The Black Civil Rights Movement

Blumberg, Rhoda Lois. *Civil Rights: The 1960s Freedom Struggle*. Boston: Twayne, 1984.

Boesel, David, and Peter H. Rossi, eds. *Cities Under Siege: An Anatomy of the Ghetto Riots, 1964–1968*. New York: Basic Books, 1971.

Brooks, Thomas R. *Walls Come Tumbling Down: A History of the Civil Rights Movement, 1940–1970*. Englewood Cliffs, N.J.: Prentice-Hall, 1974.

Carmichael, Stokely, and Charles V. Hamilton. *Black Power: The Politics of Liberation in America*. New York: Random House, 1967.

Carson, Clayborne. *In Struggle: SNCC and the Black Awakening of the 1960s*. Cambridge, Mass.: Harvard University Press, 1981.

Clarke, John H., ed. *Malcolm X: The Man and His Times*. New York: Macmillan, 1969.

Cleaver, Eldridge. *Soul on Ice*. New York: McGraw-Hill, 1968.

Donner, Frank I. *The Age of Surveillance: The Aims and Methods of America's Political Intelligence System*. New York: Vintage, 1981.

Foner, Philip S. *The Black Panthers Speak*. Philadelphia: Lippincott, 1970.

Forman, James. *The Making of Black Revolutionaries: A Personal Account*. New York: Macmillan, 1972.

Garrow, David. *Bearing the Cross: Martin Luther King, Jr., and the SCLC*. New York: Morrow, 1986.

Garrow, David. *The FBI and Martin Luther King: From "Solo" to Memphis*. New York: Norton, 1981.

Gilbert, Ben W., and the *Washington Post* Staff. *Ten Blocks from the White House: Anatomy of the Washington Riots of 1968*. New York: Praeger, 1968.

Harvey, James C. *Black Civil Rights During the Johnson Administration*. Jackson, Miss.: University and College Press of Mississippi, 1973.

Killian, Lewis M. *The Impossible Revolution? Black Power and the American Dream*. New York: Random House, 1968.

Knight, Janet M. *Three Assassinations*. New York: Facts on File, 1971.

Lewis, David L. *King: A Critical Biography*. New York: Praeger, 1970, 1978.

Marable, Manning. *Race, Religion and Revolution: The Second Reconstruction in Black America, 1945–82*. Jackson, Miss.: University and College Press of Mississippi, 1984.

National Advisory Committee on Civil Disorders. *Report* [Kerner Report]. Washington, D.C.: Government Printing Office, 1968.

National Committee on the Causes and Prevention of Violence. *Final Report*. Washington, D.C.: Government Printing Office, 1969.

Platt, Anthony M., ed. *The Politics of Riot Commissions, 1917–1970: Official Reports and Critical Essays*. New York: Macmillan, 1971.

Powers, Richard Gid. *Secrecy and Power: The Life of J. Edgar Hoover*. New York: The Free Press, 1987.

Seale, Bobby. *Seize the Time: The Story of the Black Panther Party and Huey P. Newton*. New York: Random House-Vintage, 1970.

U.S. House of Representatives, Select Committee on Assassinations. *Final Report*. Washington, D.C.: Government Printing Office, 1979.

U.S. Senate, Select Committee to Study Government Operations with Respect to Intelligence Activities. *Report*. Washington, D.C.: Government Printing Office, 1976.

Washington, James M., ed. *A Testament of Hope: The Essential Writings of Martin Luther King, Jr*. New York: Harper & Row, 1986.

Whalen, Charles, and Barbara Whalen. *The Longest Debate: A Legislative History of the 1964 Civil Rights Act*. Cabin John, Md.: Seven Locks Press, 1985.

Wilkins, Roy, with Tom Mathews. *Standing Fast: The Autobiography of Roy Wilkins*. New York: Viking, 1982.

VI. *The Student Movement, the New Left, and Columbia University*

Ali, Tariq, ed. *The New Revolutionaries: A Handbook of the International Radical Left*. New York: Morrow, 1969.

Annals of The American Academy of Political and Social Science. "Students Protest," Vol. 395 (May 1971).

Avorn, Jerry L., and Members of the Staff of the *Columbia Daily Spectator*. *Up Against the Ivy Wall: A History of the Columbia Crisis*. New York: Atheneum, 1968.

Bacciocco, Edward. *The New Left in America: Reform to Revolution, 1956–70*. Stanford, Calif.: Hoover Institution Press, 1974.

Bloom, Allan. *The Closing of the American Mind: How Higher Education has Failed Democracy and Impoverished the Souls of Today's Students*. New York: Simon & Schuster, 1987.

Breines, Wini. *Community and Organization in the New Left, 1962–68: The Great Refusal*. New York: Praeger, 1982.

Crisis at Columbia: Report of the Fact-Finding Commission Appointed to Investigate the Disturbances at Columbia University in April and May 1968 [Cox Commission Report]. New York: Vintage Books, 1968.

Decter, Midge. *Liberal Parents, Radical Children*. New York: Coward, McCann & Geoghegan, 1975.

Bibliography

Feuer, Lewis S. *The Conflict of Generations: The Character and Significance of Student Movements.* New York: Basic Books, 1969.

Fitzgerald, Frances. *America Revised: History Schoolbooks in the Twentieth Century.* Boston: Little, Brown, 1979.

Flacks, Richard, ed. *Conformity, Resistence, and Self-Determination: The Individual and Authority.* Boston: Little, Brown, 1973.

Fraser, Ronald, et al. *1968: A Student Generation in Revolt.* New York: Pantheon, 1988.

Gitlin, Todd. *The Sixties: Years of Hope, Days of Rage.* New York: Bantam Books, 1987.

————. *The Whole World Is Watching: Mass Media in the Making and Unmaking of the New Left.* Berkeley, Calif.: University of California Press, 1980.

Goode, Stephen. *Affluent Revolutionaries: A Portrait of the New Left.* New York: New Viewpoints, 1974.

Heirich, Max. *The Beginning: Berkeley 1964.* New York: Columbia University Press, 1971.

Isserman, Maurice. *If I Had a Hammer: The Death of the Old Left and the Birth of the New Left.* New York: Basic Books, 1987.

Kahn, Roger. *The Battle for Morningside Heights: Why Students Rebel.* New York: Morrow, 1970.

Kellner, Douglas. *Herbert Marcuse and the Crisis of Marxism.* Berkeley, Calif.: University of California Press, 1984.

Keniston, Kenneth. *Youth and Dissent: The Rise of a New Opposition.* New York: Harcourt Brace Jovanovich, 1971.

Kunen, James S. *The Strawberry Statement.* New York: Random House, 1969.

Lipset, Seymour Martin, and Philip G. Altbach, eds. *Students in Revolt.* Boston: Houghton-Mifflin, 1969.

Lothstein, Arthur, ed. *"All We Are Saying . . .": The Philosophy of the New Left.* New York: Putnam's, 1970.

Marcuse, Herbert. *One-Dimensional Man.* Boston: Beacon Press, 1964.

Mehnert, Klaus. *Peking and the New Left.* Berkeley, Calif.: University of California Center for Chinese Studies, 1969.

Miller, James. *Democracy Is in the Streets: From Port Huron to the Siege of Chicago.* New York: Simon & Schuster, 1987.

Rothman, Stanley, and S. Robert Lichter. *Roots of Radicalism: Jews, Christians, and the New Left.* New York: Oxford University Press, 1982.

Sole, Kirkpatrick. *SDS.* New York: Random House, 1973.

Unger, Irwin. *The Movement: A History of the American New Left, 1959–72.* New York: Dodd, Mead, 1974.

Wallerstein, Immanuel, and Paul Starr, eds. *The University Crisis Reader* (2 vols.). New York: Random House, 1971.

Westby, David L. *The Clouded Vision: The Student Movement in the United States in the 1960s.* Lewisburg, Pa.: Bucknell University Press, 1975.

Young, Nigel. *An Infantile Disorder?: The Crisis and Decline of the New Left.* Boulder, Colo.: Westview Press, 1977.

VII. *France*

Aron, Raymond. *The Elusive Revolution: Anatomy of a Student Revolt.* New York: Praeger, 1969.

Bourges, Hervé, ed. *The French Student Revolt: The Leaders Speak.* New York: Hill & Wang, 1968.

Cohn-Bendit, Daniel. *Obsolete Communism: The Left Wing Alternative.* New York: McGraw-Hill, 1968.

Fišera, Vladimir, ed. *Writing on the Wall: France, May 1968, a Documentary Anthology*. New York: St. Martin's Press, 1979.

Hoffman, Stanley. "The French Psychodrama: De Gaulle's Anti-Communist Coup." *The New Republic*, 31 Aug. 1968, 15–21.

Mehnert, Klaus. *Moscow and the New Left*. Berkeley, Calif.: University of California Press, 1975.

Revolt in France, May–June 1968: A Contemporary Record. New York: Les Evans, 1968.

Schnapp, Alain, and Pierre Vidal-Naquet. *The French Student Uprising, November 1967– June 1968: An Analytical Record*. Boston: Beacon Press, 1971.

Seale, Patrick, and Maureen McConville. *Red Flag/Black Flag: French Revolution 1968* New York: Putnam's, 1968.

Servan-Schreiber, Jean-Jacques. *The Spirit of May*. New York: McGraw-Hill, 1969.

Singer, Daniel. *Prelude to Revolution: France in May 1968*. New York: Hill & Wang, 1970.

Touraine, Alain. *The May Movement: Revolt and Reform*. New York: Random House, 1971.

VIII. *China*

Bernstein, Tom. *Up to the Mountains, Down to the Villages*. New Haven, Conn.: Yale University Press, 1977.

Central Committee of the Chinese Communist Party. *Resolution on Certain Questions in the History of our Party Since the Founding of the PRC*, 27 June 1981. Beijing: Foreign Languages Press, 1981.

Chan, Anita. *Children of Mao: Personal Development and Political Activism in the Red Guard Generation*. Seattle: University of Washington Press, 1985.

Doubier, Jean. *History of the Chinese Cultural Revolution*. New York: Vintage, 1974.

Esmein, Jean. *The Chinese Cultural Revolution*. Garden City, N.Y.: Doubleday-Anchor, 1973.

Fairbank, John King. *The United States and China*, 3rd ed. Cambridge, Mass.: Harvard University Press, 1971.

Guillermaz, Jacques. *The Chinese Communist Party in Power*. Boulder, Colo.: Westview Press, 1976.

Hinton, Harold C. *The People's Republic of China, 1949–1979: A Documentary Survey*, (4 vols.). Wilmington, Del.: Scholarly Resources, 1980.

Hinton, William. *Hundred Day War: The Cultural Revolution at Tsinghua University*. New York: Monthly Review Press, 1972.

Hsia, Adrian. *The Chinese Cultural Revolution*. New York: Seabring, 1972.

Karnow, Stanley. *Mao and China: From Revolution to Revolution*. New York: Viking, 1972.

Karol, K. S. *The Second Chinese Revolution*. New York: Hill & Wang, 1974.

Lifton, Robert J. *Revolutionary Immortality: Mao and the Chinese Cultural Revolution*. New York: Random House, 1968.

Liu Guokai. *Brief Analysis of the Cultural Revolution*. Armonk, N.Y.: M. E. Sharpe, 1987.

Meisner, Maurice. *Mao's China: A History of the People's Republic*. Madison: University of Wisconsin Press, 1978.

Milton, David, and Nancy Milton. *The Wind Will Not Subside: Years in Revolutionary China, 1964–1969*. New York: Pantheon, 1976.

Myers, James T., Jurgen Domes, and Eric von Groeling eds. *Chinese Politics: Documents and Analysis*. Los Angeles: University of Southern California Press, 1986.

Nee, Victor. *The Cultural Revolution at Peking University*. New York: Monthly Review Press, 1969.

Rice, Edward E. *Mao's Way*. Berkeley, Calif.: University of California Press, 1972.

Bibliography

IX. Czechoslovakia

Brassey's Annual: The Armed Forces Yearbook, 1969. London: Clowes, 1969.

Dawisha, Karen. *The Kremlin and the Prague Spring.* Berkeley, Calif.: University of California Press, 1984.

Fišera, Vladimir, ed. *Workers' Councils in Czechoslovakia: Documents and Essays, 1968-1969.* New York: St. Martin's Press, 1979.

Golan, Galia. *Reform Rule in Czechoslovakia: The Dubček Era, 1968-1969.* Cambridge, Engl.: Cambridge University Press, 1973.

Institute of History of the Czechoslovak Academy of Sciences. *The Czech Black Book,* edited by Robert Little. New York: Praeger, 1969.

Kunin, V. V. *The Intellectual Origins of the Prague Spring: The Development of Reformist Ideas in Czechoslovakia, 1956-1967.* Cambridge, Engl.: Cambridge University Press, 1971.

Levy, Alan. *Rowboat to Prague.* New York: Grossman, 1972.

Mastny, Vojtech, ed. *Czechoslovakia: Crisis in World Communism.* New York: Facts on File, 1972.

Maxa, Josef. *A Year Is Eight Months.* Garden City, N.Y.: Doubleday, 1970.

Mlynář, Zdeněk. *Nightfrost in Prague: The End of Humane Socialism.* New York: Karz, 1980.

Mnačko, Ladislav. *The Seventh Night.* New York: Dutton, 1969.

Remington, Robin A. *Winter in Prague: Documents on Czechoslovak Communism in Crisis.* Cambridge, Mass.: MIT Press, 1969.

Šejna, Jan. *We Will Bury You.* London: Sidgwick & Jackson, 1982.

Shawcross, William. *Dubček.* New York: Simon & Schuster, 1971.

Skilling, H. Gordon. *Czechoslovakia's Interrupted Revolution.* Princeton, N.J.: Princeton University Press, 1976.

Smrkovský, Joseph. *An Unfinished Conversation.* Sydney: Red Pen Publications, 1976.

Szulc, Tad. *Czechoslovakia Since World War II.* New York: Viking, 1971.

Valenta, Jiři. *Soviet Intervention in Czechoslovakia, 1968: Anatomy of a Decision.* Baltimore: Johns Hopkins University Press, 1979.

Zeman, Z. A. B. *Prague Spring: A Report on Czechoslovakia 1968.* New York: Penguin Books, 1969.

X. Chicago

Casey, William Van E., and Philip Nobile, eds. *The Berrigans.* New York: Avon, 1971.

Converse, Philip E., Warren E. Miller, Jerold G. Rush, and Arthur C. Wolfe. "Continuity and Change in American Politics: Parties and Issues in the 1968 Election." *American Political Science Review* 63 (Dec. 1963): 1083-1105.

Dellinger, David. *Revolutionary Nonviolence.* New York: Bobbs-Merrill, 1970.

Farber, David. *Chicago '68.* Chicago: University of Chicago Press, 1988.

Frady, Marshall. *Wallace.* New York: World, 1968.

Hayden, Tom. *Rebellion and Repression.* New York: World, 1969.

Hayden, Tom. *Trial.* New York: Holt, Rinehart & Winston, 1970.

Kunstler, William M. *Trials and Tribulations.* New York: Grove Press, 1985.

Lukas, J. Anthony. *The Barnyard Epithet and Other Obscenities: Notes on the Chicago Conspiracy Trial.* New York: Harper & Row, 1970.

Mailer, Norman. *Miami and the Siege of Chicago: An Informal History of the Republican and Democratic Conventions of 1968.* New York: World, 1968.

McGinniss, Joe. *The Selling of the President 1968*. New York: Trident Press, 1969.

Myrus, Donald, ed. *Law and Disorder: The Chicago Convention and Its Aftermath*. Chicago: Donald Ulysus and Burton Joseph, 1968.

Royko, Mike. *Boss: Richard J. Daley of Chicago*. New York: New American Library, 1971.

Schultz, John. *Motion Will Be Denied: A New Report on the Chicago Conspiracy Trial*. New York: Morrow, 1972.

Schultz, John. *No One Was Killed: Documents and Meditations: Convention Week, Chicago, August 1968*. Chicago: Big Table Publishing, 1969.

Sorensen, Theodore. *The Kennedy Legacy*. New York: Macmillan, 1969.

Stein, David Lewis. *Living the Revolution: The Yippies in Chicago*. New York: Bobbs-Merrill, 1969.

Walker, Daniel. *Rights in Conflict*. New York: Grosset & Dunlap, 1968.

(*See also* section IV, "The Presidential Campaign.")

XI. *Other Movements*

Berryman, Phillip. *Liberation Theology*, New York: Pantheon, 1987.

Cleary, Edward L., ed. *Shaping a New World: An Orientation to Latin America*. Maryknoll, N.Y.: Orbis Books, 1971.

De Bray, Regis. *Strategy for Revolution*. New York: Monthly Review Press, 1968.

Gott, Richard. *Guerrilla Movements in Latin America*. Garden City, N.Y.: Doubleday, 1971.

Gutiérrez, Gustavo. *A Theology of Liberation: History, Politics, and Salvation*. Maryknoll, N.Y.: Orbis Books, 1973.

Huberman, Leo, and Paul Sweezy, eds. *Regis Denbray and the Latin American Revolution*. New York: Monthly Review Press, 1968.

Khadduri, Majid. *Socialist Iraq: A Study in Iraqi Politics Since 1968*. Washington, D.C.: Middle Eastern Institute, 1978.

Kostash, Myrna. *Long Way from Home: The Story of the Sixties Generation in Canada*. Toronto: Lorimer, 1980.

Revueltas, Jose. *Mexico '68: juventud y revolución*. Mexico City: Ediciones Era, 1979.

Sullivan, Martin. *Mandate '68*. Toronto: Doubleday, 1968.

Uwechue, Ralph. *Reflections on the Nigerian Civil War: Facing the Future*. New York: Africana, 1971.

INDEX

Abernathy, Ralph, 95, 97–98, 121, 216
Abrams, Creighton, 232
Acheson, Dean, 39, 77–79, 83
"Action Program," 190, 200–201, 203
Adler, Renata, 30n
Africa, 239–240
Agnew, Spiro, 103
Aiken, George D., 32, 33, 232
Albania, and Czechoslovakia, 192
Albert, Carl, 218, 219
Ali, Muhammad, 34, 120
Alioto, Joseph, 44–46, 117, 218
Americans for Democratic Action, 89
Anarchism, 139, 151, 161
Antiwar movement, 5, 7, 32–34, 72, 92, 113, 224;
    and counterculture, 56–57; and student re-
    volts, 8, 136, 137, 139–142, 243
Apteker, Herbert, 137
Army, People's Liberation (China): and "Cultural
    Revolution," 167, 169, 171, 175, 178, 236
Army, Soviet: and intervention in Czecho-
    slovakia, 187–192, 195, 196; see also Czecho-
    slovakia
Army of the Republic of Vietnam (ARVN), 18,
    20–21, 23–24, 26, 29, 35, 40
Army, U.S.: and black riots, 100–103; and drugs,
    52, 54; at Little Rock, 105; see also Tet Offen-
    sive; Vietnam War
Atlanta, Georgia, 106
Atlanta Constitution, 98

Baader-Meinhof Gang, 162, 242
Baldwin, James, 117
Ball, George, 33, 231
Baltimore, Maryland: black riot in, 103
"Baltimore Four," 224
Bao Dai, 27
Beat Generation, 47, 48, 55
Beatles, The, 48, 55–56, 58, 61, 65
Beijing, *see* Peking
Berlin, West, 162
Berrigan, Daniel, 224
Berrigan, Philip, 224
Berman, Edgar, 91, 231
Bilak, Vasil, 190, 206
Birmingham, Alabama, 107–108
Black nationalists, 3, 116, 241, 243; *see also*
    "Black Power"
Black Panther Party, 111, 116–120, 227, 229
"Black Power," 10, 99, 103, 104, 110, 114–116;
    see also Black Panther Party

Blacks, 91, 92, 230, 233, 237; and New Left, 135,
    136; riots of, 8, 45, 98–99, 109, 110, 112; and
    student revolts, 127–131, 133, 141–142, 145;
    and Vietnam War, 33, 103; *see also* "Black
    Power"; Civil rights movement; King, Martin
    Luther, Jr.; Washington, D.C.
Boggs, Hale, 222
Bork, Robert, 124, 244
"Boston Five," 34, 224
Boutin, Bernard, 69
Branigin, Roger D., 88
Brezhnev, Leonid I., 195, 196, 198, 199, 205, 207
"Brezhnev Doctrine," 208, 210
Brinkley, David, 213
Brooke, Edward W., 111
Brown, Bailey, 95, 97
Brown, H. Rap, 117–120, 130
Brown, John M. G., 21, 103
Buddhists, and counterculture, 61; in Vietnam,
    21
Bulgaria, *see* Warsaw Pact
Bundy, McGeorge, 39
Bundy, William, 22, 41
Bunker, Ellsworth, 18, 30, 39, 80, 83
Burger, Warren, 124
Burnham, James, 183

California, presidential primary in, 76, 87, 90
Calley, William, 31
Calvert, Greg, 33
Cambodia, 78, 83, 182, 238, 240
Canada, 224, 240–241
Carmichael, Stokeley, 99, 100, 103, 106, 110,
    111, 116–119, 130
Carter, Jimmy, 93, 242
Castro, Fidel, 3, 28, 140, 164, 192, 238
Catholics, 33, 91, 204, 224, 239
"Catonsville Nine," 224
Ceauşescu, Nicolae, 205, 209
Central America, 8, 243, 246
Central Intelligence Agency, 20, 23, 30, 38, 52,
    197, 245
Černik, Oldřich, 189, 190, 194, 202, 210, 211
Charlton, Michael, 36, 73
Chennault, Anna, 232
Ch'en Po-ta, 171–172, 181
Chervonenko, Stepan, 189, 190, 194, 208
Chester, Lewis, 217, 218
Chiang Ch'ing (Mme. Mao), 172, 177, 179, 181
Chiang Kai-shek, 171, 177
Chicago, Illinois: and civil rights movement, 103,

Chicago, Illinois (*continued*)
109; demonstrations in, 3, 214–217, 225–228, 233; *see also* Daley, Richard J.; Democratic National Convention (1968); Police
"Chicago Eight," trial of, 119, 229; *see also* "Chicago Seven"
"Chicago Seven," trial of, 65, 123, 215, 229–230
China, 157, 170–171, 184, 237, 247; and Czechoslovakia, 192, 209, 238; and USSR, 14, 28; and Vietnam, 26; *see also* "Cultural Revolution"; Mao Tse-tung; Peking
Chou En-lai, 168, 174, 175, 181
Christopher, Warren, 101
Civil Rights Act, of 1957, 105; of 1964, 108; of 1968, 121, 122
Civil rights movement, 104–111, 114–116, 123–125; and revolution of the 1960s, 4, 11, 13, 243–244; and student rebellions, 132, 138, 139; *see also* "Black Power"; Blacks; Kerner Commission; King, Martin Luther, Jr.; Poor People's Campaign
Clark, Blair, 73–74
Cleaver, Eldridge, 117–119, 229
Cleveland, Ohio, 109
Clifford, Clark, 39–41, 70, 77–79, 83, 84
Coffin, William Sloan, 34, 224
Cohn-Bendit, Daniel, 149, 151–155, 158, 160
Cohen, Wilbur, 122
Coleman, Henry, 128, 129
Columbia Broadcasting System (CBS), 19–20, 29–30n, 38, 86
Columbia University: and anti-war movement, 224; uprising at, 3, 8, 127–132, 134, 137, 140–145
Commission on Violence in America, *see* Eisenhower Commission
Committee on Assassinations (U.S. House), 111, 121
Committee on Assassinations (U.S. Senate), 111–112, 120
Committee on Un-American Activities (U.S. House), 228
Communes, 54, 59–60, 130, 156, 165, 171
Communist Party: of China, 174, 175, 180–181; of Czechoslovakia, 189–190, 193, 194, 196, 199–202, 210–211; of France, 151, 154, 155, 157–160, 184, 192; of Italy, 192; of U.S., 107, 133, 145, 146, 192; *see also* Old Left
Conference of Concerned Democrats, 72, 73
Congress of Racial Equality (CORE), 98, 106, 110, 116, 119, 128, 129
Connally, John, 223
Connor, Eugene ("Bull"), 107
Cooper, John Sherman, 37–38
Cordier, Andrew, 144
Cornell University, 145
Counterculture, 7, 15, 47–49, 57–65; and New Left, 135, 139, 147; and religion, 55–56, 60–62, 65; and revolution of the 1960s, 3–5, 8, 92, 245–246; theorists of, 48; *see also* Beat Generation; Drugs; Haight-Ashbury; Hippies; Rock music
Counterrevolution (post-1968), 3–4, 10, 12, 15, 160, 233, 241–242, 244, 246
Cox, Archibald, 143, 144

Crime Control Act of 1968, 122–123
Cronkite, Walter, 38, 71
Cuba, 119, 242; *see also* Castro, Fidel
"Cultural Revolution," 9, 13, 28, 135, 167–185, 245; foreign influence of, 164, 240; *see also* Maoists
Curtis, Kenneth, 220
Czechoslovakia: and Democratic National Convention, 219, 223; Nazi occupation of, 196–198; negotiations with Soviet Union, 195–196, 208–209; and "normalization," 195, 203, 209–211; and revolution of the 1960s, 9, 11; Soviet intervention in, 3, 184, 187–194, 236–238; and Soviet reforms, 198, 245; and student revolts, 163, 198, 199; *see also* "Prague Spring"

Da Nang, 19, 29
Daley, Richard J., 70, 103, 213, 214, 217–219, 224–226, 228–230, 233
Davis, Rennie, 34, 136, 214, 215; *see also* "Chicago Seven"
Dawisha, Karen, 205, 207, 208
DeBray, Regis, 134, 140
de Gaulle, Charles, 8, 150, 151, 153, 154, 158–160
Dellinger, David, 34, 214–216; *see also* "Chicago Seven"
Democratic National Convention (1968), 7, 213–214, 217–219, 222–223, 227–228
Democratic Party, 7, 70, 92–93, 227, 233; Platform Committee, 222–223; *see also* Democratic National Convention; *individual leaders*
Department of Defense, U.S., 31, 39–41, 82, 127
de Tocqueville, Alexis, 155, 156, 185
Detroit, Michigan, 110
Diem, Ngo Dinh, 21, 27
Dien Bien Phu, 26, 27, 35
Diggers, 50–51, 60, 225
District of Columbia: presidential primary in, 88
Djilas, Milovan, 182
Dobrynin, Anatoly, 192
Dohrn, Bernadine, 146–147
Donovan, 57
Drugs, 44–45, 52–58, 62–63, 247; and New Left, 139; *see also* LSD
Dubček, Alexander, 189–191, 193–195, 197, 199–211
Dulles, John Foster, 27
Dutschke, Rudi, 161–162, 164
Dylan, Bob, 57, 65, 146
Dzur, Martin, 189

Eastern Europe, 3, 15, 163; *see also individual countries*
Eastland, James, 38
Eisenhower, Dwight D., 27, 36, 106
Eisenhower Commission, 114, 217
Ellington, Buford, 103
Ellsberg, Daniel, 38, 40
Enthoven, Alain, 39, 40
Esalen Institute, 48, 62

Index

Eskridge, Chauncey, 95, 97
Evars, Medgar, 108

Fanon, Franz, 117, 139, 238
Farmer, James, 98, 106, 110, 120
Faubus, Orval, 105
Fauntroy, Walter, 99
Federal Bureau of Investigation: and assassination of Martin Luther King, Jr., 111, 120–121; and civil rights movement, 107, 109, 111–112, 118, 120; and South Vietnam, 232; see also Hoover, J. Edgar; King, Martin Luther, Jr.
Ferlinghetti, Lawrence, 48
Feuer, Lewis S., 14, 47, 132, 185
Fitzgerald, Frances, 139
Flacks, Richard, 133–134
Fonda, Jane, 147
Forman, James, 117
Fortas, Abe, 123–124
Fowler, Henry, 39
France: and student revolts, 8–11, 137, 157–160, 183, 237, 238; and Vietnam, 26, 27; see also de Gaulle, Charles; Paris; Revolution, French
Fraser, Ronald, 138, 139
Freedom and Peace Party, 119
Free University of Berlin, 161–162
Froines, John, see "Chicago Seven"
Fulbright, J. William, 37

Galbraith, John Kenneth, 75
Gallup Poll, 61
Gandhi, Mohandas K., 105
"Gang of Four," 180, 181
Gans, Curtis, 74
Gardner, John, 122
Gavin, James, 33, 40, 72
Geneva Conference (1954), 27
Georgia, 106
Germany, East, 188, 205; see also Warsaw Pact
Germany, West, 9, 138, 161–162
Giap, Vo Nguyen, 32
Ginsberg, Allen, 48, 215
Ginsberg, David, 111, 223
Gitlin, Todd, 134, 137
Gleason, Ralph, 57
Goldberg, Arthur, 78
Goldwater, Barry, 4, 32, 76, 85, 221, 233
Gomulka, Wladyslaw, 163, 205
Goodwin, Richard, 68–70, 74, 219
Gorbachev, Mikhail S., 198, 200, 247
Gore, Albert, 37, 38
Gottwald, Klement, 196, 197
Goulding, Phil, 39, 41
Government of Vietnam (GVN), see Vietnam, South
Grateful Dead, The, 54, 55, 143
Great Britain, 27, 140; see also Revolution, English
Great Society, 80, 88, 122, 136, 244, 245; and Kerner Commission, 112, 113; opposition to, 12, 221, 242; and revolution of the 1960s, 4–5; and Vietnam War, 15, 28, 39, 78
Grechko, Andrei A., 206

Greens, 138, 160
Greensboro, North Carolina, 105
Gregory, Dick, 119, 215, 227
Gruening, Ernest, 32
The Guardian, 82
Guevara, Ernesto ("Che"): death of, 140, 238; influence of, 33, 128, 134, 139, 145, 156, 164
Gulf of Tonkin Resolution, 26, 32, 37, 78

Habib, Philip, 84
Haight-Ashbury, 8, 43–56, 62–64, 103, 149
Haight-Ashbury Maverick, 43, 46
Haight-Ashbury Oracle, 43, 51, 53
"Hair," 57–58
Hampton, Fred, 120
Hanoi, see Vietnam, North
Harriman, W. Averell, 81, 83–84, 154, 220
Harris, Fred R., 86, 111, 113
Harris Poll, 78, 87
Harvard University, 52, 145
Hayakawa, S. I., 145
Hayden, Tom, 6, 132, 147; and antiwar movement, 34, 137; and Chicago demonstrations, 214, 215, 226; and Columbia University uprising, 127, 129, 142, 145; and SDS, 135–136, 146; see also "Chicago Seven"
Head magazine, 56
Hell's Angels, 50, 58
Herr, Michael, 25, 103
Hersh, Seymour, 31, 74
Hershey, Lewis, 33
Hill, Gerald, 90
Hinton, William, 170, 172, 173
Hippies, 47, 49, 50, 59, 63, 226; see also Counterculture; Haight-Ashbury
Ho Chi Minh, 22, 26, 27
Hodgson, Godfrey, see Chester, Lewis
Hoeh, David, 74, 213–214
Hoff, Philip, 219, 220
Hoffman, Abbie, 58, 65; see also "Chicago Seven"; Yippees
Hoffman, Dustin, 67
Hoffman, Julius, see "Chicago Eight"; "Chicago Seven"
Hoopes, Townsend, 40–41
Hoover, J. Edgar, 89; and civil rights movement, 107, 109, 111, 112, 120; and SDS, 145, 146; see also Federal Bureau of Investigation; King, Martin Luther, Jr.
Howard University, 100, 141–142
Hué, 21, 26
Hughes, Harold, 220
Humphrey, Hubert H.: and civil rights movement, 104, 113–114; at Democratic National Convention, 218–219, 223, 227–228; and Eugene McCarthy, 72, 74; and Lyndon Johnson, 80, 102, 114, 220, 223; in presidential campaign, 83, 230–233; and primary campaigns, 76, 82, 85–89, 91, 92, 220, 222
Humphrey, Muriel, 81
Hungary, 197; and Czechoslovakia, 188, 193, 209; see also Warsaw Pact
Husak, Gustav, 196, 197, 210, 211

I Ching, 61
Imperialism: and anti-imperialist movements, 6,
13–14, 28, 137, 139–140, 146, 164, 246; and
Soviet intervention in Czechoslovakia, 188,
204, 209; *see also* Third World
Indiana, presidential primary in, 88
Indra, Alois, 189, 190
Institute for Defense Analysis (IDA), 127, 130,
132, 142, 144
Interstate Commerce Commission, 106
Israel, 198, 246
Isserman, Maurice, 134, 138
Italy, 9, 138, 162–163

Jackson, Jesse, 97, 107, 121
Jackson State College, 141
Jacobson, George, 18–19
Japan, 138, 161
Jefferson Airplane, The, 55, 56, 62
Jews, 49, 133
Johnson, Lyndon B., 4–7, 72, 93, 123; and civil
rights movement, 101, 105, 108, 109, 111,
113–114; and Czechoslovakia, 192, 209, 223;
and Democratic National Convention,
222–224; and Hubert Humphrey, 72, 80, 220,
231; and Martin Luther King, Jr., 98, 120; and
New Hampshire primary, 67–70, 76, 77; and
Vietnam War, 26–32, 35–39, 41, 68, 71, 75,
77–84, 220, 231–232, 250n49; withdrawal
from campaign, 79–85, 87–88, 91, 224; *see also*
Great Society
Joint Chiefs of Staff, 35, 36, 38
Jones, Le Roi, 117, 137
Joxe, Louis, 152

Kadar, Janos, 205, 209
Kafka, Franz, 197
Kansas City, Missouri, 103
Karenga, Ron, 118, 119
Karnow, Stanley, 32, 169, 180
Kaufman, Arnold, 33, 136
Kearns, Doris, 28, 80, 82
Kempton, Murray, 216
Kennedy, Edward F., 70, 71, 89, 214, 218
Kennedy, Jacqueline B., 104
Kennedy, John F., 73, 89; assassination of, 7, 55,
90, 108, 245; and civil rights movement,
106–107; election of, 5, 71, 76; and revolution
of the 1960s, 4, 5, 10; and Vietnam War, 29,
75, 88
Kennedy, Robert F.: assassination of, 90, 92,
219–221; and civil rights movement, 104, 106,
107, 113; decision to run, 70–79, 84; impact of,
92, 202, 227; and Lyndon Johnson, 28–29, 80,
82, 250n49; and primary campaigns, 68,
85–90; and Vietnam War, 37, 70, 77
Kent State University, 132, 147, 243
Kerner Commission, 7, 75, 111–114, 122
Kesey, Ken, 49, 50, 53
Khanh, Nguyen, 22
Kheel, Theodore, 131
Khe Sanh, 35, 78, 79
Khmer Rouge, *see* Cambodia
Khrushchev, Nikita S., 171, 198, 199
King, Alfred Daniel, 95
King, Coretta, 109

King, John W., 67
King, Martin Luther, Jr.: assassination of, 8, 86,
97–100, 103, 104, 112, 120, 244, 245; and civil
rights movement, 95–96, 104–111, 114, 116,
117, 124; and FBI, 107, 109–112; funeral of,
102–104; and Kerner Commission, 112–113;
Mao Tse-tung on, 183; and Vietnam War, 33,
109, 113; *see also* Nonviolence; Southern
Christian Leadership Conference
King, Martin Luther, Sr., 104
Kirk, Grayson, 128–131, 142–144
Kissinger, Henry, 232
Klonsky, Michael, 146
Kolder, Drahomir, 190, 197
Komer, Robert, 24
Korean War, 26, 27
Kosygin, Alexei N., 195, 206, 208
Kriegel, Frantisek, 190, 196, 202
K'uai Ta-fu, 167–169, 172, 173, 176–178
Kundera, Milan, 197
Kunstler, William, *see* "Chicago Seven"
Kuomintang (Chinese Nationalist Party), 176,
177, 181
Ky, Nguyen Cao, 22, 23
Kyles, Samuel ("Billy"), 95, 97

Laos, 19, 83
Latin America, 9, 238–240
Latin Quarter, 3, 149–154, 157, 158
Leary, Timothy, 48, 52, 53, 55
Lee, Martin, 43, 47, 52, 54, 56, 63, 64, 65, 137
LeMay, Curtis, 231
Lenin, Vladimir I., 128, 134
Levesque, René, 241
Levison, Stanley, 107
Lewis, John, 110
Liberalism, 13, 93; *see also* Great Society; New
Deal
Lindsay, John V., 111, 113, 129
Lin Piao, 171, 174, 181, 183
Lippmann, Walter, 68
Lisagor, Peter, 75
Little Rock, Arkansas, 105
Litvinov, Pavel, 195
Liu Shao-ch'i, 3, 171, 172, 174–176, 179, 182
Liuzzo, Viola, 109
Loan, Nguyen Ngoc, 23
Lodge, Henry Cabot, 39
Loeb, Henry, 103
Long, Russell, 38
Los Angeles: and Black Panthers, 118; and Watts
riot, 101, 109
Lowell, Robert, 67, 90
Lowenstein, Allard, 72, 73, 108, 219, 226
LSD, 48–54, 56, 225; *see also* Drugs
Lynd, Staughton, 136, 137

McCarthy, Abigail, 71, 82, 91
McCarthy, Eugene J.: and civil rights movement,
104, 113; and Czechoslovakia, 223; decision to
run, 72–74; and Democratic National Convention, 214, 218, 226–228; and Lyndon Johnson,
77, 82; and Robert Kennedy, 70–72, 75–76;
and presidential campaign, 230, 262n33; and
primary campaign, 67–69, 77, 84, 87–91, 93,

Index

219, 220, 222; and revolution of the 1960s, 9, 202, 204
McCarthy, Joseph, 69, 88
McConville, Maureen, see Seale, Patrick
McCulloch, William, 111, 114
McGovern, George, 72, 73, 75–76, 93, 218, 230, 233
Machočová, Božena, 193
McIntyre, Thomas, 67
McKissick, Floyd, 98, 110
McLuhan, Marshall, 237
McNamara, Robert, 32, 38, 39, 250n49
McPherson, Harry, 77–79
Maddox, Lester, 104
Mailer, Norman, 34, 107, 215
Malcolm X, 116, 117, 128
Mannheim, Karl, 165
Mansfield, Mike, 37
Manson, Charles, 50
Maoists: in Europe, 164, in France, 151, 155; in Germany, 161, 162; in U.S., 146; see also Progressive Labor Party
Mao Tse-tung, 9, 11, 167–177, 179–183, 242
Marcuse, Herbert, 48, 134, 137, 164, 243
Marines, U.S., 17, 18, 26, 29, 35–36
Marx, Karl, 134, 161, 164, 165, 197
Masaryk, Jan, 201
Masaryk, Thomas, 201
Massachusetts, 87
Massu, Jacques, 159
Mays, Benjamin, 104
Media, mass: in China, 174, 237; and counter-culture, 57, 58, 63, 64; in Czechoslovakia, 189, 191–193, 204, 210, 211, 237; in France, 153, 237; and revolution of the 1960s, 6; and Vietnam War, 29, 31–32, 35, 39; see also Television
Mehnert, Klaus, 133, 138
Memphis, Tennessee, 95–96, 103; see also King, Martin Luther, Jr., assassination of; Police
Mendès-France, Pierre, 159
Meredith, James, 106, 110
Mexico, 138, 239
Miami, Florida, see Republican National Convention (1968)
Miami Herald, 75
Michels, Roberto, 145
Middle East, 28, 239–240
Military Assistance Command, Vietnam (MACV), 36–37
Mills, C. Wright, 134, 183
Mills, Wilbur, 122
Minh, Duong Van, 22
Mitterand, François, 159
Mlynář, Zdeněk, 189, 194, 198, 200–201
Mondale, Walter, 86
Montgomery, Alabama, 104–106, 109
More, Dan, 218
Morehouse College, 104
Morse, Wayne, 32
"Motherfuckers," 137, 146
Muhammad, Elijah, 116
Murphy, George, 38
Murphy, Patrick, 100, 101
Muskie, Edmund, 219, 227
My Lai, 30–31
Myrdal, Gunnar, 115

Nader, Ralph, 138
Nanterre, see University of Paris
National Advisory Commission on Civil Disorders, see Kerner Commission
National Assembly (Czechoslovakia), 193–194, 201, 202, 206, 207
National Association for The Advancement of Colored People (NAACP), 98, 105, 108, 111
National Front (Czechoslovakia), 204
National Guard: Alabama, 107; District of Columbia, 100–102; Illinois, 103, 215, 217, 219, 227; Ohio, 147, 243; Tennessee, 103
National Liberation Front (NLF), 21, 22, 32, 82, 84, 140
National Mobilization Committee to End the War in Vietnam ("Mobe") 33, 34, 214, 215, 225–229; see also Chicago, demonstrations in
National Security Agency (NSA), 19, 231
National Security Council, and Czechoslovakia 192–193, 223
National Student Association, 72
National Urban League, 98, 108, 111
Nation of Islam, 116, 120
Nebraska, 89
Newark, New Jersey, 110, 136
"New Class," 182
New Deal, 7, 13, 93, 124, 221; New Deal coalition, 92, 233
New Hampshire, presidential primary in, 7, 41, 67–69, 74, 76–77, 84
New Left, 13, 64, 92, 133–136, 183; and anti-imperialism, 139–140; and civil rights movement, 119, 124; collapse of, 65, 93, 137, 138, 236, 245; and "Cultural Revolution," 168, 170, 183–185; and Czechoslovakia, 191, 197, 202–203; in Europe, 163–165; in France, 150, 157; and revolution of the 1960s, 10, 11, 134; and Yippees, 225; see also Old Left; Students for a Democratic Society
New Left Notes, 141
Newman, Paul, 67
New Right, 246
Newton, Huey, 117–120
New York, New York, 48, 137; see also Columbia University; Police
New York Times, 30, 41, 68, 69, 113
Nhu, Madame, 21
Nhu, Ngo Din, 21
Nieh Yuan-tzu, 178
Nitze, Paul, 39, 41
Nixon, Richard M.: and civil rights movement, 104, 113; election of, 4, 7, 232, 233; as president, 93, 114, 119, 124, 242, 245; and presidential campaign, 83, 230–231, 242; and primary campaign, 68, 69, 76–77, 80, 85, 87–90; and Republican National Convention, 219–221; and student revolts, 144–145; and Vietnam War, 40, 78
Nobel Peace Prize, 108, 109
Nonviolence, 98, 100, 104, 105, 108–110; see also King, Martin Luther, Jr.
North Atlantic Treaty Organization, 187
North Korea, 192; see also Korean War
North Vietnamese, 19, 23–26, 29n, 32, 35, 40, 78, 83; see also Vietnam, North
Norwalk, Connecticut, 59

Novotný, Antonin, 163, 197–202, 204, 205, 207
Nugent, Luci Baines (Johnson), 81
Nugent, Patrick, 81

Oakland, California, 117, 118
O'Brien, Lawrence, 79, 85, 87–88, 223, 231
O'Dell, Jack, 107
O'Donnell, Kenneth, 86
Oglesby, Carl, 140
Old Left, 13, 113–135, 139, 163, 226; *see also* Communist Party; Trotskyists
O'Neill, William, 61, 91
Orangeburg State College, 141
Oregon, 87, 89–90
Organization of Afro-American Unity, 116

Page, Bruce, *see* Chester, Lewis
Palach, Jan, 210
Paris: negotiations in, 83–84, 154, 231–232; uprising in, 8, 9, 84, 149–154, 158, 160, 161; *see also* Latin Quarter; Sorbonne
Paris Accords (1972), 232, 243
Paris Commune, 172, 175
Parks, Rosa, 105
"Participatory democracy," 135–136
Pavlovsky, Ivan, 187, 190
Peace and Freedom Party, 119, 229; *see also* Freedom and Peace Party
Peking, 176; *see also* Peking University; Tsinghua Technical University
Peking Revolutionary Committee, 177, 178
Peking University, 172, 177–179
Pennsylvania, 86–87
Pentagon, 34, 75; *see also* Department of Defense, U.S.
Pentagon Papers, 38, 39, 41
People's Daily (Peking), 184
Perry, Charles, 44, 50
Peyrefitte, Alain, 150
Phillips, Channing, 218
"Phoenix," Operation, 29, 83
Piller, Jan, 194
Pleiku, 26
Poland, 197; and Czechoslovakia, 188, 205; student revolts in, 163, 205
Police: in Alabama, 107, 109; in Berkeley, 133; in Chicago, 103, 214–217, 224–229; in Czechoslovakia, 199; in Great Britain, 121; in Maryland, 102; in Memphis, 96–98; in Mexico, 239; in New York, 128–131, 143–144; in Oakland, 117, 118; in Paris, 150–153, 156–158; in revolution of the 1960s, 236; in San Francisco, 44–46, 62–63, 117; in Washington, 99–101
Pompidou, Georges, 150, 154, 156, 159, 160
Poor People's Campaign, 110, 111, 120–122, 216
Portugal, 240
Prague: and Soviet intervention, 188, 190–195, 210; and youth culture, 198, 199, 202; *see also* Czechoslovakia
"Prague Spring," 9, 163, 184, 189, 190, 195, 196, 201–206, 237; *see also* "Action Program"
Pravda, 210
Presley, Elvis, 55
Progressive Labor Party (PLP), 146, 184

Psychedelic Rangers, 49, 50, 53
Psychedelic Shop, 49, 51, 54
Pueblo Affair, 35

Quebec, 241

Rainbow Coalition, 138
Ramparts magazine, 65
Randolph, A. Philip, 108
"Rap Brown Law", *see* Civil Rights Act, of 1968
Rather, Dan, 214
Ray, James Earl (alias John Willard, alias Ramon Sneyd), 96–98, 121
Reagan, Ronald W., 27, 66, 87, 90, 124, 221–222, 242, 243
"Red Army Faction," 162, 242
Red Brigades, 163, 242
Red Flag, 180
Red Guards, 167, 169, 172–176, 179, 180, 182, 185, 241, 245; *see also* "Cultural Revolution"
Reeb, James, 109
Republican National Convention (1968), 221, 222
Republican Party, 76, 93, 233; *see also* Republican National Convention (1968); *individual leaders*
Republic of New Africa, 111, 119
Revel, Jean-François, 64
Revolution: American, 12; and counterculture, 63–64; of 1848, 6, 161; English, 10, 12, 48, 50; French, 10, 12; of 1960s, 3–6, 8, 204–205, 235–239, 241–242; process of, 9–12, 91, 114–115, 123, 139, 184, 236; results of, 242–247; revival of, 246–247; Russian, 6, 10, 12–13
Revolutionary Action Movement, 119
Revolutionary Youth Movement, 146
Ribicoff, Abraham S., 218
Riesman, David, 91
Riots, *see* Blacks; Police; *individual cities*
Robb, Charles, 81
Robb, Lynda Bird (Johnson), 81
Roche, Jean, 150, 152
Rockefeller, Nelson, 68, 69, 76, 77, 87, 90, 221
Rock music, 48, 54–58; in Czechoslovakia, 199; groups, 55–58, 65
Rolling Stone magazine, 44, 57
Roman Empire, 48, 60
Romania, and Czechoslovakia, 188, 192, 193; *see also* Ceauşescu, Nicolae
Romney, George, 69, 76, 77
Roosevelt, Franklin D., 13, 93; *see also* New Deal
Rostow, Walt, 20, 39, 41, 79, 82
Roszak, Theodore, 48, 61
Rowe, James, 78
Rubin, Jerry, 217, 228–229; *see also* "Chicago Seven"; Yippees
Rudd, Mark, 127–128, 131, 137, 141–144, 146
Rusk, Dean, 39, 41, 77, 82, 89
Russia, revolutionary movement in, 11; *see also* Revolution, Russian; Union of Soviet Socialist Republics
Rustin, Bayard, 105

Index

Saigon, 18, 20, 83; *see also* Tet Offensive; Vietnam, South

Šalgovič, Viliam, 187, 195, 202

"San Antonio Formula," 29, 81, 231

San Francisco, black riot, 103; *see also* Haight-Ashbury; Police

San Francisco Chronicle, 46, 63

San Francisco State College, 145

Sartre, Jean-Paul, 156, 158

Sauvageot, Jacques, 154, 155

Savio, Mario, 132, 133

Schandler, Herbert, 35, 36, 41

Schlesinger, Arthur M., Jr., 89, 241

Seale, Bobby, 117, 119, 227; *see also* "Chicago Eight"

Seale, Patrick, 150, 153, 156, 157

Šejna, Jan, 201

Selma, Alabama, 109

Senate, U.S., and Vietnam War, 37–39; *see also* Committee on Assassinations

Servan-Schreiber, Jean-Jacques, 163

Sexual revolution, 15, 59, 62, 64; *see also* Counterculture; Women's rights movement

Shanghai, 175, 176, 181, 183

Shaplen, Robert, 25

Sheehan, Neil, 20, 41, 68

Shlain, Bruce, *see* Lee, Martin

Shriver, Sargent, 122

Shultz, George, 82

Sidey, Hugh, 75, 113

Šik, Ota, 198, 210

Šimon, Bohumil, 190

Sirhan, Sirhan, 90

Slánský, Rudolf, 197

Slovakia, 194, 197–199

Smith, David, 45

Smith, Hedrick, 41, 68

Smrkovský, Josef, 190, 193, 202, 206

Socialism, 13–14; in Latin America, 238–239; in Middle East, 28, 240; "Socialism with a human face," 3, 201, 245, 247; and Warsaw Pact, 206, 208, 210; *see also* Union of Soviet Socialist Republics, Soviet model

Socialist German Student League (SDS), 161, 162

Socialist Party, U.S., 133

Solberg, Carl, 80, 223

Solzhenitsyn, Alexander, 198

Sorbonne, 149–152, 154, 156–157, 160, 164

Sorensen, Theodore, 70

Southeast Asia Treaty Organization (SEATO), 27

Southern Christian Leadership Conference (SCLC), 95, 99, 105, 108, 110, 111, 121

Soviet Union, *see* Union of Soviet Socialist Republics

Spaček, Josef, 190

Speck, Ross, 49, 54

Spender, Stephen, 164

Spock, Benjamin, 34, 224

Springer Press, 162

Stalin, Joseph, 197, 198

Stalinism, and Czechoslovakia, 210

Stanley, Augustus Owsley, IV, 53

Statera, Gianni, 162, 165

STB, 187, 190

Stevenson, Adlai, 73, 88, 91

Strougal, Lubomir, 195

Studds, Gerry, 74

Student Afro-American Society (Columbia University), 127, 141

Student League for Industrial Democracy, 135

Student Nonviolent Coordinating Committee (SNCC), 99, 100, 105–106, 108, 110, 116–118; and student revolts, 128, 133, 135

Students, 11, 13, 161; in China, 4, 171, 179; in Czechoslovakia, 198, 199; in Eastern Europe, 163, 205; in France, 151, 154–156; in Italy, 162–163; in U.S., 4, 5, 8, 10, 15, 33, 124, 132, 137–140, 243; in West Germany, 161–162; *see also* Antiwar movement; Columbia University; "Cultural Revolution"; New Left; Paris; Students for a Democratic Society

Students for a Democratic Society (SDS), 33, 134–137, 140, 141, 145, 226; at Columbia University, 127–128, 130, 131, 134, 140–142, 144; decline of, 145–147

Sullivan, Ed, 55

Sulzberger, Cyrus L., 34

Supreme Court, 59, 105–107, 123–124, 244

Suslov, Mikhail, 208, 209

Sutton, Percy, 129

Svoboda, Ludvik, 188–190, 194–197, 201

Taylor, Maxwell, 39

Tate, Sharon, 50

Television, 3, 233, 237–238; in Chicago, 215–218; in France, 158; and Vietnam War, 19, 26; *see also* Columbia Broadcasting System; Media, mass

Teng Hsiao-p'ing (Deng Xiaoping), 174, 181

Tet Offensive, 7, 17–27, 20–32, 34, 40, 41; and U.S. presidential campaign, 74, 75, 78

Theology of Liberation, 239

Thieu, Nguyen Van, 22, 23, 84, 220, 232

Third World, 13, 117, 139–140, 146, 164, 238–240; *see also* Imperialism

Thoreau, Henry David, 47, 105

Thurmond, Strom, 85, 87, 221

Time magazine, 71

Tito, Josip Broz, 163, 205, 209

Townshend, Pete, 65

Transcendental Meditation, 61

Trotsky, Leon, 197

Trotskyists, 133, 139, 151, 152, 155, 161, 163, 226

Trudeau, Pierre Elliott, 241

Truman, David, 128–130

Truman, Harry S., 26, 86

Tsinghua Technical University: battles at, 167–170, 178, 179; and "Cultural Revolution," 172–176, 180

Tupamaros, 138, 146, 238

"Two Thousand Words," 207

Ulbright, Walter, 205, 206

Union of Soviet Socialist Republics (Soviet Union): and Cuba, 164; and Czechoslovakia, 190, 195–196, 247; dissidents in, 192, 195–196; negotiations with Czechoslovakia, 195–196, 208, 209; and New Left, 13, 135; and "Prague Spring," 205–207, 245; and reform,

Union of Soviet Socialist Republics (Soviet Union) *(continued)*
198, 245; Soviet model, 13, 134, 170–171, 180, 195, 200, 238; and UN, 193; and Yugoslavia, 163; *see also* Czechoslovakia, Soviet intervention in; Gorbachev, Mikhail S.
United Nations, 193
United States: and Chile, 240; economy, 11; and revolution of 1960s, 3–8, 10, 14–15, 236, 244; revolutionary process in, 10–12; social problems, 12; *see also* Civil rights movement; Counterculture; Media, mass; Revolution; Students; Vietnam War
Universities, and student revolts, 132–133, 147, 161–163, 180, 243, 245; *see also individual institutions*
University of Alabama, 85, 106
University of California, Berkeley, 132–133, 145
University of Michigan, 33, 135, 136
University of Mississippi, 106
University of Paris, 149; at Nanterre, 149, 155–156; *see also* Sorbonne
Urban Coalition, 113
Unruh, Jesse, 90
Uruguay, *see* Tupamaros
U.S. Organization, The, 118

Vaculik, Ludvik, 207
Valo, Josef, 193
Vance, Cyrus, 84, 101–102
Vanden Heuvel, William, 74
Vann, John Paul, 20
Vietcong, 7, 17–26, 28, 29–30*n*, 30, 32, 40, 83; *see also* National Liberation Front; Tet Offensive
Viet Minh, 26–27
Vietnam, North, 7, 22, 27, 28, 34, 81, 238, 240; bombing of, 26, 29, 32, 28, 41, 78–81, 83, 84, 223, 231, 232; and Czechoslovakia, 192; and New Left, 146, 164; and peace negotiations, 82–84, 231–232; *see also* North Vietnamese
Vietnam, South, 21–24, 27–29, 32, 37, 41, 81, 83, 84; and Paris negotiations, 231, 232; *see also* Saigon; Tet Offensive; Vietcong; Vietnam War
Vietnam War, 28–30, 35–41, 82–83; and Democratic National Convention, 214, 222, 223, 237; effect of, in U.S., 5–7, 10, 11, 14–15, 47–48, 245; end of, 232, 240, 243; and student revolts, 127, 132, 136–138, 140, 147, 155, 161; and television, 19, 26; and U.S. presidential campaign, 68–78, 91, 220; *see also* Antiwar movement; Johnson, Lyndon B.; My Lai; Paris, negotiations in; Tet Offensive
Volpe, John A., 87
Voting Rights Act of 1965, 109

Wallace, George C.: and civil rights movement, 85, 104, 106, 113; and counterrevolution, 4,
11; and presidential campaign, 4, 69, 76, 85, 91–93, 120, 230–233
Wall Street Journal, 38
Wang Kuang-mei (Mme. Liu Shao-ch'i), 175
Warhol, Andy, 58
Warnke, Paul, 39–41
Warren, Earl, 123, 124
Warsaw Pact, 188–189, 193, 205–208
Washington, D.C., 99–103, 108, 112
Washington, Walter, 100–102
WASPs, 49, 133
Watts, *see* Los Angeles
Weathermen, 146–147
Weiner, Lee, *see* "Chicago Seven"
Western civilization, rejection of, 246, 247
Westin, Alan, 129, 130
Westmoreland, William, 18–20, 27, 29–30, 35–36, 38–41, 79, 80, 82, 83
Weyand, Frederick, 18, 20
Wheeler, Earle, 23–24, 35–37, 39–41, 79, 80
White, F. Clifton, 221
White, Theodore, 72, 221, 227
Whittemore, L. H., 44, 63
Wilkins, Roy, 98, 111, 113
Williams, Hosea, 98
Williams, Robert, 119
Wisconsin, 68, 79, 87–88
"Wise Men," 39, 78, 79, 81, 83
Wolf, Leonard, 50–52
Women's rights movement, 11, 13, 15, 104, 244
Woodstock Rock Festival, 58, 65
Workers: in China, 11, 157, 167–170, 179; and counterrevolution, 11; in Czechoslovakia, 11, 203; in France, 11, 154, 157–160, 165; in U.S., 11, 157, 165
Writers' Union (Czechoslovak), 197, 198, 204

Xuan Thuy, 154

Yankelovich, Daniel, 245
Yao Wen-yuan, 179–181
Yippees, 64–65, 118, 135; in Chicago, 214–215, 225–226
Young, Andrew, 95, 97
Young, Nigel, 139, 147
Young, Whitney, 98
Youth: in Czechoslovakia, 191, 197–198, 202, 203; and revolution of 1960s, 4, 8–11, 15, 47, 69, 91, 92, 132, 165, 235; *see also* Counterculture; "Cultural Revolution"; New Left; Students
Yugoslavia: and Czechoslovakia, 188, 192, 193, 198, 200; and student revolts, 163, 205; *see also* Tito, Josip Broz

Zionism, 197, 205